VICTORIAN
REFORMATIONS

VICTORIAN REFORMATIONS

Historical Fiction and Religious Controversy, 1820–1900

MIRIAM ELIZABETH BURSTEIN

University of Notre Dame Press

Notre Dame, Indiana

Manufactured in the United States of America

Library of Congress Cataloging-in-Publication Data

Burstein, Miriam Elizabeth, 1971–
Victorian Reformations : Historical Fiction and Religious Controversy,
1820–1900 / Miriam Elizabeth Burstein.
     pages   cm
   Includes bibliographical references and index.
ISBN-13: 978-0-268-02238-9 (pbk.)
ISBN-10: 0-268-02238-0 (paper)
   1. Christian fiction, English—History and criticism.   2. Religion in
literature.   3. English fiction—19th century—History and criticism.
4. Historical fiction, English—History and criticism.   5. Christianity in
literature.   6. Books and reading—England—History—19th century.
I. Title.
PR878.R5B87   2013
823'.8093823—dc23
                                                              2013029850

FOR MY PARENTS

Contents

Acknowledgments

I am grateful to my colleagues at the College at Brockport, State University of New York, for providing a most congenial place to work, and to the college itself for funding multiple research trips in both the United States and abroad. The interlibrary loan department at Drake Library was, once again, indefatigable in turning up even the most obscure novels.

The research for this project was undertaken at the Bobst Library, New York University; the British Library; the Harry Ransom Center, University of Texas, Austin; the Huntington Library; the New York Public Library; the Charles E. Young Library, University of California, Los Angeles; and the Union Theological Seminary. I am further indebted to the legions of workers who have digitized texts for Google Books, HathiTrust, and the Internet Archive; without them, this book would have been considerably more difficult to write.

My colleague Stefan Jurasinski kindly read the entire manuscript and ensured that this Victorianist's grasp of the Lollards did not go too far afield. The Victorian Studies Reading Group of Western New York commented extensively on what is now chapter 2. Audiences at the British Women Writer's Conference, the Modern Language Association, the North American Victorian Studies Association, the Northeast Modern Language Association, and the Pacific Coast Conference on British Studies all offered gracious feedback on this project during its earlier stages. I am grateful to the readers at the University of Notre Dame Press for their helpful observations. Over the years, I have benefited from conversations and communications with Alison Booth,

James Chandler, Lynette Felber, Elaine Hadley, Michelle Hawley, Elizabeth Helsinger, Diane Long Hoeveler, Arnold Hunt, Teresa Lehr, Karen Lunsford, and a number of visitors, many pseudonymous, to my blog, *The Little Professor*. Ralph Byles pointed me to background regarding Esther Copley; Ken Hillier suggested some more fictional Lollards; and Daniel Mills supplied information about Emma Leslie, along with a digital copy of one of her rarer novels. As always, my parents, Dorothy and Stanley Burstein, enjoyed reminding me that for an English professor, I was doing something that looked remarkably like history.

Part of chapter 2 originally appeared in much different form as "Counter-Medievalism; Or, Protestants Rewrite the Middle Ages," in *Beyond Arthurian Romances and Gothic Thrillers*, ed. Jennifer A. Palmgren and Lorretta M. Holloway (Palgrave Macmillan, 2005), reproduced with permission of Palgrave Macmillan. An earlier version of chapter 4 was published as "Reinventing the Marian Persecutions in Victorian England," in *Partial Answers: Journal of Literature and the History of Ideas* 8, no. 2 (2010) 341–64. Copyright © 2010 The Johns Hopkins University Press. Revised and reprinted with permission by The Johns Hopkins University Press.

INTRODUCTION

Victorian Protestants of all denominations insisted that without the Reformation, there would be no economic success, no intellectual and scientific growth, no political liberty—in other words, no modern Britain. And yet, the Reformation's success apparently foretold its undoing. "As Protestants we had greatly lost, through disuse and long ease and prosperity, the armour of the Reformation," thundered the evangelical Edward Bickersteth, exploding into a battery of mixed metaphors. "While we slept the enemy has been busy sowing tares, and the tares are rapidly multiplying. The plague of popery is spreading through the camp, and it is needful to make haste and withstand it."[1] By the end of the nineteenth century, praising the Reformation and mourning its incipient loss had become one of the leading hallmarks of popular anti-Catholic discourse, spilling into tracts, lectures, poems, catechisms, histories, biographies, and novels. Nor were Protestants alone in worrying about the Reformation's cultural significance: increasingly as the decades wore on, Roman Catholic and Anglo-Catholic historians, controversialists, and novelists appropriated the Protestants' favorite topic in order to narrate an entirely different history, one in which the Reformation's "success" actually marked the beginning of widespread cultural and political collapse. Writing about and debating the Reformation became one of the Victorian era's most popular, and most loaded, national pastimes.

This phenomenon, however, is virtually unknown in literary studies, even though the heat of the debates fueled poetry, drama, and (most importantly for my purposes here) several dozen novels. The reason is not hard to find: this popular obsession with the Reformation, so crucial for Protestant and even Catholic identities, was carried on not by now-canonical authors but by some of the most successful religious novelists—figures like Deborah Alcock, Elizabeth Rundle Charles, A. D. Crake, Lady Georgiana Fullerton, Emily Sarah Holt, Emma Leslie, George E. Sargent, and Frances Taylor. Their work was widely reviewed in the leading Christian periodicals, pirated in the United States, and translated into languages ranging from French to Bengali; some of the most successful were reprinted well into the twentieth century. For example, Charles's *Chronicles of the Schönberg-Cotta Family* (1863), in which Martin Luther plays a leading role, went through over a dozen editions in Britain and as many in the United States; was translated into German (also going through multiple editions), French, and Arabic; and was re-released as late as 2003, in an edited version, by an evangelical small press. John Scott Lidgett, a leading Methodist activist and theologian from the late Victorian period to the mid-twentieth century, remembered his father reading *The Pilgrim's Progress* with as much fondness as he remembered him reading the *Chronicles*.[2]

Thus, this book insists not only that controversial fiction played a crucial role in nineteenth-century popular religious and literary cultures, but that any study of religion and literature that dismisses them in favor of canonical works will badly skew our understanding of the Victorian religious landscape. Although such familiar figures as Walter Scott, Charles Dickens, and George Eliot will appear in the course of this study, when it comes to understanding the complexities of Victorian religious narratives, close reading of classic works for traces of religious controversy is not, in the end, the most productive strategy.

Working with popular religious fiction poses its own problems, such as a nonexistent canon, frequently unanswerable questions about authorship, and difficulties in establishing reception histories. Moreover, by their very nature, these works push an explicit rather than an implicit agenda; theoretical approaches that emphasize decoding or a "hermeneutics of suspicion" founder when faced with a text that, at first, seems all surface.[3] For this reason, the chapters that follow will combine close reading with the interrelations of novelistic groups, as narrative patterns and thematic elements emerge, consolidate, and eventually disperse across time.

More specifically, this study focuses on how such popular religious fictions—by authors of any denomination—imagine historical processes at work, processes that, for these authors and their readers, led beyond nineteenth-century national history to the apocalypse itself. It is by now a commonplace that the Victorian era was quintessentially "historical" in its attitudes, seeking to position every political, economic, cultural, or religious event against a sweeping, explanatory backdrop.[4] These novels, however, narrate the past in accord with a providential, eschatological framework that often remains buried in modern studies of both Victorian historiography and Victorian fiction. George Levine has recently argued that Victorian fiction "tends toward the secular even as it insists—as it so often does—on the providential order of things"; "virtue" cannot succeed in due course without breaking all "the rules of the novel, the canons of plausibility."[5] I argue in this volume, by contrast, that religious historical novelists pushed the historical novel's "secularity" to the breaking point, often by rewriting its fundamental epistemological and moral assumptions. For these novelists, history's core drama lay in the transformative potential of individual, national, and even global conversion, one of the core emphases of pan-evangelical belief in the nineteenth century.[6] Such fictions do not, as Elizabeth Deeds Ermarth argues of conversion narratives more generally, "do away with the need for history"; instead, they narrate the convert's coming to grips with the authentic, providential history underlying all human action through the self's realization of error and consequent transformation.[7] To modern readers, the sheer repetitiveness of this patterning across novels set in wildly different time periods soon comes to seem tediously predictable—yet that predictability is precisely the point. These novels lay out a universal plot, one that repeats itself across time and space; its universality means that the reader, too, can transform him- or herself along the convert's model. At the same time, this plot's apparent suitability for all historical moments yokes past and present together, so that the "historically radical" becomes the "contemporaneously orthodox"—an apparent difference that is, in fact, not one.[8]

It would be difficult to find a nineteenth-century historical novel that did not touch, even superficially, on religion, whether it be W. H. Ainsworth's *Windsor Castle* (1842), Edward Bulwer-Lytton's *The Last Days of Pompeii* (1834), or Robert Louis Stevenson's *The Master of Ballantrae* (1889). This study, however, takes a more tightly defined form of religious historical fiction as its province: the controversial historical novel, a subgenre that has been virtually written out of mainstream literary-historical narratives about the fate of the genre after Sir Walter Scott. By *controversial* historical fiction I mean historical fiction that explicitly foregrounds questions of faith—whether in an obviously doctrinal fashion or not—in order to *convert* the reader.[9] These novels situate and attempt to historicize contemporary theological debates in narrative form. At the very least, like controversial novels more generally, they "seek to prove the truth of a particular understanding of Christianity [or any other religion, for that matter] at the expense of others."[10] They frequently incorporate catechetical dialogues, staged trials, scenes of biblical reading and exegesis, and sermons. These discursive moments exist in a larger providential framework, which the characters themselves must learn to decode; in fact, learning to interpret apparently secular events according to their proper providential signification is frequently one of the controversial historical novel's key lessons.

From its very beginnings in Grace Kennedy's *Father Clement: A Roman Catholic Tale* (1823), the controversial novel often *was* a historical novel. This choice of genre was not incidental: setting theological debates in the past validated or invalidated the present state of religious affairs, identified significant moments of origin, and highlighted connections between religious opinions and their sociopolitical equivalents. Thus, Kennedy wraps her Presbyterian catechetical dialogues in a combination conspiracy and inheritance plot set during the Jacobite Rebellion of 1715, indicting the Catholic clergy as conspirators. Moreover, her final vignettes include a Roman Catholic tourist heaving a "sigh" as he ponders his near-vanished church, "almost forgotten" in Britain.[11] Both Kennedy's politicized setting and her self-conscious dwelling on Catholic loss banish Roman Catholicism from nineteenth-century British culture: the Catholic tourist is posed on the brink of his own eradication, trapped in a nostalgia unshared by his Protestant neighbors. Kennedy repurposes Sir Walter Scott's famous evocations of cultures vanishing under the pressure of modernization to proclaim that Roman Catholicism constitutes an improper anachronism in modern British culture. Her numerous Catholic respondents evidently noted the anti-Catholic politics involved in her choice of genre, for the several responses that followed were all pointedly set at least within a decade of their publication: far from vanishing into the unstable past, nineteenth-century Catholics insisted that they were there to stay.[12]

In Search of the Controversial Historical Novel

But calling these controversial fictions *historical novels* raises questions about our definition of the genre itself. From Georg Lukács to present-day postmodernists, theorists of the historical novel have stipulated that it is a secular, post-Enlightenment form, defined by historical relativism, proto-anthropological cultural awareness, realism, and materialism—although, ironically, some of Scott's contemporaries thought his work was a brilliant exemplar of religious argumentation.[13] Even the most recent poststructuralist scholarship, which emphasizes what Linda Hutcheon calls "historiographic metafiction" (that is, fictions that reflect on the narrative construction of history itself), continues to rely on these basic presuppositions.[14] From Lukács onward, most theorists of the historical novel have argued that it is about *transformation*—in Lukács's words, "a clear understanding of history as a process, of history as the concrete precondition of the present."[15] In Sir Walter Scott's fiction, Lukács argues, we see the emergence of new social, political, and cultural conditions out of a Hegelian dialectic of warring forces, channeled through one of Scott's bland but nevertheless historically "typical" protagonists. While some have suggested that Scott's practice may be less representative than it at first appears, Lukács's identification of the historical novel with narratives of how the present necessarily came to be remains attractive, even when Lukács's interest in the historical novel's implicit politics goes by the wayside.[16]

Controversial historical fiction—especially in its Protestant incarnations—explicitly calls into question this argument that past and present must be *different*, that the past is the necessary "prehistory" of modernity and not identical to it. Against Lukács, Fiona Price has recently suggested that we think about a religiously inflected model of historical fiction that, far from chronicling the rise of modern commercial culture, instead "attempts to construct a tradition of continuous heroism and self-sacrifice."[17] Price describes this alternative model as "the other historical novel." Like Price, I agree that for the controversial historical novelist, economics and ideology do not define history, and the "past" very well may be fundamentally identical to the present. But the novels I discuss do not *assume* continuity so much as they seek to teach the reader how to reconstruct it. In one sense, the sixteenth-century past is "lost"; in another, it remains alive through an untiring and ever-watchful project of storytelling, memorialization, and reenactment.[18] Moreover, history's true "author" or "maker" in these texts is God, not the people or even "Great Men"; men and women act out their destinies with greater or lesser degrees of free will but always in accordance with the greater, if ever only retrospectively glimpsed, design of divine providence. The historical novelist may represent economic or ideological differences in all their complexity, and yet those differences are not themselves important or even necessarily determinant of what follows. And this relative lack of importance has significant moral implications, for the religious historical novel strips the secular, material world of significance in order to direct the reader to an historical narrative that normally escapes human representation—what the Anglican novelist Elizabeth Rundle Charles calls, in a meta-fictional moment, "Church history," which "is being silently lived on earth, is being silently written in heaven."[19]

Tellingly, the only book-length study of historical fiction with an overt religious bent, Royal W. Rhodes's *The Lion and the Cross: Early Christianity in Victorian Novels* (1995), is by a historian of religion, not a literary historian; and the two best-known studies of evangelical fiction more generally, Margaret Nancy Cutt's *Ministering Angels: A Study of Nineteenth-Century Evangelical Writing for Children* (1979) and Elisabeth Jay's *The Religion of the Heart: Anglican Evangelical-ism and the Nineteenth Century Novel* (1979), have virtually nothing to say about historical fiction. Yet the historical novels that the Victorians produced and consumed in mass quantities frequently flout all of modern criticism's ground rules for the genre, and they persist in doing so until the end of the century, long past the purported terminal date for "literary" fiction with religious overtones.[20] For that matter, they do so despite what some have diagnosed as a significant *historical* difficulty in late-Victorian theology: "If a religion was founded upon events in history, and the events possessed the particularity which all events must possess, how could they be of universal, redeeming sig-nificance?"[21] These novels do not neatly adhere to the timeline scholars have established for religious crises in either high literature or high the-ology. And yet, the Victorians themselves saw no necessary contradic-tion in calling both controversial and "secular" historical fiction *his-torical fiction*. I therefore address what is becoming a core problem in literary history: understanding the complicated interface between liter-ary and religious discourses. Our attention to the "high" literary tradi-tion of historical novels obscures the centrality of explicitly *religious* definitions of historical change to the historical novel's development.

Whether or not such texts had the intended effect on their target audiences, needless to say, is an open question.[22] For example, *Father Clement* proved to be an exceptionally successful novel, remaining in print until the end of the century, but while Edmund Gosse suggested that it determined his father's rabid anti-Catholicism, the novelist Lady Georgiana Fullerton claimed that it contributed to her eventual conversion to Catholicism.[23] The level of theological sophistication in such texts varies wildly. By the same token, the Catholic historian John Lingard's *History of England* (1819–30) sometimes shows its influence in unexpected places—especially in more nuanced depictions of Mary I, something I shall discuss in chapter 4.[24] Moreover, these novels frequently offer an extreme position on *sola scriptura* that makes the Bible astonishingly easy to understand, thereby sidestepping the heated disputes on biblical hermeneutics taking place in nineteenth-century Britain and, of course, Germany. Elisabeth Jay's observation that "most novelists found it easier to concentrate on the way in which Evangelicals 'used' the Bible rather than dealing with the thorny topic of Biblical inspiration" extends well beyond literary figures like the Trollopes.[25] Such occluded religious boundaries enabled writers to address an amorphous range of readers—children, adults, working class, middle class—without stepping on too many sensitive toes, an approach encouraged by ecumenical Protestant publishers like the Religious Tract Society (RTS).

This stripped-down theology was a generic fictional "Protestantism" that, in practice, did not embody the values, practices, beliefs, and norms of any given denomination. Although there were certainly fictionalized polemics devoted to topics like baptism,[26] controversial fiction did not necessarily want to stir up *intra*-Protestant controversy: many historical novelists tended to either avoid or play down subjects of a hotter sort, whether paedobaptism, predestination, or eternal damnation. ("I certainly do not go blindly over hedge and ditch after the opinions of John Calvin," one of the pro-Calvinist novelist Emily Sarah Holt's characters remarks.[27]) Protestantism may have been the means of "encouraging" the British people to "unite against its own and other outsiders," but how could such a strategy be put into practice without alienating the very insiders one was supposed to unite?[28] Instead of thinking of these texts as oversimplified and overheated Protestantism, we might consider the productive aspects of such an approach. Sarah C. Williams warns historians of religion that merely invoking "evangelicalism" conceals "the varieties of theological position, ecclesiological structure, religious disposition and denominational milieu which co-existed throughout this period and which together shaped the religious culture of the nation."[29] But by constructing an entirely Bible-centered narrative of Protestantism's clash with Catholicism, novelists could point readers toward a vision of a fully unified—or, at least, a fully cooperative—Protestant community. It was no accident that in its initial ecumenical phase, the British and Foreign Bible Society forbade opening prayers at its meetings.[30] More specific theological controversies, such as those over the Eucharist, predestination, or justification and sanctification, were divisive among even evangelicals in a way that appeals to the Bible were not, and they often vanish from or are downplayed in novels where they really ought to take pride of place. Protestants cast the Bible in the role of "open" text, accessible to any and all comers, whose presence reinstated the "original" promise of Christianity. A bibliocentric history invoked the prospect of a *possible*, fully purified Protestantism, one that could stand firm against the coming of Antichrist. In many ways, the ideal endpoint of these narratives is not Protestant religion as it is, but Protestantism as it is to come.

Not surprisingly, given their purpose, controversial historical fiction generally appeared in an inexpensive single-volume format from explicitly religious publishers, who by midcentury had clear theological "brands."[31] The novels in this study were published by a variety of publishers, ranging from the ecumenical Protestant Religious Tract Society, one of the Victorian era's great publishing concerns, to smaller presses like John F. Shaw (evangelical), R. Washbourne (Roman Catholic), and the Parker brothers (Anglo-Catholic). Only a few books in this study, like Anna Eliza Bray's *The Protestant* (1828), were published in double- and triple-decker format by "secular" publishers like Richard Bentley or Henry Colburn. The majority were single-volume novels, sometimes quite slim, published on low-quality paper, and few boasted extensive illustrations. Their audiences were loosely defined: many surviving examples are school prize books, suggesting a younger audience, but some authors (for example, Charles Edmund Maurice or Emily Sarah Holt) include elaborate footnotes that also target adults. Several novelists, including Crake, Holt, Leslie, and Charles, wrote novels either intended as series (Leslie's "Church History" tales) or packaged as such (Holt's "Tales of England in the Olden Days"), and thus could be read as virtual substitutes for the more complex fare of Reformation and ecclesiastical history. Of the novels discussed in this study, some originated in religious serials and were later reprinted in volume form. Many were pirated in the United States, where there was a strong market for British didactic texts. These were cheap novels, sometimes retailing for no more than one shilling, that were inexpensive enough to be purchased by parents, churches, and schools (the latter two for libraries and prize books), and not necessarily by the circulating libraries.[32] And they are novels with a mission.

Controversial Fiction, Religious Upheaval: Reaction and Revision

Depending on the novelist's theological and political affiliations, that mission meant anything from saving the Reformation (and Britain) from its detractors to salvaging the Catholic Church (and Britain) from its Reformation antagonists. Anything about the Reformation was fair game. A number of historians have traced the changing fortunes of the Reformation in political and ecclesiastical history, focusing primarily on the work of gentleman scholars, clergymen, and professional academics. In recent years, revisionist historians have challenged the assumption that the Reformation emerged from a decadent and irrelevant medieval Catholicism, pointing out that such Protestant narratives of the Reformation imagine it "as an inexorable process, a necessary sequence unfolding easily to a predetermined conclusion."[33] Protestant historical fiction shaped popular fantasies of this "necessary sequence" for their readers, while Anglo-Catholic and Roman Catholic historical novelists seized the opportunity to invent very different narratives of the Reformation's effects, whether to challenge its effects on the Church of England or to dismiss it altogether as a violent break in the very fabric of British national history. In and of themselves, neither the narratives nor the obsessions were new: the Reformation was a recurring canker in the British historical and political imagination, its significance always becoming the subject of passionate investigation during times of religious upheaval. For our purposes, four significant movements, or religio-political events, motivated much of the anxiety about the Reformation and its possible disappearance at the hands of Catholics, both Anglo and Roman.

First, in 1829, after years of campaigning, Catholic Emancipation enabled Roman Catholics to once again sit in the House of Commons. Although Emancipation was welcomed by some Protestants, many saw in it the imminent destruction of every effort made to secure Protestant ascendancy in the wake of the Reformation. Reminiscing some years later, one would-be Protestant versifier found the Catholic "brute" all too "eager for its prey": "The deadly Bill of Twenty-Nine! — / Ah, well-a-day, the deed! — / My Christian brother! yours and mine / May be the hearts to bleed."[34] This "deadly Bill" was more than just bad politics. It directly flouted the revelation of God's will manifested in the Reformation and thereby invited unimaginable — or all too imaginable — acts of divine chastisement.[35] Its very legislative success, hard-line Protestants argued, demonstrated that Protestants had cut themselves off from their own historical origins. And in so doing, Protestants had not just enabled Roman Catholicism to succeed but also had damned themselves. It did not help that the Catholic population in England was growing by leaps and bounds, thanks to a combination of clergymen reenergizing their congregations, reconversion and conversion, and immigration. The Catholic claim to "Protestant" space was increasingly hard to ignore.[36] As Catholicism made headway in English culture in the 1830s, apocalyptic speculations about the approaching end of days became common currency among all Protestant denominations. Although Protestants had long identified the pope with the Antichrist, Emancipation suggested that the millennium itself was at hand.[37]

Second, as the anguished response to Emancipation unfolded, John Keble's sermon "On National Apostasy" (1833) energized what would coalesce into the Oxford Movement. Traditional High Churchmen (as historians now call them) still insisted that the Church of England was a *Protestant* church, albeit one whose Protestantism was thoroughly English—"moderate and orderly," "episcopal"—instead of the more radical version from abroad.[38] The Oxford Movement argued that the Church of England still retained its status as a "doctrinally sound expression of the church catholic," and sought a renewed emphasis on "liturgical worship, eucharistic communion, and intercessory prayer."[39] The Reformation might have separated the Church of England from the Church of Rome, but the Church of England was no less Catholic for that. More immediately, they opposed erastianism, or government intervention in church matters. Hence Keble's sermon, which reacts to the "enfranchisement of non-conformists, Catholics and shopkeepers" as a danger to the viability of an established church; under such circumstances, only by liberating the church from the state could the church retain its theological cohesion and "apostolic integrity."[40] Initial approval from within the Church of England gave way to growing apprehension, however, once readers of the *Tracts for the Times* (1833–41)—the movement's self-explanatory publications written by Richard Hurrell Froude, Keble, John Henry Newman, and E. B. Pusey, among others—began to suspect that Newman and E. B. Pusey in particular wished not just to restore continuity but to restore the actual Roman Catholic Church itself.[41] Newman's notorious Tract XC, *Remarks on Certain Passages in the Thirty-Nine Articles* (1841), which closely analyzed the Thirty-Nine Articles to show that an "Anglo-Catholic" could read them in a Catholic, and not Protestant, sense, was understood to encourage essentially Roman Catholic clergy to take over the Church of England from within. It did not help that Newman and James Mozley had co-edited the letters and journals of his fellow Tractarian Richard Hurrell Froude, the *Remains of the Late Reverend Richard Hurrell Froude*, which, despite its preface disclaiming any Roman Catholic tendencies in the text, included such pull quotes as "The Reformation was a limb badly set—it must be broken again in order to be righted," and "You will be shocked at my avowal, that I am every day becoming a less and less loyal son of the Reformation."[42] This was bad press, and it reinforced anxieties that the leaders of the Oxford Movement and their followers constituted a fifth column within the Church of England.

Third, although Newman and many of his fellows from the movement converted to Roman Catholicism, another contemporaneous movement within the Church of England sought to maintain its Anglican allegiances while also reviving traditional liturgical forms—the Anglo-Catholics, pejoratively known as "Ritualists." The Anglo-Catholic movement looked back to seventeenth-century Anglicanism and its renewed emphasis on the "beauty of holiness," in which the decoration of the altar, vestments, and the church itself all came in for new aesthetic care.[43] More seriously, Anglo-Catholics called for more attention to the liturgical rubric of the Book of Common Prayer, to the sacraments, to auricular confession, to the role of the Virgin Mary, and to the church's role in interpreting the scriptures; some Anglo-Catholic churches conformed so closely to Roman practice that it was necessary to warn unwary Roman Catholics that they were not about to enter one of their own churches.[44] As historians, Anglo-Catholics insisted that the Reformation had not, in fact, severed the Church of England from its Catholic roots but that its hierarchy had deliberately set out to preserve that connection despite the ongoing threats from the more reform-minded.[45] And Anglo-Catholics also began establishing brotherhoods and sisterhoods, with at least ninety sisterhoods alone established in the second half of the nineteenth century.[46] Such apparent returns to the Catholic fold elicited reactions both legislative and violent. In 1859 the congregation of St. George's, for example, regularly rioted during services against its Anglo-Catholic minister, Bryan King, and was aided and abetted by visitors who came solely for the purpose of making things worse.[47] The government eventually sought to restrain Anglo-Catholic practices by passing the Public Worship Regulation Act (1874), which did not have the desired effect: five Anglo-Catholic clergymen, thanks no doubt to their "devout pugnacity," opted for jail rather than conformity, and the law eventually lapsed into disuse—in part because it made the more hardcore Protestant organizations look rather cruel.[48]

Finally, the 1850s proved to be the high-water mark for anti-Catholic agitation, thanks to the ugly press surrounding the restoration of the Catholic hierarchy in late 1850. English Protestants misunderstood the process of establishing new Catholic dioceses as an actual territorial land grab; indeed, Lord John Russell complained that it was impossible to find in the orders anything other than "an assumption of territorial sovereignty."[49] To make matters even worse, the newly appointed Nicholas Cardinal Wiseman's pastoral address, "From the Flaminian Gate of Rome," took a triumphalist tone that, as Richard J. Schiefen delicately puts it, "was, to say the very least, unfortunate in its consequences."[50] Quickly dubbed the "Papal Aggression," the decision to establish a new hierarchy was cast by even such normally level-elheaded individuals like Russell as a direct assault on the Church of England in general and quite possibly the Queen in particular.[51] The conflict energized anti-Catholic political agitation for the remainder of the decade, until popular interest eventually faded.[52] In addition, the Papal Aggression crisis appeared to signify to Protestants that Catholics would simply not be *content* with whatever the British chose to offer them. The government, one Presbyterian journal complained later, had "but encouraged a system which is never satisfied, but cries for more, more, saying Give, give"—catering to a party that, as far as they were concerned, aimed at "Popish rule."[53]

Even as anxious Protestants complained that England was drifting Romeward, they were also seeking commemorative strategies for reminding fellow Protestants of their endangered religio-cultural heritage. Most prominent among these were celebrations of the Reformation tercentenary, beginning in 1817 with Lutheran observances in Germany, Sweden, the Netherlands, and the United States to mark the Ninety-Five Theses.[54] Thanks to Anglican clergyman Thomas Hartwell Horne (1780–1862), the commemorations arrived in England in 1835 to mark the anniversary of Myles Coverdale's Bible (1535), England's first full, published, vernacular Bible.[55] Horne took the opportunity to supply the *Protestant Memorial* (1835), intended as a unilateral defense of Protestantism *in toto* from Roman Catholic assault.[56] The core of Horne's argument, which also became the core of the many Reformation tercentenary sermons that appeared in print, was that "*in every age* there has been a religion similar to that which is now called the *Religion of Protestants,* and which has been professed by those, who, by their separation and their conduct, have protested against every erroneous innovation, whether they were those who were '*first called Christians at Antioch,*' '*Children of Israel*' in and after the time of Jacob, or '*Sons of God*' before the deluge, until we arrive at the first man to whom the Almighty made known His will" (40; emphasis in the original). "Protestantism," in this line of reasoning, is thus less a set of denominations than it is monotheism, belief in the Holy Spirit, and a Trinitarian faith in Christ (41–46), all of which somehow manages to encompass not only Christianity but also Judaism and, apparently, Adam and Eve. Repeatedly, Horne hammers in the message that Protestantism of whatever flavor owns allegiance *only* to the Bible, and is thus antecedent to Roman Catholicism, rather than vice-versa. Intended to wipe out at one blow Catholicism's critique of Protestant schism and Protestant novelty, Horne's message has the further effect of gathering up all Protestant denominations under one generous roof—the strategy that would prove so attractive to the Protestant novelists who followed him.

Three years later, the indefatigable anti-Catholic campaigner Charles Golightly tackled the Oxford Movement closer to home by putting forward a then-unusual proposition: erect a memorial to the Oxford Martyrs of 1555–56, Thomas Cranmer, Hugh Latimer, and Nicholas Ridley. The commission went to a young George Gilbert Scott, inspired by the medieval Eleanor Crosses (built in 1291–94 as a memorial to Eleanor of Castile), who began working on the monument in 1841 and finished it in 1843. All and sundry immediately concluded that the memorial was intended as an insult to the Oxford Movement, but as Golightly's biographer Andrew Atherstone points out, Golightly first floated the idea (unsuccessfully) in 1836, when he was still on decent terms with Newman and his associates—suggesting that Golightly had originally had Roman Catholicism in his sights.[57]

What all of these debates had in common was a shared sense that Protestantism had somehow become inextricably identified with modernity. For Anglican and Dissenting novelists, the Reformation defined the horizon of a new age, one defined by widespread biblical literacy, liberty (political and religious), "natural" gender relations (valuing the family instead of celibacy), patriotism, and spiritual instead of corporeal discipline.[58] In their narratives, the Reformation literally domesticates Christianity, removing it from elite or homosocial circles and locating it within the bosom of the heterosexual family.[59] As we shall see, novelists repeatedly imagine this transformation in terms of the reading habits of women, children, and the poor. And it is worth noting that despite the relative paucity of women in public anti-Catholic agitation, the controversial novel afforded them a considerable outlet to influence public opinion—indeed, given the prominence of Grace Kennedy's *Father Clement*, women arguably invented the genre.[60] Yet such phenomena were always trembling on the brink of appearance, reappearance, or disappearance; the modernity promised by the Reformation had never absolutely arrived. Rather than "instinctively" or "naturally" rehearsing Reformation battles, evangelical Protestants believed that they needed to make their contemporaries *self-consciously aware* of the presentness of the Reformation process.[61] Protestant forgetfulness, then, was yet another symptom of the past's fragile hold on the present. In turn, Catholics argued that Protestant narratives rested on a series of strategic omissions. For Catholic controversial novelists like Fanny Taylor or E. C. Agnew, Protestantism would necessarily implode once the self-inflicted gaps in its historical memory became clear. Far from celebrating the Reformation as the source of modern British freedom, Catholics pointed to it as the moment in which Protestants began undermining the very nature of history itself; to that end, Catholic novelists presented their fictions as attempts to demonstrate that Catholic history *was* British history.

Controversial historical fiction, especially in its evangelical form, sought to remedy this perceived cultural amnesia through a course of historical pedagogy: the reader had to be taught how to reinterpret the *present*. The evangelical novelist does not simply read the Reformation as an allegory or analogy for Victorian cultural and religious controversies; instead he or she (frequently, she) fictionalizes Reformation crises so that the reader may learn to recognize that the present threatens to *repeat* the worst aspects of the past. In that sense, these novels sometimes dovetail strikingly with the Gothic—another genre dominated by endless repetitions and returns of the past—in form as well as content. These authors turn to historical fiction in order to avoid living out what they feared might be the return of sixteenth-century persecution from the dead, a real-life Gothic repetition. At the same time, repetition remains built into the evangelical model of history, for Victorian Protestant-Catholic controversies enact, again and again, the unceasing struggle between Christ and Antichrist. By returning to the past in order to reread the present, the novelist invites his or her audience to think of themselves as potential actors in the grand drama of Reformation—simultaneously a historical moment and an ongoing transformational process—that either heralds or prepares the way for the millennium.

Finally, controversial historical novelists, like didactic authors generally, intended their fictions to *reshape* how the reader understood both everyday experience and the relationship between past, present, and future. Protestant novelists do not represent martyrdom as a far-off possibility, but instead as a very real danger. Catholic Emancipation might very well mean that Protestant liberties would vanish, Protestant children would be suborned, and Protestant heads would roll. Writing of an *auto da fé*, the novelist W. H. G. Kingston gloomily prognosticated that "With a few years' judicious educating by the Jesuits, and a continuance of supineness and incredulity as to Rome's designs on the part of British Protestants, of which all denominations are guilty, it is not at all impossible that similar scenes may be enacted in England."[62] Religious novels model possible actions, even though material circumstances seem, at first, to be so very different—the ground on which Catholic novelists would dispute Protestant claims. Such concerns profoundly affected how writers manipulated narrative voice, appropriated other genres (sermons, spiritual journals, conversion narratives, letters), and situated their own fictions in relationship to predecessors like Scott. In particular, writers dramatized over and over again how disseminating the vernacular Bible itself marked an epoch in historical consciousness. For Protestants, the

Bible was simultaneously the key to history, History (with a capital *H*) itself, and the model of all historical narrative; for Catholics, Protestant "biblicism" disrupted organic communities organized around the sacraments. Writers on both sides dramatized how persecuted religious groups could consolidate themselves around sacred texts and sacred rites. In both cases, to forget the Reformation and what it wrought, then, meant forgetting not just *one* event but the meaning of *any* event.

Forging Fictional Reformations

But what were they trying not to forget? Novelists (and, for that matter, writers in other genres, such as poetry or children's history) did not offer a narrative of the Reformation that mapped precisely onto either old or new scholarship. The core problem in thinking about the Reformation historically—for Protestants, at least, and especially evangelicals—was that it was always understood as a *return* to the truths of a purely scriptural Christianity. In the words of the ardent anti-Catholic campaigner Hugh M'Neile, "We invented nothing. We added nothing. Nay, we altered nothing. We did but clear away the accumulated rubbish of the middle ages, and reach and rest upon the old foundations."[63] Far from being an innovation—a very dirty word in both Protestant and Catholic polemic—the Reformation returned to Christianity's origin, an origin that was apparently lost but, in fact, present within the Bible all the time. Protestantism thus becomes both "modern" and universal, restored in part because of material circumstances but not produced by those circumstances. As Grant Wacker notes, many Protestants assumed that "saving knowledge of divine things had been given to human beings directly, unmediated and uncontaminated by the historical context in which it was received."[64] Protestantism escapes cultural and historical relativism because culture and history do not *make* the Protestant faith; rather, Protestantism is God's revealed Word *concealed* beneath the historical accretions of ages (the [Catholic] "rubbish").

This paradoxically ahistorical historiography did not lend itself to complex narratives about Protestantism's relationship to its Roman Catholic forebears (or, for that matter, to its growing Anglo-Catholic counterparts). Margaret Nancy Cutt remarks that evangelicals "oversimplified history in the defence of Protestantism," and the novelists' need to rework facts in order to fit the polemical goal extended to historiographical theory as well.[65] In this historical mode, Protestants interpreted heretical movements like the Lollards of fourteenth-century England or the Waldenses of twelfth-century Lyons as proto-Protestant. That is, they traced Christianity's lineage not through the institutional churches—the visible church—but through successive communities of saints united by true belief rather than geography—that is, the invisible church.[66] There was absolutely nothing original about this grand metanarrative of Christian history, which had its antecedents in the twelfth-century prophecies of Joachim de Fiore and became fully entrenched in self-justificatory Protestant narratives of the sixteenth century. Rosemary Mitchell's observation that the "dominant national narrative of Protestant historians . . . was based largely on the texts of their sixteenth-, seventeenth-, and eighteenth-century predecessors, rather than on any original research," can be stretched well beyond historians to encompass both novelists and popular controversialists.[67] It is possible to overstate this point—after all, after midcentury, writers frequently announced their indebtedness to the Swiss Presbyterian J. H. Merle D'Aubigné, whose *History of the Reformation of the Sixteenth Century* (1846) became a bestseller. Nevertheless, authors regularly turned to classic older texts, all of which were easily available in full-length, abridged, and sometimes expanded versions, such as Joseph Milner's, Isaac Milner's, and John Scott's *History of the Church of Christ* (1794–97, 1826) and Gilbert Burnet's *History of the Reformation of the Church of England* (1679–1715). Similarly popular, although sometimes considered problematic because of its apparent rationalism, was the German Lutheran J. L. Mosheim's *Institutionum historiae ecclesiasticae libri IV* (1726), translated as *Ecclesiastical History, Ancient and Modern*. Finally, one of the most popular sources for evangelical historical fiction was Foxe's *Book of Martyrs*, which enjoyed a publishing renaissance in the nineteenth century. Novelists, poets, dramatists, and controversialists most commonly drew their materials from dated but nevertheless "religiously correct" sources; there is a time lag built into the discursive field.

Although this book emphasizes the evangelical Protestant novels that dominated popular religious publishing, I also examine traditional High Church, Anglo-Catholic, and Roman Catholic counterfictions that critique both the evangelical worldview and evangelical historical thinking. This book traces these disputes and points of agreement across a broad range of sometimes ephemeral and frequently anonymous works—works that, nevertheless, occupied considerable territory in the nineteenth-century literary landscape.[68] Given that most of these novels are only now being reread by modern scholars, my readers may find that the "mainstream" positions I discuss here will be nearly as unfamiliar as the minority voices. Finally, I have not attempted to replicate the extensive body of scholarship devoted to representations of Mary, Queen of Scots and Elizabeth I, although the latter will put in an appearance as more a function than a person; however, I will spend considerable time on figures central to popular thought about the Reformation but not yet studied in quite so much detail, like John Wycliffe and Mary I (dubbed "Bloody Mary" for the Protestant persecutions that marked her reign).

Over the course of this book, I will repeatedly return to four themes: forgetting, martyrdom, conversion, and Bibles. The shifting intersections of these four themes characterize both Protestant and Catholic historical novels, acting as privileged moments of *origin*: the origin of individual faith, of national identity, of modernity itself. In chapter 1 I begin with the paradigmatic historical novelist, Walter Scott, whose duology *The Monastery* (1820) and *The Abbot* (1820) revised the emotionally fraught, traumatic narratives of the Reformation inherited from the Gothic novel. Read together, these two novels celebrate the unqualified birth of Protestant modernity out of the Catholic ashes, insisting that Catholicism is not just over and done with but literally unthinkable; the novels insist that the modern Protestant mind cannot fully approximate Catholic spiritual and imaginative modes. But although Scott's novels codified many of the tropes of Victorian Reformation tales, especially gendered accounts of conversion and Bible reading—themselves inherited from older polemics in other genres—his deeply politicized reading of Protestantism's emerging dominance made the implications of his work more appealing to Catholic novelists than Scott's co-religionists.

Thus, chapter 2, which analyzes Victorian attempts to locate the Reformation's essence in the Middle Ages, shows how quickly Scott's confident link between Protestantism and modernity became untenable in the post–Catholic Emancipation decades. Proto-Protestant novels about the fourteenth-century Lollards insisted that the sixteenth-century Reformation was just one more attempt to heal the English church's alienation from its core identity and fulfilled an opportunity begun but ultimately derailed two centuries before. The "forgotten" Lollard martyrs executed for reading the Bible laid bare the structures of repression that would once again, Protestant novelists assured their readers, be in place if a revivified Catholicism came to power. The Bible itself comes to the fore in chapter 3, which analyzes representations of vernacular Bible reading during the sixteenth century. Such representations attempt to recreate the *shock* of the biblical text: arguing that the very omnipresence of the Bible in nineteenth-century culture turns it into "just another book," novelists turn the history of Bible reading into a clarion call for recognizing its crucial role in shaping modernity. Chapter 4 examines one of the greatest bugbears of Victorian culture—namely, the memory of the persecutions during the reign of Mary I. Drawing on Foxe's martyrologies, Protestant novelists implored their readers to perceive the deadly similarities between Mary's reign and an increasingly Catholicized England. This leads us to the Anglo-Catholic and Roman Catholic novelists who feature in chapter 5. Unlike their Protestant counterparts, Catholic novelists draw on elements of Scott's historicism—in particular, anachronism and cultural relativism—to insist that the persecuting past is *lost*; at the same time, Catholic novelists turn to persecutions under the Elizabethan settlement to identify organic, transnational connections among Catholics of all time periods. Nevertheless, where Anglo-Catholic novelists stop short at a call for mutual toleration, Roman Catholic novelists argue that a historical awakening will ultimately lead to England's re-conversion.

Not everyone was content with either Protestant or Catholic narrative strategies, however. In chapter 6 I examine the *difference* of controversial historical fiction through the lens of a novel that might, at first, seem to belong to the same category: Charles Dickens' *Barnaby Rudge*. *Barnaby Rudge*, I argue, unilaterally rejects both the historical novel according to Scott *and* the models of historical memory propounded by evangelicals. In its celebration of historical silencing and even forgetfulness, it declares a pox on both Protestant and Catholic houses. Finally, my coda reads Victorian narratives of the controversial Italian reformer Girolamo Savonarola, including George Eliot's *Romola*, and suggests that they tell us something about a more anxious strand of Reformation fiction, one in which victory may not, after all, be assured.

Chapter One

SCOTT'S REFORMATIONS

In *The Monastery* (1820) the Protestant evangelist Henry Warden and the Catholic priest Father Eustace (old acquaintances, as it happens) prepare to square off for a no-holds-barred controversial spat over a prooftext. Warden yearns to offer Father Eustace help to "lay hold on the Rock of Ages"; Father Eustace, icily, declares that "my faith is already anchored on that Rock on which Saint Peter founded his church." And Warden, not to be outdone, declares that this reading of the Rock is a "perversion of the text . . . grounded upon a vain play upon words—a most idle paronomasia."[1] The two are promptly interrupted, and all for the good, as far as the narrator is concerned; after all, "what can ensure the good temper and moderation of polemics?" (*TM* 303). This thwarted exchange both references what was a still fiery debate in nineteenth-century controversy—the nature of figurative language in the Bible and its role in shaping doctrine, especially of the Eucharist—and promptly sidelines it in favor of "moderation," which is apparently incompatible with any passionate theological discourse (let alone dueling prooftexts). At the same time, the narrator's weary observation situates him very clearly in a *post*-Reformation historical moment, when prooftexting is no longer a matter of life and death (Warden, after all, is being hunted through Scotland) and polite "good temper" counts for more than theological correctness.

Strategies such as this have led modern critics to praise (or blame) *The Monastery* and its sequel, *The Abbot* (1820), for their "profoundly non-partisan vision of the Reformation," noting in particular the effect produced by what Lionel Lackey calls Scott's "unwillingness to scrutinize fine points of theology."[2] Even those who have noticed that the novels obviously tilt toward the Protestant perspective suggest that they do so in the most unexceptionable and unremarkable of ways; Scott's post-Reformation world is "a new enlightened age in which Christianity has been stripped of trappings designed to control the popular imagination and returned to some putative essentiality derived from Scripture."[3] Given the speed with which controversialists like Henry Warden are bundled off each time they begin to wax too warm, such responses are understandable. Even though the quarrel between Protestantism and Catholicism looms large in each novel, the uninformed reader would come away not knowing much about what either religion was, or why their adherents were fighting. And yet, this brief eruption (and squashing) of formal theological controversy easily distracts us from the duology's more subtle questions, here creeping in through the narrator's voice: What does it mean to *think* as a post-Reformation Protestant, for whom this debate is not only decided but rather stale? What role does reading—above all, reading the Bible—play in shaping this new Protestant subject? Last but not least, who *reads*?

Despite Scott's nineteenth-century reputation as safe for evangelical consumption,[4] these questions both underpin Scott's mapping of sixteenth-century religious and political chaos and set up the terms against which Victorian controversial fiction will revolt. Some time ago, Judith Wilt found in these novels "evidence for a deep confusion or anxiety in Scott about the Protestant right-side upping of the Christian religion which he championed."[5] But although Scott makes no attempt to cover up the complexity, ambiguity, and even ugliness of the Reformation in Scotland, his duology asserts something very different from what we normally take to be his goal as a novelist: an imaginative reanimation of the past. Instead, the novels insist that the Catholic past *cannot* be successfully retrieved or imagined in a post-Reformation Protestant world, no matter what the narrator's sympathies. The coming of Protestantism, which Scott plays out in dramas of gendered reading and interpretation, turns out to also be the limit to our horizon of understanding. In narrating the dispersal of Catholicism and its past, Scott's duology also eradicates even the faintest possibility of its revival in or danger to the present.

Traumas and Ambiguities: Fictions of the Reformation before Scott

Scott's duology lies on the other side of the Catholic Emancipation barrier from the Victorian novelists of the rest of this study. His confidence in Catholicism's slide into merely antiquarian interest derives, in a very large part, from this pre-Emancipation moment. In 1820 Catholic Emancipation (or the "Catholic question") was certainly under intense discussion, and had been for some years; after all, it had been one of the original bargaining chips in the 1801 union of Great Britain and Ireland, until it was suddenly removed from the table when George III refused to countenance it. The arrival of French Catholic refugees during the Revolution and Napoleonic Wars, including religious houses and clergymen, had accustomed the British to think about Catholics with at least more sympathy than they had before, and by 1812 parliamentary motions for Catholic relief were being treated with greater and greater seriousness. In 1819, in fact, one such motion had just missed passing by a hair's breadth in the House of Commons.[6] But in 1820 the pro-Emancipation Whigs had other things to be thinking about, and Scott's novels predate the birth of Daniel O'Connell's energetic Catholic Association by three years. At the same time, the novels also postdate the notorious Peterloo Massacre of 1819, to which Scott had responded by lauding the government's treatment of the protesters. Scott himself was not pro-Emancipation in 1820, although he grudgingly converted to the cause some time later out of sheer pragmatism: given that the "old Lady of Babylon's mouth" had not been "stopd," Scott wrote in his journal in 1829, "I cannot see the sense of keeping up the irritation about their right to sit in parliament."[7] Scott's sympathy for monks subjected to Protestant depredations tells us far more about his attitude to ungovernable mobs than to Catholicism; indeed, it was shared by even doughty pro-Reformation historians like Gilbert Stuart, who several decades earlier had derided attacks on churches and monasteries as "acts of outrage and violence" or "mischief and destruction."[8]

This sense of the popular chaos always lurking beneath Reformation movements, though, also derives from earlier fictions of the Reformation, which invested it with the emotional pressures of the gothic and sentimental modes. Unlike Scott's duology, these earlier novels, such as Rosetta Ballin's *The Statue Room* (1790) or the anonymous *Lady Jane Grey: An Historical Tale* (1791), conspicuously resist attempts to identify the Reformation with the birth of modernity. Indeed, they decouple Protestantism and "progress" in ways that contrast sharply not only with Scott but with Victorian narratives as well. *Lady Jane Grey* ends not with the triumph of Protestantism but with the surviving characters in European exile and Mary I still on the throne; *The Statue Room* celebrates Mary's virtues and renders Elizabeth monstrous, while killing off its characters in progressively baroque ways. But the novel we know influenced Scott the most deeply, Sophia Lee's epistolary *The Recess; Or, a Tale of Other Times* (1783), offers a more complex vision of Protestantism's contingencies. *The Recess* imagines that Mary, Queen of Scots secretly bore two children, Matilda and Ellinor, and had them secreted away in an underground hideaway (the eponymous Recess), owned by Lord Henry Scrope. The two sisters marry (also secretly) prominent members of Elizabeth's court, Leicester and Essex, and find themselves entangled in court intrigues, attempted assassinations, shipwrecks, and even the occasional slave rebellion; by the end, after a veritable orgy of evidentiary destruction, Ellinor has died insane, Matilda's daughter Mary has also died, and Matilda herself is on the verge of death. As modern critics have repeatedly noted, one of the most striking things about the novel's practice is how it consistently undermines each viewpoint character's reliability. After observing Matilda drool over Lord Leicester at some length, the reader is taken aback to find Ellinor bluntly declaring that Leicester's sole "charm" is physical.[9] But Ellinor herself tellingly substitutes fantasy for reality when it comes to her love for the Earl of Essex, whose goals another character describes as "romance" (220). Ellinor and Matilda both badly mistake their respective husbands' virtues, or lack thereof, prefiguring Mary's similar error in her choice of lover (James I's favorite Robert Carr, Viscount Rochester), and, as a result, the reader can never be quite sure how to understand their evaluations of Mary, Queen of Scots, Elizabeth I, or James I.[10]

For both Ellinor and Matilda, the Reformation registers as a series of disconnected psychic traumas. Even though both of them somehow become Protestants, suggesting that the Catholic cause has already lost its traction, their Protestantism does not align them with Elizabeth (who emerges as one of the villains of the piece) or a well-defined national identity. Because they spend most of the novel shuttling from one enclosed space to the next, including repeated returns to the Recess (which, symbolically, grows more and more tattered as the novel continues), their sentimentally inflected views of history remain subjective in more than one sense of the word. Ellinor and Matilda understand history through their investments in the heroic actions of their idolized husbands, actions that turn out in the end to be neither particularly heroic nor even particularly effective; in the words of their friend Lady Pembroke, Ellinor's understanding of Essex is at best "partial" (256). They themselves, while potentially history-altering, are systematically erased, until James I finally destroys the remaining documentation that proves their identities. Everyone, Protestant and Catholic, unites in betraying the heroines. Recusant Catholicism offers no nostalgic vistas of a harmonious British culture; Elizabethan and Jacobean Protestantism may generate private virtues in a few individuals but does nothing to constrain the evils disseminated by the royal court. The clash between Catholic and Protestant never emerges as a coherent national *plot*, securely grounded in biblical allegory or typology. Instead, the novel makes Protestantism's moral effects purely personal and contingent, while it denies Catholicism any counter-weighing authority or historical significance. Ellinor and Matilda, Protestants both, find Protestant monarchs of no help at all, while Catholicism, in the person of their relative Lady Mortimer, turns out to be at best a "narrow faith" (128).

April Alliston comments that Ellinor's eventual "madness" consists, in part, of a "recognition of the gap, of the contradiction between the reader's demand for 'truth'—the truth in this case being itself an abyss, the very placelessness of women in a patrie—and the social demand for a unified narrative which would deny the truth of the abyss."[11] The formal fragmentation Alliston notes in Ellinor's narrative characterizes the novel as a whole, which not only highlights how women defined primarily by their mothers silently vanish into historical thin air but also denies that the usual stabilizing categories of Reformation history, already long operational by the late eighteenth century, have much, if any, meaning. In that sense, the episodic nature of Ellinor's and Matilda's extreme psychological trials reappears at the level of national history: there is no progress, no change, no greater meaning to events, no organized story to tell. Indeed, Diane Long Hoeveler suggests, gothic works such as this "actually seem to be mourning the loss of Catholicism as the state religion" or, at least, its "'porous selves,' magic, superstition, and irrationality."[12] The gendered historical disorder of Sophia Lee's Reformation depends, in part, on the fragmented and frequently traumatized perspectives of her protagonists, who can only ever observe, not participate. When it comes to subjectivity, the shift from Catholic to Protestant appears to have little to no significance—so little, indeed, that in both daughters' cases the narrative erases the actual moment of conversion.

Catholicism's Vanishing Trace

Unlike *The Recess*, Scott's duology seeks to differentiate between Catholic antiquity and Protestant modernity, and in so doing it historicizes what Lee represents as a transhistorical condition. *The Monastery* and *The Abbot* offer us different modes of confusion and enlightenment: one enabled by the "enchanted," romance-permeated world of *The Monastery*, in which the mysterious, fairy-like White Lady of Avenel figures prominently and, as Charles Taylor puts it, "the boundary between agents and forces is fuzzy"; and the other enabled by the "disenchanted," more deliberately realist world of *The Abbot*, in which characters find themselves adrift in a feminized political landscape where appearances are nearly impossible to decode.[13] The novels closely follow the fate of the Avenel family and their associates across two generations in mid-sixteenth-century Scotland, during the heat of the early Reformation; in both cases, the male protagonists find themselves traversing an often violent Scotland, caught between the Catholic old regime and the increasingly powerful, but decentered and disorganized, Protestant insurgency. In *The Monastery* young Mary Avenel, orphaned early in the novel, is loved in different ways by two brothers, Halbert and Edward Glendinning; the more brutish Halbert, eventually refined by literacy and the soldier's life, joins Mary in converting to Protestantism, whereas Edward remains Catholic and takes vows. Throughout, the Avenels (and their Bible) come under the protection of the White Lady, who is magically linked to the House of Avenel's fate. Years later, in *The Abbot*, Halbert's and Mary's marriage, while generally happy, has been marred by childlessness and frequent absences. Into it enters the mysterious and apparently illegitimate Roland Graeme, who has been secretly groomed by his grandmother, Magdalen, to liberate Mary, Queen of Scots from Elizabeth's control. By the end, however, Roland turns out to be both a true Avenel and a true Protestant, even as he achieves some sort of delicate balance between being "loyal to Queen Mary" and having some "influence . . . with the party in power."[14] The contentious threads of Reformation history intersect through Roland and his alliances, but as in *The Recess*, his love for the deposed Scottish queen silently rests on the loss of her Catholic cause.

Not surprisingly, the duology frequently finds that the Reformation seems hardly more organized from within than without. The "spirit of the times," thinks one character in *The Monastery*, may best be summed up by "the unhallowed and unchristian divisions of the country" (92): the Reformation *zeitgeist* warps and deforms its sometimes unwitting participants, whose minds are not so much converted as perverted to ungodly ways. As the speaker, Father Eustace, is Catholic, his point of view might understandably be somewhat jaundiced— and yet, Scott denies much in the way of sacredness to the Protestantizing process. Dismissing *The Monastery*, Donald Cameron complains that the driving force of Scott's Reformation is "general greed," and certainly both novels devote much of their energy to insisting on the Reformation's basest motivations.[15] Both Catholic and Protestant forces seem primarily bent on stealing as much as they can from the remaining monasteries, while one of *The Monastery*'s most important converts, the fearsome Julian Avenel, turns to Protestantism explicitly for political and worldly reasons: "we of the laity care not what you set up, so you pull merrily down what stands in our way" (224). Julian's self-interested conversion, which will be echoed by the plotter Magdalen Graeme's deceptively enthusiastic conversion in *The Abbot*, suggests deeply ominous conversion plots—conversions that not only produce no difference but, in fact, are either willfully read or innocently misread as authentic by "fellow" Protestants. Here, the Reformation sounds suspiciously like a pretext for the mobs that Scott so loathed.[16] Similarly, *The Abbot* notes Protestant court intrigues, attacks Protestant would-be terrorists (one of whom tries to assassinate the Queen of Scots) alongside Catholic conspirators, and registers how Protestant iconoclasm destroys Catholic spaces. Reformation Scotland is violent, in flux, and frequently difficult to parse.

In both novels the sense that the Reformation constitutes progress emerges only as an effect of the novels' explicitly Protestantized narration; that is, the warrant for the Reformation's success is the novels' own attitude to it. And in the beginning, this attitude emerges from a fiction of an explicitly masculine and homosocial literary network. *The Monastery*'s introductory frame openly and self-reflexively parodies the gothic "found manuscript": the editor (Scott) receives the manuscript from Captain Clutterbuck, who receives it from a

Benedictine. The Benedictine, in turn, completed the manuscript left unfinished by his uncle, and both of them based it on "authentic materials of that period" (21). When Captain Clutterbuck expresses some anxiety about the propriety of a good Protestant like himself taking on this project, the Benedictine assures him (prefiguring the narrator, much later on) that "no matter of controversy" (21) is involved—that, indeed, he has indicted his Catholic ancestors for the "decay of discipline" (22) that partly prompted the Reformation (or, as he puts it, the "great schism" [22]), no doubt to the annoyance of modern Catholic readers. In Fiona Robertson's words, he has "modernized and Protestantized" the tale "to suit contemporary taste."[17] Scott quite dryly informs Clutterbuck that this found manuscript scenario seems remarkably familiar in the course of hinting that Clutterbuck himself is a mere fiction (27–28); in any event, Scott takes the liberty of rewriting the manuscript whenever it seems too pro-Catholic. This rather dizzying record of provenance thus culminates by asserting the narrative's location in the present—in other words, a Protestant fiction of a Catholic setting out to Protestantize the narrative! In the context of a different Scott preface with similar strategies in play, Caroline McCracken-Flesher suggests that Scott "draws attention to the irrecuperability but also the complexity of its telling, and raises the problem not just of truly telling a tale, but of telling it once and for all."[18] On the one hand, that is the case here as well: the Catholic origin story exists as both presence and absence, imaginable only as the opposite of the obviously pro-Protestant text on the page. On the other, the preface insists that Catholic writing in modern culture must already be necessarily formed (or deformed) by Protestant norms—the Benedictine has, after all, indicted his own faith—and thus has been rendered unreadable as such. The Benedictine remains as a trace of the lost Catholic past, but only insofar as he has been imagined into being *by* a Protestant; Catholic texts are no longer possible except as artifacts of a rational Protestant mind.[19]

Jerome McGann argues of Scott's "spurious texts" that their job is not "vindicating probabilities" but rather acting as an "authenticating sign—a true index—of Scott's powers of historical invention."[20]

In this case, the found manuscript trope—which we shall meet again in a very different register—testifies that in post-Reformation modernity, an unmediated Catholic point of view turns out to be fundamentally unimaginable (even, one notes, to a Benedictine, fictional or otherwise). This shift becomes even clearer in *The Abbot*, in which the White Lady of Avenel, a key agent in *The Monastery*, is as noticeable for her absence as she had previously been for her presence. More than one critic has objected that the White Lady violently ruptures Scott's historicist frame, charging that it is difficult to reconcile the real presence of the supernatural with the otherwise materialist workings of the plot.[21] Others, seeking to find a more organic explanation for her role, have suggested that the White Lady is an "impersonal, inevitable historical will instead of a romantic, mood-creating presence," or perhaps a "figure" of "Imagination as a power for attaining knowledge of self, other, and the past."[22] To make matters even more complex, her role in the text is suspiciously reminiscent of the sacred (or at least supernatural) *genius loci* that were still appearing in Catholic texts through the early modern period—making her an apparently ineradicable trace *of* the Catholic past, the sign of the Protestant future *within* the Catholic past, or perhaps a combination of both.[23]

Her abrupt disappearance from *The Abbot*, though, is as startling as her role in *The Monastery*—all the more so because her erasure seems so very casual. As Scott explains to Captain Clutterbuck in the preface to *The Abbot*, he has simply "struck out" the White Lady, as "public taste" is no longer quite so keen on such "legendary superstitions" (3). This response to real-life criticism not only Protestantizes the narrative further but insists that the very capacity to enjoy a mix of supernatural and realistic elements has vanished along with Catholic power. "Miracles, visions, necromancy, dreams, and other preternatural events, are exploded now even from romances," Horace Walpole ironically assured the first readers of *The Castle of Otranto* (1764), casting all such things as pre-Reformation rubbish (all to be resuscitated by his novel, of course).[24] Ironically, Scott winds up confirming Walpole's preface (apparently, readers really *didn't* want to find "preternatural events" cropping up in their historical novels) while in the act of preserving Walpole's quasi-historicist gothic practice, which identified the "reality" of supernatural events with the supposed moment of writing. The White Lady exists in the first novel as one of the traces of its Catholic authorship: her supernatural status, far from being some bizarre rupture of a realist text, testifies (as the supernatural does in *The Castle of Otranto*) to the novel's Catholic origin story. The supernatural thus functions naturally as historical evidence—what E. J. Clery calls "exemplary historicism."[25] Scott recuperates the White Lady's critical failure as proof that, in fact, Protestantism has won the day. Indeed, Scott adds, he has erased explorations of Catholic "enthusiasm" on the ground that "we do not feel deep sympathy at this period" with such religious sentiments, profound as they once were (*TA* 3). Modern Protestant context rules out the possibility of reconstructing its Catholic equivalent, or even of preserving traces of Catholic "superstition" within the novel's form. The duology turns out to be not just about how the Reformation came to Scotland but about how a particular way of writing about the Reformation came to be.

Yet erasing the traces of Catholic supernaturalism also leads to chaotic plots. Without trying to force the issue of the White Lady's success—or lack thereof, given that even Scott conceded that she was rather a flop—she renders causality *visible*, or at the very least points beyond herself to its existence. Despite the contention of one irate correspondent to the *Gentleman's Magazine*, who felt her "presence was no where required," the White Lady acts as both connector and corrector, forcibly ensuring that the narrative's supposedly "inevitable" (as Lionel Lackey puts it) Protestant plot goes according to plan.[26] The White Lady's frequently prophetic presence indicates to her friends (or victims) that a particular historical plot is in operation, albeit without explicitly specifying what that plot is; even as she confuses, she explicates. Thus, after coaching the illiterate Halbert on how to retrieve the Avenels' Bible from the mystic flames guarding it deep in the mysterious cavern, she counsels him to "[w]ith patience bide, / Heaven will provide / The fitting time, the fitting guide" (*TM* 119). Even in the most bizarre circumstances, in other words, she points to the possibility of divine order, of a world that functions according to a necessity that cannot always be perceived by mere mortals but the knowledge of which comforts nevertheless. Fallen man may never be able to grasp divine providence in its full meaning, but he may at least rest secure that it is there.

Unlike God's providence, the White Lady's agency in the narrative does not need to be taken on faith, but it does provoke speculations about the nature and possibility of miracles. Like the quarrel over figurative language, the controversy about the White Lady's miraculous (or not) interventions indexes the decay of modern theological heat—in this case, the so-called disenchantment of the world, in which God no longer manifests himself by disrupting nature's laws and spirits depart from once-sacred spaces. In practice, disenchantment and sacramental enchantment continued to coexist, despite the Reformers' best efforts at drawing a neat line between the two; although the sixteenth-century Reformers argued that miracles had long since ceased to happen, substituting special providence (in which "God demonstrated a particular concern for a specific person or community") instead, in practice it was difficult to keep the two concepts apart, and a number of Protestant churches insisted that miracles were still possible.[27] Strictly speaking, however, the established churches maintained that "true miracles were no longer to be expected in the Church," including exorcisms and, of course, transubstantiation; God's Word was sufficient to make His point.[28]

Notably, the disenchanted readings in this novel initially derive from the skeptical Father Eustace, who reads poor Father Philip's story of his damp disgrace at the White Lady's hands in "less than miraculous" (*TM* 75) terms, decoding it as a potentially scandalous narrative about a monk making merry with the miller's daughter. Later, he tries to read his own vision of the White Lady as the aftereffect of the "impression" Philip's story had made (*TM* 79), only to finally be convinced of her reality when she magically saves him from murderers (*TM* 94). Ruefully, he confesses to his Abbot that this was divinely ordained "penance" for disbelieving Father Philip, a warning that God "can at pleasure open a communication betwixt us and beings of a different, and, as we word it, supernatural class" while penalizing intellectual pride (*TM* 103). Yet this Catholic reading of events, which interprets the White Lady as an agent of divine grace, is promptly dispelled by the Lady herself, who tells Halbert she is "Something betwixt heaven and hell— / Something that neither stood nor fell—," who has "[h]elp nor hope beyond the grave" (*TM* 114). The narrative thus unfolds toward a Catholic position, only to shunt matters off into a less familiar and less classifiable direction. She may be part and parcel of the "irrational and therefore false consciousness of a moribund feudal order" that also generates a "myth of supernatural necessity," as James Kerr observes of gothic in *The Bride of Lammermoor*, but she cannot be so easily sorted into either pre- or post-Reformation mindsets.[29] Simultaneously in awe of the God whose book she preserves and unable to receive the gift of grace herself, the White Lady stubbornly refuses to be reduced to either Catholic or Protestant narratives of how the supernatural *ought* to function in the natural world.

There is no evidence to interpret her interference as Father Eustace does—that is, as punishment directly inflicted by God—and yet she cannot be reduced to mere "superstition," as a Protestant reading might have it. Michael Gamer, in one of the most thoughtful examinations of Scott's vexed relationship to gothic, notes of his ballads that "[i]n making the past simple and chivalric yet supernatural and senselessly violent, his poems can hardly be said to advocate a return to the historical venues that they inhabit."[30] Although the world of Scott's Reformation duology hardly qualifies as either simple or chivalric, something very similar is at stake here. The White Lady's reality within the text reveals a now-exploded (from the novel's point of view) Catholic understanding of how the supernatural may incarnate itself but without confirming the disenchanted mainstream Protestant perspective, in which natural and supernatural are severed in postbiblical times. As she moves through the plot, the White Lady enables the narrator to suggest how narratives of miraculous events might come into being and proliferate, without ever *validating* such narratives. When the White Lady puts miracles in play, she also renders them problematic, frustrating attempts to bring both her and them under a neat theological roof; any attempt to explain (and, thus, tame) her turns out to be fatally fragmented, introducing the possibility that both Catholic and Protestant systems, applied too strictly, may fall apart under pressure.

Biblical Enchantments and Disenchantments

The White Lady's agency manifests itself most startlingly (and, perhaps, most frustratingly) in one of *The Monastery*'s most prominent subplots: the perambulations of Lady Avenel's Bible. As it moves through the novel, this Bible is glimpsed, hidden, stolen, returned, mystically preserved, and even read. This surprisingly mobile text reenacts the fictional circulation of *The Monastery* and *The Abbot* in a distinctly feminized register—even in the various priestly attempts to gain control of it. Father Philip, who first absconds with the Bible, calls it a "perilous volume" and warns Elspeth Glendinning that "it is rendered into the vulgar tongue, and therefore, by the order of the Holy Catholic Church, unfit to be in the hands of any lay person" (*TM* 60). The vulgar *vulgarizes* the text, not least because it removes it from elite, homosocial control and renders it accessible to women, children, and the poor (or, at least, those who can read). The second person to make off with the Bible, Father Eustace, offers Mary Avenel and Halbert and Edward Glendinning a missal "curiously illuminated with paintings" and promises to "come myself, or send some one at a fitting time, and teach them the meaning of these pictures" (*TM* 86). Edward, the next novel's eponymous abbot, willingly hands over the Bible because it "has no such goodly shews in it" (*TM* 91). In both instances, invoking standard anti-Catholic tropes, the priests disallow independent reading and interpretation: vernacular Bibles are dangerous because they are too easily consumed by the ignorant laity, who need guidance from authorized clergy, while the pretty pictures in the Catholic missal are not only obviously infantilized and infantilizing but also require expert decoding to render the iconography fully meaningful. Moreover, Edward's delighted response to the missal, and concomitant boredom with the Bible, suggests that Catholicism is a religion of immature pleasures, of relatively unsophisticated aesthetic experience (these are images calculated for a child, after all) instead of hard textual labor. (In context this is ironic: Edward is enthusiastically literate, unlike his brother Halbert.) By prohibiting vernacular lay reading, which threatens to vulgarize (and therefore demystify) the scriptures, Roman Catholicism insists on perpetuating a perverse parent-child relationship between church and worshipper. In elevating its own sole authority to interpret the Bible, the church denies both *sola scriptura* and the right of private judgment, both of which are central to the Reformation and post-Reformation myth of liberation through literacy. Both priests *produce* interpretive difficulty as a mode of control.

This split between the Bible and the missal, the verbal world of Protestantism and the visual world of Catholicism, itself dates back to Reformation-era controversy, even as the problems it causes— "Language cannot fail to have a material dimension; it cannot avoid being flesh or image"—are just as old.[31] At one level, Scott simply rehearses the historical tropes that link the Reformation and modernity: the shift from Catholicism to Protestantism becomes one of childhood to adulthood, image to text, passive learning to active interpretation. But the mystical journeying of Lady Avenel's Bible seems at first to redefine this Bible in enchanted terms, as an object whose aura of sacredness inheres in its materiality instead of its texuality. This Bible first appears as a "thick black book wi' the silver clasps" (*TM* 55), which Lady Avenel's protector Dame Glendinning anxiously associates with faeries and bringing "ghaists and gyre carlines" into the house (*TM* 55). And yet while we appear invited to laugh at the Catholic superstition that cannot recognize the Bible for what it is, the book's afterlife turns out to be intimately bound up with the ungodly White Lady, who protects it, returns it when removed, guides Halbert Glendinning to it in a mystical underground cavern (!), and ultimately reveals it to Mary Avenel. As an *object* the Bible moves through the narrative under the aegis of enchantment; as a *text* it is invested with the power to facilitate Protestantism's disenchantment of the world. In its enchanted mode, the Bible-as-object is invested by lay and clergy alike with quasi-magical and dangerous powers; in its disenchanted mode, it potentially dismantles all of Roman Catholicism's machinery. But in order for that to happen, it must cease to be an object and, instead, become scripture—not simply a religious text but one, in theologian Wesley A. Kort's terms, that "articulate[s] the beliefs that go into the construction of the world."[32] It must, that is, be *read* so that it can become transformative.

We do not see the illiterate Halbert Glendinning reading the Bible that he so magically rescues, and as Francis Hart observed, the rationale for his conversion seems thin.[33] Instead, the drama of Bible reading plays out in an entirely feminine mode, one that contrasts starkly to Warden's and Father Eustace's attempt to duel to the death via proof-texting. Mary Avenel, the novel's heroine, is guided to her mother's Bible in a moment of profound spiritual darkness brought on by "the narrow and bigotted ignorance in which Rome then educated the children of her church" (*TM* 278). The narrator establishes an entirely clichéd opposition between Catholic legalism and Protestant spirituality. When Mary encounters her Bible, Catholicism is *already* reduced to a mere historical curiosity, an irrelevant negation of the divine; for the first time her reading makes her truly self-conscious of its spiritual deadness. But although the narrator poses Mary on the brink of a new historical epoch, his manner of projecting her into the future once again invokes the enchanted past: Mary finds her mother's concealed Bible thanks to the intercession of the White Lady, who promises that "Beneath my foot lies hid / The Word, the Law, the Path, which thou doest strive / To find, and canst not find" (*TM* 278). In Scott's reworking of St. Augustine's *Tolle, lege* ("take it and read") in the *Confessions*, Mary is incapable of "personal approach to the Divine Presence by prayer" (*TM* 278)—another familiar convention from anti-Catholic rhetoric— and yet she receives the gift of devotional language from a figure who claims to be entirely alienated from the Christian way. By positioning the White Lady at the gateway to Protestant modernity, the narrative transforms the supposedly safe Reformed future into something as potentially uncanny as the Catholicism it leaves behind.[34]

In fact, the White Lady's role in this textual transaction rewrites the novel's own masculine frame narrative, which sends the text from the Benedictine to Clutterbuck to Scott. As we saw, Scott's version of the "lost manuscript" trope posits a Catholicism only faintly visible through multiple Protestant rewritings. Here, the White Lady marks the trace of the novel's Catholic origin yet also initiates Catholicism's erasure; her agency seems to belong to some other text, now written over, but that agency tramples the "usual" explanations for any form of religious conversion. By guiding Mary to the Bible, the White Lady acknowledges the anachronism of the very mentality that produced her. At the same time, the White Lady plays the role of Captain Clutterbuck. Not only does she pass on Lady Avenel's Bible to Mary, but Lady Avenel herself has already loaded that Bible with guides to interpretation, theological disquisitions, and confessional meditations. In a feminized echo and corrective of the opening frame narrative, the textual lineage runs from the Bible to Lady Avenel to the White Lady to Mary, thereby preserving the original text alongside Lady Avenel's interventions. Such conservation stands in stark contrast to the problematic nature of the overarching historical narrative and grants women a privileged role in disseminating religious truth instead of writing original narrative.[35] The ambiguities of the masculine frame narrative appear, at first glance, to find their counterbalance in the coherence of the feminized biblical tradition. Unlike the miscellaneous source texts "adapted" into this novel, the Bible undergoes no direct revision or reorganization. But, like the Benedictine, Lady Avenel has "Protestantized" the text through her own writings, which mediate and guide Mary's encounter with the Bible.

Whereas the masculine frame narrative dramatizes the loss of the past, the feminine Bible sequence at first promises that the distance between past and present can be sutured shut. But the Bible's feminine provenance turns out to be wrapped in its own historical qualifiers. To begin with, the historical past here is represented not by the Bible's *contents* but by the *physical* Bible itself and its associations with Mary's lost mother. The question, then, is how textuality and materiality ought to properly interact. Mary's ability to engage with the Bible-as-text turns out to be predicated on the Bible-as-object:

> Ignorant in a great measure of its contents, Mary Avenel had been taught from her infancy to hold this volume in sacred veneration. It is probable that the deceased Lady of Walter Avenel only postponed

initiating her daughter into the mysteries of the Divine Word, until she should be better able to comprehend both the lessons which it taught, and the risk at which, in these times, they were studied. Death interposed, and removed her before the times became favourable to the reformers, and before her daughter was so far advanced in age as to be fit to receive religious instruction of this deep import. But the affectionate mother had made preparations for the earthly work which she had most at heart. There were slips of paper inserted in the work, in which, by an appeal to, and a comparison of various passages in holy writ, the errors and human inventions with which the Church of Rome had defaced the simple edifice of Christianity, as erected by its divine architect, were pointed out. These controversial topics were treated with a spirit of calmness and christian [*sic*] charity, which might have been an example to the theologians of the period; but they were clearly, fairly, and plainly argued, and supported by the necessary proofs and references. Other papers there were which had no reference whatsoever to polemics, but were the simple effusions of a devout mind communing with itself. Among these was one frequently used, as it seemed from the state of the manuscript, on which the mother of Mary had transcribed and placed together those affecting texts to which the heart has recourse in affliction, and which assure us at once of the sympathy and protection afforded to the children of the promise. In Mary Avenel's state of mind, these attracted her above all the other lessons, which, coming from a hand so dear, had reached her at a time so critical, and in a manner so touching. She read the affecting promise, "I will never leave thee nor forsake thee," and the consoling exhortation, "Call upon me in the day of trouble, and I will deliver thee." She read them, and her heart acquiesced in the conclusion, Surely this is the word of God. (*TM* 280–81)

Scott once again adheres to convention when he pinpoints the break between Catholic and Protestant spirituality in the act of Bible reading. In the process he implicitly genders nascent Protestant reading practices as female: even "ignorant" reverence for the Bible develops from the mother's religious instruction within the domestic sphere, not the priest's sermons or catechisms. Here, Scott draws on conventional Protestant tropes linking private religious experience through reading, as opposed to more technical doctrinal questions, with essentially feminine qualities.[36] By the same token, in feminizing Bible readership he borrows from polemical positions dating back to the Reformation itself, which insisted that "the presence in England [in this case, Scotland] of female, as much as male, readers signalled the nation's Protestant culture."[37] Although Halbert's transition to literacy constitutes one important historical marker in the text, Mary's own discovery of the Bible is arguably even *more* important from a Protestant perspective: the two taken together herald the slow growth of an authentically bibliocentric culture that spans genders as well as generations.

Protestant narrative commitments thus revise the Scott rendered familiar to us by Ina Ferris, who argues that in *Waverley* the female reader "stands *for* reading errors" and must be trumped by a masculine awareness of historical difference.[38] Here, the mother's authority trumps that of the church, but only insofar as she draws on a self-authenticating text (the prooftexting) as opposed to "errors and human inventions." Unlike the Benedictine and his uncle, who *rewrite* their sixteenth-century sources, Lady Avenel supplies her daughter with instructions about how to *read* the Bible; unlike Henry Warden and Father Eustace, Lady Avenel prooftexts only in the service of pastoral comfort, not theological warfare. Yet where *The Monastery* purports to be a unified and updated version of fragmentary sources, Lady Avenel's Bible turns out to be best read in fragments; after all, Scott highlights not Mary's cover-to-cover reading of the Bible as a whole but her emotional response to her mother's devotional *extracts*. And, specifically, Mary reacts to the extracts as her mother has copied them. Copying simultaneously preserves the original text, produces a new one, and calls forth the reader's sentimental identification with the writer. Even though Mary Avenel has no living community of readers, her mother's handwriting enables her to imagine herself into such a community—and, in turn, into the spiritual knowledge that will finally allow her to speak to God.

By emphasizing that Mary reads the Bible explicitly through Lady Avenel's mediation, however, Scott quietly torpedoes the belief that *any* reader equipped with basic literacy should be able to get at the most important points of the Bible with no trouble whatsoever. To begin with, the narrator frames Mary's access to the Bible in terms of a double age: her individual age and her historical moment. This link suggests that Mary's intellectual maturity parallels a new historical maturity, one more hospitable to the "reformers" and their emphasis on private scripture reading. Mary's religious conversion both parallels and depends on a more general historical conversion, as Scottish culture hesitantly opens itself to a new model of religious belief. But Scott makes this all-important biblical encounter depend on the nature of the *age* (in both senses). Moreover, by arguing that Mary herself needs to be of "age" to read the Bible, Scott contradicts what was becoming a staple of evangelical fiction—that is, the figure of the godly child, inspired by Matthew 18:2–5, whose innocence enables him or her to read and even expound on the Bible in a way that educated adults cannot. By contrast, Lady Avenel's prudent reserve intentionally tailors religious instruction to her daughter's life course and unintentionally to the course of history itself.

Most importantly of all, Scott emphasizes that Protestant faith emerges from a mediated encounter with the Bible—notes, prooftexts, and so forth—and not from autonomous private reading. Indeed, Scott hedges Mary's later expressions of faith with significant qualifiers: when things go right, "it *seemed* to her that her prayers had been instantly answered" (emphasis added); her sentiments evinced "a dangerous degree of enthusiasm"; she realizes that she needs a "fitting interpreter" to understand most of the text; and, warns the narrator, "[s]he was unaware of the yet greater danger she incurred, of putting an imperfect or even false sense upon some of the doctrines which appeared most comprehensible" (*TM* 301). Far from celebrating private judgment, the narrator insists that even Mary's already-mediated reading is insufficient without the intervention of a trained clergyman—the warring prooftexters of a few pages later. Not only is private judgment inadequate to dealing with the Bible's complexities, but also simple laymen cannot read and interpret the Bible for themselves. The truths necessary for salvation, in other words, are not necessarily obvious to the lay reader—and, in fact, are the ones most liable to misreading. Far from emphasizing the Bible alone, Scott emphasizes the Bible in multiple pedagogical contexts, all of them necessary to keep the reader from straying off the orthodox path. Scott's Bible must be read within a historical, doctrinal *tradition* in order for it to truly make theological sense. And, in so doing, Scott carefully folds feminine Bible reading back into a masculinized structure: women preserve, transmit, and certainly read biblical texts, but men (especially increasingly professionalized men) guard the gates of interpretation.

GENDER, DISENCHANTMENT, AND CATHOLIC PLOTS

Having mothered biblical reading into being, Scott promptly turns over the act of authoritative interpretation to fathers, figurative and otherwise, and this strategy turns out to prefigure the duology's overall gendering of history. On the one hand, as the Bible translates across vernacular languages and domestic spaces, it inaugurates a new world of interiority (again, one of the most common tropes of Protestantism's difference from Catholicism) explicitly linked to the possibility of private female reading. On the other, it insists that this feminized interior world, far from remaining wholly private and impermeable, is inextricably entwined with the still-masculine domain of theology. In reordering the gendered religious landscape, Scott invests Protestantism with spiritual complementarity, a vision of men and women collaborating on a godly society. But this complementarity simply vanishes in *The Abbot*, which erases the White Lady only to replace her by rapidly multiplying female authority figures. With the White Lady's disappearance, the debate over miracles (and the Catholic mindset enabling such debates) permanently goes out the door, replaced instead with our hero Roland Graeme's frequently ill-judged attempts to decode both gender and politics. The feminized Catholic politicking of *The Abbot* is, paradoxically enough, figured in secular terms, despite the overtly gothic heritage of the main plot.[39] There are no more mystical interventions, no more assurances of Providence at work.

This shattering of Catholic enchantment manifests itself in *The Abbot*'s Catholic spaces, which are quite literally in ruins. In Magdalen Graeme's anguished survey of the Catholic landscape, she discerns an ancient cross rendered into "a shapeless block"; "spires" stripped of their "crosses and bells . . . as if the land had been invaded once more by barbarous heathens"; and "battlements" subjected to "partial demolition." It's no wonder, she says, that saints such as St. Ringan no longer condescend to perform miracles at their shrines, for what else can the Scots expect save "vengeance" (*TA* 96)? Her violent rage suggests, in Michael Tomko's terms, how Scott links "memories of disinheritance" to "a latent desire for revenge"[40]; her similes invoke her own fantasies of Catholic rampage. This violated landscape reveals a Scotland whose sacred spaces are not merely ruined but actively disenchanted, stripped, and rendered into pure materiality. Unlike the spiritual fragments that constitute Lady Avenel's legacy to her daughter, the Catholic ruins cannot be reanimated through reading; at best, from even the most devout believer's point of view, they signify the void left by the slow withdrawing roar of enraged saints. Matters do not improve once we reach the previous novel's titular monastery, which has suffered partial disassembly at the hands of looters and now can be glimpsed awkwardly incorporated into the hovels surrounding it. This is very much in keeping with the first novel's rather sardonic take on the self-interest motivating the Reformation, if in a lower key: Protestant Scotland turns out to be Catholic bricolage, repurposing its own past without any regard for its relation to the present (other than, quite literally, to hold up the house).

Faced with this rubble, however, the antiquarian narrator intervenes to arbitrate between this wholesale wreck of the material past and the spiritual needs of the present. Arguing that the iconoclastic destruction derived from "the charge of idolatry, to which the superstitious devotion of the papists had justly exposed them," the narrator warns us that "nor, if the devastation had stopped short at this point, could we have considered the preservation of these monuments of antiquity as an object to be put in the balance with the introduction of the reformed worship" (*TA* 97). As we have already seen, Scott's prefaces deny the possibility of truly reconstructing Catholic subjectivity in a post-Reformation context; here, the brutal reduction of Catholic culture to unreadable and recyclable fragments suggests the *material* impossibility of reconstructing it as well. Performed in such a space, littered with the "rubbish" (*TA* 99) of broken saints, Catholic ritual literally lacks a context. Sliding from simile to simile, the narrator compares the installation of a new abbot, once an act of spectacular pageantry, to a gothic haunting, a procession of "spectres"; to "bewildered travellers," lost in the desert; and to a "shipwrecked crew" (*TA* 100). Whereas Mary Avenel's reading of the Bible constructed a newly coherent life narrative for herself, the monks' worldview turns out to be as fatally broken as their church; as the similes suggest, they are undead, anachronistic, estranged. (When, much later, Father Ambrose tries to revitalize Roland's flagging faith, he pointedly does *not* offer him a Bible [*TA* 266].) The sudden appearance of the carnivalesque Abbot of Unreason and his motley crew accentuates the point: their destructive desires, initially inculcated by the church as a means of crowd control, become in a Reformation world a series of pointlessly monstrous acts that threaten to bring down the monastery altogether—until Halbert Glendinning, cropping up out of nowhere, tartly reminds them that "what you now practise [*sic*], is one of the profane and unseemly sports introduced by the priests of Rome themselves, to amuse and to brutify the souls which fell into their net" (*TA* 115). In an ironic conjunction, Protestants and Catholics find post-Reformation Catholicism equally unthinkable.

During a significant encounter between Roland and Protestant clergyman Elias Henderson, some time after Roland takes up service with the Queen of Scots, Henderson reworks Magdalen's almost postapocalyptic view of the terrain. Henderson shows Roland Graeme a "pleasant prospect," dotted with homes and churches, all speaking of the "dwelling-place of peace and unity." "What would he deserve," Henderson asks,

> who should bring fire and slaughter into so fair and happy a scene—
> who should bare the swords of the gentry and turn them against

each other—who should give tower and cottage to the flames, and slake the embers with the blood of the in-dwellers?—What would he serve who should lift up again that ancient Dagon of Superstition, whom the worthies of the time have beaten down, and who should once more make the churches of God the high places of Baal?" (*TA* 232–33)

Where Magdalen sees sacrilegious devastation, Henderson perceives a pastoral space dominated by the signs of domestic cheer, and her vision of Catholic restoration turns here into the idolatrous return of the false Old Testament gods. Magdalen's crosses, cathedrals, and icons transform into private habitations scattered across an agriculturally improved landscape, suggesting a culture in which home-based affections trump the sacralized and spectacular spaces of the church. In and of itself, Henderson's vision of Reformation comfort sits awkwardly with the rest of the duology, with its skepticism about the purity of the Reformers' motives—even, in fact, within this very novel, which features a would-be Protestant assassin. Although the occasionally tedious Henderson is nowhere near so fanatical as Magdalen, his perspective (literally, in this case) is as suffused by his Protestantism as hers is by Catholicism. And yet, Henderson's apocalyptic vision of a Catholic future that actually slingshots Scotland back to the premonotheistic past also echoes, in a far more colorful vein, the narrator's own decisive vote in favor of iconoclasm.

Thus, even if this were not a historical novel, the project to restore the Queen of Scots seems doomed by the novel's own logic. Suspense is the last thing on the narrator's mind; modernity requires permanently disassembled ruins. Yet even though the profaned church reminds us that Reformation Scotland has been forcibly disenchanted, a very different kind of magic threatens to sneak in through the back door—one that threatens even the supposedly well-Protestantized narrator (and even occasionally trips up our evangelical clergyman, Henderson). The ambivalent, in-between White Lady mutates into the decidedly feminine Catholic network of Magdalen Graeme, Roland's love interest Catherine Seyton, and the Queen of Scots—what Jayne

Lewis calls the "sensuous, imagistic, and even quasi-mystical past under the sway of female desire" in conflict with "a constitutional present in fact dominated by coalitions of Protestant men."[41] The Queen thus manages to entrap George Douglas, the son of her own jailer, in a web of romantic longing that runs to an extreme that ultimately renders even the Queen anxious and results in his death. This desire, one might add, extends to the present; dreamily pondering portraits of the Queen, the narrator sighs, "no small instance it is of the power of beauty, that its charms should have remained the subject not merely of admiration, but of warm and chivalrous interest, after the lapse of such a length of time"—an interest felt, he goes on, by even those who take the "unfavourable view" of the Queen (*TA* 188). The Catholic Queen's allure sneaks in through the figure of the male historian's erotic desire for his subject. Even preserved solely in print, female beauty temporarily upsets the modern moral order.

The Abbot's feminization of Catholicity thus figuratively weakens it in the face of what is, when done "correctly," an indubitably masculinized Protestantism—notably, the Queen's jailer, the Lady of Lochleven, echoes "in her ideas of reformed faith the very worst errors of the Catholics" (*TA* 186). It also, however, suggests the possibility of a secularized equivalent to the first novel's magic. *The Monastery*'s White Lady repeatedly intervenes in the narrative, whether by dumping priests into the river or protecting the family Bible; *The Abbot*'s supernatural feminine vanishes, to be replaced by multiple controlling female figures whose plots to rescue and restore Mary, Queen of Scots to power consistently spiral out of control. The White Lady directs the plot, but in a disenchanted world of feminine plotting, history's signs become hard to interpret—not least because the novel's Catholic women demand that Roland obey without thinking, in an echo of the priestly claims to control biblical interpretation from the previous novel. "What avails it that you might perchance adopt the course I propose to thee, were it to be fully explained?" Magdalen lectures Roland. "Thou wouldst not yet follow my command, but thine own judgment; thou wouldst not do the will of Heaven, communicated through thy best friend, to whom thou owest thine all; but thou wouldst observe the blinded dictates of thine own imperfect reason" (*TA* 72). In stereotypical Catholic form, Magdalen demands slavish obedience while erasing the believer's potential for interior dissent; poor fallen Roland, incapable of transcending the gap between "imperfect reason" and divine realities, must submit patiently to instruction. (By contrast, *The Monastery* identifies Protestantism as the "more reasonable" religion [325].) Unlike the riddling White Lady, who tells Halbert to patiently await divine providence, Magdalen perceives herself as God's authoritative channel, fully capable of unfolding his "will" as if no mediation existed at all—a woman "foredoomed by Heaven" to restore the Catholic faith (*TA* 94). Roland's often comical uncertainty thus derives from Magdalen's far more dangerous fantasies of absolute certainty.[42] Magdalen's frequent prophetic eruptions about the "vengeance" awaiting those Scottish Protestants who have betrayed their Catholic roots contrast starkly with the narrator's cool assessment of Catholic anachronism; she dwells in a future history on which the narrator has already foreclosed and which the very existence of the novel disproves. She believes in an enchanted world; Roland exists in one where enchantment no longer functions as an explanatory strategy.

Indeed, Roland Graeme, bereft of anything resembling supernatural intervention, is so adrift that he fails to realize that he is in a plot in the first place. This-world Catholic plotting turns out to be indecipherable in a way that divine providence is not: a fully disenchanted environment bodies forth confusion rather than truth. For much of the novel, Roland occupies the same position as Ellinor and Matilda in *The Recess*; he is unable to decipher the events unfolding around him, let alone understand his own implication in the plot masterminded by Magdalen, the Queen, and Catherine. Taunted for his apparent vacillation by the Catholic Catherine Seyton, his co-conspirator (or she would be, if he were aware that a conspiracy existed), an annoyed Roland asks "[h]ow can I withdraw . . . from an enterprize which has never been communicated to me?—has the Queen, or have you, or has any one communicated with me upon any thing for her service which I have refused? Or have you not, all of you, held me at such distance from your counsels, as if I were the most faithless spy since the days of Ganelon?" (*TA* 229). His vacillations, Catherine will sneer later, are themselves "womanish" (*TA* 257). And yet, Roland is in trouble precisely because he has followed orders by maintaining his faux Protestant façade—orders which, ironically, have resulted in him listening with more attention to Henderson, the "natural consequences" (*TA* 222) of such exposure. Feminine craft in the cause of Catholicism inadvertently leads to its subversion by Protestant masculine discourse.

As it turns out, Henderson successfully breaches Roland's Protestant defenses because Roland has only been advised to *listen* to him, rather than to "repeat within his mind *aves*, and *credos*, and *paters*" (*TA* 222) to ward off any evangelical infection. Roland's confusion thus partly derives from exiting a monologic Catholic discourse—one that Scott represents as suspiciously close to nonsense language, repeated as a ritualized, magical charm against the divine Word—and engaging instead with its dialogic Protestant alternative. In that sense, confusion becomes necessary: it indicates a rational subject seeking to make sense of his spiritual alternatives. This confusion, masculinized once again, stands over and against the mess that the female plotters make of things; Roland is neither supposed to evaluate nor to think about the unfolding chain of events. Female plotters leave Roland in a "land of enchantment," where he is apparently not granted "free-will and human reason" and finds himself "like one who walks in a weary and bewildering dream" (*TA* 260). Post-Reformation enchantment descends from spiritual presence into deceitful magic, the very mode of superstition against which Henderson has already cautioned him. No godliness infuses this space, only irresolvable mysteries that give way to yet more mysteries, in much the same way that all the Queen's plots end in the chaos of bloody battle and death.

As the novel's Catholic plot dies out in yet more confusion, it puts an end to the old religion's disruptive, feminized revolutionary potential and promises instead a new world based on the "true Gospel" (*TA* 374). All of the plotting women are either dead (Roland's fanatical foster mother Magdalen), domesticated (Catherine), or disempowered (Mary), while the White Lady reemerges as a set decoration "by her haunted well" (*TA* 375). Pointedly, Magdalen inadvertently dies in her own act of ascetic "penance" (*TA* 374), her religion literally proving to be a religion of death. Amidst all this, the now-converted Roland's interfaith marriage with Catherine (rapidly dispatched in the space of a couple of paragraphs) seems, at first glance, to echo the nationalist symbolism of marriages such as Ivanhoe's and Rowena's in *Ivanhoe*, here yoking the two religions together in a show of liberal tolerance. But this is a marriage predicated on individual Catholic defeat: the collapse of the Queen's plot, Catherine's own disappointment in her immediate afterlife, and Catherine's father's eye to the main chance when it comes to Roland's political connections. It is not even immediately obvious that this is a marriage of "shared moderation,"[43] as is so frequently the case in Scott's symbolic unions; we have seen little sign that Catherine's devotion to the cause has evaporated, or that her opinions of Protestantism have undergone much in the way of change. The marriage suggests less a yoking of equal faiths than the death knell for Catholicism's cause, as worldly and masculine interests finally trump the feminized quest for absolute power. At the same time, this interfaith marriage hints at the true ground on which Catholicism can be tolerated: at the moment it accepts its own failure.

CONCLUSION

Even though Scott turns out to be skeptical about the motivations underlying Protestant reforms, in the end his Reformation duology embraces the shattering religious conflicts of the sixteenth century as the beginnings of his own modernity. *The Monastery* and *The Abbot* stage themselves as post-Catholic novels, as denials that it is possible to think or even fantasize in an early modern Catholic mode. This lost Catholic past, a world of moldering ruins and broken icons that gives way to the textual world of the Protestant Bible, poses no danger to modern Britain; even the novel's own contemporary Catholics wind up estranged from the history of their faith. At the same time, the novels also domesticate religion's potentially anarchic feminine valences.

Women reading (and transmitting) the Bible marks the break between Catholic past and Protestant future, but such women turn out to be in need of formal guidance from male theologians and clergymen; similarly, women trying to reinstate Catholicism, to reverse the forces of history, turn out to self-destruct in the dizzying arabesques of their own elaborate plots, leaving Protestant men to reorganize the pieces. But Scott's vision of a world in which the Catholic past is not only irretrievable, but inconceivable, relies on a conviction that Catholicism no longer has any role to play in the nineteenth-century British polity. As Alison Shell reminds us in a very different context, "[t]he notion of a Catholic 'past' is loaded, and sometimes even impertinent, if one does not qualify it with the consciousness of a Catholic present."[44] For Victorian Protestant novelists working in the wake of Catholic Emancipation, the incursion of the Catholic past into the modern present was all too frighteningly palpable. It is to them that we now turn.

Chapter Two

THE "MORNING STAR" OF THE REFORMATION

The Victorian Cult of John de Wycliffe

The Lollards are gone to their rest; but they have bequeathed their cause.
Four centuries have rolled away, and times and fashions have altered;
but the cause essentially is now what it was then,—of Christ against
Belial—of the Church against the world—of truth against error—
of the Bible against Rome. Theirs was severer—ours is easier work.
　　　　　—"The Lollards (IV)," *The Evangelical Magazine*
　　　　　　　　　　and Missionary Chronicle (1862)

Walter Scott may have been skeptical about at least some of the Reformers, but he nevertheless insisted that Protestant modernity put a convenient end to Catholic medievalism—indeed, made Catholicism irretrievably medieval. Such a strategy played into the fantasy that Catholicism had little to do with Protestantism per se, that Protantism was a *departure* (or, rather, a return to primitive origins); it owed more to the legacy of Protestant polemic and martyrology, which sought to sharply differentiate the post- and pre-Reformation historical landscape, than it did to the rather messier history of Catholic-inflected practices in Protestant worship.[1] But as the nineteenth century wore on, Protestants, especially Nonconformists and their sympathizers, returned to the Middle Ages, not to recuperate Catholicism but to unearth its Protestant (or, rather, "Protestant") counter-element. After Catholic Emancipation in 1829, no one could deny either Catholicism's *presentness* or its believers' insistence on their historical priority. Protestants of all stripes, then, sought for narratives that would show that the Church of England had always been Protestant . . . even when Catholic. And in the post-Emancipation era, they found one of their most popular solutions to this historiographical crisis in the fourteenth century.

The theologian John de Wycliffe (1328–84) and his followers, known as the Lollards, seemed to many to herald a native English Reformation that was *revived*, not *inaugurated*, in the sixteenth century, and was centered on the widespread dissemination of the vernacular scriptures.[2] The rise, fall, and resurrection of Lollard "Protestantism" was a story of naturally English spirituality done in by dangerously cosmopolitan Catholic forces answering to Roman instead of English interests. Even better, this was a proto-Protestant story that prefigured and even appeared to double modern cultural conditions. Excitedly pointing to fourteenth-century chronicler Henry Knighton's objections to Wycliffe's Bible, one early Victorian polemicist declared that "[t]he reader cannot fail to remark the exact similarity between these arguments of the Romish priests in the fourteenth century, and those which are urged by the same class of individuals at the present day."[3] Norman W. Jones has recently cautioned that the process of identification "does not enact transparent sameness but rather a self-challenging encounter with an other—with difference."[4] In Victorian Lollard texts, though, the potential challenge posed by historical difference—that was then, this is now—frequently vanishes under the pressure to admit *sameness* not only in dogmatic pronouncements but also in any future that might come about as a result of their utterance. No longer was British Catholicism still safely banished to Reformation ruins; now it threatened its own Gothic return, repeating itself in the apparently antibiblical pronouncements of post-Emancipation priests. Far from becoming safely unthinkable, Catholicism reappears and spreads.

Under the circumstances it was only fitting that the Victorians, already obsessed with the Reformation's legacy, would gladly seize on one of the Reformation's pet projects: turning Wycliffe and his followers into stalwart forebears of Protestant thought. The Lollards seemed tailor-made for Protestant progenitor hunting: they celebrated popular access to the Bible in English (or appeared to, anyway), savagely denounced the Pope and the mendicant orders, and were skeptical about transubstantiation. Their less convenient ideas—such as those about when the state had the right to appropriate the church's property, a notion blamed for inciting the Peasants' Revolt (1381)—were treated rather more gingerly by later enthusiasts, and theological positions that might undermine interdenominational Protestant cooperation, like predestination, were frequently underplayed.[5] "Rhetorical sleight of hand," Alexandra Walsham says of John Foxe, "converted radical sectaries who had little in common with the followers of the New Gospel apart from being victims of persecution by the Church of Rome into their direct ancestors and brethren"—a proceeding which, to be fair, has not altered in the past few centuries.[6] In turn, Victorian Lollard narratives, both fictional and non-, appropriated and reworked such Reformation theological magic, making the Lollards not only "Protestant" but also participants in the ongoing war against Catholic influence in and on the Church of England.

Despite a relative lapse of interest in Wycliffe in the late eighteenth and early nineteenth centuries—a period corresponding to a relative lapse of interest in the Reformers more generally—he roared back to life with Robert Vaughan's *Life* (1828) and the scholarly editions, lives, poems, plays, paintings, and novels that eventually followed. Although one of the earliest novels about the Lollards, Thomas Gaspey's *The Lollards: A Tale*, appeared in 1822, and Lollards featured sporadically thereafter (for example, in William Howitt's *Jack of the*

Mill [1848]), most Lollard novels were published in the mid-1860s and later—especially in the 1870s and 1880s. In other words, the drive to *fictionalize* Wycliffe coincides with growing anxieties about the Anglo-Catholic movement in the Church of England. While it is too much to assume a neat one-to-one correspondence between the phenomena, at least some Anglo-Catholics themselves took note. One such commentator, very likely Charlotte Mary Yonge, tartly observed of Lollard tales that "I don't think the good ladies who write them have much knowledge of what most Lollards really did wish or believe; and there is no good ground for representing them as good evangelical Christians."[7] This did not stop Wycliffe fans. By the end of the century, Wycliffe-worship would become an evangelical shibboleth; it is no accident that when Anglican evangelicals founded a new Oxford theological college in 1877—which promulgated an explicitly "Protestant interpretation of the atonement, justification, the sacraments, priesthood, and the Bible" right alongside the Thirty-Nine Articles—they dubbed it Wycliffe Hall.[8]

Rescuing Wycliffe from the supposed jaws of popular forgetfulness, then, was meant to assert the Englishness of English Protestantism. But it also delimited the tensions between Protestant-identified members of the Church of England and their Nonconformist brethren, for Wycliffe's attack on ecclesiastical property and hierarchical church government struck right at the heart of the Anglican establishment.[9] Here, the celebrations of Bible reading and vernacular translation, which seemed to image forth the possibility of a postdenominational Protestantism, smashed into both Wycliffe's own legacy and the state of Victorian religious and cultural politics. Victorian narratives of Lollardy tried to rewrite the Reformation in a purely English key while celebrating the rebirth of "true" holiness through the reader's personal, emotional encounter with the vernacular scriptures. Under the eventually thwarted Lollard regime, new forms of interiorized spirituality become available to both men and women, reshaping subjectivity and domesticity while enabling national liberties. But for authors who were far less sanguine about evangelicalism's influence, casting Wycliffe as a point of narrative origin turned out to cause as many problems as it theoretically solved.

The Victorians Rediscover the Lollards

The martyrologist John Foxe said of Wycliffe that he "by Gods prouidence sprang and rose vp: thorough whom, the lord would first waken and rayse vp agayne the worlde, which was ouer much drowned and whelmed in the depe streams of humain traditions"—a sentiment later echoed by Milton.[10] Foxe was among the first of many later polemicists to turn Wycliffe into the mirror of their own minds and, in the process, grant him the status of original Reformer. Wycliffe unsettled any historiography that grounded the Reformation in sixteenth-century Germany; later evangelical partisans and popularizers followed Foxe in regarding Wycliffe and the Lollards as the heralds of not simply English Protestantism but of the Reformation *in toto*. By the nineteenth century, this all seemed very commonsensical. Thus, the children's novelist Anna Maria Sargeant cheerfully informed her young readers that the English Reformation "may be said to have commenced in the middle of the fourteenth century" with Wycliffe and his followers, well before it started overseas.[11] In drawing a clean line from Wycliffe to the Reformers, Victorian Protestants were merely rehashing positions already taken by the very first sixteenth-century critics of the new theology afoot, including no less a luminary than Henry VIII—even though Wycliffe's actual work was by then exceptionally difficult to find.[12] But for devout Wycliffe fans like John Foxe, albeit ones not necessarily well-read in his writings, Wycliffe and the Lollards originated the Protestant tradition. Though Catholics might claim they were heretics, Foxe argued that the Lollards stood side by side with the elect within the institutional churches—already a sign of the problems that this narrative would pose for churchmen of a Higher bent, as it suggested that apostolic descent (the belief that the church was authorized by a continuous chain of ordinations stretching back to one of the Apostles) was not very relevant.[13] Nevertheless, Wycliffe enjoyed considerable praise from the sixteenth century onward, although outside the Protestant fold commentary was not always positive. G. R. Evans, characterizing Wycliffe's up-and-very-down career, quips that "[t]he man on his way up is generally willing to tolerate, in his own interests, things he does not entirely approve of.

The able man with no prospects may discover his principles and become a danger to the Establishment."[14] This assessment is by no means new. David Hume wryly observed that Wycliffe "seems not to have been actuated by the spirit of martyrdom," while later an even less enthusiastic John Lingard painted Wycliffe as a thwarted place-seeker whose opinions were variously characterized by "violent hostility," "bitter and envenomed invectives," and "quibbles and evasions."[15] It was against opinions such as these, enshrined in best-selling popular histories, that nineteenth-century pro-Wycliffites took up their pens.

Looking back on Wycliffe's nineteenth-century reputation and the Wyclif Society's (1882) role in shaping it, Rudolf Buddensieg, one of the society's founding members, sighed that "[u]ntil within the last fifteen years the opinion prevailed among Protestant scholars in England, as well as on the Continent, that John Wyclif's country had been singularly neglectful of the memory of one of its greatest men."[16] As was often the case, such claims for cultural amnesia were strategic rather than accurate, for if it were difficult for Wycliffe to be very much *read*, he had nevertheless served as a Nonconformist and Low Church rallying point for decades, even centuries. Nevertheless, the Independent Robert Vaughan sparked Wycliffe's Victorian renaissance with *The Life and Opinions of John de Wycliffe* (1828; 2nd ed., 1831), which was based on extensive manuscript research and intended to correct the eighteenth-century life by John Lewis. In England the scholarship advanced further with Forshall and Madden's edition of the Wycliffe Bible in 1850, but German Protestants, especially G. V. Lechler, rapidly established themselves at the forefront of Wycliffite studies.[17] However, Vaughan's study reignited the project to turn Wycliffe into a thoroughly Protestant hero, and to turn the Reformation into a thoroughly English, domestic affair. Coming to press right as debates over Catholic Emancipation were intensifying, Vaughan's claims for Wycliffe's significance were highly topical; they were also rooted in a Congregationalist vision of Protestant worship, emphasizing local self-control by individual churches as opposed to an overarching hierarchy.

Vaughan detected a neat progression in Wycliffe's theology, arguing that over the course of his lifetime, Wycliffe moved away from his youthful, medieval Catholicism and toward a position close to that of post-Reformation Protestantism. Out went centralized ecclesiastical authority; in came the right to private judgment and *sola scriptura*—the latter argument of which would prove crucial to later Protestant narratives, despite its dubious accuracy.[18] Moreover, by insisting that Wycliffe pioneered what looked like sixteenth-century reforming theology, Vaughan nationalized and naturalized the Protestant strand of English thought. Like Foxe and Milton, Vaughan proudly declared that when it came to comparing Wycliffe and Luther, "the claim to originality and enterprise, must be certainly awarded to the Englishman"—a claim that would later be echoed in the work of even German theologians and historians like Buddensieg and Johann Loserth.[19] The English had no need to *import* the Reformation; it was already at work in the English consciousness, only temporarily suppressed by foreign Catholic oppressions.

For popularizers, this argument could lead to some rather hyperbolic assessments of Wycliffe's legacy, like the novelist Anne Manning's assertion, in her history of England for children, that Wycliffe was "a very good man" who "translated the whole Bible" (all by himself?) so that everyone might have one.[20] As modern scholars have established, some of the adulation was based on false attributions. It is not clear how much, if any, actual work Wycliffe did on the Bible translation that bears his name, and one text popular with Victorians, *Wycliffes Wycket*, may not be his at all.[21] But, as Manning's cheerful praise suggests, Wycliffe's work as a translator enabled his popular transformation into a model Protestant before Protestantism. It is this Wycliffe that Ford Madox Brown immortalized in his painting *Wycliffe Reading His Translation of the Bible to John of Gaunt, in the Presence of Chaucer and Gower* (1847–48), which positions the Bible almost exactly in the center of the canvas.[22] This deliberately uncomplicated version of Wycliffe makes him available for modern identification precisely because he signifies in no way other than in Protestant shorthand. At the end of the century, the biblical scholar and textual critic Frederic George Kenyon put his finger on the core issue: "his championship of the common people led him to undertake a work which entitles him to honourable mention by men of all parties and all opinions,—the preparation of an English Bible which every man who knew his letters might read in his own home."[23] This elides the complexities involved in the history of medieval vernacular texts, and not just the Bible.[24] The Wycliffe legend rests on his image as a scriptural Robin Hood. Wycliffe's purportedly democratic sympathies take acceptable form in his translation work, which promises to reinvent man's encounter with God's word in terms of private reading instead of public, institutional worship. In this idealized vision of Wycliffe's project, the translator *domesticates* the text, removes it from the pulpit— where it is doled out in weekly fragments—and transforms it into a book for personal ownership, study, and desire.

In addition to the obvious class connotations, this narrative carries with it another story about gender and age, for once removed from clerical control, the Bible freely circulates among not just all sorts and conditions of men but of women and children as well. We have already seen Walter Scott working through the implications of this plot; Victorian evangelicals and Dissenters, however, would adopt it with considerably more enthusiasm and with much less anxiety about reabsorbing either feminine or juvenile reading into masculine authority. In Frances Eastwood's *Geoffrey the Lollard* (1870), for example, young Hubert, one of the novel's three juvenile Lollard protagonists (and the novel's chosen infant "martyr"), is an enthusiastic reader of his father's scraps of biblical manuscript, but he is positively thrilled to have the chance to read "a *whole Bible*"—an enthusiasm, the narrator comments with some asperity, that "would shame many a Christian of the present day, whose legible, perfect Bible is ever *at* his hand, but seldom *in* it."[25] Child readers, female readers, uneducated readers—all serve as potential models for modern Protestants too at ease with their post-Reformation vernacular Bibles. Eastwood's child readers decode the major lessons of scripture without too much in the way of assistance; we are no longer in Scott's world of extensive qualifications about mature reading practices, let alone theological mastery. Biblical interpretation becomes quite literally a homely thing, associated with everyday family life.

Such domestication was the *sine qua non* for the development of a recognizably modern (that is, Protestant) Britain: Wycliffe's Bible frees everyone, but especially women and children, from the theological and political tyranny of Rome.[26] A more polemical and less academic historian, Henry P. Cameron, linked Wycliffe's translation work to Revelation, proclaiming that the "unsealing of the Book of books" initiated a centuries-long work of national labor that, in Cameron's own present, still manifests itself in Protestantism's "complete emancipation" from Rome.[27] In Cameron's exalted account, Wycliffe's Bible ignites the birth of modern Britishness; the shift from oral Catholic culture to textual Protestant culture both liberates British citizens from priestly deceptions and supplies them with the wherewithal to resist further oppression. Without Wycliffe, in other words, there could be no independent Britain. Thus, when Protestants pointed to Wycliffe in order to argue that "when tracing the history or influence of Divine Truth throughout Europe, the habit of ascending no higher than *Germany* is past, or passing away," they celebrated the intrinsically British nature of both the Reformation and of Protestantism itself.[28] The lesson to be learned from Wycliffe's example was a pointed one, according to yet another Congregationalist, John Stoughton: Wycliffe "promoted the policy of liberal English statesmen of the fourteenth century, who aimed at maintaining, as far as possible, the independence of their country."[29] According to such arguments, Wycliffe was protonationalist as well as proto-Protestant: his interest in "independence" explicitly separated the English nation-state from the trans-European Catholic hierarchy and its unwelcome interference in local government and worship.

Needless to say, not everyone found this to be a convincing argument, whether, like Francis Massingberd, their churchmanship was too high to approve of Wycliffe's teachings on church authority and property or, like another anonymous and probably independent essayist, because they felt Wycliffe's reforms did not really anticipate modern Protestantism.[30] Even an admiring Robert Southey, attempting to hold off the bugbear of Catholic Emancipation, admitted that "Wicliffe held some erroneous opinions, some fantastic ones, and some which, in their moral and political consequences, are most dangerous."[31] Such dissents point to the politics involved in turning Wycliffe into "the" medieval exponent of Protestant practice: because he appealed more to Dissenters and Low Churchmen than to those concerned with defending the Church of England against assault from both Roman Catholicism and Dissent, invoking the Wycliffe shibboleth often meant implicitly or explicitly attacking High Church exponents, whether traditional or Anglo-Catholic. Nevertheless, evangelicals seized on Wycliffe as proof that essential Protestant doctrines such as *sola scriptura* and justification by faith alone were inculcated in England long before they were heard of abroad.

PLAIN SPEECH AND LOLLARD HEROICS

As celebrations of the Wycliffite tradition go, Thomas Gaspey's *The Lollards* (1822) is probably not what evangelicals had in mind.[32] An awkwardly plotted and awkwardly written farrago of historical facts, gothic horror, and romance, *The Lollards'* willingness to engage in homoerotic titillation when one of its female protagonists dresses as a page no doubt sent shudders down the spine of any evangelical who picked it up. Nevertheless, the novel's interest in the rise of print culture does foreshadow later (if perhaps no more sophisticated) attempts at rendering the significance of Wycliffe's Bible. For Lollard tales imagined a marginalized truth battering against the walls of a now-institutionalized and corrupt Christianity—a call to arms against the progress of Anglo-Catholic attitudes within the established church. And authors crystallized access to that truth by representing the translation, dissemination, and consumption of the biblical text itself. In these texts, Bible reading takes on new importance as not just the means of salvation but also as the historical marker of a new inwardness—an inwardness that problematizes the categories of "masculine" and "feminine" when it comes to religion as emotional experience. By this, I do not mean the model of "manhood fused with female *suffering*" that James Eli Adams has found at work in mid-Victorian texts like *In Memoriam*.[33] Instead, narratives of biblically induced feeling imagine that both men and women transition to an almost Wordsworthian response—that is, spontaneous and sympathetic—to biblical narrative. It is as if Lollard reading ceases, at a certain moment, to be interpretation at all.

Victorians of evangelical and Dissenting stripes seized on Wycliffe because his translation of the Bible (whether or not "he" is the actual translator) seemed to promote, as Vaughan put it, "the right of private judgment" and "the duty of a devout attention to whatever may promote their [the laity's] faith in the grace of the Saviour and obedience to his will."[34] In Lollard tales, as so often in evangelical fiction, "words spoken by the blessed Lord himself" are "so deep, so pure, so simple, so divine—children might understand them": the scriptures are calibrated to the understandings of even the youngest and most innocent.[35] Novelists sometimes encouraged their readers to identify with Wycliffe's contemporaries and near-contemporaries by quoting Wycliffe's translations and sermons directly instead of modernizing his prose; the sudden appearance of "authentic" medieval English in a nineteenth-century narrative invites readers to contemplate the sameness of Protestant (or would-be Protestant) truths within even a momentarily alienating form of English.[36] In a very real sense, the scriptures are supposed to speak directly and plainly to the mind of any honest inquirer. By translating the scriptures, Wycliffe makes their transparency visible to the laity's eyes and hence brings down upon himself the persecutions of the Roman Catholic Church. Wycliffe's crime, in other words, is that he dismantles the "privilege" involved in reading and interpreting scriptural texts. He is spiritually but not politically democratic—a necessary qualification for those who needed to distance him from such radicals as John Ball, Wat Tyler, and the anti-taxation Peasants' Revolt of 1381. Neither Ball's leveling doctrines nor revolutionary mobs found much favor in the post-1848 literary world.[37] All of the evangelical Lollard novels, whether by Nonconformists or members of the Church of England, anticipate or adopt the position codified by the leading Wycliffe scholar of the later nineteenth century, G. V. Lechler: namely, Wycliffe's goal was to make scripture "the common property of all."[38] That is, Wycliffe advocated private judgment and the ease of scriptural interpretation, both of which Protestants took to be the guarantors of civil liberty. Translated into English, the Bible takes on superhuman power, eradicating error through the sheer force of a Word that seems to require no interpretation whatsoever. Whereas the scriptures represent divine truth, the Roman Catholic Church represents the allure of human desires; the former chastises in order to heal, but the latter pleases in order to imprison.

This approach endorses Paul's observation that "while knowledge puffs up, love is what builds up" (1 Cor 8:1): the humblest believer proves more capable of biblical interpretation than the most learned scholar. Access to biblical truths becomes easier from the margins than from the center. A case in point is Emma Leslie's *Conrad* (1881), earlier known as *Before the Dawn*, which was an entry in Leslie's evangelical "Church History Stories."[39] Over the course of the novel, Conrad transforms from peevish young cripple to scholar, only to find himself repeatedly learning lessons of humility from the poor and the meek. As a child, Conrad has a difficult time appreciating that God's definition of good is not the same as man's; he is unwilling to admit that when it comes to human suffering, "God keepeth the help in his own hands that we may seek him only for it, and because we might wear out the patience of the saints by our impatient cries, and they should give us what we cry for, though it should do us harm" (92). In this conventional evangelical explanation of pain, God is simultaneously parent and doctor: pain reminds the sufferer of his sinful human nature, and the sole "medicine" for this pain lies in total faith in God. Because the Roman Catholic Church urges prayer to the saints or to Mary, however, the sinner finds himself disbarred from the proper medication for his physical and spiritual pains.[40] Leslie shows particular distaste for what one character calls the "accommodating" (97) nature of Roman Catholic doctrine, which relativizes Christian practice to the worldly desires of the sinner (the wealthy sinner in particular) rather than preaching absolute scriptural truth to all men.

Conrad's own problem lies in his unwillingness to relinquish his desire for academic advancement; he yearns to be learned, but as a youth he sets out about it on the negative path, seeking "for things to find fault with" (115). Despite his enthusiasm for Wycliffite doctrines, however, only "[h]is reason and his intellect had been convinced" (241)—that is, he finds himself very close to the position of Charlotte Brontë's St. John Rivers, that philosophical "follower of the sect of Jesus."[41] Much to his astonishment, an "honest old mason" (241) he has known from his childhood manifests far greater strength than he. Leslie's point is an evangelical truism: if the meek shall inherit the Earth, then it ought not to be surprising that the meek shall have an easier time understanding the Gospels. When shaped into historical narrative, however, this truism goes further. Insofar as the Roman Catholic Church emphasizes Aristotelian logic, controversial debate, and so forth, it institutes a deliberately *anti*-Christian regime—for all such intellectual acquirements lead the practitioner to self-contemplation rather than self-abnegation. "I have thought I deserved *more* than God hath given me," moans Conrad, "and so how can I go to him confessing I am unworthy, when I feel almost as though God were my debtor for doing what I have to help Master Huss here in Bohemia?" (249) All of Conrad's training, even when turned to the Wycliffite good, nevertheless does not teach him to understand his own total depravity, his essential weakness and worthlessness: that Christ's grace is *given* but never *deserved* is a lesson he cannot bear to learn until the very end, precisely because it threatens to level all distinctions between the learned elite and the unlearned populace.

Such leveling requires that the scriptures have an *immediate* effect on the honest inquirer. Elizabeth Rundle Charles's "A Story of the Lollards" meditates on precisely this point: to what extent can acquaintance with the scriptures awaken human beings to their personal call to labor for God? Charles divides her story into two journals, one belonging to Cuthbert, a friar, and the other to his sister, Cicely. Cuthbert begins and ends in prison, first as an accused follower of the twelfth-century mystic and apocalypticist Joachim of Fiore and last as a Lollard; his sister, meanwhile, grows up in a household divided between her father's partly political and partly emotional enthusiasm for Wycliffe and her mother's attempts to remain orthodox. Cuthbert's apparently circular journey from prison to prison actually maps out a spiral of enlightenment; if he begins by moaning that "[t]he gloom of this prison is nothing compared with the horror of great darkness in my soul," he concludes "[o]nce more in prison, but no more in darkness,— never more in darkness" (343, 384). His original and metaphorical imprisonment partly derives from what, in Protestant eyes, was a peculiarly Catholic misreading of Matthew 10:37: he flees to the convent *from* personal feeling, thereby undercutting rather than strengthening his faith (356).[42] Cuthbert thus finds himself facing the abyss of skepticism as he literally and figuratively travels to Rome, until he hears Joachim's "Everlasting Gospel." Yet this, too, fails him, for he has no assurance of its divine inspiration (351–52).

It is only when his cousin Richard reads to him from a manuscript copy of Wycliffe's Bible that Cuthbert discovers true peace. "I could scarcely account for it," he says, in a passage worth quoting at length:

> I lay still quietly weeping as of old when my mother told me some touching sacred history. Doubtless I was weak with my hurt, and with prison fare, and with long anguish of mind. But it was long since tears had risen to my eyes. And this was no tale of woe, no story of wrong and agony to harrow the heart, no appeal such as the Friars' Preachers make on Passion Week or on Martyrs' Festivals,— appealing with quivering voices, clasped hands, and streaming eyes, to the blood-stained crucifix, the pierced side, the nailed hands and feet, until the people sobbed, and wailed, and beat their breasts, as I had seen them often in Italy. Richard's voice was calm and steady, the story was cheerful and quiet, the words of comfort very simple and very few. Yet I could do nothing but cover my face for shame at these childish tears and weep, so deep did the soft, slow-falling words pierce into my inmost heart. ("Story," 388)

This passage relates the discovery of religion as *inward feeling*, inspired not by rhetorical persuasion or the literature of complaint but by the greater meaning of an otherwise "cheerful and quiet" narrative. Notably, Cuthbert's response to the Wycliffe translation echoes his sister's response to hearing Wycliffe himself: "I hid my face and wept quite gently, lest I should miss one of the precious words, until he once more prayed for a blessing on the sufferer and on me, and left" (378). Again, gender differences blend in authentic spiritual experience (although Cuthbert, unlike his sister, is partly ashamed of his response). Roman Catholic experience is not just corporeal but founded on visible signs of pain; it is literally sensational. Cuthbert identifies Italian religious experience with a kind of group hysteria, derived from repeated appeals to the gory and scarred representation of Christ on the cross. Worshipping this tormented, brutalized body elicits only crescendos of improper identification—sobs of personalized agony with no redemptive Passion in sight. By contrast, the "natural" response to scripture and scriptural doctrine comes from the "inmost heart" and is accompanied by a desire to privatize the experience by hiding the face. Such inwardness is associated with maternal care, as Cuthbert figuratively returns to childhood innocence in the moment of listening; even though the actual reading encounter is homosocial, the reader himself momentarily takes on the role of feminized nurturer. This stands in stark contrast to the vibrantly physical Catholic male speakers, whose oral narratives incite their audiences to spectacular demonstrations of pain. In subjugating the male voice to the biblical text, Richard does not merely appeal to Christ's pierced side but relays words that themselves "pierce." This repetition of "pierce" identifies the true conversion experience with Christ's own sufferings on the cross: Cuthbert does not *contemplate* Christ's sufferings, but he (in a very small way) experiences an *echo* of those sufferings.

Fictional representations of Wycliffe himself, such as those in Emily Sarah Holt's *The Lord Mayor* (1884) and W. Oak Rhind's *Hubert Ellerdale* (1881), dwell on Wycliffe as almost Protestant, one for whom *sola scriptura* is the sole route to authentic religious experience (even if he was a bit shaky on other Protestant "essentials").[43] In these texts the question of identifying modern Protestant experience with medieval Catholic heresy more obviously takes center stage. Like Walter Scott, Holt engages in antiquarian thick description of medieval social and religious practices, from worship to clothes to what was served at dinner, constantly defamiliarizing even minor matters such as hygiene and the meaning of the daily menu. But unlike Walter Scott, this attention to the chaos of historical difference counterpoints the narrative's assessment of spiritual development: the shift from one mode of dining to another constitutes neither progress nor regress but simply pure difference in action, whereas the religious narrative repeatedly slips into the present tense. Speaking of a lukewarm reformer, the narrator sententiously observes that "[t]he world teems with such men," suddenly abstracting the historical figure from his hitherto contextualized existence.[44] As the narrator shuttles back and forth, she provocatively undermines gender difference alongside historical difference when it comes to heroic Christian strength, at one point identifying Wycliffe with Florence Nightingale (59–60). (Later, her protagonists Alice and Edmund admire each other for reasons that similarly undermine stereotypes: he her "heroism" and she his "warm affections" [141].) The true Christian occupies a subject position that is both *and* neither male or female, insofar as s/he seeks always to emulate Christ. By the same token, the "then" of mundane life in the fourteenth century interfaces with the "now" and even "forever" of humanity's ongoing struggle between God and world, Christ and Antichrist. Unlike Scott, Holt refuses either to endorse the "moderate" religious position or to make scriptural faith the *effect* of any historical context. Far from being of mundane or profane time, the true Christian is spectacularly *out* of time, belonging to the very different historical order of God's providence.

In Holt's narrative both Wycliffe's Bible and his sermons function primarily as quotable texts rather than as movable objects. The reader is asked to treat such texts' materiality as transparent, in much the same way that they are invited to think of scriptural meaning (and, for that matter, the meaning of Wycliffe's sermons) as entirely pellucid. For Alice, the Lord Mayor's daughter and one of the novel's protagonists, the first encounter with Wycliffe constitutes a generic break with her previous existence. Alice has previously been exposed primarily to sermons on "older legends of the saints"; while the stories "were perhaps true, and were pure, beautiful, and touching in themselves, when they came from pure lips," they were frequently transformed

from "pure" to "coarse," and from "romance" to "buffoonery" (26).
Putting to one aside the qualified "perhaps," hagiography proves dismayingly vulnerable to oral deformation. Wycliffe arrives in an age of
priestly aesthetic degeneracy, all the more degenerate because it is primarily an aesthetic in operation. By contrast, the narrator celebrates
Wycliffe for the near-transparency of his vernacular sermons, which
bring their audience to an immediate sense of Christ's presence. Speaking of Wycliffe and the poor priests, Holt remarks that "[t]hey had the
virgin honey; why should they present it in vessels of painted porce-
lain, so that men would stop to admire the jar and would *not* taste the
contents?" (27; emphasis in the original). Both rhetoric and a yen for
the aesthetic—the beauty of holiness—interfere with the listener's
ideal communion with the very Word of God, which, again, seems to
transcend interpretation itself. The obvious retort to Holt's position—
that Wycliffe was hardly anti-rhetorical and that even "plain style"
may require rigorous analysis—is never raised as a question within the
narrative. As becomes clear during one pointed exchange, Wycliffe's
meaning may exceed its expression, but in general Wycliffe "meaneth
so much as he saith"—even when hurling insults (47).

It is in Wycliffe's plain speech itself that the novel locates the turning point between Catholic "superstition" and Protestant modernity.
The truth Wycliffe speaks turns out to be "an absolute, imperial, everlasting certainty" (266). Whereas, Holt argues, Catholics and Ritualists
take "The Church" (268) as their rule of law, Wycliffe elevates God's
revelation above all human tradition and thus sets the rule of moral action on a transcendent plane; indeed, Holt makes Wycliffe explicitly re-
ject his earlier Marian theology (267) on the grounds that it contradicts
scripture. Again, Holt shifts her arguments from past to present: faith in
Mary, sneers the narrator, requires "Romanists" and "Ritualists" alike
to "divest [themselves] of common sense in reference to religious matters" (270). In her reading Catholics occupy an alternate universe in
which the "logic" of incarnation might as well be the product of Mad
Hatters and March Hares. Catholic theology turns out to be unspeakable, not because (as in Walter Scott) the modern reader can no longer
identify with it, but because it obeys arbitrary rules of speech laid down

by the equally arbitrary rule of fallen man; "common sense," as far as Holt is concerned, is scriptural sense. Those who do not join the Lollard cause wholeheartedly wind up unable to speak at all, like poor Father Hunt, who finds himself incapable of even saying "good morning" lest he be roped in as a heretic (329). Or, alternately, they fatally distort the historical record, like those "contemporary monks" whose attacks on Richard II the narrator dismisses (337). Instead of Scott's fiction of a Protestantizing Benedictine, we have here instead Protestants who unwittingly pollute their narratives with the remnants of Catholic bias. Bad theology makes for bad historiography.

By figuring proto-Protestantism in terms of Christian plain speaking, accessible to all comers of whatever gender, age, and class, Holt imagines Wycliffe inaugurating a new discursive world in which all Christians collaborate for their general good. While Holt hardly evacuates gender differences under this new regime—one of her subplots involves a woman learning to properly obey her husband—striving to identify with Christ opens up gendered emotional and psychological spaces that escape strict historical determination. The "domestication" of religious experience liberates women, children, and the poor into true Christian subjectivity, but it also endorses a masculinity based on sentiment rather than physical strength. For W. Oak Rhind in *Hubert Ellerdale*, Wycliffe himself manifests the link between scriptural reading and tender feeling: he is "stern" when rebuked by the friars but "full of sweetness and tenderness when he talks to us about the Gospel; and so gentle does he become under the influence of the sublime words of Christ, I have seen his eyes moisten when he has touched upon some more than usually loving promise of the Saviour."[45] By contrast, Hubert's friend Walden (sister of his beloved Edith) initially professes himself bored by Wycliffe, preferring sports instead (25); to make matters worse, he contemptuously refers to the poor as "wretched serfs" (127). This ethic is all part of the "merrie England" (165) with which the novel has no truck. Such purportedly bluff masculinity, linked to Walden's military vocation, stands in stark contrast to the affective, sympathetic appeal of Wycliffe's carefully restrained weeping. It's no accident that soldierly Walden loses interest in now-Wycliffite priest Hubert and winds up feeling only "hatred" for the Lollard movement (200). The trajectory of Catholic teaching in this novel is toward a kind of jovial brutality, a send-up of medieval merrymaking. But it also parodies muscular Christianity: the sporting soldier, far from exemplifying a moralized English masculinity, turns out to signify its collapse into too, too solid flesh. Although for Broad Church novelist and clergyman Charles Kingsley, one of the theorists of that Christianity frequently dubbed muscular, "violence, like sex, becomes a sanctified force of male behavior, a definitive quality of 'real' men," Rhind and many other Protestant novelists harshly critiqued such supposed ideals.[46] True Christian feeling legitimates manly tears, especially in response to what one character calls the "pathos" of the Bible, which would make the "heart . . . melt with love for God" (19).

In this mode the true warrior-patriot is actually the sentimental priest. Thus, Wycliffe remains weak from a stroke, but he still gives "himself little rest" and, more importantly, "spent much of his time in translating the Bible—it being the dearest wish of his heart to give England an English Bible before he died" (99). Physical strength transmutes into strength enough to hold a pen; the militant saves his country through an assault on the Vulgate. Rhind's decision to emphasize Wycliffe's illness is important, since it strips Wycliffe's writing of any purely careerist motive. Instead, Wycliffe's desire is salvific but also nationalist: it is a wish for England. When he arrives to preach, he thrills to the "cheers" of his auditors, not because they are celebrating him but because they prove that his "beloved England" will be in good hands (22). He is, in fact, "our English Wycliffe" (256), yoking together proto-Protestant belief and nationalist feeling. Wycliffe's Christianity is not incompatible with devotion to his country—an important point when one of the key charges against Roman Catholicism was that it undermined civic loyalty. Rhind, somewhat more willing to entertain the notion that Wycliffite doctrines might have encouraged the Peasants' Revolt of 1381, nevertheless argues that at its heart the revolt was prompted by the desire for "freedom" (152). Wycliffe's emotionally fraught doctrine of divine love turns out to stimulate such modern sentiments as "'Liberty of conscience!' 'Down with the oppressors!'"

(38); biblical faith makes for something that sounds pleasantly liberal, in the philosophical sense, but also very stereotypically English. Even if such sentiments ran too dangerously rampant, they were nevertheless deeply English at their core.

Against Lollard Liberties

Rampant freedoms, however, signified very differently amongst those whose churchmanship was higher or High. Holt, among many other evangelicals, was certainly aware of Lollardy's potentially radical political valences, which she took care to defuse by invoking the "no true Lollard" fallacy. In her Lollard novels politicians appropriating Lollard doctrines for their own purposes are treated as inauthentic; only those with purely "spiritual" goals in mind count as real Lollards. This strategy enables her to neatly sidestep Walter Scott's messier, more skeptical reading of Reformation history, as she hives off the more inconvenient (historiographically speaking) Lollards into their own enclosed category. But not everyone was so willing to draw such neat genealogical lines. Some, like Charles Edmund Maurice (son of the liberal theologian Frederic Denison Maurice), imagined how the purported rhetoric of Lollard liberty, featured so prominently in *Hubert Ellerdale*, might easily be harnessed in the fifteenth century by a rebel like Jack Cade. Maurice's Richard de Lacy, a man of the landed gentry who winds up as a merchant's apprentice after he helps a persecuted Lollard friend escape from Oxford, comes to identify the Catholic regime with immorality and tyranny, but the shape-shifting Cade—"Why doth your leader call himself Mortimer, that late called himself Aylmere, and once he was known as Cade?"—embodies the amorphousness and instability of the uncontrollable crowd.[47] As is so often the case in Victorian fiction (Dickens's *A Tale of Two Cities* and *Barnaby Rudge* being two of the most obvious examples), rebellion does not institute not a new beginning, let alone civil liberties, but collapses into chaos. Richard, who abandons ship just before everything goes wrong, suffers the providential punishment of his mother's collapse and death (274); in the end, he and his new wife Alice abandon the country altogether and shift their allegiances to an entirely new mode of social reform—the printing press (283). In other words, political instability resides within Lollardy itself, and the responsible proto-Protestant must *choose* between violent radicalism or the gradualist reforms of the mind.

For High Churchmen, though, the Lollard inheritance inevitably inscribed chaos at the very heart of Protestantism. We have already seen some examples of High Church skepticism about evangelical attempts to wrest the Lollards into their own narratives of religious development. But what happened if one returned to the very foundation of Lollard popularity with evangelicals: that Wycliffe's movement consolidated authentic "Protestant" resistance to Roman Catholicism, even before Protestantism *per se* existed? One answer to that question came from Henry Cadwallader Adams, an Oxford fellow turned schoolmaster, country clergyman, and novelist for boys. Adams's novella *Mark's Wedding, or Lollardy* (1877) was one of the four he printed in the third volume of publisher James Parker's series *Tales Illustrating Church History*, a six-volume collection that also included contributions from the embattled Ritualist priest and hymnodist J. M. Neale (1818–66). The overarching theme of Adams's volume is the difficulty of establishing a delicate balance between the national imperative of escaping papal claims to supremacy and the spiritual imperative of retaining those liturgical practices inherited from antiquity. Unfortunately for England, what frequently ensues instead is sectarian violence and fanaticism, thanks to man's fallen nature; as a result, the collection tends to skew toward a pessimistic, unsettled reading of the Reformation's effects.

Like both Walter Scott and the other High Church novelists I will discuss later, Adams strives for ostensible "balance." His conclusions, however, are very much not Scott's. The Lollard activists in this novel all do too much, but the Catholic Church is equally culpable in repressing them; the result, Adams concludes with a sigh at the end, is not a "mild and beneficent reform" but a "sweeping revolution" that leaves the Church of England in a state of permanent lack.[48] Violent fanaticism meets violent repression and produces a modern world in a state of permanent dysfunction—all the more dysfunctional because Protestants fail to recognize it as such. Echoing Scott's notoriously wobbly protagonists, Adams's eponymous Mark finds himself caught between the opposing forces of Catholicism and Lollardy, and he spends much of the novella showing a conspicuous lack of good judgment. Lollardy turns out to be riven between an inward mode and a more violent, semimilitarized one—between private contemplation and political or rebellious action. The former is accessible to both sexes, the latter figured as exclusively male. Despite yearning for the comic resolution of marriage to the lovely Lettice, Mark is also a partisan of the embattled Sir John Oldcastle. The promise of contented domesticity, so frequently held out in Protestant fiction as the product of a Bible-centered Christianity, is continually deferred (as, for that matter, is the presence of the Bible itself). Mark repeatedly opts for his homosocial entanglements with Oldcastle and the novel's most prominent Lollard figure, the ominously named Jasper Graves, an evangelical fanatic who yearns for "the fire and faggots" of martyrdom (154).

Graves's impassioned devotion to Lollardy parodies the very self-discipline that James Eli Adams identifies as a primary component of the Victorian masculine ideal as formulated by Thomas Carlyle: the "ascetic program" shapes a man "alien to all human customs and ties, responsive instead solely to divine imperatives."[49] Here, the man who acknowledges only God's regime turns out to embody homosocial masculinity run amok. As one character puts it, Graves speaks "[m]anfully, but not wisely" (190). Significantly, when Henry Chicheley, the archbishop of Canterbury, is moved to pity on Mark's behalf late in the novella, it is because the woman pleading for Mark is, unknown to herself, Chicheley's old playmate; the archbishop's nostalgic, tender sentiment, harkening back to a presexual innocence, signifies virtue in a way that Graves's ferocious devotion to his cause does not. Graves's furious preachifying and lust for martyrdom indicates a black hole at the very center of the novella's vision of the Lollard project, just as his support for the expropriation of church property suggests how religious reform and social unrest could go hand in hand. Such a position, the narrator declares, is not "reason, but fanaticism" (185). David Vallins's Coleridge-inspired definition of fanaticism—"the fanatic is effectively empty, and can only find or have meaning in conjunction with others of his class"—nicely sums up Graves, who empowers himself by parasitically appropriating other minds to do his bidding.[50] Like Charles Edmund Maurice's endlessly mutable Jack Cade, Adams's Graves suggests the instability of a moral world uprooted from its traditional grounding in the church. When Graves and Mark collaborate on a scheme to break Oldcastle out of prison, they do so by pretending to be the very pilgrims that Graves so despises; Graves's casuistical self-justification ("our purpose is a very different one from that of these benighted souls" [173]) promptly infects the weak-minded Mark, who knows perfectly well that such a lie would upset his friends. The fate of Mark's morals, effectively buried in Graves, suggests that fanaticism exerts an irresistible pull that nevertheless undermines a very different form of masculine morality.

In Adams's critique of evangelical crusading, reform must be stripped of any connection to political action. Slowly pulling away from Graves, Mark realizes that "unless he should be called upon openly to deny what was true, or profess what was false, it was his duty in life to remain quiet" (206). Masculine inaction turns out to be the proper order of the day; the ideal reforming mode is to work silently and conservatively within the constraints of church discipline. Even the sentimental priest-warrior goes by the wayside. Pointedly, Mark agrees to attend church services once again, even professing himself willing to take Communion (despite his disbelief in transubstantiation) (211). Yet Graves, the serpent in the novella's garden, reappears shortly after Mark turns to his newly inward Lollardism and convinces him to help liberate Sir John Oldcastle from prison. In a neat moment of symbolic retribution, Mark is arrested several months later in the midst of his own eponymous wedding, as if opting for Graves was a form of "cheating" on his bride-to-be; again and again, radical action defers the promised comic resolution to the plot. Indeed, the comic resolution proves not to resolve anything at all, for even after Mark marries Lettice, he still finds himself pursued by Graves. It is only his mature realization that Graves and Oldcastle are engaging in "treason," under a divinely approved pretense of not being interested in "any distinction between man and man, such as those you speak of" (274), that enables Mark to jettison Graves altogether.

Adams, who denies Graves his martyrdom (he pulls out a sword and dies fighting), begins to wrap up his narrative with a series of reflections about Protestant distortions of the historical record. It is only in "the times of Bale and Fox" that anyone doubted Oldcastle's conviction for treason (278); the martyrological narratives that celebrate Oldcastle's witness to the truth at the gallows either contradict themselves, cannot be verified from "historians of the times," or are distinguished by "partisanship" (279). This sudden breach in the narrator's otherwise predominantly omniscient voice leads us back to Scott's play with prefaces in his own Reformation duology. In Scott the dizzying multiplication of "Protestantizing" narrators leaves the reader uncertain where a "Catholic" past can be found. There is no Catholic story left to tell. Here, Adams shifts focus from fictional narrators to actual martyrologists and inverts Scott's point: Scott turns Protestantism's erasure of the Catholic worldview into a sign of modernity (in the end, "losing" Catholicism is no cause for distress), but in Adams's hands it becomes a warning about evangelicalism's unwillingness to confront the artificial, rather than the providential, attributes of its own historical narratives. The Victorian author, confronted with a heap of Protestant narratives, is left with something that signifies not nothing but merely itself; such texts are simply pure presentism in action. Instead of the violence inflicted on the martyr or pseudomartyr, we have the violence inflicted by martyrologists on the Christian past, which is at its least recoverable when at its most relevant to religious controversy.

Conclusion

The obvious difficulty with identifying Wycliffe and the Lollards as the starting point of the Reformation was, as the Rev. Arthur Brown admitted, that "they were utterly exterminated, and their very name had become a thing of the past, before the final assault began that drove from its strongholds in England the usurping power of Rome."[51] Yet, despite the nay-saying from authors like Henry Cadwallader Adams, it was precisely their apparent defeat that made them such powerful figures in the end. For if the Roman Catholics thought they had destroyed Wycliffe's legacy, the Reformation proved not just Catholic fallibility but, more importantly, the impossibility of wholly suppressing divine truth. The persecution of the Lollards signaled not medievalism's triumph but its defeat by the once-forbidden book, the reading of which makes "life, and death, and things present, all [seem] to be nothing, and Christ alone [seem] to be everything."[52] If this proto-Reformation only proved semisuccessful, it nevertheless demonstrated (to evangelicals) that access to the Bible always generated something that looked suspiciously like modern evangelical Protestantism; modern faith existed within the historical detritus of Catholic ritual, ready to be released once readers and audiences finally had access to the vernacular scriptures. For the Victorian evangelical author, the only thing about Catholicism that transcended its original context was negative: its status as eternal oppressor or Antichrist, forever seeking to undermine true godliness whenever it can. Moreover, at a time when Protestants anxiously contemplated the resurgence of modern Catholicism, tales of the Lollards attempted to reconsolidate the "Britishness" in British Christianity. It was not that medieval dissenters from orthodoxy were "Protestant" (although some certainly went so far as to argue that they were) but that *Protestant* was simply another way of speaking the word *Christian*. Protestantism might be modern, but its modernity was just a new instantiation of Christianity's antiquity. Mainstream Catholic orthodoxy became a dangerous detour from the "strait gate" through which the heretics entered the gates of Heaven.

Chapter Three

"THE WORD OF LIFE
LIES OPEN BEFORE US"

Reading the Reformation Bible
in the Nineteenth Century

As we have seen, Wycliffe's fascination for Victorian readers derived, in part, from his role as Bible translator and disseminator of the scriptures to the common people. But, paradoxically, a number of Victorians complained that the Wycliffite and Reformation projects had been *too* successful: the Bible had turned into just another object *because* it was omnipresent. Reflecting glumly on the Bible's place in contemporary culture, the noted missionary Alexander Duff asked, "how often is it treated as nothing better than an insignificant toy, or converted into a mere gilded ornament, or removed, as an indispensable piece of sacred lumber, to collect the dust in some corner of our libraries?"[1] In Duff's early Victorian lament over the rise of what Mary Wilson Carpenter calls "consumer Christianity," the Bible decomposes from message into object, and an object for the middle-to-upper classes at that: Duff's examples involve leisure (the toy), superficial aesthetics (the ornament), dedicated space (the personal library), and an income sufficient to provide luxuries (all three).[2] Moreover, the Bible has become interchangeable with what ought to be very different classes of objects, whether the toy or the ornament; not only has it lost its particularity as the Word, it has apparently lost its particularity as a book. Reduced to "sacred lumber" and banished to "the corner," the Bible is more of a collectible figurine than a text for careful reading. For Duff, the Bible now derives its value from its ability to take on the characteristics of some other material object, and therein lies the problem. Those who turn the Bible into "gilded ornament[s]"— aesthetically pleasing books addressed to the eyes instead of the mind— presume that the Bible-as-book is itself valuable. But what about the Word within? Is it possible to offer a strict valuation of man's salvation?

Although, as Michael Ledger-Lomas notes, Victorian Bibles "became important physical symbols" available in every bookshop and found in just about every family library, many evangelicals nevertheless suspected that the Bible had gained bestseller status but lost all of its readers.[3] Patrick Brantlinger's quip that late-Victorian authors saw "the very success of culture leading to a sort of collective suicide" applies here as well: Bible readership falters and dies under the weight of the one thing necessary for maintaining moral order.[4] What has been lost, in other words, is the *shock* of the Bible. Protestants insisted that one of, if not *the*, most important contributions of the Reformation was taking the Bible out of its institutional and linguistic shackles and making it available to all seekers of salvation. This tight focus on popular Bible reading as *the* historical event erases all traces of Roman Catholic vernacular Bibles while it downgrades or deliberately ignores both the other theological controversies of the period (such as Eucharistic controversy) and Victorian Protestant infighting.[5] Instead, telling the story of the Bible and lay readership makes the widespread distribution of both the Bible-as-book and the Bible-as-Word crucial for maintaining Protestantism's strength—and, along with it, the nation's strength. Yet, spreading the Word reduces the Word to mere words. In its triumph Protestantism transforms the scriptures into just another material object, and thus carries within itself the seeds of its own potential degeneracy. As Duff's gloomy assessment suggests, once the Bible turns into something that is entirely material, its meaning ceases to circulate.[6] The Bible's capacity to not only energize history, but actually interpret it, vanishes in an age of comfortable Protestantism and equally comfortable capitalism. And with it goes the core of Britain's national identity.

Complaints about nonreaders, however, presume a desire for readers—and yet, a widespread readership, or at least *potential* readership, appears to be part of the problem. This interest in a mass lay readership for the Bible leads our authors down some perhaps unexpected paths. As we have already seen, these novels emphasize the accessibility of the Bible to *all* readers, insisting that key truths are plain to even the youngest and least educated student of the scriptures. This is *sola scriptura* in action: all things essential to salvation are accessible to individual readers—with or without additional help—and all interpretive problems can be resolved by comparing problematic passages to others *within* the Bible. But precisely because these tales argue that the shock of Bible reading ultimately produces conversion, they deemphasize the difficulties expressed in the many available manuals devoted to lay Bible reading, just as they paper over the divisions among sixteenth-century and Victorian Protestant denominations. As Scott Schofield reminds us, sixteenth-century readers would not have been expected to read the Bible unassisted; instead, they had to "confer with printed commentaries or 'interpreters' and attend sermons, i.e., 'preaching.'"[7] Such textual or verbal aids tend to be quietly suppressed in Victorian fictions of Bible reading. Only a few novels address the question of difficulty, choosing to dwell instead on the instantly transformative possibilities of the biblical encounter.

In fact, the novels' emphasis on *sola scriptura* not only elides the existence of vernacular Catholic Bibles but also obscures the extent to which readers—especially young readers—primarily encountered the Bible in rewritten, excerpted, and abridged form. As Ruth B. Bottigheimer notes of European Protestants more generally, Victorian novelists helped construct a story about the "hunger for Scripture" that purportedly characterized Protestants alone, even though considerable demand had always existed among Catholic readers as well.[8] The extensive literature on representations of reading, though, alerts us to the numerous anxieties about who was reading what when—particularly when the "who" in question was female, young, or working class. Novels were problematic, but as Kate Flint reminds us, the Bible was "the most important text" for any woman's education.[9] The obvious antidote to the wrong sort of reading was the Bible, but even Bible reading could meet with objections when the reader in question was female or otherwise unqualified for theological pursuits.[10] As the earlier quotation from Brantlinger suggests, widespread literacy was not necessarily considered an ideal state of affairs for the national or cultural health. How, then, did the utopian dream of universal Bible reading signify in religious fiction?

Whereas the previous chapter emphasized celebrations of Wycliffe as *translator*, this chapter turns at greater length to the fictionalized Reformation *reader*, whose yearning for the scriptures models the right way of forming good Protestant subjects. Reformation tales reinvent moments of "first contact" between the reader and the scriptures, the better to re-enchant a modernity sadly lacking in reverence for the Bible. These novels depend on the reader's prior acquaintance with the Bible, given their frequent use of biblical quotations and allusion without any direct citations, but they seek to construct this prior knowledge as *historically determined*—without arguing that Protestantism itself is historically determined. Reformation tales take the nineteenth-century reader back to the original point of contact, the better to translate the shock of Bible reading from past to present. I begin with responses to the scholarly and popular historiography of the Bible, a field that expanded rapidly in the nineteenth century. Histories of the Bible normally focused on translators and the accompanying philological problems of translation, whereas novelists emphasized individual (or group) readership and reception. I then return to the problem of the Bible as object, as novelists insist on the shock of having—even touching—a Bible in the sixteenth century. Finally, I emphasize the role of gender in these narratives, particularly in representations of popular, frequently feminized reading communities that arrive at an authoritative interpretation of the scriptures.

The English Bible in History

Histories of the English Bible flourished in the nineteenth century, thanks to the intense combination of increasing evangelical influence, anxieties about Catholic inroads into popular consciousness, and the cheap publishing technologies that enabled more and more readers, the poor included, to own their own copy of the scriptures. Peter J. Thuesen sums up the defining features of these histories as "anti-Catholicism," "ethnocentrism," "hagiography," and "evolution" (in the sense of steadily improving translations).[11] Despite wide-ranging differences in scholarship and originality, most of these histories normalized a Protestant reading of British (or Anglo-American) history: the Roman Catholic Church was corrupt; the laity yearned for firsthand access to the Bible; such access was both subversive (to the established order) and community building (for the invisible church of the elect); and, last but not least, the widespread distribution of the Bible undergirded modern civil liberties. These assumptions structured even the most scholarly of works on the topic, such as Brooke Foss Westcott's standard *A General View of the History of the English Bible* (1868). Westcott, one of the nineteenth century's most eminent textual critics and editors, announces in the first paragraph of his introduction that "A people which is without a Bible in its mother tongue, or is restrained from using it, or wilfully neglects it, is also imperfect, or degenerate, or lifeless in its apprehension of Christian Truth, and proportionately bereft of the strength which flows from a living Creed."[12] For Westcott and most of his contemporaries, the vernacular Bible provides the fundamental growth solution for an organic community, united in its common reading from the Book of Life—a claim already circulating during the sixteenth century and used to justify vernacular Bible translations.[13] As Westcott's insistence on the "mother tongue" suggests, each community must access the universal "Christian truth" through a particularized and nationalized version of it. What Benedict Anderson famously proposed for the function of novels and newspapers, Westcott proposes for the vernacular Bible, which unites all readers through a shared spiritual identity discovered in the firsthand encounter with the sacred text.

But beyond this invocation of the reading public, Westcott's real interest lies in the *production* of the English Bible, not its *consumption*, an interest that characterizes both other scholarly accounts like the Baptist Christopher Anderson's *Annals of the English Bible* (2 vols., 1845) and popularizations like William Fiddian Moulton's *The History of the English Bible* (1878). Hence the near-universal focus on biographical accounts of the major translators—with John Wycliffe and William Tyndale attaining heroic status—accompanied by bibliographical data and philologically based comparisons of translations across multiple texts. After midcentury this celebration of the translator's work reflects an increasing consciousness of potential difficulties with the King James Version; it was no coincidence that both Westcott and Moulton were themselves translators who collaborated on the Revised Version (1881).[14] Within the overarching Protestant narrative described above, these minutely detailed accounts slowly accrete into a story of translation as progress—Thuesen's "evolutionism"—as each translator corrects and builds on the work of his predecessors. If anything, dissatisfaction with the current state of Bible translation demonstrates a people's healthy engagement with the text: each generation should *want* to bring the full weight of modern knowledge to bear on the Bible, with the goal of inching closer and closer to the perfect Book of Life. After all, as the Congregationalist John Stoughton cheerfully noted of those who preceded the nineteenth-century advocates of a revised translation, "Every merely human work—and translation is necessarily such a work—it was felt must admit of improvement, and that a careful distinction should ever be made between the perfect writings of men inspired, and the rendering of them into a modern tongue by men uninspired."[15] The labor of translation and revision renders the vernacular Bible eternally transcendent and yet eternally up-to-date, always in the process of being brought closer to its national audiences.

Those audiences, nevertheless, were almost always missing from the historian's narrative. One exception to the rule was the American historian and translator Hannah Chaplin Conant's *The English Bible* (1856), which, in addition to its sentimentalizing and sometimes sensationalizing rhetoric, did not shy away from flights of imaginative fancy:

Many a touching scene might be imagined, of rustic groups by the wayside, in the churchyard, or around the peat fire at evening, listening for the first time to the words of the Bible in their mother tongue. Then, how would the beautifully written manuscript be passed round, from hand to hand, to be admired and wondered at; and not seldom to be wet with tears from eyes that beheld for the first time, in English characters, the name of Jesus![16]

Mrs. Conant, happy to suggest elsewhere that the "historical novelist" might find ample source material in Tyndale's history,[17] here injects the kind of scene that *would* be crucial to historical novelists. In bracketing this "touching scene" as an explicit fiction, Mrs. Conant simultaneously highlights the absence of a particular kind of biblical communal audience—impoverished, probably illiterate—from the record and insists on the integral nature of this imaginary audience to her historical project. In question is not the first encounter between listener and Bible but the first encounter between listener and vernacular Bible. Like Westcott a dozen years later, Mrs. Conant insists that authentic, affective Bible reading can only happen in the "mother tongue." Clearly, these readers did not *know* Jesus until they saw his name "in English characters"; the shock derives from God's word suddenly descending into everyday English. Notably, all of these imaginary encounters occur outside the Roman Catholic Church, both conceptually and physically, where Latin still reigns supreme. Mrs. Conant thus proposes a moment in which the vernacular Bible is simultaneously central (as the Word of God, speaking to the elect) yet culturally marginal (because exiled from the physical house of God). As the Reformation unfolds, the vernacular Bible will move from margin to center. But can it do so without losing the shock of familiarity that makes it so powerful in these first moments?

Mrs. Conant's need for this primal scene of reading crosses over into historical fictions and fictionalized histories proper, which sought to imagine how communities might be constituted around biblical reception history. Candy Gunther Brown notes that "[n]ineteenth-century evangelicals simultaneously narrowed the focus of Christian fellowship from church to home and expanded it out again to encompass all participants in a textually defined community," and the very possibility of women and children reading the Bible *at home* itself becomes a key historical marker.[18] In one of the most popular Protestant narratives, which remained consistent across the nineteenth century, modernity emerged as the Bible moved from the homosocial, elite Catholic monastery and university to the heterosocial home. For example, in Selina A. Bower's pedagogical dialogue *"Let There Be Light"; Or, the Story of the Reformation* (1883), a mother quotes John 4:24 and then reminds her children that such scriptural knowledge would have been unavailable a few centuries previously: "But as the Scriptures were not only scarce, but were also forbidden books to the laity, the people knew not the will of God, nor the way to Heaven." This sad state of affairs, she goes on, was because "[t]he Church of Rome professed to be infallible, and usurped the entire right of explaining God's Holy Word."[19] This is a narrative for children, and yet it inculcates a number of core assumptions about Protestant historical process. To begin with, history begins and ends with the Bible, the source of all essential knowledge about the will of God; the "people" can neither know nor fully participate in God's sacred plan without access to the divine word unmediated by institutional interference. More specifically, the people have a "right" to read and interpret the scriptures for themselves, a right that the Roman Catholic Church wrongly appropriates to itself. A scriptural reader sets down the road to becoming a historical agent at the moment of reading the text, which reveals both the "will" and the "way." (If, as James Simpson notes, such reading turns out to have unforeseen complications, the complications are not yet visible in our example.[20]) The people have a right, then, to *read*, to *interpret*, and, not least, to *own* the scriptures. Without this right as a possibility, the people perceive history as, for lack of a better term, a closed book; indeed, many will have no sense that there is an authentic historical narrative from which they have been summarily disbarred. Our mother and her children, however, exist in a world in which the scriptures can be read, quoted, and analyzed—all within the comfort of a safe, clearly feminized domestic sphere. In the words of Colleen

McDannell, "Protestantism changed the ritual [of worship] from one of sacrifice to one of instruction," an instruction that takes place at the entirely textual "altar of the Protestant home."[21] Mrs. Conant's narrative trajectory has been realized: the post-Reformation world has relocated the Bible from the dreaded "Church of Rome" to the private household.

This private scene of Bible reading carries its own historical weight. Considered in terms of genre, *"Let There Be Light"* is the British equivalent of what Sarah Robbins calls the American "domestic literacy narrative," in which the mother or "motherly teacher" educates children (or, in some cases, adults) into their national responsibilities through some form of "storytelling text." Literacy becomes the prerequisite for virtue in general and responsible political participation in specific.[22] Here, literacy points beyond national culture to a universal divine providence. In Bower's dialogue the mother and her children, both male and female, have read the Bible closely enough that all of them can summon up prooftexts. As we have seen both in Scott and in the proto-Protestant novels discussed in chapter 2, Protestant reading is associated with domesticity and femininity; however, unlike in Scott, the mother's instruction is entirely sufficient for the child's needs. The mother takes it upon herself not just to explain the Bible to her children but, more importantly, to *historicize* the very possibility of such reading and explanation. As she triumphantly proclaims at the end of Bower's narrative, "The good and brave men who lived and died in defence [*sic*] of the faith which that Word declares can alone save sinful man, read the Bible amidst difficulty, danger, destruction, and death. We can read it in ease, comfort, peace, and safety" (78–79). Her narrative of the Reformation leads up to these scenes of maternal pedagogy—which nevertheless are figured as both privileged and "lesser" than what has gone before.[23] There is nothing heroic about modern Bible reading, which requires neither effort nor bravery and seems to take place on a chaise lounge in front of a roaring fire. The Bible has become mundane, as opposed to what it once was (as the alliterative account of earlier horrors suggests); Protestantism's success may well be the mark of its potential failure. In fact, the editor,

Ernest Boys, warns in his preface that the events of the Reformation "happened too long ago to have the influence they ought to have," and therefore "it is all the easier for misguided persons to be led in a backward and Rome-ward direction, as is now so lamentably the case" (vii). By situating Bible reading within its bloody historical context, however, the mother re-enchants the children's encounter with the text—even as her "secure control" over the Reformation narrative is itself historicized as a product of the story she tells.[24] Having motivated the Reformation, the scriptures now become most vivid to readers when interpreted through narratives *about* the Reformation.

BIBLES IN MOTION

Even when Reformation tales spend relatively little time on actual scenes of Bible reading, the Bible's presence as both text and object drives the narrative—even though the magical Bible of Walter Scott's *The Monastery* is nowhere to be found here. *Text* and *object* need to be interpreted loosely, for these novels offer multiple ways of engaging with the Bible (individual reading, group reading, oral transmission) and of possessing it (divided into fragments, New Testament only, print, manuscript, memorization). Nevertheless, they avoid virtually all mention of anything that might be used to help the reader *understand* the Bible, such as commentaries, let alone Bible stories or any other popular approach to the text. Moreover, they tend to leave unquestioned the overall effect of the Bible as a singular book, even as they register multiple ways of reading, encountering, and distributing it. As a result, these tales collectively generate a fiction about the history of Protestant Bible reading that implicitly links all popular aids to interpretation, along with any questions about the Bible's coherence, with Roman Catholic "tradition." Quite obviously, Reformation tales presume the reader's own acquaintance with and possession of a Bible: negotiating a novel based on the work of John Foxe, for example, requires the reader to recognize biblical patterns of martyrdom along with frequent direct quotations (usually without chapter and verse) and allusions. Ideally, whenever and however possessed, the Bible is both the story's subject and its interpretive key. Selina Bower's mother tells a story that implicitly culminates in her own ability to interpret the Bible for her children; similarly, the Reformation tale narrates its own historical possibility.

But, as Boys and Bower also suggest, the Reformation tale may well chart its own undoing, even its own misinterpretation. In *Dayspring: A Story of the Time of William Tyndale, Reformer, Scholar, and Martyr* (1883), a work contemporary with Bower's history, Emma Marshall momentarily breaks the frame to admonish readers who "look back on these times with shrinking and perhaps disgust":

> And are we not slow to deny ourselves—to sacrifice our time, our strength, and our means—in order to communicate to others the faith, which by William Tyndale's hand was first laid before the English people, and is now circulated wherever the English tongue is spoken? Read in our churches and in our families, printed in every type for the eyes of old and young, the Word of Life lies open before us. Are we so far in advance, in the faith that worketh by love, of the Lady Cranstone and Father Francis of the sixteenth century?[25]

The privileged modern reader, suspects Marshall, yearns to disavow his or her roots in sixteenth-century persecuting culture. The Bible (and one notes that Marshall collapses "the faith" into the Bible itself) percolates throughout all of English-speaking culture, not just the United Kingdom; it transcends differences of institution, space, and generations. It is, above all, *accessible* ("lies open"). Everyone reads the Bible, everyone owns the Bible, and everyone feels the effects of the Bible. And yet, the Bible's omnipresence does not, after all, signal Protestantism's triumph; the very "shrinking" and "disgust" with which Marshall's imagined reader reacts to the Reformation indicates that Tyndale's heroic act of translation has not, after all, ushered in an age of godliness. If anything, the Bible's availability in Marshall's text functions as a *false* historical marker. An apparent break between past and present conceals the real continuity of the sinful human heart. Read wrongly, inattentively, or not at all, the Bible fails to produce the self-sacrificing, evangelical Protestant subject; instead, it produces the overly sensitive, self-satisfied "Christian" as incapable of properly interpreting the historical past as any of Marshall's Catholic villains.

What novelists like Marshall wanted to do, then, was reclaim the Bible from its own success, the better to consolidate a unified Protestant community in the present. In this case the novelist compensated for what Mrs. Conant found absent from the nonfictional documents by dramatizing the moment of first encounter with the Bible as both text and material object. Interpretation was not the only issue at stake; it was necessary to estrange the possibility of actually possessing or having access to a Bible, in whatever form. We see this process at work in one of the Victorian period's most popular Protestant books for children: the short-story collection *Historical Tales for Young Protestants* (1857), which was used as a Sunday school and missionary text for decades after its publication (although High Church readers often found the book deeply objectionable in tone and content).[26] The book's narratives of biblical reading and circulation elide denominational conflicts, helping to shape an idealized "Protestant/Christian" readership; notably, one print ad includes pull quotes from Church of England, Baptist, and Methodist sources, among others.[27] And in the 1850s, when anti-Catholicism was at its Victorian high point, the author's or authors' turn to stories of religious persecution canonized in John Foxe's *Book of Martyrs* (itself undergoing a publishing renaissance, as we shall see in more detail in the next chapter) was hardly coincidental. As the editor, John Henry Cross, explained in the preface, the book's treatment of "the dark deeds of the papacy" sprang from a "conviction that the principles and spirit in which they originated in former ages are not extinct in the present day."[28] But the tale I would like to discuss in detail, "The Youthful Martyr," does not merely copy. Instead, it revises John Foxe's account of the martyrdom of nineteen-year-old William Hunter so as to make his "crime" the act of scripture reading itself. Beginning with the 1570 edition, Foxe established that Hunter, an apprentice, initially journeyed home after his employer made it clear that Hunter's refusal to take communion was endangering the household.[29] Caught reading a Bible in a Brentwood church, Hunter was soon caught up in a debate, first with a Father Atwell and then the Vicar of Southweild, about scriptural interpretation—in particular, scriptural justification for the Mass. Brought before Bishop Bonner, Hunter continued to hold his original position, and so, after Bonner repeatedly failed to convince him to change his mind, he was condemned to death (1751–55). "The Youthful Martyr" deletes all references to the Mass, to transubstantiation, and even to the Bible verses under discussion in Foxe's text. Instead, it stages Hunter's fatal encounter with the church authorities as a conflict between open and closed texts, a conflict that emblematizes the core historical difference between the Edwardian and Marian regimes: while "[i]n the days of the young king Edward the Sixth, a Bible was placed on a desk in every church of the land, for the use of the people," Queen Mary, "a stern papist, ascended the throne of England, and quickly ordered the removal of the Bibles."[30] In making it appear as though Mary's very first act as Queen was to remove the Bible, the anonymous author suggests that Catholics perceive the Bible and its communities as a challenge to both theological and social order. As Father Atwell's initial questions suggest, the threat derives not just from private judgment but from literacy itself: "Why meddlest thou with the Bible? . . . Knowest thou how to read? And canst thou expound the Scriptures?" (68). Hunter, a literate adolescent, challenges the clerical elite's control over scriptural interpretation by displacing the priest's exposition with his own private judgment, overturning the spiritual (albeit not the social) distinctions between both clerical and lay *and* adult and child. The priest's misplaced anger, in fact, confounds the difference of social and spiritual that "The Youthful Martyr" carefully maintains.

Hunter's sufferings, then, follow entirely from his refusal to "give up the Bible, and deny its truths" (71) rather than from his opposition to transubstantiation. In suppressing Hunter's argumentation, "The Youthful Martyr" elevates private reading above public exposition— as Hunter tells Atwell, "Father Atwell, I take it not upon me to *expound* the Scriptures; but, finding the Bible here, I *read* it for my comfort" (68)—while, in turn, making such reading the key to the *imitatio Christi*. For Hunter, all historical narrative flows, in effect, from the knowledge of "what his Saviour had suffered for him" (72); unlike the materialistic Bishop Bonner, who offers material rewards in exchange for Hunter's conversion, Hunter understands both that his own works are useless to achieve salvation and that his true "career" is to be "faithful" (72) whatever the circumstances. The old clerical elite fails in the face of *sola scriptura*, which teaches that the Bible's teachings on the essentials of salvation are accessible to all honest inquirers. The tale's materialist, blasphemous Catholics, who refuse to read, blind themselves to the narratives that structure a devout Christian's life and death.

But it was not enough to remove biblical interpretation from the sphere of "licensed" readers. Once again, in these narratives Protestantism domesticates the Bible by translating it into the vernacular, relocating it to private spaces, and/or privileging modes of reading conventionally linked with women and children. The writer who dramatized this narrative in the greatest detail was Elizabeth Rundle Charles, a classically educated novelist, poet, translator, and hymnodist who made her reputation with *Chronicles of the Schönberg-Cotta Family* (1863), one of the Victorian era's most successful Reformation tales. As one reviewer approvingly concluded, it was excellently suited for "indoctrinating the young into the principles of the Reformation, and for showing the unnaturalness into which a religious system falls when its mission becomes one of class ambition."[31] *Chronicles* is the first book in a series of historical novels about the emergence of Protestantism and its spread across the Continent, to England, and across the Atlantic; the series is pointedly ecumenical, reflecting Charles's wide-ranging theological and devotional interests, and praises High Church as well as evangelical worship.[32] Here, religious history turns entirely domestic, encapsulated within the autobiographical narratives, frequently by women, of a single family; this is Protestant narrative as the purely quotidian. The *Chronicle*'s first two narrators are Friedrich and Elsè, brother and sister, who begin the novel in their late teens; later, they are succeeded by their mother and younger sister.

They and their family develop a close relationship to the young Martin Luther, and Friedrich's and Elsè's mutual coming-of-age dovetails with conversion to the new faith. But in both instances, this conversion comes after long, hard engagements with the Bible—a process that dramatizes the problems of interpretation for both learned (Friedrich) and unlearned (Elsè), men and women, readers. For that matter, Charles insists that this process begins with the realization that there *is* a text that requires interpreting. What Charles historicizes, then, is not just the shock I have delineated above but also how biblical readership was constructed at a particular epoch—a set of norms only partially visible to the characters, even when they seek to contest them.

Much of the novel is about chasing a fragment: being struck by the fragment, finding its context, interpreting it, resisting it. Elsè's and Friedrich's younger cousin, Eva, remembers only part of the sentence her imprisoned father taught her before he died: *"God so loved the world, that he gave his only son."*[33] Eva registers the link between God the Father and her own lost father (103); Elsè, however, does not believe that the most obvious meaning (God loves the world entire) can be the proper one. Eva's interpretation is both affective and analogical, an emotional response that instinctively maps the biblical text (as yet unrecognized as such) onto everyday life. This "innocent" mode of reading stands in stark contrast to Elsè's more sophisticated *un*reading, as it were, which seeks alternative contexts (the creed) before giving up in despair. But both modes of reading remain within the province of the Roman Catholic Church. In fact, Eva believes for some time that she can live a religious life only by becoming a nun (189), a position that contradicts the entire trajectory of the novel's plot. Only by returning the fragment to both the full sentence and its original biblical context, and then relearning how to read it, can the characters enter the novel's nascent Protestantism.

Elsè, who thinks little of herself as either a narrator or a spiritual being, exemplifies the sixteenth-century woman reader's ambivalent relationship to the Bible. On the one hand, the very title "Chronicle" turns out to be inspired by the biblical books of that name; on the other, Friedrich must supply Elsè with that information, for she cannot read Latin and has only encountered the Vulgate Bible as part of her father's publishing business. As in the old story about Milton's daughters, Elsè participates in a textual enterprise that is gendered masculine but without being able to decipher the strange signifiers littering the page. From Elsè's point of view, this is a purely material Bible: "Only I cannot help seeing that people do honour the bindings and the gilded titles, in spite of all my mother and Fritz can say; and I should like my precious book to have such a binding, that the people who could not read the inside, might yet stop to look at the gold clasps and the jewelled back. To those who can read the inside, perhaps it would not matter" (9). Elsè's fantasy Bible gives visual, tactile pleasure, but it also swaps aesthetics for spiritual knowledge. In making pretty covers a sufficient substitute for reading, Elsè treads perilously on the path to idolatry. She is willing to be complicit with this misguided act of "honour," which celebrates this-worldly tastes, even as she acknowledges an entirely different way of interacting with the book. But, as the qualifier "perhaps" suggests, she cannot quite think her way *into* this difference. In the novel's historical reckoning, the Bible as text must supersede the Bible as object—a transition that demands, at this point in the novel, classical literacy.

And this, of course, is the problem: classical literacy is unavailable to all but an elite, usually male, few. Elsè points out to the much more spiritual Eva, who is learning Latin, that the Bible was originally written in Hebrew and Greek—but, she goes on in her diary, "We should understand it all so much better in German; but of course Latin is the language of the blessed saints and angels, that is a reason for it" (77). As Charles's Protestant reader would immediately understand, of course, the Roman Catholic Church prefers Latin precisely so that the Bible may *not* be understood by laywomen like Elsè and Eva. The problem, however, goes deeper than that. Shortly after Elsè concludes this section of her diary by invoking the possibility of the vernacular, Fritz recounts Martin Luther's first encounter with a complete Latin Bible. In Fritz's telling, Luther comes to startled consciousness of how much the church edits the Bible for general consumption, reducing it to "the

Evangelia read in the churches, or in the Collection of Homilies" (79). For the first time, Luther discovers the Bible as *narrative*, in the story of Hannah and Samuel (1 Samuel 1–2). Narrative, as we have seen, is all-important: the Bible is not just story but *history*, and the moment that Luther reads a biblical narrative in its entirety—unmediated by the structure of Catholic liturgy—he implicitly finds himself within a much larger historical narrative than he ever knew existed. Here is the equivalent to Eva's fragment, put into its right context. Moreover, Charles's choice of text for Luther's reading implicitly links him to the biblical prophet, a point that Fritz fails to register. In other words, Fritz doubly misses the point: he neither perceives the full significance of Luther's encounter with a complete Bible nor understands the moment's symbolic import—the latter because, ironically enough, he hears the story in the "old" way, through Luther's oral retelling.

Fritz's life in the convent doubles Luther's, both literally and figuratively, and this doubling encompasses his transformation into a scripture *reader*. Like Luther, he takes a vow—in this case, to save Eva during a terrible illness—and enters the cloister because of it. He ends up in Luther's cell, has similar doubts, and shares the same confessor, a kind older man who nevertheless cannot answer Fritz's anxious questions about full atonement for sin. And when Fritz receives his first Bible, it turns out to be the one that Luther used to read. This is less the *imitatio Christi* than the *imitatio Lutheri*: it is Luther, even more than Eva, who turns out to be the novel's model reader, and to read like Luther, Fritz must learn to recognize the providential plot in which he has found himself. At first, however, Fritz attempts to organize his life according to an entirely different set of landmarks. Before his initial Bible readings, Fritz's diary entries in the cloister are nearly all written to coincide with the feast days of his patron saints, beginning with that of St. Sebastian (to whom Fritz had sworn his vow, and whose name Fritz now takes [107]). In that sense, the renamed Fritz inscribes his new identity according to the rhythms of the Roman Catholic Church's liturgical calendar. From a Protestant point of view, the dating is not a problem, but Fritz's constant requests for intercession are. Fritz's own first reading of the Bible, in fact, follows on a diary entry about spiritual doubt that concludes with an invocation of Mary and the saints (118); it is the first entry not marked as a saint's day. His unalloyed anxieties about his vocation and his soul, that is, require the help of *all* the saints, exceeding his turns from one patron saint to another. It is therefore ironic that his reflections on reading the Bible are recorded on the Feast of the Annunciation and St. Gregory of Nyssa's day. After St. Gregory of Nyssa, Fritz ceases to mark the saints' days altogether. Even if Fritz does not receive an angelic annunciation, he is greeted by his confessor, bearing Luther's old Bible, and this moment clearly marks a rupture in Fritz's spiritual history.

Initially, however, Fritz responds with doubt and anxiety instead of affirmation. On the Feast of the Annunciation, Fritz's reading fills him with nostalgia for the era *before* the Annunciation, when "there was one temple wherein to worship, certain definite feasts to celebrate, certain definite ceremonial rules to keep" (118). This moment of yearning transforms Judaism during the Temple era into an age of definite, institutionalized religious knowledge. Yet Fritz's fantasy also turns Judaism into something stubbornly material and legalistic, rooted in a specific space and practiced according to divinely ordained rules. The New Testament, he notes with some worry, "is all addressed to the heart; and who can make the heart right? I suppose it is the conviction of this which has made the Church since then restore many minute rules and discipline, in imitation of the Jewish ceremonial; for in the Gospels and Epistles I can find no ritual, ceremonial, or definite external rules of any kind" (119). Here, Charles charges the Roman Catholic Church with "Judaizing," of imposing Old Testament legalism on a New Testament that resolutely resists it. But yet again, between these two comments, Fritz notes that the Jews did not believe in the cloistered life. The church simultaneously supersedes Judaism, embraces it, *and* is rebuked by it. Suppressing the Bible means also suppressing the church's problematic negotiations with the Judaism it supposedly replaces; there can be no awareness of a history, of the law succeeded by "the heart," without the text that supplies the key.

Reading promises liberation, in part by restoring the reader to his own history. But it also disconcerts precisely because interpretation itself now has a history. This becomes all the more evident once Fritz discovers the entirety of Eva's fragment:

> I have found, in my reading to-day, the end of Eva's sentence—"God so loved the world, that he gave his only begotten Son, *that whosoever believeth in him should not perish, but have everlasting life."*
>
> How simple the words are!—"Believeth;" that would mean, in any other book, "trusteth," "has reliance" in Christ;—simply to confide in him, and then receive his promise not to perish.
>
> But *here*—in this book, in theology—it is necessarily impossible that believing can mean anything so simple as that; because, at that rate, any one who merely came to the Lord Jesus Christ in confiding trust would have everlasting life, without any further conditions; and this is obviously out of the question. (119)[34]

The difficulty with Fritz's interpretation of the text is that the text is not difficult. Fritz finds himself trapped between Eva's reading strategy, which assumes that the most evident reading is correct and proceeds from immediate emotional response, and his own prescribed "theological" strategy, which assumes that the Roman Catholic Church is the only authoritative guide to interpretation. Here, the Bible reads its readers. Charles does not merely accuse the Roman Catholic Church of promoting symbolic or allegorical readings of verses that should be taken in their obvious, mundane signification but of actually *distorting* language, effectively injecting words with meanings they do not possess. What does "believeth" mean here, Fritz wonders? It "must include contrition, confession, penance, satisfaction, mortification of the flesh, and all else necessary to salvation" (120). Reading turns into rewriting, and this rewriting constitutes an evasion of the Bible. In accepting the church's interpretation, Fritz refuses to be confronted by the Bible, to be read *by* it.

As we soon discover, Fritz's momentary inability to read the Bible also echoes Martin Luther's journey. Luther admits that he felt "angry" at the word "righteousness," which, like "believeth," contradicts the church's received interpretation of the text (159). With some assistance from Staupitz, however, he realizes that this is the righteousness by which God "justifieth us," and all is well: "Straightway I felt as if I were born anew; it was as if I had found the door of paradise thrown wide open. Now I saw the Scriptures altogether in a new light—ran through their whole contents as far as my memory would serve, and compared them—and found that this righteousness was the more surely that by which he makes us righteous, because everything agreed thereunto so well" (160). In retelling this moment of discovery (a narrative modeled on Luther's own autobiography), Luther demonstrates the right method of reading the scriptures, which is to confirm all interpretations not by references to an external tradition but by harmonizing the text.[35] Moreover, the novel attempts to distinguish between two modes of guiding interpretation: Roman Catholic rewriting and Protestant tutelage. The former disables the reader's mind by substituting one set of meanings for another; thus, before his talk with Luther, Fritz cannot square the everyday definition of "believeth" with that supplied by the church because the church's definition *cannot* be derived from the text. By contrast, the latter focuses not on final meanings but on interpretive practices. Once Luther clarifies Fritz's difficulties, Fritz can finally embrace his *own* reading of Eva's completed fragment and experience the conversion that will lead him back to Eva some years later. Reading the Bible promotes the domesticity in which the Bible can finally be read by all.

THE SHOCK OF OWNERSHIP

In its emphasis on owning and even touching a Bible, the *Chronicles* consolidated trends already at work in Reformation fiction. In Mary Atkinson Maurice's *Isabella Hamilton* (1852), a tale of the Scottish Reformation, the title character's aunt keeps her Bible, an "'invaluable treasure,'" "carefully concealed during the day, but at the dead hour of night, all her most intimate associates would assemble round her bed, and read to their sick friend the precious word of life."[36] Such feminine reading groups provide not only "a sense of nurturing companionship; freedom from the constraints of class and gender; and independence" but also—and from the point of view of these texts, more importantly—a site of potentially national religious regeneration, despite the necessary secrecy.[37] Bible reading proves simultaneously sacrosanct and scandalous, uniting a local community around the "precious" and "invaluable" text that nevertheless carries with it an aura of fatal criminality. Under these circumstances, the contrast between "dead hour of night" and "word of life" is not an accident: in the profane world, godly life really does mean death (and, in fact, Isabella will end up martyred). Similarly, in another tale published fifteen years later about the dawning of the Scottish Reformation, the Irish novelist Deborah Alcock tells her mid-Victorian readers that "[n]o one that reads these pages will be able to understand from experience what Mary felt as, loving Christ more than her life, she held in her hand for the first time the Book that contains the words of Christ."[38] Mary's awed response to the Bible as both Word *and* vessel ("Let me haud it in my ain hand, Jamie") dramatizes a historical moment in which the individual reader *expected* to be alienated from the physical book. Alcock's own readers may have been able to imagine what Mary feels, thanks to the sympathetic identification promoted through the novel's plot and characterization, but their unthinking nineteenth-century experience remains entirely other.

The message underlying all of these tales is that the Victorian reader must relearn what it means for Bible reading and ownership to be a *privilege*. Repeatedly, Bibles appear as objects of intense desire.[39] But how does divine providence guide the Bible to its readers? In some cases, by explicitly moving the circulation of biblical texts out of approved channels. As part of the process of estrangement, the reader must be reminded that the Bible was once bound up with criminality and transgression; thus, W. H. G. Kingston's *The Last Look: A Tale of the Spanish Inquisition* (1869), Alcock's *The Spanish Brothers: A Tale of the Sixteenth Century* (1871), and Charles Bruce's *The Story of John Heywood: A Historical Tale of the Time of Harry VIII* (1873?)

celebrate the role of Bible smugglers, who risk martyrdom in order to transmit the Word—and take on the aura of adventure heroes in the process. Instead of representing smugglers as threatening because "incapable of forming attachments, whether familial, communal, or national," these novels insist that Bible smugglers ground their identities in a loyalty to God that transcends mere national legal systems.[40] Early in *The Story of John Heywood*, the fugitive Oldcast recounts how "[m]any have been my dangers by sea and by land, from open violence and secret craft, from robbers and priests; but the Lord has delivered me out of them all, His arm has surrounded me, His strength has upheld me; He has been with me in the dungeon, and given courage to endure torture in His cause."[41] Oldcast's account of his life as a Bible smuggler rewrites both the boy's adventure tale and the Newgate criminal novel. His status as criminal turns the Newgate novel upside down: the Catholic culture of not-quite-Reformation England defines Oldcast as a criminal, but in Protestant terms his criminality actually derives from his willingness to *obey God's law*. By mapping Oldcast's moral righteousness onto the romance of criminality, *The Story of John Heywood* reclaims the "criminal" hero from the sensationalist Newgate genre, while simultaneously linking that hero with all the manly dangers of the adventure tale. But then, the novel pushes the reader a step further, for the actual hero of Oldcast's tale is not Oldcast but God. Oldcast's adventures, in other words, must not be read for escapist pleasure but for signs of God's agency in the world. This narrative strategy rests not on historical relativism but on a return to the very object in question: the *suppression* of the Bible is the pretext for defining Oldcast as a criminal, and its *distribution*, while it may cost Oldcast his life in the short run, provides the providential context within which Oldcast's actions may be interpreted properly.

At the same time, casting Oldcast's experiences in terms of high adventure turns the pre-Reformation Bible into divine treasure, the legendary object hidden beneath the *X* marking the spot. Alcock, who provides a very similar account of the real-life Bible smuggler and martyr Julian Hernandez, makes this link explicit: "How real and great, nay, how unutterably precious, must be that treasure which men were found willing, at such cost, not only to secure for themselves, but even to impart to others."[42] The rhetoric of adventure, exploration, and even piracy here mutates into an entirely different model of the quest romance, in which the desired "treasure" is best enjoyed not in possession but in distribution. In Kingston's *The Last Look*, Hernandez's colportage becomes shorthand for all evangelizing work; even when rendered unable to speak, he still "continued by his gestures to encourage his companions" and "bore witness to the truth" until his last moments at the stake.[43] At the moment of death, the Bible smuggler's "criminality" manifests itself in his refusal to hoard his "treasure." By embracing such criminality and its terrible results, a figure like Hernandez effectively becomes like Christ himself, dying in one of the most humiliating ways possible.

Julian Hernandez smuggled his Bibles while pretending to be an ordinary peddler, and Alcock's interest in his work carries over into other representations of both packmen and colporteurs (peddlers who specialized in religious texts), who turn more legitimate and traditional forms of trade into avenues for a very different kind of salesmanship. Emma Leslie's *Soldier Fritz and the Enemies He Fought: A Story of the Reformation* (1871?), a shilling novel aimed at younger readers, showcases Carl, who uses his pack of goods as an excuse to go about his true business, "spreading the knowledge of Christ as an all-sufficient Saviour."[44] While Carl is not first and foremost a colporteur, his sideways approach to evangelism, in which the trinkets attract potential buyers of higher truths, comes close to the religious justification for colportage offered by one reporter on Protestant missionaries in Ireland: "This system of colportage has always appeared to me to be precisely in character with the way in which the gospel has been spread—going with the bible 'in hand,' and offering it to those who probably were not thinking about it. It is in the very spirit in which our blessed Lord says: 'I stand at the door, and knock.'"[45] In this evangelical vision of religious salesmanship, the colporteur recognizes that there *is* a potential market for divine truth, which transforms the relationship between seller and buyer; in the end, the Bible buyer purchases an object that leads the reader to that which exceeds all economic valuation. Unlike all other salesmen, the colporteur never sells his books for what they are "worth," for their true worth cannot be quantified, let alone recognized, without the cooperation of divine grace. A traditional colporteur was "usually dedicated to the cause of Christian evangelism, not pecuniary profit."[46] Buying a Bible from a colporteur or other peddler momentarily interrupts everyday financial exchange, in which cost depends on supply and demand. The Congregationalist John Angell James's observation that the Bible "is the cheapest of all cheap books, in an age distinguished for cheap books" highlights the counterintuitive relationship between price and value at work here: because the Bible is the world's most valuable book in spiritual terms, it must become the cheapest book in profane terms.[47] It occupies the same market as far more scandalous reading material, only to outsell those other "cheap books" by undercutting them. Moreover, Carl's evangelization of both the masters and the servants falls in line with what a Victorian reader would have recognized as standard practice among contemporary colporteurs, who became a national fixture again at midcentury.[48] Colportage turns buying and selling into a community-building exercise in which the ultimate goal is spiritual, not material, profit.

Yet while purchasing a Bible carries considerable weight because the initial investment demonstrates that the buyer is willing to relinquish material goods in the service of a higher truth, giving and receiving Bibles as gifts is an even more loaded act, one that retains its symbolic import to the end of the nineteenth century. The gift of a Bible itself positions the recipient within a historicized and sanctified new community: the Bible that Alcock's Mary touches is a gift from the soon-to-be martyr George Wishart, while in Alice Lang's *The Adventures of Hans Müller* (1894?), which entwines Martin Luther's career with that of a family from Württemberg, Luther receives a Bible from one of his most important religious mentors, Johann von Staupitz, and then much later inscribes a copy of his own vernacular Bible as a gift to Hans's devout young daughter, Magdalene.[49] These gifts historicize similar moments from contemporary didactic literature, such as Harriet Warner Ellis's pedagogical dialogue *The Melvill Family and Their*

Bible Readings (1871), in which the giver uses the weight of the moment (dying moments, in this case) to consecrate the Bible to the recipient. In Ellis's dialogue gifting Bibles confers an obligation not to
return a gift to the recipient but instead to properly con the text: in the
words of skeptical Hugh's dying mother, "Promise me that you will
study the Bible. Not merely that you will *read* it, but that you will
carefully and prayerfully *study* it."[50] Hugh can only repay his mother's
gift with the right sort of "study," which requires him to abandon the
implicitly self-sufficient reading skills of his Cambridge education for
the divinely assisted reading skills appropriate to Bible study. To read
properly the inquiring sinner must trade his belief in autonomous reason for dependence on God's help, the only means of illuminating
what to the rationalist seem like contradictory passages. Between the
book-as-object and the right approach to the text, the recipient finds
his way to the ultimate gift of salvation.

But whereas Ellis's characters exchange Bibles without fear of re-
prisal, emphasizing that the Bible is now open to all potential converts,
such gifts in Reformation tales come fraught with danger and, just as
importantly, with a larger historical significance: each gift fractures the
clerical elite's monopoly on the Word and in the process reveals that
the Word and the clerical elite are at odds. At one level—especially in
the Wishart instance—the Bible implicitly displaces Catholic relics; the
devout exchange the Word of God instead of blood, bone, or cloth-
ing. Emma Leslie's *Daybreak in Italy* (1870) makes this substitution
explicit in a story about an unnamed reforming priest—in reality, not
a priest at all but the Italian Reformer Celio Secundo Curione—who
secretly swaps a "box of relics" on the altar for a Bible, which is described as, among other things, the "true relics of the saints."[51] At another level gift-giving extends the divine grace granted to the eminent
Reformer, who in both cases offers up the Bible for free. Lang's Magdalene calls our attention to just this point: "He has laboured, not for
the rich, who could repay him, but for the poor and ignorant, who
can give him nothing beyond their blessing and their prayers" (198).
Once again, the Reformer operates in a providential, not a market,
economy. And in working for the poor, not the rich, Luther not only

promotes biblical literacy among the common people but also imitates Christ's ministry. The gift from von Staupitz to Luther still positions the Bible within a restricted space (the monastery) and confines it to an elite, entirely male readership; by contrast, Luther gifts his vernacular Bible to a rather poor village girl. Magdalene fully recognizes what Luther's work means *because* she can interpret it in the light of scriptural knowledge. Paradoxically enough, such recognition marks her out as Luther's spiritual equal, as one of the elect capable of reading and applying their biblical knowledge properly, even as Magdalene herself pays homage to Luther as a superior.

Gender, Generations, and Bible Reading

At this point, anyone familiar with nineteenth-century anxieties about widespread literacy may feel some puzzlement. Alice Lang's late-Victorian vision of Luther's reception seems more like a potential nightmare: "Oh, Magdelene," says Hans, "you have no idea of the indignation there is about this book; for women and cobblers and children are now devouring this translation of Luther" (197–98). Luther's Bible targets precisely those impressionable audiences who, according to Victorian critics, were most inclined to consume fiction in distressing quantities; even Hans's choice of "devouring" echoes the language of literary and cultural critics who figured novel reading in terms of gluttonous consumption. Bible reading was an important part of any evangelical reforming program; earlier in the century, Hannah More made reading and memorizing the Bible a cornerstone of her Mendip Schools for the poor.[52] But the eager female, working-class, and youthful readers of the Reformation tales don't just read and memorize— they engage in feats of evangelization and biblical interpretation, borrowing from conventions of fictional anti-Catholic dialogue already established in the sixteenth century. The Reformation dialogue's regular turn to "a layman's argumentative victory over a conservative priest" recurs here in not just laymen's victories but also laywomen's (and, on occasion, laychildren's).[53] In E. H. Walshe's *From Dawn to Dark in Italy* (1864?), which chronicles the failure of the Reformation in six-teenth-century Italy, two "weak women" (ironically termed) square off against a papal nuncio. Insisting that they "are ready to be taught," provided that he "prove to us from God's Word that we are wrong," the more vocal of the two women bluntly declares that "[t]he whole system of the papacy is one vast error."[54] Moreover, such interpretive self-assertion extends to bad Protestant readings. In Emily Sarah Holt's *Robin Tremayne* (1872), set during the Marian persecutions, Thekla dis-covers that her friend has been distressed by "cold and harsh" preacher Mr. Carter's interpretation of Paul and offers a theological rebuttal based on the nature of love, supported by prooftexts that undermine the preacher's position. Afterwards, her more educated male friends affirm *her* interpretation, not the preacher's, commenting that "the fel-low knoweth not his business" and "I have little patience with such doctrines, and scantly with such men."[55] Both novelists affirm the right of women to read against male-dominated, institutional authorities— as long as these readings emerge from a strict literal interpretation of the text. Thus, the Italian women who resist (perilously) the papal nun-cio do so by reconfiguring the grounds of the debate: they will ac-knowledge his authority only *after* he jettisons the Catholic apparatus of church fathers, councils, and so forth. They demand, in other words, that he read as they do. But that is only one level of interpretive inter-ference, for in Holt's novel, Mr. Carter's failure derives from a flaw in his own subjectivity. He is a man who "hath not himself known nei-ther much love, neither much sorrow, neither much of God" (293). The negations leave Mr. Carter in an interpretive abyss, unable to sympa-thize with his parishioners (because he himself has never experienced the same feelings) but also unable to read the text properly (because he does not read with the help of the Holy Spirit). In these instances, proper reading derives neither from institutionally authorized con-texts, nor from an explicitly gendered position, but from a willingness to relinquish self in the act of interpretation.

Novelists like Holt and Walshe repeatedly insert Victorian anxi-eties about popular literacy and various sociopolitical differences (gender, class, generational) into their narratives, only to recuperate them for a celebration of an activist Bible-reading culture that frequently flaunts all the social hierarchies. In effect, Bible reading liberates potentially disaffected members of society from their merely local complaints and transforms them into a fully spiritualized and—with any luck—fully nationalized reading community. Various forms of social exclusion and oppression may produce model Bible readers, but such forms are never sufficient to explain how such readers actually approach the text. The Methodist novelist Dora M. Jones, for example, puts the following observation about the Statute of Six Articles (1539) into the mouth of a servant, Margery, whose son, now dead, had been her spiritual guide:

> And oh! sir, it is not now as it was some time since, when the Bible was open for all men, and you might go to church and hear the good words read and explained; but they have taken away the book from all that are not gentlefolks, and they have forbidden the people to speak the word of life to each other, lest they should wrest it to what they call heresy.[56]

We have already seen novelists identifying Protestantism's victory (and the rise of modern English culture) with the Bible's availability, but here we see an awareness that the Bible's *physical* presence is a volatile historical marker. For one fleeting moment, the Bible was "open" literally and figuratively to "all men"—here, clearly meaning all humankind, irrespective of class or gender—and then it was shut up again. But note that by describing the Bible as "open," Margery apparently does not reference an incidence of private meaning but rather one of communal interpretation: even though no clergymen appear to be on the scene, the people congregate not just to "hear" but to hear something "explained." Explanation implies some sort of authority, but whence? From "each other," apparently—the community of the devout. From both Margery's and the novel's points of view, true piety trumps other sorts of competencies. The Six Articles reintroduce a meaningless form of spiritual authority, based on class, into a reading community that only recognizes those who speak "the word of life." Note that the speech in question conflates Bible reading and Bible interpretation. By definition, participants in this community speak a language that is pre-authorized by the highest authority of all—namely, God himself. The government's fear of "wrest[ing]," an act of violence against the Word, is intrinsically ruled out by Margery's own understanding of how her now-lost community once operated: since the congregation utters only that which is God's, they cannot, by definition, utter anything that constitutes "heresy." In this model of communal reading, the Bible really does interpret itself, leaving the community nothing to do but confirm its transparent truths to each other.

Thus, while this representation of popular interpretation appears to authorize all sorts of previously unauthorized voices, particularly the voices of women and children, it does so only by subordinating the speaker to the content of her utterance.[57] In Emma Leslie's *The Chained Book* (1878?), for example, women become significant players in the transmission of the vernacular Bible: Anne Boleyn protects Bible smugglers and insists that Bibles be made readily available to the people, while the young Muriel Tewkesbury (supposedly related to the real-life martyr John Tewkesbury) inadvertently becomes a designated oral Bible reader for the illiterate public. Moreover, Anne first hears about the English Bible from the brilliant Marguerite d'Alençon, author of *The Heptameron* (1558).[58] We are back to Walter Scott's feminine genealogy but in another key. While this feminized genealogy of English Protestantism rules out women as *producers* of the Bible as object, let alone theologians, it nevertheless suggests that women create the conditions under which biblical knowledge is *possible*. The men generate the text, but the women read it. When the first Bible appears in a church, most of the people could "only stare at it, and wonder blankly why the priests and monks hated it so much." But once they realize that Muriel can actually read, they call on her to read aloud to them; while "Muriel looked round on the upturned faces of the little crowd and blushed . . . she could not refuse their request," and so begins reading a chapter.[59] On its first appearance, the Bible does not merely seem strange but *is* strange. It may be open, but it is not accessible.

Popular illiteracy reduces the Bible to a mere object, a spectacle that yields no more knowledge of the truth than the Catholic rituals it supposedly displaces. Muriel's literate presence in the church, however, inaugurates a new kind of speaking, one that enlightens precisely because it says *nothing* beyond what is present in the text.[60] Muriel herself reads in silence until called upon to speak, already signaling her subordination of self to text; despite her obvious embarrassment, she further subordinates her own modesty to the spiritual needs of the community. This modesty is explicitly feminine modesty, as she admits to Anne Boleyn: "It is not seemly that a maiden should be reading in a church before her betters" (58). Muriel wishes to reassert gender and class norms—to silence herself. Despite her temporary willingness to read for an illiterate community, Muriel's "I" tries to take refuge in the conventional bounds of sixteenth-century feminine selfhood. But this badly misses the point, as Anne Boleyn explains: "It will but be following in thy father Tewkesbury's steps. As thou knowest, he helped to give the New Testament to the Londoners in spite of the Pope and the cardinal, and thou mayest give the very Word of God to these poor folk who cannot read it for themselves; and thou mayest even help them to conquer the mysteries of this book-learning, that they may read it for themselves" (59). Anne Boleyn, speaking at a moment in which biblical reading has been temporarily authorized, allots Muriel's dead father a defiant heroism that flaunts the hierarchy, but she then turns literacy into its own form of historical action and, as the verb *conquer* suggests, heroism. Muriel's father distributed the Bible as object, but Muriel herself activates the Word. Within the space of the church, Muriel speaks nothing but her daily reading, yet it is that "lowly, unnoticed work" (63), and not the official rites of the church, that saves her audience.

If the history of the Bible as object necessarily interfaces with the history of literacy, then, it is nevertheless still the case that the Bible sometimes persists in these narratives through oral transmission alone—albeit an orality distinguished from the "unwritten verities" of Catholic tradition. True biblical knowledge "mobilizes" the text, disrupting Roman Catholic punishments from within: while the church seeks to separate the reader from the text, the true Protestant reader imprints the text upon his or her own mind and heart. Thus, in George E. Sargent's *Lilian: A Tale of Three Hundred Years Ago* (1864), Lilian, a young Protestant whose father has been martyred, lives with a Catholic family for several months while journeying with her grandmother (also the daughter of a martyr) to find a new home. Lilian tells her host family's children stories from the Bible, given that in the future, "they might be in the way of hearing a great many monkish fables about very questionable saints, which fables Lilian rightly believed would do them more harm than good"; having "determined that their thoughts should have something better to dwell upon, . . . she secretly prayed that God would impress his own truth on their young souls while yet the light of the gospel remained with them."[61] Lilian's memories sustain her own faith and enable her to translate the Bible into children's narratives, and thus undermine her hosts' Catholicism even without the physical presence of the dangerous text. Here, scriptural tales compete with Catholic traditions, which are downgraded to "monkish fables"—fictions, in other words. Biblical memories serve as inoculations of sorts, guarding the children's souls against the moral and spiritual threat posed by those ambiguously "questionable" saints. This critique of "monkish" tales itself recycles standard Reformation polemics against medieval hagiography; thus, as Helen Parish notes of William Tyndale, "[t]he authority of Scripture lay in its immutability and its status as the written word of God, in sharp contrast to the legends contained in medieval chronicles and hagiography, which Tyndale argued had been deliberately invented and perverted by the clergy."[62] By orienting the children toward the Bible and away from the saints, Lilian seeks to ground them in the only authentic history known to man while diverting them from the perhaps more spectacular pleasures of the saints' lives. Like Muriel, Lilian's authority as educator derives both from her own literacy and from her willingness to subordinate her speech to God's: her prayerful tale-telling marks her out as a vessel for God's language, not as a "monkish" creator of unreliable, possibly poisonous fictions. Lilian *adapts* the Bible to the youthful mind of her audience; she *invents* nothing. In that sense, the actual transmission of biblical/historical knowledge both is and is not gendered feminine, for while the circumstances of the Reformation displace true religious knowledge to outside the boundaries of masculine clerical discourse, it only passes through feminine and youthful agents *because* they are willing to de-self themselves in the act of speaking. The fiction-making monks put too much of themselves—that is, their fallen human nature—into the text.

CONCLUSION

The Reformation tale's logic not only pushes it toward the inevitable victory of *sola scriptura* over Catholic tradition, then, but also toward a privatized and feminized model of textual interpretation. And yet, once victory has been achieved, it threatens to self-destruct. Novelists thus urge their readers to remember the shock of Bible reading in the sixteenth century in order to estrange them from the Bible's boring omnipresence in the nineteenth century. In these novels reading the Bible is a good independent of historical context or the reader's age; moreover, while the novels do note the importance of group reading, they nevertheless argue that the Bible's capacity to authenticate and explain itself makes formal, "professional" intervention almost entirely unnecessary. Ideally, the reading community solves its own problems; even when outside aids to interpretation become necessary, they remain subsidiary to the individual reading *process*. Most importantly, as we also saw in the previous chapter, Protestantism (stripped of its actual denominational conflicts) is, quite literally, *in* the Bible. By discarding Catholic tradition in favor of scriptural faith, the reader exits a merely profane historical narrative, shaped entirely by fallen human desires, and enters into the sacred historical narrative authorized solely by God. Those who read the Bible catch glimpses of the providential organizing principle otherwise hidden from man's gaze. In other words, they alone achieve historical consciousness. As we shall see in the next chapter, however, such reading also leads to the greatest test of faith: the prospect of martyrdom.

Chapter Four

REINVENTING
THE MARIAN PERSECUTIONS
IN VICTORIAN ENGLAND

Surveying the religious landscape of Victorian England, Protestants saw no heretics burning at the stake, no racks, no fearful imprisonments. In mainstream culture this provoked a rather skeptical, even sardonic, take on the minor deprivations that constituted what passed for nineteenth-century martyrdom, along with a more intense debate over whether the term could be applied to those Anglo-Catholic clergymen imprisoned for Ritualist offenses under the Public Worship Regulation Act (1874).[1] Yet amongst evangelicals, this absence of violent martyrdoms prompted two very different, and very paradoxical, reactions: that the absence of martyrs was a danger in and of itself, and that martyrdoms might resume at any moment. Even more specifically, they feared that England was reversing religious course, mutating into the England of 1555 to 1558—the years in which Protestant heretics were burned during the reign of Mary I. Thus, the popular evangelical Irish novelist Charlotte Elizabeth [Phelan Tonna] warned parents and children of the threat in her pedagogical dialogue *Alice Benden; Or, the Bowed Shilling, and Other Tales* (1846), which retells the martyrdom of Alice Benden (betrayed by her own husband) in 1557. But why did this story need to be told in the mid-nineteenth century? Explains the dialogue's evangelical Mamma, "The greatest danger lies in our having so entirely forgotten its [Catholicism's] real character, and being so willing to judge of it by what we see around us, not from what we know, from past history."[2] Far from being a positive feature, this disappearance of martyrdom into the apparently safe confines of historical narrative endangers England's national stability. Modern Englishmen mistake their comfortable encounters with nineteenth-century Catholics for authentic *knowledge*—knowledge that derives not from what only appears to be empirical evidence from the present but instead from the authenticated witness of the past. Personal experience erases Catholic history—and thus the nature of Catholicism's "essence"—from the Protestant mind.

In this account Protestantism's "victory"—and, with it, the disappearance of Protestant martyrs—trembles on the verge of self-destruction. For novelists, historians, and poets, the reign of Mary I (1553–58) epitomized the physical and spiritual violence finally suppressed—but, Protestants feared, not eradicated—by English Protestant policy under Elizabeth's regime. Invoking the Marian persecutions against the dreaded Catholics was hardly a Victorian Protestant innovation; the very nickname "Bloody Mary" emerged in the seventeenth century and became entrenched in the 1670s as polemicists anxiously contemplated the likelihood of having the Catholic James II succeed Charles II on the throne.[3] The "vivid, lurid and crude" terms of the nineteenth-century debate about the persecutions, however, pointed to a lurking threat to British national stability within the very nation itself, one apparently enabled by the events of Catholic Emancipation (1829) and after.[4] By granting Catholics seats in Parliament, a supposedly Protestant government instead subjected the country to foreign papal rule. Later, the expansion of the Oxford Movement and the Anglo-Catholic and Ritualist movements suggested that hot warfare was already being waged inside the supposedly safe territory of

the Church of England. In fictionalizing the persecutions, often by explicitly adapting John Foxe's martyrologies, Protestant authors tutor
their audiences in the proper way of interpreting contemporary events.

This strategy plays out, I argue, in a conflict between the queen's
body and the martyr's body. In chapters 1 and 2 we saw novelists linking proto-Protestant faith with new modes of masculine identity, frequently substituting church militancy for the more violent variety. But
in these Marian novels the battle plays out across the bodies of women
and children, whose battered and burnt extremities warn of Catholicism's slide into a kind of depraved materialism. At one level, these
narratives clearly participate in what Billie Melman has identified as
the Victorian taste for "Tudor horror," to satisfy which authors like
W. H. Ainsworth located "[i]mprisonment, punishment, and torture . . .
at the heart of the state, the monarchy, and the nation."[5] But they also
appropriate and rework much older narratives about the significance
of martyrdom for the nation. For Victorian Protestants, Mary I's excessive erotic attachment to Philip of Spain and her false pregnancy
give rise to a deranged mentality that defines religious persecution,
even as it threatens English nationhood itself. The queen's body becomes simultaneously hypersexualized and pathological, in a riot of
excessive feeling that will spawn the injuries inflicted on Protestant
martyrs. These injuries suffered by martyrs' bodies—in particular,
the female martyr's body, even though such martyrs were actually in
the minority[6]—testify to the horrors of Catholic persecution and to the
universal truths of Protestant faith. But they also affirm the martyr's
physical and spiritual chastity, self-control, and containment.[7] In both
cases history plays out on the body through emotional trauma, spiritual devotion, sexual desire, principled resistance, and unprincipled
violence. Not surprisingly, these works stage martyrdom as itself
the test case of historical interpretation; if, as Brad Gregory notes and
nineteenth-century Catholics and Protestants alike would have agreed,
martyrdom "meant conformity to an ancient course of action, grounded
in scripture and epitomized in the crucifixion of Christ himself," then
the ability to recognize the true witness of Protestant martyrdoms
became key to any historical consciousness whatsoever.[8]

Yet Protestant texts were not free of Catholic influences. In the first section of this chapter, I analyze how the Catholic historian John Lingard's revisionist portrait of Mary insinuated itself into even evangelical texts, thanks largely to the work of Agnes Strickland. This Mary, fundamentally virtuous but weak, threatens the nation through her perverse sexuality and equally perverse religious obsessions. In the second, I turn to the popular martyr Rose Allin, whose resistance to torture suggested very different possibilities for heroic female bodies. Rose Allin's story was twice granted novel-length treatment, once by the folklorist-*cum*-novelist Anna Eliza Bray and again by the prolific evangelical historical novelist Emily Sarah Holt; as I argue, the two novelists' very different revisions of Rose Allin's story demonstrates how evangelicals felt increasingly embattled over the course of the nineteenth century.[9] Finally, I turn to a novel critical of evangelicalism that tries to rewrite the history of the Marian persecutions in order to at least theorize how Catholics might be safely incorporated into a firmly Protestant nation.

THE QUEEN'S BODY

Mary I's short reign generated a long shadow over the Protestant imagination. David Loades reminds us that when she came to the throne, most of her subjects would have associated her with Henry VIII's limited understanding of religious reform and not necessarily full-blown reunion with Rome; they were soon disabused of their beliefs.[10] Protestant recalcitrance led the hierarchy and the government to pursue a system of persecution starting in 1555, with approximately 275 believers eventually executed. Later historians, the Victorians included, have long debated how much responsibility Mary actually bears for the persecutions.[11] Mary's reign was not, however, characterized by good relations with the pope, despite what polemicists might argue.[12] In fact, the return to Catholicism under Marian rule was deeply inflected by Protestant, humanist, and Continental Counter-Reformation developments, such as a new prominence for the Bible in personal piety.[13] Moreover, it remains unclear how effective the persecutions actually were. While certainly Victorian Protestants believed, with the martyred Hugh Latimer, that "[w]e shall this day light such a candle, by God's grace, in England, as I trust shall never be put out," more recent historians have suggested that Mary's death was the problem, not her policies.[14] That being said, Mary's reputation as "Bloody Mary" had been well-cemented by the seventeenth century, and her polemical value for Protestants was equally established.

The most enduringly popular source for thinking about the Marian persecutions was John Foxe's *Acts and Monuments*, better known as the *Book of Martyrs*, which experienced a notable publishing revival in the nineteenth century. Until midcentury Protestants had little access to the texts of even the major Reformers, such as Martin Luther.[15] The Parker Society reprints (1841–53), dedicated to creating a library of English Reformers for an audience bewitched by the Tractarians, was intended to stem that gap for at least a middle-class readership. Against this background evangelicals pushed to reprint Foxe in order to establish their sixteenth-century roots for a modern audience—an audience whose openness to Catholic toleration signified considerable historical amnesia. Evangelicals suspected that the lack of a complete, modern Foxe signaled much greater cracks in the ecclesiastical foundation; as the Rev. John Stock sighed in 1835, "the good old family book, the Book of Martyrs, is now laid aside, and with it much, if not all that sterling abhorrence of error, which once proved our high esteem of the work of the Reformation."[16] As Stock's complaint suggests, to not *know* the Reformation intimately—the Reformers, the martyrs, the deeds of Rome, and so forth—was tantamount to abandoning the Protestant project entirely. In a sense, Stock was correct about access to Foxe. Prior to the Stephen Cattley-George Townsend edition of 1837–41, the *Book of Martyrs* had been simultaneously omnipresent but absent in British culture: the last complete edition had appeared 153 years earlier, even though portions of the text remained easily available in abridged or retold form.[17] But in the nineteenth century the *Book of Martyrs* appeared in a wide range of publishing formats, ranging from multivolume complete editions to adaptations, updates, excerpts, and serials; it was priced for and marketed to multiple reading publics, ranging from the wealthy to the working classes. In turn, Anglo-Catholic and Roman Catholic controversialists, including Samuel Maitland and William Eusebius Andrews, attacked Foxe's work and/or the new editions on grounds ranging from inaccuracy (correctly, in the case of Cattley-Townsend) to bigotry.[18] Protestants themselves reacted to the *Book of Martyrs* in complex and not always respectful ways—for example, the shoemaker John Askham seems to have remembered the book for its exciting and gory woodcuts, not its religious significance[19]—but they nevertheless read and discussed it avidly. Perhaps not coincidentally, Devorah Greenberg counts seven editions of various types appearing in 1851 alone, a year of intense anti-Catholic sentiment thanks to the Papal Aggression—the public outcry whipped up by Lord John Russell after the reestablishment of the Roman Catholic hierarchy in England.[20]

As the 1851 surge suggests, Foxe's new attraction for the Protestant reading public derived in part from anxieties about the more and more obvious Roman Catholic revival; in addition, Peter Nockles argues, Foxemania was further stoked by internal warfare within the Anglican camp between evangelicals and both traditional and Oxford Movement High Churchmen. The evangelical and traditional High Church wings, though not exactly fond of each other, nevertheless agreed that the Church of England was, in essence, a Protestant institution; those invested in the Oxford Movement, however, wanted to restore the Church of England's pre-Reformation liturgical continuity with the Roman Catholic Church, even if they otherwise intended the churches to remain separate.[21] But this explosion of interest came accompanied with an interesting paradox: as Foxeite material proliferated, evangelicals complained more and more loudly that the martyrs themselves were forgotten or, what was just as bad, subjected to unfriendly criticism. Anxiously contemplating a Roman Catholic onslaught, the Church of Ireland-turned-Anglican polemicist M. Hobart Seymour mourned that

> we, as if they had no echo among us, as if there were no memory of their names among us, as if there were no esteem for their martyr-

doms among us, as if there were no love to the precious truths which they conveyed unto us—we are looking upon the advancing strides of Popery and upon the decay of our Protestantism, with a coldness that seems to argue that "the sighing" of our land hath "ceased."[22]

(Not incidentally, Seymour produced his own abridged edition of Foxe in 1838.) Nearly thirty years later, W. Jay Bolton detected the ongoing workings of a dangerous historical revisionism among his fellow Anglicans: "The Reformation, it is said, was a 'blunder' and a 'merited chastisement;' and the principal movers in it, whom we have been used to regard as holy men, were only 'hypocrites,' 'unredeemed villains,' and wretches worse than Robespierre and the assassins of the French Revolution!"[23]

Both Seymour and Bolton clearly sense a crisis in what they retrospectively construe as a unified, self-evidently true orientation to the past, one that must now be explicitly marked as *Protestant* in part because it has new and unwanted competition. Revisionist approaches to the Reformation do not just threaten the Reformation legacy—they threaten historical consciousness itself. For Seymour, writing midway through Cattley-Townsend's printing, the very success of Catholicism correlated with Protestantism's historical failure. In his mournful parallel clauses, Seymour invokes what he hopes to be a hypothetical ("as if") failure of both memory and affect, warning "us"—that is, the Protestant community—that our own historical lapses will have a lethal effect. Without the martyrs and their "precious truths," there is no "us." Bolton, meanwhile, suggests that the very foundations of Protestant belief have been shaken by his unnamed sources, who deface history instead of write it. The Reformation itself slowly vanishes under the combined weight of the Protestant readers' apathy and the historians' suspect theological biases. Modern historical narrative, in other words, does not lead the reader to remember the Reformation so much as to dismember it.

Under the circumstances the Marian persecutions, in which nearly three hundred Protestants were executed as heretics, exerted a powerful and allegorical attraction. The comparison would take on added pungency once Victoria ascended to the throne. Mary was a paradox but an admonitory one. John Cunningham Geikie, summing up her reign, commented that "Well educated, rigidly honest, simple in her tastes, and pure in her life, she ruined all, and made herself an everlasting abhorrence to England, by the one fact that she was an abject slave of the priests."[24] If Victoria appeared to be Mary's Protestant and virtuous opposite—a protector of true religion instead of its destroyer—Catholicism's increasing visibility and confidence suggested that Mary might be the age's fearsome ruling spirit. In 1852, during the uproar over the Papal Aggression, an article pointedly entitled "Popish Tortures, Massacres, and Persecutions" declared that "[t]he whole system of Rome . . . is essentially bloody and intolerant, and to give it power is only to prepare for our own destruction."[25] "Bloody Queen Mary" and the number of her victims feature prominently in the article's list of Roman Catholic enormities (which concludes with a total of 16,390,277 victims!). As the overlapping adjective "bloody" suggests, in this list Mary organically expresses Catholicism's "essence." Yet while some authors felt no compunctions about declaring that "the previous reign of the bloody Mary gives one the best idea which history presents of the fiendish spirit of Rome," her image remained contested even among Protestants.[26] Did Mary persecute because she was Catholic? Because she was female? Because she married a Spaniard? Or, perhaps, some combination of the three?

Although Catholics had long challenged the more demonic accounts of Mary's reign, Victorian Protestant ambivalence about Mary initially derived from the work of the Catholic historian John Lingard. Lingard's popular *History of England* (1819–30) obtained a broad ecumenical readership, despite its attack on the mainstream Protestant account of English history in general and Hume's *History of England* in particular.[27] Lingard argued against triumphalist interpretations of the Reformation that represented medieval and early modern Catholicism in terms of moral degradation and decay; far from understanding the Reformation as an inevitable response to the needs of a spiritually starved population, Lingard and later Catholic historians saw it as a radical rebellion against divine authority fueled by personal ambition, wayward sexuality, and sheer greed. Lingard's work participated in a larger Whig and Catholic attempt to develop a new history of the Marian persecutions that would situate them in an early modern context and thus demonstrate their irrelevance to modern Catholic culture—thereby justifying the repeal of the Test Acts, which kept Catholics (and, as it happened, many Dissenters as well) out of public office until their final repeal in 1828 and 1829.[28]

Certainly, in early modern romances Mary "oscillated between different poles . . . for example, her representation as Queen by God's grace and as the epitome of women's monstrous rule, as Queen of England and as the wife of Philip I, the real King of England, or ultimately between her representation as *victimizer* and *victimized* (bloody/unhappy)"[29]—in which figures of her emotional vulnerability contended with figures of her religious violence. But in the context of early nineteenth-century debates over Catholic Emancipation, Lingard popularized the practice of de-exemplifying Mary, insisting that the Marian persecutions were an anomalous response to Reformation violence with no predictive value for the present. The sixteenth century was an age in which the Reformers readily "displayed the same persecuting spirit which they had formerly condemned"; there was nothing Catholic per se about executing heretics.[30] But while admitting that "[t]he foulest blot on the character of this queen is her long and cruel persecution of the reformers" (5:259), Lingard invokes the "more moderate of the reformed writers" (5:259) to substantiate her practice of the holy virtues, such as charity and humility, and decouples her acts of persecution from Catholic modes of thought.[31] In Lingard's hands the sixteenth century does not give birth to modernity but rather stands out as a radically disjointed moment full of near-gothic chaos; the queen's "blot," far from being an individual moral failing, is the gory stain of an entire century, wrongly imputed to a single religious tradition. Pointedly, Lingard tells the reader that the thoughtful mind contemplating the sixteenth-century historical spectacle "learns to bless the legislation of a more tolerant age, in which dissent from established forms, though in some countries still punished with civil disabilities"—a sharp glance in England's direction—"is nowhere liable to the penalties of death" (5:239). Lingard's understanding of modernity relegates violent martyrdom to the gothicized past, while folding Protestantism itself into that age's unspeakable "horrors." In a moment of sly reversal, the Henrician and Edwardian Reformations, far from erasing the Catholic "blot," in fact contribute to it.

Catholic apologists would recuperate Mary's reputation as a virtuous queen besieged by traitorous Protestant subjects, as would canny political agitators like William Cobbett. But the most influential reassessment of Mary came from the popular historian Agnes Strickland, whose *Lives of the Queens of England* (silently co-authored with her sister Elizabeth) further popularized Lingard's Catholic revisionism while offering a more psychological interpretation of the persecutions—despite Lingard's own reservations about the final product.[32] (Strictly speaking, *Strickland* here refers to *Elizabeth* Strickland, who wrote Mary's life.) Strickland's generally positive assessment of Mary forms part of what Mary Spongberg has termed her practice of "sympathetic history," which "allowed women to critique patriarchal privilege, while simultaneously recording the trauma women suffered as a result of their participation in the great events of history."[33] In Mary's case, as elsewhere, Strickland genders persecution as an essentially masculine practice. Like Lingard, Strickland historicizes sectarian violence as the product of a mindset in which "toleration" functions "to denominate a crime."[34] The executions embody a universal, not a Catholic, tendency. But she also argues that the persecutions were a delayed effect of Henry VIII's own executions of Mary's close friends and associates. In Strickland's reading Mary reworks and augments the damaging lessons she learned from her father's example:

> Dr. Fetherstone, suffered the horrid death of treason, in company with Abel, her mother's chaplain, and another zealous catholic. They were dragged to Smithfield with fiendish impartiality on the same hurdles that conveyed the pious protestant martyr, Dr. Barnes, and two of his fellow-sufferers, to the flaming pile. Scarcely could the princess have recovered the shock of this butchery, when the frightful execution of her beloved friend and venerable relative, the countess of Salisbury, took place. She was hacked to pieces on a scaffold,

in a manner that must have curdled Mary's blood with horror, and stiffened her heart to stone. The connexion of these victims with Mary has never been clearly pointed out, nor the consequent effect of their horrid deaths on her mind properly defined, nor her feelings analyzed, which were naturally excited against those who were in power at the time of their destruction. (5:230)

Strickland's sixteenth century is even more explicitly gothic than Lingard's. Executions are "horrid" and "frightful," the mentality (Henry VIII's) is "fiendish," and the effect on Mary herself is sensational. The atmosphere suggests a charnel-house run by a madman. In a world in which even women can be subjected to brutalities of the most spectacular sort, it is no wonder that the queen's mind warps; her "curdled" and "stiffened" interiority will become permanent. To make matters worse, Mary cannot escape her father, even after his death. The moral and economic corruptions that emerge during his reign produce a state of "national depravity" (5:415) in hers. Thus, Henry VIII haunts Mary's reign, as his daughter simultaneously confronts the ballooning effects of his misrule and reenacts his violence on the English public.

Unlike Strickland's beloved Victoria, acclaimed by a "united nation" (1:xviii), Mary exists at cross-purposes with her degraded government. Like Lingard, Strickland refuses to make Mary embody national disorder, turning her instead into an idealized figure of queenly chastity whose values fail to influence the public. The persecutions thus signify the fatal split between the nation and its monarch, a split exacerbated by Mary's failed maternal impulses. Without directly arguing for causation, Strickland notes that Mary's false pregnancy coincided with the beginnings of the persecutions—a monstrous birth: "Her hope of bringing offspring was utterly delusive; the increase of her figure was but symptomatic of dropsy, attended by a complication of the most dreadful disorders which can afflict the female frame, under which every faculty of mind and body sunk, for many months. At this time commenced that horrible persecution of the protestants, which has stained her name to all futurity" (5:413). Thomas Betteridge has demonstrated that sixteenth-century Protestant controversialists like John Foxe and Robert Crowley established the false pregnancy as "a metaphor for the sterility and corruption of the Marian regime," and centuries later authors were still unpacking not only its figurative potential but also its psychological ramifications.[35] Thus, David Hume proposed a connection between the false pregnancy and the persecutions, but only to the extent that it exacerbated her preexisting disposition to persecute Protestants, not altered it.[36]

Strickland, however, suggests cause and effect. Neither a physical nor a national mother, the queen finds herself at war with her own body in a fashion that parallels her struggles with the nation itself. What Mary "births" instead is not just blood but her own future as Bloody Mary—the stain that parallels Lingard's blot. And yet, as Strickland's phrasing suggests, Mary is a virtual sacrifice *to* the persecutions, a point Strickland reiterates by twice calling Mary the "half-dead queen" (5:413, 5:415). Hovering between this world and the next, the queen disappears offstage in Strickland's analysis, to be replaced by the politicians of "selfish interest" who "were dishonest, indifferent to all religions, and willing to establish the most opposing rituals, so that they might retain their grasp on the accursed thing with which their very souls were corrupted—for corrupted they were, though not by the unfortunate queen" (5:415).[37] In this Strickland follows the general tendency of Catholic historians, like Charles Butler, who strategically displaced any blame for the persecutions from Mary to other leading figures of her reign, like Bishops Gardiner and Bonner.[38] Thus, Strickland turns from a feminized monstrous birth to a masculinized political disorder, reinventing the Bloody Mary legend as the paradoxical result not of religious controversy but of rampant self-interest grounded in all the vices of which the virtuous queen is innocent. The persecutions are neither "Catholic" nor "Protestant" in nature but rather derive from childhood trauma, disrupted maternal desires, and a perverted, male regime of unenlightened self-interest.[39]

Strickland's Mary I resonated even with evangelicals, some of whom sought to rescue the woman from the legend—the better to insist on Catholicism's essentially anti-English character. Even toward the end of the century, an anti-Catholic novel like Miss Pocklington's

The Secret Room (1884) still urged readers to remember that far from being "the hard, unfeeling woman that history too often paints her," Mary was the product of a wretched upbringing and terrible illness.[40] Pocklington "rescues" Mary from the accumulated legends about her evil nature, only to make her incapacity as a queen the result of her bodily weakness. It is, Pocklington argues, "Philip of Spain" and Mary's cabinet who must be blamed for the persecutions (187). Pocklington's Mary is still domestic enough to care for the children she cannot have, but her tender femininity lacks the strength that authors found only in Protestantism. For many evangelicals or more moderate Protestants, such appeals to Mary's goodness serve as a dangerous apologia for the revival of Catholic domination. Instead of sentimentalizing Mary's weak femininity and its violation by foreign invaders, writers instead called for her to be represented as a deadly manifestation of Catholicism's worst features. But authors who sought to cleanse both Mary and Catholicism from the taint of blood insisted, like Pocklington, that the Spanish were to blame—a staple of anti-Catholic polemic even before John Foxe's *Acts and Monuments* first appeared.[41] In this reading Mary's failed marriage to Philip of Spain symbolizes Catholicism's attempted takeover of a naturally Protestant England: England rejects Catholicism just as Mary's body rejects Philip's attempt to inseminate it. The persecutions result from a combination of thwarted romance and biological sterility, which, taken together, unhinge Mary's mind even as they providentially strip Catholicism of any future on English soil.

While Sabine Müller argues that early modern representations of Mary insisted on her "fundamentally Spanish body and soul," Victorian authors often insisted on Mary's fundamental but vulnerable *English* nature.[42] In these texts Englishness quite literally cannot reproduce with the Spanish Other. Such arguments, themselves inherited from the sixteenth-century "Black Legend" of the religious, sexual, and political corruptions of Spain, circulated through British and Irish texts written in the wake of Emancipation and the Oxford Movement; they seek, but do not always find, a space for an "authentically" native English Catholicism.[43] Sir Aubrey de Vere, an Irish Protestant whose sons later converted to Catholicism, authored a lengthy two-part tragedy, *Mary Tudor* (posthumously published in 1847, in the wake of several Oxford Movement conversions), that suggests that the persecutions derive from the fatal intersection of Spanish rule and Mary's emotional fragility.[44] In this clash the queen represents a threatened but essential Englishness, endorsing "English law" in its clemency for "traitors" over classical precedents that call for them to be "crushed" (2. II.iii). But Mary's fragile grasp of both rule and sanity collapses once Protestants install Lady Jane Grey on the throne, disrupting both the divine order of succession and the queen's emotional stability. Still, her English mercy and virginal chastity are no match for the designing Philip, whose interest in virgins proves far more general: "Egmont! methinks I spied a pretty maid / At Hampton in the church of Holy-rood, / Where we made our thanksgiving—Many such / They say this England nurtures. That is well" (2. III.i). Philip's introduction in the second act marks him out as the true villain, hypocritically using the church as a pick-up spot while associating England with maidens ready to be ravished. He proceeds to assault most of Mary's ladies-in-waiting, only to accuse Mary herself of dallying with Cardinal Pole (2. IV.i). De Vere thus transforms the court into a site not of feminine monstrosity but of rampaging masculine heterosexuality, which violates virtuous Englishwomen much as Spanish Catholicism violates English moral sensibilities.

Philip's brutality exacerbates Mary's preexisting mood swings, in which her emotional excesses turn into a Lady Macbeth–like obsession with the blood she spills. The first part of the drama concludes with Mary's horror at the thought of Lady Jane Grey's execution, as she imagines herself drowning in blood that fills her mouth and covers the floor (1. V.vii). Later, warned by Cardinal Pole that the persecutions are furthering the Protestant cause, she moans, "What mean you? / Think you I love to kill? It is—It is— / A terrible duty! Pole, I cannot sleep / Yet dreams are not more hideous than my thoughts" (2. V.i). As her stutter suggests, the persecutions enact the queen's warped desires, in particular her thwarted, dangerously idolatrous love for Philip. As in the act 1 hallucination, the queen's purportedly authorized acts of violence shatter her own psyche, even as they disrupt the order she seeks to impose. A weak monarch, veering in and out of madness by the end of the play, Mary prophesies her horrific afterlife in English popular memory:

> Shame's never dying echoes
> Shall keep the memory of the bloody Mary
> Alive in England. Vampyre calumny
> Shall prey on my remains. My name shall last
> To fright the children of the race I love.
>
> (2.V.vi)

Mary's prophecy transforms history into gothic fable. Immortalizing her for "shame" rather than fame, popular tradition simultaneously transforms Mary into the undead herself and into dinner for a peculiarly necrophiliac verbal "vampire"; far from resting comfortably in her tomb, she will be ravaged by history itself. Once turned into a bogeyman, her political power mutates into pure sensationalism. The queen's identity becomes synonymous with terror itself, but it is a terror torn away from its original context and reduced to a momentary thrill for "children." And yet, she retains her patriotic love for the English, even as she imagines their violent rejection.

Mary's problematic, sterile relationship with Philip highlights the apparent incompatibility of Catholicism with domesticity itself, an anti-Catholic trope already popular by the seventeenth century.[45] By transforming Mary's sterile Spanish marriage into a figure for both national disorder and Catholicism's lack of a British future, writers associated Roman Catholicism both with "failed" womanliness and with the dangers of improperly managed womanly rule. Alfred, Lord Tennyson's verse drama *Queen Mary* (1875) casts the Queen as a pious Catholic whose reign is nevertheless defined by a drive toward annihilation.[46] This, Tennyson's first (failed) attempt at drama, was topical: although the more lurid elements of 1850s anti-Catholicism had died down by the end of that decade, anxieties had been revived, yet again, by the combination of the Ritualist movement in the Church of England (heir to the Oxford Movement, which the government had attempted [unsuccessfully] to put down with the Public Worship Regulation Act of 1874) and the First Vatican Council, which had made papal infallibility a matter of dogma. Despite its ongoing legislative advances, Catholicism continued to seem decidedly foreign.[47] At the same time, by the 1870s Queen Victoria had slowly begun reappearing in public, most notably at the ceremony of thanksgiving for her and the Prince of Wales's health in 1872, after a long and increasingly scandalous absence as she mourned for Prince Albert after his death in 1861. This absence, some critics have suggested, fundamentally altered how she was represented in both the verbal and the visual arts: she became "spectator to the spectacle of her loyal people more than . . . spectacle herself," not so much private mother as "mother England," even "the spirit of the age."[48] In Tennyson's rendition, the literally and figuratively sterile Mary I, by contrast, cannot properly nurture her nation. Betrayed by her unrequited passion for Philip and beset by broadsheets that announce the people's loathing for their queen, Mary tells her friend, Lady Clarence, "My people hate me and desire my death"; "My husband hates me, and desires my death"; and finally, "I hate myself, and I desire my death" (V.vii). The queen's quasi-suicidal urges work themselves out in the persecutions, which undo the country instead of unifying it. On her deathbed the queen can still imagine England's future only in apocalyptic mode, mourning that burning "[t]he heretic priest, workmen, and women and children" (V.v) has been insufficient to ensure England's spiritual safety. Nor does Tennyson embrace the prospect that Elizabeth's coming will make Catholicism, quite literally, history. "God save the Crown! the Papacy is no more," cries one character; "Are we so sure of that?" another wryly inquires. In this moment of prophetic doubt, the play's ending calls into question England's own supposedly permanent "Protestantism"—an ironic reflection on the nation in the aftermath of both the Papal Aggression and the rise of Anglo-Catholicism.

This strategy of separating Catholicism from both symbolic and literal maternity persisted through the end of the century. As we have already seen in Pilkington's *The Secret Room*, novelists continued to purvey the fantasy of a sadly misguided yet basically virtuous Queen well into the 1880s; by this point, Queen Victoria had assumed the (rather politically vexed) title of Empress of India, consolidating her symbolic function as both global and national mother. Against that background, Mary's failings suggest Catholicism's danger not only to England but to England's imperial sway. Not only does Mary fail to mother but she fails to mother *Englishness*. Emma Leslie's *Cecily: A Tale of the English Reformation* (1881) is moderately sympathetic to the young Princess Mary, whose attitude to Protestantism has been permanently tainted by the sufferings of her mother, Catherine of Aragon. But the embittered princess' obsession with her mother renders herself unfit for either wifehood or motherhood. In a moment reminiscent of Robert Browning's "My Last Duchess," Mary "[draws] aside a richly embroidered curtain, disclosing a life-size portrait of Catherine of Arragon (*sic*)."[49] Mary, attempting to convert the title character, uses this portrait as the pretext for an encomium to Catherine's virtues as a "saint" (70). The list that follows—fasting, long hours praying, asceticism—inadvertently sums up the standard Protestant objections to Catholic spirituality: it emphasizes ritual performance and bodily discipline over Bible reading. As Cecily points out, however, Catherine Parr abstained from such things because Henry VIII "would have complained that she did not perform her duty as a wife and Queen" (71); so much time in church would have required "the neglect of some other duties" (72). Mary's devotion to her mother, embodied in the quasi-iconographic portrait, idolatrously conflates maternal and spiritual love, even as it also inadvertently indicts the queen as a failed role model.

While the novel does not conceal its contempt for Henry VIII's treatment of his first wife, it nevertheless suggests that Catholic motherhood quite literally cannot reproduce itself: Mary explicitly rejects Cecily's vision of domestic sanctity, in which "a wife caring for her husband and children, or a daughter dwelling with her father" (74) is superior to even the most virtuous nun.[50] Mary's inability to understand Protestant domesticity, rooted in marital and filial obligations, turns out to prefigure her inability to be a successful mother herself.

Even worse, the Catholicism that shapes Mary's antidomesticity turns out to be antidomestic in another way. As one of Cecily's friends later remarks of Philip of Spain, "the Queen will be only too willing" to help him undermine the country, which he will effectively "rule" in her name (211). By marrying Philip and acceding to his desires for power, Mary reveals that her contempt for private domesticity also extends to domestic policy; in effect, she rejects her duties to the nation at the same time that she misunderstands her proper wifely role as a queen regnant. Instead of mothering her country into global greatness, she threatens to subordinate it to a different empire altogether.[51]

THE MARTYR'S BODY

Representations of Mary warned of the threat posed by feminine ritual and erotic excess; representations of those martyred during Mary's regime demonstrated how a God-given self-control could inspire an equally feminine resistance to religious oppression. But such resistance needed historical awareness in order to work. In the Protestant narratives discussed thus far, the Reformation emerges from a growing sense of Catholicism's own blindness to itself and its history; thus, Mary's failed pregnancies conjure up not just the Catholic regime's figurative sterility but also its own historical blindness. Quite literally, Mary believes in a fiction (the false pregnancy) that turns out to have no future whatsoever. Cristina Mazzoni has recently argued that quickening is "an explicitly sexualized knowledge that stages a sexed corporeality as constituting and constituted by a particular subjectivity: the pregnant woman's," but in these pre-psychoanalytic texts, Mary's inability to decode the signs to which she has *privileged* access simultaneously figures her failures as woman, as ruler, and as religious authority.[52] Her inability to recognize herself as the subject of her own knowledge is not so much an allegory as it is an analogy: under a Catholic regime different forms of knowledge all fall apart in the same way. In turning to Foxe authors hope to stave off a reverse Reformation, in which Protestantism's own historical blindness might precipitate a new reign of terror under Catholic control.

By memorializing the Marian martyrs, then, controversial writers hoped to rehabilitate Protestant historical consciousness by fixing their audience's attention on the Christian witness of the tortured body—in particular, the tortured woman's or child's body. Mary's sterile body and her improper marriage to Philip both indict a Catholicism that perversely rejects domestic heterosexuality even as it scandalously embraces it elsewhere. By contrast, the Protestant female martyr understands the distinction between suffering pursued for its own sake and suffering sent by the will of God. Thus, Edith Dolnikowski reminds us, apropos of Foxe's *Acts and Monuments*, that if "authority is a revelation from God to the individual believer," then the believer's obligation to testify means that "gender, wealth, or social status should not be barriers to Christian witness"; the heroism of women, children, and the poor imitated Christ's scandalous death on the cross—the death, after all, of a common criminal.[53] In fact, such "meek" bodies, as it were, in and of themselves are witnesses to the truth of Protestant faith. The uneducated, impoverished, or underage believer challenges an elitist (and male) Catholic hierarchy that claims absolute control over biblical reading and interpretation. Cultural marginality turns into a mode of authority in its own right. Pointing to women readers in early modern Protestant polemic, Edith Snook observes that "[t]he Protestant Christian displays all the virtues conventionally denoted as feminine and speaks in a language of piety, simplicity, and unlearnedness that women inhabit by virtue of their gendered social position and which men—at least upper class men—employ only with more vexatious negotiations of the structures of masculinity, class, and education."[54] Such gendered qualities extended beyond reading into the experience of martyrdom itself. In dying for their faith Protestant women like Alice Benden or Anne Askew could embody the same heroic role as Thomas Cranmer or Nicholas Ridley—and be the more exemplary for it, precisely because their femininity made such heroism all the more obviously a testimony to divine grace.

The story of Rose Allin (sometimes Allen) offered an especially potent opportunity for representing such heroism in action. Rose Allin's martyrdom was roughly contemporaneous with Alice Benden's: she was executed at the stake in 1557, after Edmund Tyrrel horribly burned her hand while trying to force her to persuade her mother and stepfather, the Mounts (or Munts), to recant.[55] By the nineteenth century, narratives of Rose Allin's fearlessness in the face of both torture and persecution had transformed her into an exemplary Protestant virgin martyr, whose death at the stake ended in "realms of perfect peace, and endless day!"[56] Unlettered and apparently impoverished, Rose Allin demonstrated that authentic belief—and, therefore, authentic Christian heroism—required no guidance beyond that of the scriptures. Victorian aficionados of abridged editions of Foxe inherited an already elevated account of Allin's heroism. Beginning in the 1570 edition Foxe had noted the parallel between Allin's torture and that of the (probably mythical) Roman hero Gaius Mucius Scaevola, who was at least allowed to decamp alive; he used the comparison to make Bishop Bonner, whom he accused of having a habit of this sort of thing, look even worse.[57] Thomas Fuller, however, rewrote the parallel so that it referred to Allin's heroism, and by the early nineteenth century the pseudonymous John Milner was excitedly announcing that female Christian virtue trumps any heroics in the classical Republican vein.[58] By 1851, in the heat of the Papal Aggression controversy, Rose had become, in the words of one enthusiastic poet, "but a simple peasant; truth in its simplicity, / Truth she lov'd as Jesus gave it; 'but believe and follow me.' / Truth she learn'd not from tradition; hers the faith that God reveals / By his spirit to the childlike, from the worldly-wise conceals."[59] This accumulation of Christian clichés is precisely the point: Rose Allin's life and death exemplify the radical *accessibility* of the Protestant message, as well as its potentially infinite reproduction across apparently ineluctable boundaries of gender, class, and culture. She is both of her time and of the mid-Victorian era, a heroine suitable for emulation by beleaguered nineteenth-century Protestants. At the same time, as Maria LaMonaca reminds us, "[t]he martyr was, without exaggeration, the only truly heroic literary prototype for women, suggesting a courageous, active femininity which legitimately transgressed traditional gender norms and expectations."[60] Called by God, the female martyr engages in feats otherwise disbarred to "normal" women. Moreover, Rose Allin's "bodily decorum" under torture, as well as her resistance to improper sexual advances, demonstrated that she was an appropriately chaste virgin who was emphatically not, nevertheless, vowed to a life of celibacy.[61] Rose does not die *for* her virginity; instead, she dies *while* a virgin. And, significantly, she suffers because her filial loyalties cannot be separated from her religious faith. Her martyrology soon dovetailed with other midcentury polemical narratives about Catholicism's innate violence. And even as she became an icon of maidenly Protestant heroism, her persecutors turned into case studies in wayward, deformed masculinity.

In the novelist and folklorist Anna Eliza Bray's *The Protestant* (1828), published just a year before Catholic Emancipation, Foxe's Rose Allin material is adapted to the figure of Rose Wilford, who is tormented not by Tyrrel but by the historian and polemicist Nicholas Harpsfield, Thomas More's biographer and author of a blistering attack on the *Book of Martyrs*. (Bray appears to be conflating Rose Allin's torture with the near-identical experience of Thomas Tompkins, which was carried out by Harpsfield.[62]) By transposing her villains, Bray turns Harpsfield's critique of Foxe's text into a direct attack on the martyr's body itself, while further sexualizing what is already in Foxe a "sexually obscene" encounter.[63] The novel traces the persecution of a married Protestant priest, Owen Wilford, who is imprisoned (along with his wife and daughter) during the Marian regime and sentenced to execution, only to be reprieved at the very last moment by Mary's death and Elizabeth's providential accession to the throne. Contemporaries interpreted the novel as an intervention in Catholic Emancipation debates, although Bray herself insisted that the novel's political overtones were the work of her publisher, Henry Colburn—an argument which, as Irene Bostrom notes, seems "somewhat disingenuous."[64] Rose's torture and heroic resistance appears in the second volume, approximately midway through the novel, and occurs in two parts: first, an attempted seduction by John Thornton, the Bishop of Dover (Bray's invention); next, the actual assault by Harpsfield. Rose's miraculous resistance to both men provides the feminine counterpart to her father's own Protestant steadfastness and suggests that the obverse side of persecution on theological grounds is persecution on erotic grounds.

Rose's sexual trial prefigures her trial by fire. Initially, the drunken Thornton calls Rose a "pretty damsel," praises her "pretty little hand,"

and indicates that she could save herself by becoming his "lady-love."[65] Contemptuous, Rose refuses him, and he storms off, "incensed at the unshaken firmness of her manner" and "maddened by the just, but severe reproaches she had cast upon him" (2:111). The encounter miniaturizes several Protestant talking points. Thornton's wayward and obviously inappropriate sexual desires indict the failings of clerical celibacy; similarly, his willingness to exchange sex for safety reveals the obsession with the body lurking at the heart of Catholic faith. He promises clemency not for abjuring Protestantism but for abjuring virginity—a move that profanes the Catholic Church's desire to reclaim its lost souls. Unintentionally, Thornton makes illicit sex the functional equivalent of Catholic belief. Rose's resistance to his advances, meanwhile, turns Rose into the Protestant equivalent of a Catholic virgin saint, thereby putting Thornton into the awkward position of pagan tormenter. Finally, Thornton's insane rage as he exits suggests how male Catholic consciousness, supposedly unshaped by the scriptures, fractures at the appeal to conscience. Despite the hierarchical imbalance of the confrontation—young, imprisoned, female Protestant versus older, empowered, male Catholic—the speaker grounded in scriptural authority easily trumps the one equipped with all the privileges of approved religion, gender, and wealth.

While Harpsfield's direct attack further tightens the link between sexual and purportedly religious violence, it also prefigures what the reader expects will be Rose's eventual martyrdom by fire. The physically and psychologically monstrous Harpsfield undertakes his work in a spirit of "savage exultation" (2:112), transforming persecution into perverse pleasure. When Rose refuses to "kiss the cross" (2:112), Harpsfield decries her as a "harlot" (2:113) before searing her hand with a "flaming candle" (2:114). Despite the pain, Rose silently calls on God, then "stood with a noble constancy and an unchanged mien, in deep silence, enduring the burning flame" (2:114)—keeping so still that she spills none of the water she carries. As is the case with Thornton, the persecution rebounds on the perpetrators. While one man "turned aside his head, as if ashamed to witness the scene," Harpsfield is completely overcome:

At length the sinews of her hand, that were withered by the flame, cracked, and burst asunder. Rose only turned her eyes for a moment and looked upon her hand. Awe-struck, confounded, and even abashed by her magnanimity, Harpsfield dashed the candle on the ground, uttered a horrid oath, and walked towards the lower end of the room. (2:115)

Given Rose's encounter with Thornton, Harpsfield's demand that Rose "kiss the cross" sexualizes ritual obeisance, and this burning duplicates Thornton's seduction attempt at another level. Thornton treats Rose as a potential "harlot," while Harpsfield sneers that, as an unregenerate Protestant, she *is* one; Thornton offers the two alternatives of sexual exchange or martyrdom, while Harpsfield similarly offers the alternatives of ritual submission or torture. But in resisting Harpsfield, Rose specifically witnesses to the authority of *Protestant* belief, for Harpsfield burns her to make her "disclaim her faith." Neither Harpsfield nor Cluny, the witness, can interpret the physical proof of this faith, manifested in her perfect stillness, although Cluny's refusal to gaze on the scene offers its own testimony to the power of the martyr's witness. In fact, Cluny is moved enough to volunteer medical assistance afterwards, a moment of charity implying that the martyr's witness may lead to a fleeting awareness of true Christian love. By contrast, Harpsfield's "horrid oath" doubles and intensifies Thornton's mad ravings. In this novel Catholic speech is always just one step away from devolving into the unprintable (literally) disorder of a religious regime grounded in human desires. Harpsfield's total confusion in the face of faith in action, which leads him to denounce Rose as "woman, angel, or devil—for I know not what you are . . . for something more or less than human you must be" (2:115), demonstrates how badly fallen man falters when he interprets the effects of authentic belief without the framing narrative of the scriptures.

And yet, Rose and her family are never martyred. Instead, Elizabeth ascends to the throne and saves everyone at the last minute, an evasion of the historical record that attempts to preempt the possibility of Catholic Emancipation. "God bless Queen Elizabeth!" says Owen Wilford, toasting the new queen, "and may England for ever preserve that liberty gained for Englishmen by the Reformation of the Church!" (3:280–81). This Elizabeth *ex machina*, a common trope in novels about the Marian period, simultaneously rewards the would-be martyr's constancy and imagines the Elizabethan settlement as the *end* of Catholic history in England—thereby cheerfully sidestepping sixteenth- and seventeenth-century Puritan responses to what they saw as the still too "Papist" quality of the Church of England. Unlike such eighteenth-century fictions as *The Recess* or *The Statue Room* (discussed in chapter 1), Elizabeth's accession fully puts paid to the Catholic historical menace, even though, in the novel's historical context, her intercession seems to have had a sell-by date. The novel's Elizabeth *ex machina* invokes past triumph to halt what appears to be a present-day slide down the religious slippery slope.

Sixty years later Emily Sarah Holt's own novel about Rose Allin, *The King's Daughters: How Two Girls Kept the Faith* (1888), warned that such claims for historical closure were unwarranted. Unlike Bray, writing just before Catholic Emancipation, Holt writes in the wake of Emancipation, the Papal Aggression, and the Ritualist controversies; equally unlike Bray, Holt, who wrote tracts for the anti-Catholic and anti-Ritualist Church Association, does not flinch from casting herself as a hardboiled antitolerationist.[66] "If these times of ours were suddenly changed to a storm of persecution, how should we stand?" Holt demands in the preface to one novel, sounding the alarm that rings through all of her work.[67] Whereas Bray rescues the Wilfords with the aid of an Elizabeth *ex machina*, thereby suggesting that Protestant power brings Catholic persecution to a crashing halt, Holt argues for the power of necessary martyrdom as the nineteenth century draws to a close.

Holt's account of Rose Allen's torture both hews closer to Foxe and dwells in more detail on its historical and theological implications. Following Foxe, there is no seduction scene and Edmund Tyrrel carries out the burning. In this case, the burning constitutes multiple interpretive failures on Tyrrel's part:

> Mr. Tyrrel was in the habit of looking with the greatest reverence
> on certain other young girls, whom he called Saint Agnes, Saint
> Margaret, and Saint Katherine—girls who had made such answers
> to Pagan persecutors, twelve hundred years or so before that time:
> but he could not see that the same scene was being enacted again,
> and that he was persecuting the Lord Jesus in the person of young
> Rose Allen.[68]

To begin with, Tyrrel fails to draw the appropriate analogy between
past ("twelve hundred years") and present, suggesting that tutelage in
saints' lives does not, in fact, prepare him to recognize either saints or
persecutors. The latter misreading further suggests that Tyrrel has not
learned to engage in self-critique; the situation repeats itself identi-
cally, and yet the Catholic reader cannot perceive that his own traditions indict him. His "looking" paradoxically blinds him to the *lack*
of historical difference. Holt further emphasizes that paradox after
the colon, by shifting from the perhaps problematic virgin saints (the
"whom he called" implies that the saints in question might be of dubious origin) of Christian antiquity to Christ's immanent *presence*.
In fact, the "same scene" features not the saints and their resistance to
persecution but the ultimate model for all martyrdom, Christ's passion.
John R. Knott has noted, apropos of sixteenth-century martyrologies, that Protestant martyrs are important not as "intercessors with
God or conduits of supernatural power in the manner of medieval
saints but as exemplars of the heroism possible for individual protestants in a hostile world." And while Holt praises Rose Allen's power,
she does so only to point toward Christ himself, who is both the inspiration for and end of Rose's resistance.[69] Tyrrel, who cannot read
this moment in either historical or spiritual terms, cannot even man-
age the bewildered response to this event of Bray's Harpsfield.

In the end both the torture and Tyrrel's blindness to its meaning
prefigure Rose's death at the stake—although representing executions
posed problems for nineteenth-century novelists, who frequently dwell
on audience *response* rather than the martyrdom itself. In line with
Alice A. Dailey's argument that "without that audience, there is no

martyrdom, for martyrdom is a semantic distinction—an interpretive construction negotiated by victim and viewer, by historiographer and reader," in Victorian fiction the martyr's embodied sufferings take second place to fictions of the model audience.[70] Ideally, the spectacle of martyrdom instructs and enlightens the audience; as Alice Lang puts it in *From Prison to Paradise*, "[t]he horror of the persecution swept away all other considerations, and every death at the stake won hundreds to the cause for which the victims died."[71] In Lang's formulation the Catholic audience's visceral response to exemplary punishment leads them to properly interpret these deaths as martyrdoms, and not as criminal executions. Providence becomes visible as God thwarts Mary's desire to reestablish Catholicism in England by multiplying Protestants by the very method Mary chooses to eliminate them. To spiritual seekers, martyrdom momentarily reveals that the struggle between Protestantism and Catholicism is not that of heresy versus orthodoxy but of Christ's true church versus the Antichrist.

Holt, who did not shy away from representing the physical effects of torture or long-term incarceration, adopts the comic emplotment of martyrdom familiar from Reformation polemic.[72] The martyrs go to their deaths "joyfully," cheered on by a crowd that calls on God to "strengthen them, and comfort them, and pour Thy mercy upon them!" (200). Holt follows Foxe's original, borrowing his "joyfully," the martyrs' address to the crowd, and the crowd's enthusiastic reaction to the martyrs' bravery.[73] What Holt adds to both this scene of martyrdom and the one that took place earlier in the day are other, dissonant responses, all of them female: a young girl who faints at the sight of her much-loved servant's death (199–200); Agnes Bongeor, not martyred that day, "weeping" in disappointment (201); and Margaret Thurston, who has returned to the Catholic fold and whose reaction is not spelled out (201). The primary responses to the martyrs emphasize an affective, communal response, which identifies Protestantism with a grassroots English spirituality—"Ah," says the narrator, "it was not England, but Rome, who burned those Marian martyrs!" (199)—and dissociates violent persecution from Englishness. Punitive burnings, far from ejecting Protestants from the community, instead knit the martyrs and the survivors together in a celebration of divine joy. Agnes Bongeor's reaction is entirely apropos: held back from martyrdom, she is both more "dead" and more isolated than those who have gone before. By contrast, Margaret Thurston has no voice at all; ironically noting her "better lodging" (the jailer's term), the narrator tells us that she "had shut herself out, and had bought life by the denial of her Lord" (201). Margaret follows the "wrong" biblical script, choosing St. Peter's denial of Christ. The narrator emphasizes this moral failure by playing up Margaret's free will, as the active verbs suggest, and by assimilating her to the Catholic jailer. Only Margaret's eventual decision to recant her recantation and accept martyrdom restores her textual voice, albeit in a "meek and fervent appeal" (236). But the true evangelical power of martyrdom appears in the case of Amy, who experiences the death of her servant-friend in apocalyptic terms: "I felt as if the last day were come, and the angels were shutting me out" (202). In Amy's violent reorientation toward Protestantism, the image of being shut out—already deployed by the narrator in the case of both Agnes and Margaret—takes on eschatological significance. Amy's shock at the martyr's death opens into a vision not just of personal salvation or damnation but of universal Christian history—a brief glimpse of the providential narrative in which all the characters exist but of which only a few are ever aware. It is this narrative that Holt fears modern Protestants have lost.

PHILO-CATHOLICISM?

While Holt and Bray represent the majority position in nineteenth-century religious fiction, novelists of a higher (or, at least, a different) churchmanship found that their attitude to the persecutions neither addressed their own understanding of theological tradition nor imagined suitable "futures" for Protestant-Catholic relations. I conclude this chapter by examining how the novelist and devotional writer Lady Charlotte Maria Pepys (1822–89) critiqued evangelical narratives of apocalyptic Catholic depravity in *The Diary and Houres of the*

Ladye Adolie, A Faythfulle Childe, 1552 (1853) using strategies that are in some ways very similar to Walter Scott's in his Reformation duology. In one sense *Ladye Adolie* is the ultimate Foxeite text: it is an "edited" collection of a martyr's documents, including a journal (which concludes with an entry from her grieving mother), a catechism, and a book of hours. Like the most famous diary novels of the time, including Hannah Mary Rathbone's *Diary of Lady Willoughby* and Anne Manning's *The Maiden and Married Life of Mary Powell, Afterwards Mistress Milton*, *Ladye Adolie* was published in mock-diary format and an antique font. It fictionalizes both the martyr's voice and the transmission of the martyr's narrative to a wider public, modeling not only how a Protestant female martyr should act but also how she should practice devotional reading *and* writing; it is worth noting that all of the text's authors are female, with no fictionalized intervention by a male authority figure (although there are male authorities aplenty in the narrative). The diary itself offers a fictional example of spiritual self-examination, as the teenage Adolie meditates on and castigates herself for her various sins—most frequently, pride and a lack of charity. But the novel also casts spiritual growth in terms of scholarship. Adolie's annotated outline of the church services emphasizes the continuity between the Church of England and pre-Reformation traditions, making the church's liturgy into an amalgamated, perfected anthology of the best in all Christian traditions; the church appropriates and consolidates, instead of rejects, its forebears.[74]

Given Adolie's (and the novel's) interest in the organic links between Anglicanism and other theological traditions, it is not surprising that Adolie herself advocates a strong tolerationist position. In fact, early on her dream parable of the fish argues in favor of the Christian truths to be found in all denominations. After dreaming of fishermen arguing that one fish or another was a "Poisonous sorte," Adolie has a vision of "One who from His Hande did give us some of all Kindes of Fishes to eat, and they were verie goode" (52). When Adolie points out that the giver was important, not the "Sorte," the men in her vision threaten her until the "Blessed Voice" promises that "none shall pluck Thee out of My Hande" (53). In the course of prophesying Adolie's martyrdom, the parable both advocates an irenic, ecumenical vision of Christian cooperation—the many churches pouring forth from Christ's hands—while associating persecution with the whole complex of controversial speculation and polemic. Martyrdom proves Christ's truth, not necessarily the truth of any single church. When taken together with the novel's total disinterest in lay Protestant evangelism and its attacks on the Protestant's anti-Catholic name-calling (47) and "blinde Furie" (241), the parable suggests not just that Adolie envisions a future in which all denominations realize their ultimate unity in Christ but also that Protestants are called by God to refrain from engaging in violent and disrespectful polemic against Catholic religious practices. Given that the novel was published in 1853, when Protestant agitation over the Papal Aggression was at high tide, Lady Charlotte's statement would appear to be a radical one.

And yet, *Ladye Adolie* undercuts its utopian vision of Protestant-Catholic relationships by insisting that only the *Protestants* are capable of thinking in tolerationist terms. As in Scott, the possibility of reconciling the two religions requires that Catholicism concede its failure—something that its religious adherents are conspicuously unwilling to do in this novel. Adolie's friend Alice offers Adolie protection at a convent but only if she will "give Hopes of being converted" (123); other Catholic friends try to convert Adolie after she is confined to the Tower (255, 276–77, 289–90); and Cardinal Pole, whom Adolie praises for his "kind Zeale" (293), is not so kind as to save her from martyrdom. As Adolie's mother's closing note explains, the rest of the family survives only by fleeing into exile. The novel's trajectory thus redefines the parable: there is no sign that the world of "all Kindes of Fishes" can coalesce in any nation controlled by Catholic political forces. In effect, Lady Charlotte proposes what could be called a philo-Catholic position, akin to Enlightenment philo-Semitism, which disallows overt prejudice but also makes access to political power contingent on conformity—here, conformity to what the novel casts as Protestant values, even as it critiques Protestant extremism. As in Walter Scott's *The Abbot*, Catholicism must first concede its own irrelevance before it can lay claim to any share in Protestant toleration.

CONCLUSION

In fictionalizing the Marian persecutions, Protestant novelists re-wrote the *Book of Martyrs* so that Victorian readers might see just how the Marian past ought to inform the nineteenth-century present. These novels insist that the sixteenth-century persecutions, far from being anachronistic, lie dormant within Victorian culture, ready to be awakened by the promise of toleration; Protestants who fail to re-member history are doomed to repeat it. Apocalyptic visions of the aftermath of Catholic Emancipation damned the nation on both theo-logical and political grounds. Where Mary's body testifies to the self-inflicted ignorance and moral irresponsibility of Catholic culture, Rose Allin's tortures—inflicted because she would not influence her par-ents to recant—link domestic loyalty to divinely inspired resistance. Still, the philo-Catholic position offered by Lady Charlotte Pepys sug-gests that it *was* possible, after all, for Protestants to imagine Catholic persecution in terms of historical difference. Nevertheless, even ac-knowledging the possibility that context might shape Catholic action did not extend, apparently, to imagining a future in which Catholics might have *power*. As we shall see in the next chapter, however, Anglo-Catholic and Catholic novelists soon challenged the very foundations of Protestant Reformation tales.

Chapter Five

UNNOTICED PERSECUTIONS
Anglo-Catholics, Roman Catholics,
and the Reformation Tale

*"I would rather live in rags like thee, with the memories of the past to
sweeten my hard and bitter crust, than sit on a throne without them.
They may persecute us, beggar us, trample us; but they cannot wrench
from us the history of the past—that dominion of thought—that lies
far above the earth, and far beyond the grave."*
    —Paul Peppergrass [Father John Boyce], *The Spaewife* (1853)

In this elevated declaration of faith from Fr. John Boyce's *The
Spaewife* (1853), the brave young Catholic Alice Wentworth insists
that the Catholic believer's true, inalienable patrimony lies in the domain of history. Even as the Elizabethan regime shatters their bodies
and expropriates their lands, Catholics maintain a sense of sweeping
historical time that can never be rendered vulnerable to Protestant
theft—save in the dreaded act of apostasy. Amidst the literal ruins of

Protestant rule, Alice suggests, Catholic recusants preserve the essence of a history simultaneously national and universal. The "centuries of faith, the mother of virtue and of honor" both preserve the nation and preserve the individual who, maintaining her belief, is cast out from the land of her ancestors.[1] Given that Boyce's novel revolves around a supposed conspiracy to conceal Elizabeth I's illegitimate child— an ironic nod in the direction of Sophia Lee's *The Recess*, perhaps— Alice's pure devotion to her *historical* faith suggests that post-Reformation England has fatally severed its connections to its source of strength, enraptured as it is with a court dominated by a dark, debauched parody of the Virgin Mary. Under the new Protestant regime, chastity gives way to the public performance of virginity, devotion to God to devotion to public opinion, and true religion to mere policy. Only the Catholics prove capable of resisting this erotic, relativistic modernity, maintaining as they do that their religion is living history in action, not an anachronism.

In so doing, Catholics ironically proved themselves much more open to Sir Walter Scott's narrative practice than his co-religionists did.[2] Their works insisted on a Reformation that was fatally political and material in its basis, an immoral swerve from the true faith that brought only cultural collapse in its wake. ("Will you permit me to ask you one question? Is there *more*, or is there *less virtue* since the Reformation?" a Catholic asks a Protestant in *Florence; Or, the Aspirant*. "No, my friend, we are not better, and we are every day growing worse," the Protestant concedes.[3]) Moreover, Scott's fascination with the anachronistic, so easily turned *against* Catholics, reappeared as a controversial weapon: the internecine battles of the Marian and Elizabethan periods would be repurposed as part of an "age of persecution," a strictly delimited epoch of mutual religious violence now superseded by the triumphant reign of Queen Victoria. Protestants might worry about the dangerous psychological and theological effects of having no martyrdoms at all; Catholics would celebrate their martyrs, even as they turned the age of corporeal martyrdom into a peculiar, and unrepeatable, historical moment. And more specifically still, Catholics would invoke and rework Scott's representations of violated, degraded Catholic spaces, especially Catholic churches.

But like their Protestant counterparts, Catholics also revisited tropes popularized by their own Reformation and Counter-Reformation forebears. In particular, what Gary Kuchar describes as "the sense of fragmentation and inner division that characterized the experience of Elizabethan Catholics who were alienated from the liturgical life that grounded the integrity of both self and community" returns in Catholic historical novels, although re-inflected: not only do Catholic novelists represent Protestant historical narratives as themselves fragmented and perpetuating fragmentation, but they also insist that Catholics experience this rift at the level of national identity.[4] For would-be honest Englishmen and women, their devotion to Catholic liturgical and sacramental practices leaves them in a state of unsettled exile, both internally and externally.

This chapter analyzes how Catholic novelists pulled apart the neat connections between modernity and Protestantism, arguing instead that Protestantism deformed historical thinking itself. "To be deep in history is to cease to be a Protestant," John Henry Newman declared in 1845—a pronouncement that, at first glance, runs counter to the obsessive self-historicizing already documented in this volume.[5] Newman's argument, however, is that Protestants fear *church* history and desperately reach for their Bibles because church history merely records their absence. Whereas Protestant novelists argued that the Reformation returned to Christianity's original biblicism, Catholic novelists narrated how recusants struggled to maintain the traces of sacramental order, signifying the continuity of the Catholic Church *as a Church*. In this sense, Catholics cast Protestantism as a deadly fracture between past and present, one that made it impossible to "think" the self in relation to history. Summing up the architect A. W. N. Pugin's own historical analysis of the Reformation, Corinna M. Wagner describes it as a "familial rupture" (thanks to Henry VIII, a "counterfeit political father") that could not be resolved by a merely "surrogate religion" such as Protestantism.[6] The Protestant regime ushers in a world without the divine, but Catholic historical narratives point to the possibility of a new Counter-Reformation, as it were, healing the literal and figurative wounds of post-Reformation Britain.

I begin by sketching out the poetics of Reformation rupture in Catholic historical narratives, emphasizing the problematic reign of Elizabeth I. Next, I analyze the breaking points between Anglo-Catholic and Roman Catholic fictions of the Reformation, contrasting novels by the clergymen William Gresley and Augustine David Crake to the two most popular Catholic historical novels about the Elizabethan period, Frances (Mother Mary Magdalen) Taylor's *Tyborne* and Lady Georgiana Fullerton's *Constance Sherwood*. Although all of these novelists work against the Marian novels from the previous chapter, historicizing persecution in order to clear the way for a revived Victorian Catholicity, Gresley and Crake ultimately undercut their critique by resorting to a mild theological relativism, whereas Taylor and Fullerton insist that Protestant ideology disrupts historical consciousness. Finally, I turn to Catholic conversion fiction, which dramatizes the effects of Catholic historical consciousness on the English landscape itself. If Protestant novelists turn to history in order to teach readers to see that the present always threatens to *reenact* the past, Catholic novelists do so to suggest that they are the true bearers of historical awareness in a world that yearns to kill the past entirely.

Sex, Violence, Theft, and the Reformation Rupture

In the Catholic Reformation tale, *Reformation* signals not the rise of biblicism but, instead, the perverse liberation of humanity's worst impulses—a chaotic explosion of sexual libertinism and uncontrollable violence. C. J. Mason's popular *Alice Sherwin* (1857), written during arguably Britain's worst decade for anti-Catholic propaganda, imagines the full blossoming of Henry VIII's reforming project in near-apocalyptic terms:

> The carrying out [of] an organised system of plunder was about to be intrusted to Cromwell; Luther's orgies at the hostelry of the Black Eagle at Wittemberg were re-acted at Whitehall; the most gross slanders against the monastic establishments were rife amongst Henry's

boon companions; and ere the axe had emptied the state-prisons of the victims to the oath of supremacy which they enclosed, the bloodhounds of Cromwell were let loose, the banner of religious reform was unfurled, and the peaceful homesteads of England became the prey of lawless rapine and desolation, which rendered her a spectacle to all Europe. Men gazed in astonishment at the monarch, whose fiery passions once let loose left their seared and blackened traces over the unhappy kingdom whose laws he had set at naught, and with still greater astonishment at the weak and degraded sons of those mighty barons who had wrested from the weak yet less guilty John the glorious charter, now so unblushingly outraged.[7]

Mason reads the English Reformation as a concerted attack against the very fabric of Englishness itself. Inverting Protestant attacks against Catholicism's "foreign" nature, Mason insists that the King de-Englishes himself in aping Martin Luther's nights of singing and drinking at the Black Eagle tavern; as Mason's overheated "orgies" suggests, "Lutheranism" consists in the triumph of the body's worst impulses. In effect, the King imports not Luther's theology but Luther's stomach. Of Henry's "two bodies," only one remains: his riot of (unnamed) excesses first corrupts the court, then devastates the core of English domesticity, and finishes by both literally and figuratively scarring the landscape. As Europe's "astonishment" suggests, the resulting "spectacle" is a monstrosity, a record of kingly and aristocratic crime previously unknown in Christian history. The Henrician Reformation carries with it only national decadence and decay, embodied most clearly in Henry's violation of the Magna Carta itself. Post-Reformation England may not be "England" at all.

Mason's novel is unusual in its focus on the Henrician Reformation; the majority of Catholic novelists instead staked their turf on the Elizabethan era, the better to counter Protestant obsessions with the Marian persecutions. This approach was in line with mainstream English Catholic historiography, which from the late eighteenth century onward took the Elizabethan regime as the key to making sense of the Reformation.[8] While most novelists were not interested in the

complex ins and outs of Elizabethan politics, they seized on the willingness of Protestants to violate recusant domesticity in search of
priests. John Lingard, the nineteenth century's most instantly recog-
nizable Catholic historian, argued that "[n]o man could enjoy security
even in the privacy of his own house, where he was liable at all hours,
but generally in the night, to be visited by the magistrate at the head of
an armed mob."[9] The Elizabethan Catholic's home is presumed open
to all comers, whose visits can only with difficulty be distinguished
from criminal invasions. Far from being a sacred domestic space, the
Catholic's home is legally subject to violation—both its objects and its
women, "whose reasons and lives were endangered from the brutality
of the officers" (6:166). In effect, the Elizabethan regime devotes itself
to rendering Catholics both literally and figuratively homeless. Even
those Catholics who remain in England instead of going into exile find
that their homes are, in fact, no homes at all (a situation soon to be lit-
eralized under the Penal Laws that prohibited Catholics from owning
property). Concluding his assessment of Elizabeth's reign, Lingard
notes that the emergence of "new families" from the shattered remnants of Catholic estates represents "not the prosperity of the nation" but rather "that of one half obtained at the expense of the other"
(6:324). The modern Protestant aristocracy rests on a calculated act of
erasure: far from being a stable ground for the nation, its very existence announces England's violent repression of its true Catholic past.
It is precisely this past that the novelists will recuperate.

According to many Victorian Catholics, while early modern Protestants expropriated Catholic property, sundering lands from their traditional families and uses, they also instituted the project of deforming
historical narrative—a charge, of course, that Protestants themselves
made against Catholics. The incendiary priest Thomas Flanagan complained that beginning with Polydore Vergil, historians showed a dis-
maying "want of independence," not to mention a "too evident change
in their estimation of truth."[10] For Flanagan, the Elizabethan age was
important not only for its oppression of the recusants but because it
is ground zero for Protestant narratives of modernity; put simply,
Flanagan argued, "[t]he predominating idea in the busy, but not al-

ways profound, researches of that age, was, therefore, to make out that Rome was not the fountain-head of Britain's Christianity" (2:5). For Flanagan, Protestant historiography to virtually his own time follows Reformation historical protocols, transforming Catholics into illegitimate, marginalized voices on the boundaries of a history that properly belongs to them. Whereas Protestant authors feared that modern readers were apt to forget the Reformers, Catholics were apt to remind them that the Reformation had come to occupy the entirety of the historical field, to the extent that no other narratives seemed possible, let alone visible. Thus, the convert Frances Taylor (later Mother Mary Magdalen Taylor, founder of the Poor Servants of the Mother of God) observes in her pioneering novel about the Elizabethan persecutions, that "religious persecution" has led readers to empathize with the Albigensians, Huguenots, and Covenanters—all of whom Taylor finds theologically and politically dangerous. And so, she wryly asks, "[i]s it not, then, wonderful, that when the persecutions under Mary Tudor have been written indelibly on the page of history, the long, the terrible, the patient sufferings of Catholics in the succeeding reign should remain unnoticed?"[11] Turning the Protestant rhetoric of Christian amnesia on its head, Taylor promises to undo centuries of anti-Catholic silencing and thus produce an alternative narrative of English national identity. Moreover, Taylor further attempts to seize the countercultural high ground from staunch evangelicals like Charlotte Elizabeth Tonna (discussed in chapter 4), for whom Catholicism posed an imminent apocalyptic threat. Taylor and fellow novelists like Lady Georgiana Fullerton restored the Catholic voice—and tormented Catholic body—to the supposedly golden age of the Elizabethan regime. For Catholic novelists, then, the Reformation tale provided an opportunity to reinvent mainstream Protestant narratives—not only to undermine the dominant voice, but also to assert Catholic claims to Englishness.

It is worth noting, however, that in casting themselves as the unbiased critics of Elizabeth's reign, these Catholic novelists ignored mainstream attitudes to the queen, which often ranged from uneasy to passionately negative. In fact, the Elizabeth *ex machina* co-existed with a considerable body of verbal and visual material devoted to critiquing or outright denigrating the Gloriana legend.[12] As Thomas S. Freeman and Alexandra Walsham have both pointed out, Elizabeth's status as England's Protestant savior required ongoing finagling during the sixteenth and seventeenth centuries, not least because the Elizabethan settlement's *via media* failed to satisfy more ardent Puritan voices.[13] By the Victorian period Elizabeth's failure to live up to modern feminine ideals—especially those personified in the figure of Queen Victoria herself—made it difficult for many writers to reconcile the glorious sovereign and the apparently immoral, not to mention unchristian, woman. Or, as one biographical sketch remarked, "[a]s a sovereign, Elizabeth was resolute and sagacious, but personally she was odious."[14] Even from the point of view of more liberal Protestant historians, like Henry Hallam or T. B. Macaulay, Elizabeth's reign, including her treatment of Roman Catholics, was problematic. Far from regarding the Elizabethan persecutions as justified, Hallam and his peers argued that Catholic "dissatisfaction" "proceeded mainly from the penal rigors to which they were subject and not from the principles of their religion, as was so frequently alleged."[15] To appropriate Elizabeth as the providential marker of the glorious age of Protestantism was, therefore, a fraught project, even for evangelicals; some of them, like Emily Sarah Holt, could muster only half-hearted praise of the queen, even when admitting her importance for the Protestant cause.[16] As we have already seen, Lord Tennyson queried the myth of Elizabeth as the Protestant point of no return, implying that such an interpretation of the past failed to take into account the far more volatile and unsettling presence of Catholics in the present. In this instance, evangelical fictions of the Reformation really did contain the seeds of their own self-deconstruction.

This revisionist approach also highlights another characteristic of the Catholic Reformation tale: while historians of the historical novel often link the genre to the rise of the modern nation-state, both in its moment of origin and in its frequent subject matter, Catholic novels set during the age of the Penal Laws are frequently tragedies of national *disidentification*. Kevin Morris remarks that "[t]he Victorians believed that Catholicism was unpatriotic, that the Catholic Church was trying to exert political power in England, and so it was important to exonerate Catholics from the charge of being un-English and treacherous."[17] In the Catholic historical novel characters try to assert patriotic English identities, only to be thwarted by their own government. Under the new Protestant regime, characters who might otherwise embody a "deep" national history, grounded in the very landscape, find themselves uprooted and permanently dislocated. In that sense, the novels participate in a tradition of English Catholic writing, dating to the sixteenth century, in which "Catholics perceived themselves as historical exiles from the time when England belonged to the true faith, and—in a unique intensification of the Christian commonplace—as spiritual exiles from heaven."[18] Such narratives persisted to the end of the nineteenth century, as legislative advances in England—such as those allowing Catholics to matriculate at Oxford and Cambridge (although the hierarchy prevented them from doing so until 1895)—were promptly counterbalanced by Protestant anxieties over events in the Catholic Church abroad, most notably the First Vatican Council's conclusions about papal infallibility. For many British readers it remained unclear if Catholics could truly be domiciled within a Protestant national space; Catholics responded by warning that "Protestant national space" was both illusion and self-delusion.

We see this critique of Protestantism's appropriation (or expropriation) of the landscape in Alice O'Hanlon's *Erleston Glen: A Lancashire Story of the Sixteenth Century* (1878), which tracks the ruinous effects of the Elizabethan settlement on a formerly idyllic rural village. Both the churches and the local manor, Erleston Grange, are reappropriated for greedy Protestant purposes. Erleston Grange, the narrator tells us, has been owned by the Anderton family "from time immemorial," and its architecture is practically an anthology of historical styles.[19] Simultaneously all-historical and transhistorical, the Grange and its occupants cannot be disentangled from the birth and growth of the English nation. At the beginning of the novel both the Grange and its neighboring church offer what appears to be the final refuge for English Catholicism—the last geographical location not tainted by the Reformation. But by the end of the novel both have been emptied and despoiled. Protestants intrude into Catholic space by literally smashing it to pieces, as in an iconoclastic orgy that climaxes with the destruction of the Sacred Host (72). Moreover, in an ironic and pointed juxtaposition, the first time the church bells ring under Protestant control also marks the first time the Catholic Walter Willoughby spots the Protestant Caroline Winwood, for whose hand Walter will eventually betray the Anderton family (103). Once Protestantism moves into Catholic sacred space, it releases uncontrollable erotic and violent energies that bring once close-knit communities to their knees. Not surprisingly, Caroline Willoughby eventually elopes with the brother of the Protestant buyer of Erleston Grange, while the Anderton family itself does not survive its youngest generation. Decoupled from their land, the Andertons have a higher spiritual future in store for them but no national future; the novel's end asks us to return to the beginning, a view of Erleston Glen as it appears in nineteenth-century industrial Lancashire. The signs of modernity—factories, railroads, "[g]ood, substantial roads" (1)—that link the once-isolated village to the rest of modern Britain also write over the erased Catholic spaces, signaling, perhaps, a world in which "humans are bound to a landscape blighted by the spread of urban manufacture."[20] Modern Britain, that is, does not incorporate its past so much as it displaces it altogether.

Constructing Catholic Reformations I: Anglo-Catholicism and Toleration

Anglo-Catholic and Roman Catholic novelists both sought to undermine mainstream narratives of Protestant liberty. While it is useful to remember that both groups "shared cultural values based on a common theology, one evident in advanced Anglicans' belief that they belonged to the universal Catholic Church," Anglo-Catholic revisions of the Reformation ultimately sought to undo mutual prejudice, *not* the Reformation.[21] Despite their renewed emphasis on sacramentalism, they began to run aground on the question of the miraculous, of an enchanted universe. Devon Fisher has recently suggested, in fact, that the still-Anglican John Henry Newman's attempt to publish a full *Lives of the English Saints* provoked multiple spiritual crises in the series' authors, in part because the gap between the source material attesting to miracles (the "collective memory of the church") and rationalist historiography could not be reconciled.[22] As we shall see, Anglo-Catholic and Roman Catholic novelists tend to separate on exactly this question of God's ongoing willingness to manifest himself in the world through miracle.

To establish what makes Roman Catholic novelists so different, let us examine two of the better-known Anglo-Catholic novelists, William Gresley and Augustine David Crake. While both Gresley and Crake were prolific didactic novelists, they were well-known outside of novel-writing circles: Gresley was a Tractarian and advocate for aural confession, while Crake, one generation later, wrote devotional manuals and ecclesiastical history from an openly Anglo-Catholic point of view.[23] Crake himself argued that Gresley pioneered the sympathetic representation of Catholics who "could not disguise their convictions or transfer their allegiance to a lustful tyrant"—phrasing that accurately identified Crake's project as well.[24] Both novelists participate in the well-known Tractarian and Anglo-Catholic critique of the Reformation as a largely destructive force that undermined the catholicity (that is, the universality) of the Christian church. The Tractarians saw themselves as the heirs to seventeenth-century Anglicanism, but their historical project "entailed a conscious marginalisation of the Reformation and most of the Elizabethan epoch from [their] vision of the foundations, identity and integrity of Anglicanism."[25] In particular, they attacked the bibliocentric focus of the evangelical Reformation narratives and argued instead for a return to church authority grounded in tradition derived from the early church fathers. Like Evangelicals, the Tractarians saw themselves returning to the fount of "antiquity"; unlike Evangelicals, they did so by "idealiz[ing] a Church grounded in the unaltered and unblemished precepts of the church fathers and without mediation," jettisoning the Reformers in the process.[26] At the same time, the Tractarians insisted that even though their movement sought to restore England's awareness of what her established church owed to the Catholic tradition, their purpose was to *prevent* conversions to Roman Catholicism; revitalizing Anglican Catholicity, despite the claims of their detractors, would keep the national church safe from the pope.[27]

In *The Forest of Arden: A Tale Illustrative of the English Reformation* (1841), Gresley—the less sophisticated novelist of the two—narrates the rise of an ideally "Catholic" Church of England while simultaneously decrying "that antipathy against the Romish Church" and "that schismatical spirit with which so many eminent Reformers were infected."[28] Despite the presence of a subsidiary romance plot, the novel's real project is to offer an alternative history of the entire sixteenth century from Henry VIII onward. Borrowing from Walter Scott's narrative repertoire, the novel is structured on the equivalence of Roman Catholics and evangelicals: while Catholics may believe in papal infallibility, warns Gresley, "[t]he ultra-Protestants consider each man to be a pope himself, and at liberty to take the Scriptures and interpret them according to his own fancy; hence the variety of sects into which they are divided" (266). Private judgment, integral to *sola scriptura*, here becomes as arbitrary an exercise of authority as that bugbear of anti-Catholic polemics, papal infallibility. Although Gresley believes that the Catholics are frequently at fault in their reasoning, he nevertheless finds Protestantism to be a more negative than positive force. To establish this point, Gresley frequently breaks away from straightforward narrative into often-unresolved dialogue exchanges, in which the participants model the conceptual limits of their beliefs. For example, in a debate on the dissolution of monasteries between Hugh Latimer and Father William, the Abbot of Merevale, the narrator informs us that Latimer's reasoning about monasteries inheriting estates fails because "[q]uestions of abstract justice are not much heeded by men whose minds are made up to the expediency of a certain course" (84); but, then again, Father William "could not deny this charge" about monastic corruptions (86). In the end, the narrator concludes,

> Such are the arguments which were employed on the question of the dissolution of the monasteries by two honest and moderate men, whose habits of thought were different;—the one being what some

might call, though unjustly, a bigot,—the other an utilitarian; the
one accustomed to see and admire what was good,—the other
prompt to detect and remove what was amiss; the one willing to reform when too late,—the other careless of destroying, in his anxiety to reform. (88)

This summation, typical of the novel, promises to unite Father William
and Latimer ("two honest and moderate men") but tips the scales
slightly in Father William's favor. Father William, after all, is on the
receiving end of the qualifiers and the positive verbs, while Latimer
emerges as an entirely negative force; it's clear that Father William's
not-bigotry is superior to Latimer's purportedly "utilitarian" outlook,
which implies that a creeping secularism accompanies the Reformation
movement. Nevertheless, Father William is also, quite literally, belated,
and in that sense fails to realize that this dialogue exchange is *pointless*:
his arguments have already been tried, found wanting, and discarded.
The future lies with the Hugh Latimers of the world, who will simply
dismantle that with which they cannot argue. In reconstructing Father
William's voice, however, the narrator identifies a potentially opposi-
tional voice granted authority from historical tradition. Although both
Father William and Latimer are "the past," it is only by remembering
both men that the Church of England can become what Gresley calls
"the mother of us all," both Protestant and Roman Catholic (278).

Writing a generation later, A. D. Crake sought more explicitly to
construct an organically unified narrative that would incorporate both
Protestant and Catholic voices, although again his novels skew notice-
ably toward their Catholic characters. *The Last Abbot of Glastonbury:
A Tale of the Dissolution of the Monasteries* (1883), set in the 1530s and
early 1540s, and *The Heir of Treherne: A Tale of the Reformation in
Devonshire and of the Western Rebellion* (1889), set mostly in the late
1540s, both employ allegorical "lost heir" plots—probably modeled
on Sir Walter Scott's *Guy Mannering*—to think about the relationship
between religious faith and national identity. In both cases, the rightful
heir is partly or entirely raised by a priest and adheres to the Roman
Catholic Church, whereas the false heir adopts Protestantism for purely

political reasons; again, the false heir dies not at the protagonist's hands but as an unintended consequence of his own evil actions. And both novels end with the narrator breaking frame to explain the afterlife of his characters. Cuthbert, the protagonist of *The Last Abbot of Glastonbury*, is rescued after his mother dies in a snowstorm and raised by peasants (with help from the titular Abbot); after the Abbot's death, Cuthbert is adopted by Sir Walter Trevannion, who is actually a priest, Prior Ambrose. Cuthbert knows one important secret, the whereabouts of the monastery's church plate, but is unaware that he is the heir to the property of his uncle, Sir John Redfyrne, who is also one of his primary persecutors. In *The Heir of Treherne*, Mervyn (a.k.a. Pixie) has been raised by the Zingari (gypsies), who throughout the novel offer a virtuous counter-example to that of the novel's frequently decadent Catholics and Protestants. As it turns out, Mervyn should have inherited the Earldom of Treherne but has been displaced by the religiously indifferent—not to mention illegitimate—Roger, whose evangelical father never married his mother. Cuthbert ultimately goes into exile and never lays claim to his property, unable to reconcile himself to the Elizabethan settlement; Mervyn, who conforms as far as he is able to the Elizabethan church, temporarily loses claim to his property under the reign of Edward VI but has it restored to him at Mary's accession to the throne.

In both novels Crake draws on the long medievalist tradition, shared with both Walter Scott and Crake's own Catholic contemporaries, of reading the Reformation as a politically and financially motivated attack on both wealthy monasteries and wealthy Catholics.[29] For Crake, Reformation history is, in effect, a cash transaction: sacred objects mutate into profane consumer goods, while aristocratic titles (and the land that supports them) jump the entail's tracks. In this new world of exchange, the very ability to judge values, moral and otherwise, disappears. For example, Cuthbert keeps the secret of the monastery treasure chest, which contains both "golden and jewelled [*sic*] treasures," and extremely important, potentially life-threatening documents (31). When the Abbot goes on trial, along with a number of others, one of the charges is that of concealing the treasure—not the documents—and thus "depriving our sovereign lord the King of his rightful property, conferred upon him by Act of Parliament" (55). But as the Abbot points out, the true crime lies with the government, which seeks to "take to itself the houses of God for a possession" (56). In this new economic landscape, the very idea that certain spaces and objects cannot be owned or exchanged by man has gone by the wayside; instead, everything circulates according to human whim and can be repurposed (quite literally, in this instance) as need or desire requires. By erasing this notion of sacred space, however, Parliament also elevates the temporal monarch over the divine king, in an act that could be read as either idolatrous or atheist. When Henry VIII lays claim to God's property, he ejects God from the world; material things, now disenchanted, no longer enjoy any connection with the divine. Only the Catholics preserve the notion that those things consecrated to God cannot be alienated from him. When, years later, Cuthbert and Father Ambrose return to the hidden chest, they "borrow" (223) some of the gold to help them escape the country but burn the documents (which were actually far more important) and leave the rest until their longed-for restoration of the Catholic Church in England (224). Sir John Redfyrne, however, who scouts out the hiding place shortly afterward, winds up accidentally imprisoned there and dies of starvation (227). Sir John's greed leads him to a literal dead end, but it also suggests the spiritual emptiness of the new world order: the abbey's treasures, improperly understood, fail to nurture those who seek them.

It's no coincidence, then, that Crake chose the inheritance plot. In these novels, the Reformation deforms the customary bonds of inheritance, transforming the rightful stewards of the land into outcasts and substituting false masters in their place. As the Catholic Church loses its divinely ordained role in guarding God's property, so the aristocracy becomes vagrant; similarly, as the reformers eliminate all but two of the sacraments, so their followers find themselves wandering into moral territories left unsanctified by the divine. Roger's predicament in *The Heir of Treherne*, for example, arises because, as the evangelical Barnaby forthrightly explains, "we consider the mutual agreement between man and woman, made in the fear of God before chosen witnesses, to live only for each other, is enough," since marriage is not a sacrament; thus, Roger's illegitimacy is an inconvenient by-product of English "superstition."[30] An antisacramental society such as this promptly dissolves what was once the holy bond of matrimony. The reformers have literally *disinherited* their followers—not from their physical property but from the ecclesiastical traditions that joined them to the divine. If Crake frowns on Roman Catholicism *per se*, he nevertheless insists on the Anglo-Catholic position that the Reformation wrongly severed the English Church from its roots in the universal (Catholic) church; it is no accident that Cuthbert chooses to shelter in Catholic France and accept a landed estate there, rather than return to England, or that the more flexible Mervyn needs Mary before he can finally lay hands on his own property. Roman Catholicism may be wrong, according to Crake, but it nevertheless supplies the chain of authority that the Protestants conspicuously lack. Yet, like Gresley, Crake pulls back from a full-blown critique of either side, opting for a more irenic position. Cuthbert is "[u]ndoubtedly" wrong for believing in the papal supremacy (*Glastonbury* 236) but deserves praise for his wholehearted commitment to his faith, just as the otherwise unpleasant (and martyred) Barnaby should not be condemned, but "was a good man according to his lights" (*Treherne* 332). Even as Crake imagines post-Reformation England as a loose collection of disinherited Christians, he tries to reunite the country on the basis of a shared *subjective* sense of righteousness. The reader should sympathize with Cuthbert and Barnaby not because they *are* right, but because they subordinate all else to their *belief* that they are right.

Constructing Catholic Reformations II: Roman Catholicism's English Pasts and Presents

While Catholic novelists obviously shared this revisionist, tolerationist project with their Anglo-Catholic contemporaries, they did so in order to insist on the Catholic martyrs *as* martyrs. Being good "according to his lights" was no substitute for staunch faith in the one true Church. This claim was explicitly countercultural: where Protestant novelists insisted that their antitolerationist position ran against the grain of indifferentism, and thus claimed the countercultural mantle for themselves, Catholic novelists could point to anti-Catholic sentiment as a sign that their *own* voices were systematically suppressed in modern culture. By celebrating sixteenth-century Catholic martyrs, Catholics both reminded readers that their own martyrological traditions preceded the Protestant variety and installed Catholic faith at the heart of English religious experience—what Thomas Woodman describes as the "faith of our fathers" strategy, which is still popular in twentieth-century Catholic fiction.[31] At the same time, Catholics used martyrdom and the miracles surrounding it to point to what we now call the still-"enchanted" nature of the world.

The most influential of the Catholic novels in this vein was Frances Taylor's *Tyborne: "And Who Went Thither in the Age of Queen Elizabeth"* (1859), also known as *Father de Lisle*; in addition to a French translation, it was reprinted at least five times in England and nine in the United States, the last time in 1994.[32] Taylor, a prominent convert who had been a nurse during the Crimean War, was well-connected in Catholic literary circles: she edited one of the best-known Victorian Catholic magazines, the *Lamp*, and went on to pioneer another, the *Month*.[33] Taylor deliberately echoes the Foxeite novel by using Richard Challoner's *Memoirs of Missionary Priests* for her source material, drawing on the lives of such noted martyrs as Edmund Campion and Robert Southwell for her characters' adventures. As a result, her heroes' lives becomes synthetic martyrologies, uniting multiple martyrs' lives into a few exemplary figures. For example, an imprisoned priest, Father Gerard, finds that his chains "always fell off" (140), and he describes a "glorious" visitation of the "Mother and Child," in which "this dark dungeon is full of heavenly light, and she bids me be of good cheer, and confess to the end the faith of her Son" (140–41). As Taylor points out in a footnote, Gerard's prison experience derives from that of Thomas Atkinson; Challoner's own life of Atkinson borrows from multiple texts, with the visitation and the miracle of the irons mentioned only at the end, in a brief summary of a Latin account from 1617.[34] In transposing Challoner's secondhand summary into direct speech, Taylor replaces the martyrologist's explicit discussion of sources and authorities with narrative immediacy. By fictionalizing the martyr's experience and eliminating the textual apparatus, the novel grounds martyrological authority in the reader's sympathetic identification with Gerard's plight. In a sense, Taylor's hero becomes an epitome of the Catholic hagiographical tradition, in which the same deeds and miraculous happenings may be ascribed to saint after saint but God's divine action in the world remains constant.[35]

As a revisionist text, *Tyborne* performs two different acts of appropriation: it *reappropriates* martyrology (from Foxe and his nineteenth-century Protestant readers) and *appropriates* the Reformation tale (from Protestant controversial novelists). The enthusiastic reviewer for the *Dublin Review* singled out this project for special praise, complaining that in the Protestant literary world, "[t]here have been no martyrs but Bible-readers, and Tyborne is a name unknown."[36] When one character tells the protagonist, Walter de Lisle, that his sufferings are "not witnessing for Christ" because Walsingham will rewrite this event as treason, Walter serenely replies that "[i]n His own good time the truth shall be told, and England know for what cause we suffer" (194–95). Protestant rewriting cannot permanently overwrite the truths of Catholic witnessing.

Taylor structures her plot around the Penal Laws, in particular, the Acts of 1581 and 1585 that forbade Catholic priests from residing in England and punished sympathizers who tried to conceal them. Each chapter traces the effect of one aspect of the acts, supported by a lengthy note appended at the end; the endnotes mainly draw from Richard Burn's *Ecclesiastical Law* (1760) and Richard Robert Madden's more recent (and far more polemical) *History of the Penal Laws Enacted against Roman Catholics* (1847), both standard sources at the time. The novel thus diversifies its call for sympathy: readers disinclined to believe in Catholic martyrology may nevertheless be reached through the more secular—or, at least, more neutral—ground of legal history. As Maureen Moran points out, Taylor insists on a "sympathetic, articulate hero to argue that religious and civil obedience are separate and distinct."[37] Taylor's characters would obey if the government allowed them to do so; it is a persecuting government that paradoxically produces Catholic disobedience. Given Taylor's interest in restoring Catholic experience to English national history, remembering the Penal Laws becomes both a political and a historiographical project. If, as Taylor claims, the "name of Catholic is yet hated and despised, and they who wear it wear also a mark of their Master's scorn" (xii), then narrating the Penal Laws rewrites English history in a far more inimical mode of continuity: post-Reformation culture inherits not Protestant liberty but the much more problematic inheritance of ongoing persecution. Clearly, excessive toleration is not the problem.

Like her Protestant contemporaries, Taylor insists that one of the chief signs of Christian heroism is putting faith above mere physical safety. Her hero, Walter de Lisle, has no initial interest in martyrdom, but when his beloved Constance, a Protestant, urges him to Nicodemism—"Surely the prisoner who feigned in order to outwit his jailor, and escaped, would be fully justified, and England now is one great prison, where we dare not say or do as we list, but as pleasures the queen" (71)—he realizes that he cannot betray his faith. Abandoning all hopes for Constance, Walter goes abroad, becomes a Jesuit, and returns to England as a missionary priest and eventual martyr. His embrace of divine over earthly love rebukes Protestant critiques of priestly celibacy. Repeatedly described as "joyous" or "joyful" in his reactions to impending death, Walter models an ideal Catholic masculinity, in which celibacy merely forms part of a greater self-abnegation before Christ and the good of His church. In abandoning Constance for the church, Walter does not abandon marriage but rather chooses the true marriage of man and God: "Let me be well apparelled for my bridal day," he says as he prepares for execution (224). Such language originates not with Taylor but with the martyrological tradition she fictionalizes. In its Victorian context, however, the traditional rhetoric undermines anti-Catholic attacks on celibacy as perverse and antisocial. Walter's ability to endure vividly described tortures of various sorts, as well as his gory execution (which culminates with his "quivering heart" being "torn from its place and held before the fast glazing eyes" [240]), quite literally embodies the triumph of Catholic devotion and heroism in the face of Protestant monstrosity.

By contrast, Walter's sister, Isabel, chooses the path that Walter rejects. Despite her contemptuous claim that "Isabel de Lisle is too proud to be a renegade from the faith of her fathers and the traditions of her house" (41), the pride in question ultimately leads her to conform. The results are catastrophic: she is visited by a series of clearly divine punishments, beginning with childlessness and ending with years of dementia. It is her own husband, in fact, who engineers Walter's capture and execution. Only at her death, when she regains awareness, fully repents, and reconciles herself with the church, is Isabel rewarded with a glorious vision of her sainted mother and brother awaiting her in Heaven (259). Isabel's fall into Protestantism, an example of sinful frailty, and even her eventual redemption stand in bleak opposition not only to her brother's exalted call to martyrdom but also to the heroism of other Catholic women in the text, including her mother, who resists all pressure to conform after her husband is executed; her cousin Blanche, who is horribly crippled after she saves all the "vessels and vestments" of a mass from being taken by Protestant officers (113); and Constance herself, who converts and lives the rest of her life in suffering and penance.

The sufferings of *Tyborne*'s characters suggest the complexity of national identification in the Catholic Reformation tale. Constance and her female friends and family spend the remainder of their lives in Belgium; Walter goes abroad for training as a missionary priest and then returns to his true home, a journey with predictably lethal results. Even as *Tyborne* and other Catholic Reformation tales insist that English national identity and Catholic history cannot be separated, they also remind their readers that Catholicism is not simply English. Christopher Highley observes that the early modern Catholics were hostile to Protestant models of England "as a self-sufficient and inward-looking island nation" because their own "idea of England had to accommodate the country's separate identity with its place in the international structures of the Catholic church."[38] The internationalized Catholic faith enables its English adherents to identify themselves *as* English, but it also enables them to transform alien lands into spiritual homes. While Constance does not become a nun, she still transforms her Belgian convent into a site of English community:

> She was kind to all; but when, as it sometimes happened, refugees from England came for shelter, her sympathy poured itself forth upon them with infinite tenderness. The sick valued the touch of her cool hand, and the sound of her soft voice. The sorrowful raised their heads as they looked at her, bearing her bitter trials so meekly; priests, who were venturing on the English mission, came to see her to beseech her prayers; for in their might, before God's throne, they had great faith. The Religious, also, of the convent, when in trouble or distress, were wont to ask their superioress's leave to beg the English lady to pray for them; but of all who loved her, and she loved, the dearest were the little children. (264–65)

Within this explicitly religious space, Constance becomes the focus of a diasporic English culture, binding it together through self-sacrificial acts of Christian charity. Constance's "infinite tenderness" to English exiles demonstrates that Christian love encompasses, rather than transcends, an explicitly English sense of self, even as it also opens out to the convent's residents and to the local children. Moreover, as Tonya Moutray McArthur notes of overseas English convents, this Belgian convent offers "simultaneous impregnability and permeability," offering a safe space for the embattled English community to reform itself around Constance's "sympathy" and, in the case of the missionary priests, to fortify themselves for the return to England.[39] Constance's universal yet English love suggests the extent to which overseas Catholic spaces maintain and fortify English Catholic identity, even as Englishness in turn enriches those same spaces.

Protestantism, by contrast, works against nurturing. Taylor's critique of Protestantism forms part of what she clearly believes is a revisionist attack on Elizabeth I. In fact, as we have already seen, Taylor's "revisionism" conforms to contemporary Victorian critiques of the queen's moral character: the volatile queen presides over a court where "license" runs wild (53). The ambiguously gendered Elizabeth has "a

woman's weakness, without, apparently, one instinct of her nature,—
a woman who had taken the hard and reasoning part of the masculine
nature, without one spark of man's tenderness or the refinement so
constantly found in the sternest characters" (160). Combining the
worst of male and female, Elizabeth embodies post-Reformation disorder, and this dangerous headship is echoed in turn by her depraved
court, full of "dangers without end or limit" (160). Taylor's Elizabeth
has little enthusiasm for women who haven't "the least taint of scan-
dal" (250), as one character notes to herself; the queen's unregenerate
nature is the essence of Protestantism in miniature. Unlike the Protestant representations of Mary discussed in chapter 4, which emphasize that her mental fragility and hysterical sexuality coexist with her
would-be moral purity, the Catholic representations of Elizabeth
render her self-consciously erotic *and* eroticizing. Once God has been
banished, only a defiled corporeality remains. Under the circumstances,
it is no surprise that Isabel's conversion to Protestantism results in
mental chaos. Indeed, all of the novel's Protestants are timeservers,
moral relativists, and libertines, implicitly taking their cue from Elizabeth. On his way to his own execution, Walter converts another condemned man, the son of a convert to Protestantism, who tartly sums
up the content of his father's religion as "nothing" (228). Protestantism is not alternative belief but simply nonbelief.

And yet, Taylor manages to wrest a sort of triumph out of the
disappearance of Elizabethan Protestantism:

> Three hundred years are past and gone! The last of the Tudors and the
> last of the Stuarts alike crumble into dust. A new dynasty holds the
> sceptre of England, and a queen, with all a woman's virtues, sits upon
> the throne. The rack and the torture-chamber are things of the past,
> and the savage laws of Elizabeth can be found only in some obsolete
> statute-book. Men walk abroad in safety, for England is free! (265)

If there is some irony at work here—after all, as Taylor argued in the
preface, Catholics are still disadvantaged—nevertheless the new queen's
"virtues" model an equally new Protestantism, one that rejects violent compulsion and dispatches "savage laws" to the junk heap of

discarded law texts. Pointedly, Taylor insists on Victoria's perfect femininity, untainted by Elizabeth's problematic gender; an orderly womanhood signals an orderly nation. Taylor's praise for Victoria carefully links Catholicism to English patriotism, even as it implicitly calls on Victoria to extend English "freedom" to her still-persecuted subjects. Unlike her Protestant counterparts, who deny that Catholicism can change, Taylor has no trouble arguing that modern Protestantism has liberalized itself. Nevertheless, the novel concludes not with a celebration of Victoria's England but, as Alice O'Hanlon would do some years later, by reminding its readers of Tyborne's Victorian existence "in the midst of bustling, rich, gay London" (267)—an emblem of Catholicism's near-forgotten presence in England's past and present alike.

Lady Georgiana Fullerton, herself a convert and one of the best-known Catholic novelists of the period, became interested in Taylor's work after reading *Tyborne*, and her own *Constance Sherwood: An Autobiography of the Sixteenth Century* (1865) is similarly set during the time of the Penal Laws. Originally commissioned by Taylor for the *Month*, the novel was brought out in three-volume form the same year not by a Catholic press but by both Richard Bentley and Bernard Tauchnitz; it was last reprinted in 1908. *Constance Sherwood* was both a financial and a critical success: Bentley paid Lady Georgiana £300 for the copyright, and the novel sold quite nicely, netting him a profit of just over £190.[40] Unlike *Tyborne*, which was primarily marketed to a Catholic readership, *Constance Sherwood* was aimed at a more ecumenical audience—although, granted, the audience was not uniformly receptive, as Protestant reviewers grudgingly praised "the style" but not the subject matter.[41] Under the circumstances, *Constance Sherwood* offers an extended dialogue with *Tyborne* that attempts to moderate the earlier novel's harsh critique of Protestant myth making.[42] Moreover, it reflects the Catholic equivalent to Protestant anxieties about forgetfulness—in this case, as Christine d'Haussy reminds us, of the English martyrs, who would not be canonized until the twentieth century and who seemed not to excite much enthusiasm among early and mid-Victorian English Catholics.[43] Like Taylor, Lady Georgiana fictionalizes Catholic martyrologies, including Challoner's *Records of Missionary Priests*, although both her secular and her martyrological research is more wide-ranging than Taylor's; in particular, she draws heavily on John Geninges' life of his martyred brother, Edmund Geninges, whose death becomes a major set-piece toward the end of the narrative.[44]

Again, Lady Georgiana shares Taylor's preoccupation with toleration and modern Catholics' vexed relationship to their native land—a set of problems channeled here through a female *bildungsroman*, as the youthful Constance converts to ardent Catholicism and, ultimately, chooses exile. Constance's autobiographical narrative details her growing consciousness of how the government produces treason rather than recognizes it. As she tells John Geninges, "their religion [Catholicism] is made treason by unjust laws, and then punished with the penalties of treason; and they die for no other cause than their faith, by the same token that each of those which have perished on the scaffold had his life offered to him if so he would turn Protestant."[45] Failing Christian unity, the Catholics call for the government to recognize civic allegiance as an essentially *secular* act—a distinction the government refuses to acknowledge.[46] Lady Georgiana unravels the much touted link between Protestantism and liberty of conscience: the true "theorists" of liberty of conscience are not Protestants but disempowered Catholics, for whom such liberty just barely holds together the bleeding wound of a fractured church. The very need to articulate such a concept, in other words, derives from the (supposedly temporary) triumph of Protestant heresy.

While *Constance Sherwood*'s Catholic characters renounce Protestantism, they become disaffected from their queen and country only against their will. Constance's future husband, Basil Rookwood, exiles himself from his home after a visit from the queen turns destructive, most spectacularly in the destruction of a much-loved statue of the Virgin Mary; this violation of the laws of hospitality, justified by Basil's recusancy, embodies the government's willingness to violate and profane Catholic subjective interiors as well. Later, when Constance prepares to follow Basil into exile, she echoes and rewrites Sir Walter Scott's paean to "my own, my native land" in *The Lay of the Last Minstrel*:

I looked at the soft blue sky and fleecy clouds, urged along by a westerly breeze impregnated with a salt savor; on the emerald green of the fields, the graceful forms of the leafless trees on the opposite hills, on the cattle peacefully resting by the river-side. I listened to the rustling of the wind amongst the bare branches over mine head, and the bells of a church ringing far off in the valley. "O England, mine own England, my fair native land—am I to leave thee, never to return?" I cried, speaking aloud, as if to ease my oppressed heart. Then mine eyes rested on the ruined hospital of the town, the shut-up churches, the profaned sanctuaries, and thought flying beyond the seas to a Catholic land, I exclaimed, "The sparrow shall find herself a house, and the turtle-dove a nest for herself—the altars of the Lord of hosts, my king and my God." (257)

Constance renders her attachment to "my fair native land" in sensual, aesthetic terms, a pastoral and picturesque moment devoid not only of people but also at first of any visible signs of human habitation. The moment has a Wordsworthian quality; Constance's apostrophe to England unites her to the natural world, not a world despoiled by recent human history. Even the far-off church is invisible. The church bells that appear to spark Constance's lamentation, however, are no longer Catholic, and the almost magical appearance of Catholic ruins in the landscape determines Constance's willingness to leave. Her instinctive possessiveness ("mine own," "my") falls apart in the face of the traces of *dis*possession. The link between Catholic tradition's physical manifestation and the English countryside has fatally disintegrated. Detaching herself, Constance shifts registers: relinquishing "mine own England," she chooses instead the "Catholic land" defined by the figurative (re)union of nature (Constance as the sparrow or turtle-dove, both familiar from Christian iconography) with the divinely infused home of the "altars." Shifting from geography (England) to creed (Catholic), Constance also shifts her allegiance from an earthly queen to a heavenly king. To be in exile, after all, is *not* to be without a home.

Although the novel rejects Protestantized Englishness, it offers a far more nuanced account of Protestant-Catholic relations than *Tyborne*.

As Kathleen Grant Jaeger notes, *Constance Sherwood* evinces an unusual "breadth of sympathy" for its non-Catholic characters.[47] It is possible that Lady Georgiana had Protestant responses in mind when she rewrote Edmund Geninges' martyrology, for she downplays or eliminates the miraculous elements that would have been most objectionable to a non-Catholic reader: for example, in the original martyrology, Geninges' thumb, which a devout Catholic detaches from the martyr's body in "miraculous" fashion with only a "little pull," here separates from the body only with a realistic tug, no miracle implied.[48] Although Lady Georgiana shares Anglo-Catholic attitudes to the Reformation—there was no reason to be Protestant except to turn a profit, usually from the literal and figurative lives of one's fellow-citizens—she insists that many Protestants aided recusants in times of need and represents some of them, like the spectacularly self-sacrificing Millicent, Lady L'Estrange, as virtual saints. Such apparent conciliatoriness is actually in service of a larger polemical point, common among early and mid-Victorian Catholic novelists, that the Roman Catholic Church did not consider many Protestants to be heretics; a heretic knew the truth but refused to acknowledge it, whereas Protestants were frequently misled by their own authorities.

Lady Georgiana reserves her real condemnation for the fanatical and easily tempted—defined by their uncharitable loathing of their opponents—whose unbalanced psyches swing naturally toward destruction. Her primary examples are Anne Bellamy, the woman who betrayed Robert Southwell to the notorious *pursuivant* (priest-catcher) Richard Topcliffe, and Basil Rookwood's rival for Constance's hand, his Byronesque brother Hubert. Lady Georgiana strongly implies that Topcliffe *seduced* Anne Bellamy, not raped her, which makes Anne an agent in her own spiritual and sexual downfall; as in Taylor, spiritual and erotic transgression go hand-in-hand.[49] Hubert offers a more complicated case: he conforms in order to receive the queen's favor and then abruptly returns to Catholicism, but he develops a "virulent hatred of those in power" (274) and is eventually executed for his participation in the Gunpowder Plot. In a familiar rhetorical strategy, Hubert's story carefully decouples Catholicism from political disloyalty by making violent rebellion emerge from a *collapse* of true faith—the novel's protagonists repeatedly insist on the need to love, forgive, and pray for one's persecutors—instead of a *sign* of faith. Similarly, while Lady Georgiana repeatedly contests Victorian Protestant commonplaces about the St. Bartholomew's Day Massacre, she nevertheless insists in a footnote that the cruelties on both sides resulted from "a blind, violent party spirit, which often acted irrespectively of all control" (279n5) and argues that more thoughtful Huguenots and Catholics were appalled by the acts of their respective co-religionists. Fanatical hatred, in other words, is a universal failing, one that can only be surmounted by truly Christian love; at the same time, persecution emerges from historically specific political contexts, not from within the religions themselves. Lady Georgiana historicizes, and therefore marginalizes, violent persecution, even as she universalizes the effects of true Christian love. Such love, the novel suggests, emerges in local and domestic action, not just (or not even) in the court; when, at the end, Constance bids "farewell" to her "pen and ink," promising to pick them up again only for "such ordinary purposes as housewifery and friendship" (274), she quietly turns away from herself and toward a community of loved ones.

RECONSTRUCTING CATHOLIC SPACES:
HISTORY IN THREE DIMENSIONS

While Catholic historical novels mourn the loss of an organic link between Catholic spirituality and English nationality, Catholic conversion novels draw on history in order to imagine how that link might be restored. Such novels simultaneously critique Protestant historical narratives and map out alternative models that affirm the convert's place within a universal church that is *also* an English, Scottish, or Irish church. In particular, Catholic conversion novels oppose the atomizing tendencies of *sola scriptura* to the community-building work of both tradition and the sacraments. Catholic novelists shift the "entry point" of historical experience, as it were, from private scripture reading to the communal experience of the Mass; Protestant characters who convert must relearn what constitutes reading, interpretation, and, indeed, historical knowledge itself. At the same time, where the historical novels dwell on the collapse of the Catholic landed aristocracy, which leaves the nation bereft of its deepest connections to the past, the conversion novels celebrate the recuperation of originally Catholic spaces: manors return to Catholic ownership and ruins transform back into functioning churches or monasteries. Whereas Scott's *The Monastery* and *The Abbot* insisted on the necessity of Catholic ruins remaining ruins, the better to mark the rupture between Catholic past and Protestant present, Catholic novelists recovered the ruins in order to manifest their very real historical presence in modern time.

In so doing, they update the early modern "sacrilege narrative," which expounded on the theme of families who turned Catholic monastic property to their own personal use—leading, as one might expect, to divinely ordained "decay."[50] In these novels the decay in question may or may not be familial, but it certainly is national. By wrecking, appropriating, and otherwise erasing its Catholic spaces, England has transgressed against God himself. Alison Shell suggests that Victorian attempts to restore Gothic architecture in "an archaeologically correct manner" might have been "motivated in part by instincts of reparation," and certainly these novelists thought that such was the case.[51] Early modern antiquarians like John Bale had already begun the process of trying to reclaim lost Catholic libraries during the sixteenth century, followed by historians, collectors, and architects recording monastery ruins and their contents—even if their motives were sometimes more aesthetic than religious.[52] But nineteenth-century Catholics undertook a large-scale program devoted to restoring and upgrading poorly built, ineptly decorated, or largely ruined places of worship.[53] And in dwelling on restoration, these novels signal an allegiance to Gothic architecture, which A. W. N. Pugin had polemically associated with an expressly *English* Catholicism (as opposed to the new trend for building churches according to neoclassical models).[54] Once again, Roman Catholicism and Englishness become inseparable. Protestant novels marked the passage of history by making the Bible *private*, but Catholics narrated the process of their *public* return to history by reconstructing places of worship.[55]

E. C.[56] Agnew's conversion novel *Geraldine: A Tale of Conscience* (1837–39) was not the first Catholic controversial novel, but next to John Henry Newman's *Loss and Gain* (1848), it was arguably the most famous—and, I will suggest, far more influential. *Geraldine*'s narrative trajectory follows what Penny Edgell Becker has dubbed, in an American context, the "adventuress tale," "pitting the demands of home against the dictates of a religiously informed conscience" to the extent that the title character eventually finds herself asking her husband for a celibate marriage.[57] Like Lady Georgiana Fullerton and Frances Taylor, Agnew was a prominently placed convert; like Taylor, Agnew's Catholicism eventually led her to become a nun, initially joining the Sisters of Mercy as Sister Mary Clare Agnew. *Geraldine*, her first novel, was released in two volumes by the Catholic firm of Booker and Dolman (later Charles Dolman), with its third volume appearing in 1839. It is not clear from internal evidence if Agnew originally intended to stop with the second volume, although if Agnew took her vows after the first two volumes were published, it is possible that autobiographical inspiration drove the third volume's appearance.[58] Although Margaret Maison glumly describes Agnew's "propaganda for the religious life" as "far too feeble and unconvincing to combat the strong and scandalous tradition of 'wicked Jesuit' and 'nunnery-tale' books in England at that time," *Geraldine* in fact sold well: it was soon reprinted in single-volume format and became a popular prize book, reaching a twelfth U.K. edition by 1875.[59] Overseas it was translated into German and French and remained in print in the United States until at least 1911. Its sequel, *Rome and the Abbey* (1849), was much less successful. Reactions to *Geraldine* ranged from wildly enthusiastic to outraged, with some, like a young and anonymous John Henry Newman, castigating it for bad characterization, simplistic theology, and poor history.[60] It was denounced in some Protestant journals and inspired the anti-Catholic author Gorges Lowther to write a novel in response, *Gerald: A Tale of Conscience* (1840), in which an Irish Catholic priest is converted—or, to be less polite, browbeaten into submission—by his evangelical nephew.

Like a number of Catholic controversial novels that preceded it, such as *Florence, or the Aspirant* (1829), *The Biblicals, or Glenmoyle Castle* (1831), and *The Converts: A Tale of the Nineteenth Century* (1837), *Geraldine* takes aim at the most famous anti-Catholic novel of the nineteenth century, the Presbyterian Grace Kennedy's slender *Father Clement* (1823). *Father Clement*, set in 1715, traces the effects of Protestant evangelization on a Catholic family and their priest, the eponymous Father Clement; the narrative consists of theological disquisitions strung along a very fragile thread of plot, climaxing with Father Clement's own implied deathbed conversion. Agnew pokes fun at Kennedy's Presbyterianism in the figure of the hotheaded and stubborn Katherine Graham, and she turns Kennedy's biblicism on its head by devoting much of her first volume to prooftexting in Catholicism's favor. Like *Father Clement*, *Geraldine* subordinates plot to theological exposition, with the "right" side of the debate either reducing the "wrong" side to silence or immediate acquiescence; in addition, like *The Biblicals* and *The Converts*, *Geraldine* sends up evangelical controversial meetings, including the nascent Reformation societies. Again, as with the other responses to Kennedy, Agnew figures Geraldine's conversion in terms of intellectual endeavor as well as affect: Geraldine reads her Bible, ecclesiastical historians like Joseph Milner and Johann Lorenz von Mosheim, and Catholic controversialists like John Milner and John Gother; writes essays on theological topics of note; and debates her findings with a series of clergymen (evangelical and Anglican) and educated laymen.[61] Significantly, unlike *Father Clement*, which represents a Catholic priest swayed by the power of young laymen and laywomen, *Geraldine* insists that its heroine can find authentic answers to her intellectual and spiritual questions only within the domain of the apostolic Catholic priesthood. By relinquishing private judgment—the novel's favorite bugbear, which reduces Protestant England to "wild, unstable conduct"—and acknowledging the Roman Catholic Church's authority to interpret scripture, Geraldine finally learns to decode the providential narrative underlying apparently meaningless moments of suffering.[62]

Agnew represents Protestant ecclesiastical history as a self-deconstructing project that witnesses to Catholicism's truth in the act of repudiating it. Geraldine's readings of Milner and Mosheim, for example, reveal that "during the first five centuries" (before the church became corrupted, according to Protestant apologetics) the Roman Catholic Church upheld such things as the doctrine of purgatory, the adoration of the Eucharist, and the like—all things rejected in practice by the Church of England, even though it claims to accept the "first four councils" that "*confirmed all these things, as articles of faith, against heretics*" (113; emphasis in the original). Far from serving as a median between two extremes, the Anglican *via media* celebrated by Geraldine's High Church uncle rests on a systematic suppression of the very doctrines it claims to uphold. Similarly, Geraldine's readings in the biographies of the major Reformers and narratives of early Protestant history, far from adding up to a triumphalist account of Protestant modernity, suggest instead that "the modern evangelical world is the only thing to which I can liken the dogmatism, coupled with unnecessary vacillation, the violence, the recrimination, and total want of brotherly love, to be found amongst the revolutionists of the sixteenth century" (114). Geraldine's analogy turns Protestant narrative on its head: where Protestant controversialists linked the sixteenth century and the nineteenth century in order to warn readers against the threat of Catholic persecution, Geraldine argues that the psychic violence of modern sectarianism derives from the evangelicals' resemblance to the early Reformers. But note that Geraldine does not turn the *likeness* into a claim for *identity*; the structural similarities do not herald a repetition of the sixteenth century. Instead, the chaos of modern Protestantism emerges from what was not a Reformation but merely a *revolution*, a horrific assault on the Roman Catholic Church traditions that maintained the stability of Christian truths. Protestant history yields no coherent historical narrative; instead, it fragments and collapses, as various incompatible sects spin off and seek to undermine each other. There is, in fact, no Protestant "identity"—just an accumulation of differences. Just as the novel argues that the Roman Catholic Church alone has the authority "to decide the obscure points of Scripture" (152), so too does it suggest that without such authority, there can be no coherent narrative of Christian identity at all. Or, to put it differently, the believer can only learn to position herself vis-à-vis past, present, and future through the medium of Catholic Church tradition, which offers both authoritative interpretations of the scriptures and an incorruptible repository of *eternal* truth.

In this context evangelical Reformation societies repeat history as farce, not tragedy. Agnew's target is the British Society for Promoting the Religious Principles of the Reformation, founded a decade earlier to evangelize in Ireland, and its various offshoots.[63] As Geraldine discovers when she attends a Reformation society meeting, the members explicitly advocate repetition as their goal: "We are here assembled, in the name of the dauntless Luther, to trace the ignorance, the superstition, the idolatry, that he once overthrew. (Hear!) We invoke the spirit of the great Reformer, for the same glorious work. What was their cause, is our cause, and their watchword is our watchword—the Bible, the whole Bible, and nothing but the Bible!!!" (217–18). But this climax from the society's opening speech inadvertently turns anti-Catholic agitation into the modern repetition of a *failed* historical epoch. "Overthrew," after all, suggests that Luther banished Roman Catholic corruptions to the historical rubbish heap, substituting the purified, primitive Christianity of the Bible on which modern Protestantism rests. And yet, the society must "trace" those very heresies that their own religion purportedly conquered. The return of Catholicism, "once" overthrown, signals its ongoing presence within modernity, not its otherness to modernity; far from installing itself as the sole possessor of the religious field the first time around, Protestantism carries forward its failures into the present. Unbeknownst to itself, the Reformation society comes into being only to announce the implosion of its own "cause"—all the more so because it yearns to declare its perfect identity with the Reformation era, down to the bibliocentrism that this novel critiques so sharply elsewhere. Notably, however, this doughty Protestant fails to register the fatal differences between past and present that troubled his real-life brethren—in particular, the disappearance of state-sanctioned violent persecution. As Geraldine quickly realizes, this fantasy of historical repetition actually takes the form of a legitimated fiction: "After the treasurer had sat down, the secretary arose, to read the report of the labours of the society during the preceding year, in which their marches, and counter-marches, being productive of but two instances of seeming success, these anecdotes were thrown into a species of historical romance, for the excited and delighted ladies of Elverton" (218). Modernity, far from yielding up the circumstances of heroic martyrdom, resolves into what looks suspiciously like boredom with the entire neo-Reformation project; the adventures of the would-be modern Reformer instead become sensationalist fodder for feminine consumers—a loaded suggestion, since both sexes are in this meeting's audience. The neo-Reformer is, in a sense, at *religious play*, transforming the life-or-death (literally) subject of man's salvation into a self-perpetuating array of pleasurable "romances."

Agnew's satire on Reformation societies goes further: not only are they farcical in their posturing, but, more seriously, they also promulgate the nothingness that Agnew finds at the heart of Protestantism. That is, the failed history that the Reformation society longs to reenact is a history of pure negativity, in stark contrast to the positive content of Catholic truth. According to an Irish priest who stands up in his church's defense at the meeting, "[f]or three hundred years have the Catholics of these realms declared their faith, and Protestants have refused to hear it! For three hundred years have Catholic books of faith been published, and Protestants have refused to open them! To what, then, have you listened?—to Protestant tradition! What, then, have you read?—Protestant dreams and fictions? and is this the way to understand the faith you condemn?" (232). Mr. O'Neil constructs a lineage of continuous Catholic witnessing, in both books and print, that contrasts sharply with the Protestant triumphalism of "overthrow": Catholicism does not disappear from English (and Irish) history so much as Protestants self-consciously negate its presence. Post-Reformation Catholics, far from being silent or even silenced, disappear from the Protestant historical consciousness thanks to a conspiracy of the "wilfully [*sic*] ignorant" (232)—that is, those Protestants who know that truth rests with the Catholic Church and yet refuse to acknowledge it. Although the priest does not spell it out here, such willful ignorance, as opposed to the ignorance of those who have had no opportunity to know the truth—for example, a child exposed to only anti-Catholic propaganda—is cause for damnation. Such willful ignorance extends not only to Catholics but to Protestant self-awareness; in a familiar trope from Catholic controversial literature, the priest points out that Protestants themselves must adhere to "tradition" in order to supplement the necessary failures of *sola scriptura*, but this tradition has been amputated from Christian history. To be Protestant, in fact, is not to know history at all, to mistake fantastic "dreams" and "fictions" for the true authority bound up with the doctrines of Roman Catholicism. As the etymology of *fiction* suggests, Protestants—victims of private judgment—insist on *making* their history instead of reading it.

Geraldine's journey toward conversion, then, is also a journey toward history, and that history emerges, quite literally, from a ruin. Near the beginning of the novel Geraldine visits the ruined castle at Abbey Hill in the company of Katherine Graham and another family friend, the irenic Mr. Everard, who dreams of reuniting the Church of England with the Roman Catholic Church. Abbey Hill was destroyed in a fit of anti-Catholicism, and thus its ruins testify both to Catholicism's grounding in the English landscape and to Protestantism's essential negativity. Despite his projects and his historical self-awareness, however, Mr. Everard thinks of the ruins primarily in picturesque terms, inviting Geraldine to "draw all this for me, and place me some holy man, engaged in orisons, just within the Abbey; for now we will go within, and decide whether a crumbling breach, or fretted window-arch, shall frame the future picture" (47). Everard's imagined painting revives the vanished past (the holy man) but juxtaposes it against the present fragment; the lost religious order must be appropriately "framed" by the ruins of what once housed it. The result is ambiguous, for although the holy man suggests that Abbey Hill still embodies the essence of Catholic spirituality, Everard nevertheless appropriates the building itself for entirely aesthetic purposes, as a convenient "frame" for an absent religious Other. The perils of Everard's vision become clearer when the explorers enter a largely intact chapel. While the chapel, hidden behind a secret doorway, suggests the possibility that Catholic spirituality persists within the shell of its outward ruin—resisting even the worst ravages of literal and figurative Protestant iconoclasm—Everard emphasizes not the religion but the art. In fact, much to Geraldine's instinctive dismay, Everard clambers onto the altar to show Katherine Graham the painting hanging above it, which he again admires in terms of its craft rather than its spiritual import (49). For Everard, the ruin has value as historical testimony rather than as a functional sacred space. This blind spot derives from Everard's own vision of a reunited church that requires Catholics to abandon such inconveniences as clerical celibacy while Protestants give up only a vague "some thing for the common harmony" (78). Everard's dream, that is, maintains the Reformation project even as it denies programmatic anti-Catholicism; he does not return to the Catholic Church so much as he projects a more appropriate future Reformation. For Everard, Abbey Hill cannot signify as anything except a witness to the ravages of the first Protestant Reformation.

As it turns out, Everard ultimately does take a hand in restoring the abbey to working order—but at the instigation of the devoutly Catholic Eustace de Grey, Geraldine's future husband. Where Everard remains an antiquarian—"And so, my lady . . . , you suppose Miss Carrington fool enough, to believe in seven sacraments, and Transubstantiation, because I have put some painted glass into an arched window?" (251)—Eustace restores the ruins in order to repair the damage done to England by the Reformation itself. Restoration denies that Roman Catholicism belongs to the sphere of antiquarian inquiry and "mere" picturesque aesthetics; instead, it testifies to a rejuvenated Catholic presence within England, one that can reappropriate places of worship from the Protestant's condescending and historicizing gaze. In fact, Geraldine's Catholic friend Lady Winefride's home, which "has never passed from the possession of Catholics," contains a once-secret chapel; as Lady Winefride assures Geraldine, "[y]ou are therefore sheltered in the very bosom of Catholicity, dear child, and may its treasures be yours in rich abundance" (310). Architecture testifies to England's hidden spiritual history, an authentic continuity between past and present that, in turn, stretches beyond England itself to all of "Catholicity." By the same token, the concealed chapels mark the limit points of Protestantism's literally and figuratively violent historicism: such Catholic spaces frustrate Protestantism's will to eradicate all traces of the faith it rejects. As even the ruins testify, Protestants cannot erase the truth, merely vandalize it. Fittingly, Geraldine's spiritual journey ends when she becomes a nun and transforms the abbey into a convent. This final transformation depends on her husband's death, which follows almost immediately after he grants her wish (which he had initially rejected) to maintain a celibate marriage; in effect, the novel's belated third volume insists that Geraldine can love God fully only once she abandons sexualized domesticity for the sanctity of spiritual marriage. Eustace begins the process of reviving Abbey Hill, but he also represents a limit—in terms of both sexual obligations and marital duties more generally—that must be transcended before Abbey Hill can be entirely resacralized. Only those who remain entirely out of the world can restore Roman Catholicism to the world. The presence of restored ruins in later conversion fiction testifies simultaneously to Catholicism's authentic Englishness and to its "sleeping" presence within the Protestant community.

By refusing to regard ruins purely in the light of potential tourist attractions, pleasurable solely because they picturesquely embody England's lost history, Catholic novelists insist that Protestantism represents a mere swerve in English national identity. Thus, Fiorentina Straker's *Immacolata, the Catholic Flower: A Convent Tale* (1860), about a saintly child born from a mixed marriage, begins by invoking those notorious cultural "memories" of convents that "form a heterogeneous mass, too painful for a sensitive mind to dwell upon, too hideous to inquire into," only to celebrate instead

> the remains of an ancient abbey, which, like so many others, had survived the faith of our fathers, and remains a tradition of those days of old when England was all Catholic. In many instances, a modern creed has profaned those walls, but in vain; the old stone is full of the memories of an undying faith, the altar breathes still of the mystic sacrifice, and the crypts, where English dust has accumulated for ages, impregnate the very air with Catholic immortality.[64]

The novel opens by invoking the stereotyped narratives that structure all Protestant encounters with convents—indeed, that render convents

Gothic spaces, impenetrable to the Protestant gaze because already described *too* clearly. Protestant culture turns the convent into a monstrous site—"Auto da fe, inquisitions, and deeds of crime" (1)—the last remnant of a purportedly long-gone history of unimaginable physical violence. The Protestants' "memories" overwrite Catholic Englishness with an astonishing hodgepodge of international bugbears; far from reading history in the ruins, Protestants ruin international borders in their rush to keep their distance. And yet, the narrator slyly remarks, these are "obsolete visions" (1), historicizing the very Protestant imagination that seeks to keep Catholic spaces in their proper places. As the narrator's description of the abbey suggests, it and its fellows not only testify to England's true Catholic origins but also *actively* resist the supposedly Protestant nature of modernity: even the "dust" cannot silence the living Catholic faith embodied in the abbeys' very walls. Protestantism is merely "modern," a temporary aberration in the historical record; Catholicism, by contrast, both is the essence of history itself and exists out of history's destructive reach.

This historical mode in conversion fiction is taken to its furthest extreme near the end of the century in Laetitia Selwyn Oliver's positively reviewed first novel, *Father Placid; Or, the Custodian of the Blessed Sacrament* (1884), which melds the Protestantized Catholic manor with a Gothic horror tale—or, at least, so it first appears. Oliver sets the tale in Trevayler Hall, occupied by the Protestant Sir Herbert Vyvyan; as it happens, Sir Herbert is "the last of his race," a historical dead end.[65] Far from being fanatically anti-Catholic, Sir Herbert makes no effort to convert his Catholic niece, Gertrude, or to interfere with the religion of his friend (and the novel's protagonist), Everard Neville, who has been disowned by his family (9). But the Vyvyans turn out to have a horrific skeleton in their closet: in 1600 the Benedictine Father Placid, who was hidden in the Hall, was betrayed and murdered by Richard Vyvyan, the heir to the estate (13). Not surprisingly, the now-Protestant Richard "died raving mad in the very room where the murder was committed" (15), and the family now believes itself to labor under some mysterious curse—not counting the ghost of Father Placid himself, still thought to remain in that room.

So far, so conventionally Gothic. Father Placid's murder marks a double betrayal: of himself and of the Catholic Church. By murdering the monk and converting to Protestantism, Richard Vyvyan apparently amputates his family from the spiritual and historical mainstream; at the same time, the very presence of the monk's ghost, several centuries later, implies that the Catholic "spirit" (quite literally) abides within the household. The Vyvyans are a family haunted and scarred by Protestantism's violent history, subject (thanks to the ghost) to repeated reminders about the criminal disgrace that allowed them to retain the Hall.

If this were a conventional gothic novel, then the haunting would signal that Father Placid's murder needs to be avenged in order to liberate the family from its curse. Instead, however, the reader discovers that interpreting the ghost in Gothic terms entirely misreads the case. Everard Neville is on the right track when he announces that "[i]f some Catholic were to give it an opportunity it might appear and speak" (17); the living Catholic elicits the voice of the supposedly dead Catholic past, turning the transaction into one of Christian charity rather than gothic terror. Both Everard and Gertrude refer to the spirit as a "martyr" (20, 23), and this insight crucially shifts the tale's genre: far from being a gothic text, it is in fact a fictional martyrology structured around a miracle—Father Placid's spirit protects a hidden cache that includes, most importantly, "the *Blessed Sacrament*" in a "jewelled [*sic*] monstrance" (42; emphasis in the original).[66] In this instance the family doesn't need to relinquish its property to the church; it needs to relinquish *itself* to the church (which will have the happy side effect of re-Catholicizing the property), in part by explicitly recognizing Father Placid's status as martyr rather than avenging spirit.

Everard had earlier mourned the relative obscurity of the English martyrs, comparing the "devotion" to foreign saints like St. Teresa of Avila with the "indifference and coldness" meted out to native heroes like Margaret Clitherow (or Clitheroe, who would finally be canonized, along with the other figures on Everard's list, in 1970) (34–35). This echo of the Protestant complaint about historical amnesia suggests that England's current state—"our benighted fellow-countrymen still wallowing in the mire of heresy and schism" (34)—derives from English Catholicism's denationalization of itself, its unwillingness to celebrate its own identity as part of, but not identical to, Continental Catholic culture. Oliver's fictional martyrology not only puts her compatriots in direct competition with their more famous counterparts, who were denied "that privilege of martyrdom" (35), but also hints at the power of an authentically English Catholic mindset. By rereading the haunting in terms of martyrology instead of the Gothic, Everard turns the ghost's presence into an act of witnessing to God's truth, not an inescapable repetition of man's sinfulness. Quite literally, Father Placid's presence represents a blessing, not a curse.

This discovery joins the dead martyr and the living man in mutual contemplation of the divine, momentarily erasing the temporal, cultural, and religious chasm dividing pre- and post-Reformation England. At the same time, this miracle changes the nature of the haunting from a stern indictment of Protestantism to, instead, a loving celebration of Catholicism's essence; far from signifying the family's unalterable affiliations with Protestant heresy, it instead demonstrates that Christ—and, by extension, Catholicism—has been harbored and protected within the Hall, merely awaiting a Catholic's right interpretation in order to awaken it. Not surprisingly, "heresy" begins to ebb away almost immediately: the entire family converts (56), along with most of their dependents, and the apparently infertile Lady Laura and Sir Hubert suddenly find themselves blessed with a surfeit of sons (57). Everard and Gertrude, far from becoming a romantic couple, both happily pursue their vocations in the church, thereby solemnizing spiritual marriages that balance the Vyvyan family conversions. While this miraculous cluster of conversions and vocations verges on self-parody, it nevertheless suggests at least two polemical points: first, that the English are instinctively attracted to the Catholic faith once it has been presented to them; second, that only the Catholic mind can truly engage with the English past. Protestantism is an unnatural religion, as it were, separating the English from their organic faith. In effect, gothic horror reigns only under the horrific, heretical sway of Protestant thinking; martyrology, by contrast, demonstrates that miracles and modernity are inseparable. If we read the novel's conclusion as unintentionally comical, we make the mistake of historicizing (or compartmentalizing) the working of miracles—and, therefore, merely repeat the Protestant's error.

It may be noticed that John Henry Newman's *Loss and Gain* (1848) has not figured in this account, and that is precisely because Newman stands *against* this historical mode in conversion narratives. As Ian Ker notes, *Loss and Gain* is about why a convert might come to accept the Catholic Church's authority, not what the Catholic ought to believe, and this shift in emphasis positions historical consciousness as the *antecedent* to conversion, not the result of it.[67] Just as importantly, by the time of *Loss and Gain*, Newman had long since shed any interest in yoking Catholicism to a singular architectural mode; if anything, he had come to feel that Pugin's Gothic medievalism mistook the right relation between the church and history by fetishizing a single past epoch instead of the living church.[68] In what looks very much like a rejection of *Geraldine*'s revived ruin, Newman has his protagonist, Charles Reding, experience his first Catholic Mass in a new building operated by the Passionists, themselves new to England in the nineteenth century. As the narrator explains,

> [i]t was a plain brick building; money had not been so abundant as to overflow upon the exterior, after the expense of the interior had been provided for. And it was incomplete; a large church had been enclosed, but it was scarcely more than a shell,—altars, indeed, had been set up, but for the rest, it had little more than good proportions, a broad sanctuary, a serviceable organ, and an effective choir.[69]

Far from emphasizing a deep continuity with the English landscape and English history, as is the case with the ruined abbeys and manor houses, Newman insists on the novelty of this unfinished metropolitan building, founded by an explicitly foreign order. There is no mention of aesthetic appeal—indeed, Newman earlier mocks the Anglo-Catholic fascination with church ornaments that have been stripped of their original theological context—and no suggestion that the architecture has anything especially noteworthy about it. Earlier, a priest tells Charles that "Englishmen have many gifts, faith they have not. Other nations, inferior to them in many ways, still have faith" (265), and his argument suggests that calls to recognize the essential Englishness of Catholicism miss the central point. The Catholic faith's purpose, after all, is not to render English history more intelligible but to lead men to salvation; the appeal to history, Newman suggests, substitutes the nationalist trees for the universal forest. In this novel it takes the *foreign* Passionists to render the absence of faith visible and to reconsolidate English Catholic worship. But Agnew, not Newman, appears to have exerted the stronger pull on later novelists.

CONCLUSION

At the end of the nineteenth century one American Catholic author, surveying with approval the effects of historical scholarship on contemporary attitudes, asked "Who would describe Henry VIII. as the 'bluff and honest Hal,' or Queen Elizabeth as the 'good Virgin-Queen Bess,' or Mary Tudor as 'Bloody Mary,' or Mary, Queen of Scots, as a 'fiend in human flesh'?" Our author was perhaps somewhat overoptimistic.[70] Nevertheless, Catholics from Lingard onward developed a counternarrative to the "official" Protestant version that, as Nicholas Tyacke points out, finds itself echoed today in the work of the revisionist school in Reformation studies.[71] Catholic fictions of the Reformation represented it as a traumatic moment in European history, yet one that could be healed by a turn away from the atomizing emphasis on the Bible and toward the communal experience of the Mass. Moreover, these novels reminded their readers that any evil attending on Catholic rule derived solely from the effect of *context*— a context long gone in the nineteenth century. Fixing history was a matter of remembering the "right" martyrs, not to mention restoring the sacred to places of worship despoiled by Protestant assaults. But as we shall see in the final chapter, Charles Dickens laid out a path for the historical novel that tried to rule out evangelicals, Anglicans, and Catholics alike from imagining the future by returning to the past.

Chapter Six

REJECTING THE CONTROVERSIAL
HISTORICAL NOVEL

Barnaby Rudge

At first glance, Charles Dickens's *Barnaby Rudge* (1841), set during the anti-Catholic Gordon Riots of 1780, maps exactly onto the intellectual and formal concerns of Reformation tales: it addresses the role of toleration in shaping religious and national identity, the historical grounds of nineteenth-century Protestant belief, and the problematic place of Catholics within a Protestant social order. Moreover, it participates in and engages with the explicitly historical arguments for and against toleration on all sides of the debate, as well as with the burgeoning trend for religious historical fiction more generally. And, quite expressly, the novel's anti-Catholic agitators represent themselves as agents of a Reformation cause—on the side of Queen Elizabeth, not Bloody Mary.

But *seems* is the operative word. Critics have frequently pointed to *Barnaby Rudge*'s paradoxical status as an actively antihistorical historical novel, particularly in its rejection of Sir Walter Scott's Enlightenment-based, contextual model of historical explanation, in which human action and agency are necessarily shaped by the immediate environment. As discussed in chapter 1, Walter Scott's Reformation duology historicized both the Reformation and its representation as the effects of an "age": just as receptiveness to Bible reading emerged from a specific sixteenth-century moment, so too do Scott's own novels emerge from an irrefutably post-Reformation Scottish Protestant culture. Scott argues, in effect, that it has become impossible to think about, let alone with, Catholicism in any meaningful way. By contrast, when it comes to Dickens and *Barnaby Rudge*, Alison Case argues that "[h]istorical consciousness is hence replaced by an ahistorical family, and by a moral code which is supposed to transcend historically conditioned, class- or culture-bound values."[1] Others have pointed out that *Barnaby Rudge* casts a skeptical eye on supposedly empirical historical narratives—even on any attempt to produce "a coherent narrative of historical events."[2] Indeed, most readers cannot help noticing that the novel consistently associates the past with death, violence, and ghostliness; characters invested in the past exist in a self-defeating half-life, verging on the undead themselves. Further, the novel echoes its willfully disruptive attitude to its own genre in its treatment of its ostensible subject. Although Dickens initially prefaced the novel with a warning against repeating the political errors of the past, his dislike for all those with a dog in the hunt makes the novel's own attitude to Catholicism in general, let alone Roman Catholic toleration, difficult to pin down. If the novel argues against the dangerous social effects of any and all raging religious agitations—Avrom Fleishman suggests that Dickens portrays the riots as a "pogrom"[3]—it also questions the justifications for the toleration it "supports." Dickens himself was a doctrinaire (even rather dull) anti-Catholic, as his travel narrative *Pictures from Italy* (1846) makes clear. D. G. Paz succinctly observes that "[a]lthough Dickens disliked Roman Catholicism, he also disliked anti-Catholicism and Evangelicalism,"[4] and this all-around disdain manifests itself in the novel's conflicted treatment of the plot's most vocal critic of anti-Catholic practices.

But *Barnaby Rudge*'s resistance to Scott does not make it a friend to religious historical fiction. *Barnaby Rudge* mounts a radical, bi-level challenge to both evangelical anti-Catholics and advocates of Catholic toleration on the bases of generic form and intellectual content. As we have seen, evangelical authors dwelt insistently on the need to obsessively *remember* Protestantism's violent sixteenth-century birth, the better to consolidate Protestant identity in the present; toleration, which evangelicals equated with historical amnesia, fractured Protestantism's ongoing narrative of historical identifications, repetitions, analogies, and typologies. And those in favor of Catholic toleration, whether liberal Protestants (with whom Dickens has been frequently identified) or Catholics themselves, called on their contemporaries to *historicize* the past. Catholic intolerance, they argued, emerged from a complex set of theological, social, political, and economic imperatives, none of which obtained in the nineteenth century; having historicized Catholic practices, then, British Protestants could "modernize" themselves (and their country) by liberating Catholics from their outmoded civil restrictions. But Dickens's critique of history and historicization disrupts any argument for or against toleration based on historical practices. By the same token, Dickens rejects not only Sir Walter Scott but the foundations of the emergent religious historical novel, which insisted on the potency of cultural memory to guard against Protestant—and, later, Catholic—collapse.

Dickens, *The Heart of Midlothian*, and Moderation

While critics have frequently noted that *Barnaby Rudge* undoes Scott's *The Heart of Midlothian*—with the Gordon Riots serving as hellish commentary on the Porteous Riots that begin Scott's work— they have not discussed the extent to which *Barnaby Rudge* also engages with that novel's narrative of religious moderation (which it holds in common with the Reformation novels of two years later). Jeanie Deans's father, Davie Deans, is a "tough true-blue Presbyterian" who maintains his allegiance to Covenanting principles.[5] By contrast, Jeanie's love interest and eventual husband, the university-educated clergyman Reuben Butler, is equally a man of "stanch presbyterian principles" (88) but nevertheless a minister in the established Church of Scotland. As his domestic tragedy plays out, Davie grumpily gains sympathy for Reuben, finally joining Reuben's congregation while vocally refusing to "compromise[e] any whit of his former professions, either in practice or principle" (449). While Scott plays the resulting familial strife for gentle comedy, he nevertheless does so by figuring Davie as a historical relic, capable of adapting only so far to the mildly cosmopolitan (albeit still strict) outlook of his son-in-law's more theologically and culturally informed Presbyterianism. Jeanie herself tries to smooth things over through a narrative of modern decline, in which the age of ministers receiving "downright revelation" gives way to those who search the scriptures for divine guidance (450). The narrative folds Davie's militant, intransigent beliefs into the established church without moderating them, while it finds the temporary solution to the resulting conflicts in domestic affect: mutual toleration derives not from any change in principles but from the routines of everyday family life. At the same time, Davie remains a relic. His namesake and grandson David Butler inherits the "military spirit" of his Covenanting ancestor, "Bible Butler," but apparently not his religious practices (506). But while the protagonists quietly assimilate themselves to polite conformity, the fallen Effie, now Lady Staunton, can only assuage her grief and guilt by converting to Catholicism and immuring herself in a Continental convent (507). Butler's response succinctly illuminates the nature of moderate Presbyterianism: for him, "any religion, however imperfect" is better than no religion at all (507). By the same token, Scott sanctions an interfaith marriage at the end of *The Abbot*, but only after ensuring that Catholicism as a political and cultural force has been thoroughly delegitimized. Scott's modernizing Scotland apparently has little to no *physical* space for Catholics, but it manages to find *conceptual* space to identify Catholic religious sincerity.

Scott's narrative of religious modernization relies on a gendered division of spiritual labor. Men perform public and professional religious duties, such as preaching, but they also carry on outright theological warfare (and, in the case of the Covenanters, literal warfare). But such public religion rests on the private, affective work of women like Jeanie, whose domestic interpretations of scriptural lessons calm the troubled waters of theological debate. Without Jeanie's unofficial intervention, the intergenerational strife between Davie and Reuben might explode into a dangerous repetition of outright Covenanting principles; her "unprejudiced and attentive ear" (450) allows Jeanie to productively transform unbending Presbyterian positions into something more workable. Jeanie's "practical" Christianity, while not rooted in Reuben's book learning, serves the conservative function of substituting historical *change* for historical *rupture*. After all, even the story she tells Davie implicitly casts him as the product of a bygone radical age, in which God spoke directly to mankind. In effect, Jeanie's account of her father's circumstances reconciles him to his place as the last authentic voice of Covenanting principles in a degraded world, which he restrains himself from using only because it would cause distress within the household. Davie still yearns for the good old days, in which couples who had sex out of wedlock could be punished even if they got married afterwards, but he relinquishes his dream of a thoroughly public Presbyterianism in favor of private harmony. Effie's retreat to a convent, however, abjures the feminine role of peacemaker altogether; instead, as Magdalen Graeme will at the end of *The Abbot*, she chooses an extreme penitential self-discipline, defined by Roman Catholicism's "formal observances, vigils, and austerities" (507). Unlike the discursive and emotional activity of Jeanie's Presbyterianism, which transforms religious practice even as it preserves it, the explicitly ritualized, entirely feminized world of Effie's Catholicism substitutes endless repetitions for historical process. Moreover, Effie's choice does not assimilate her father's Covenanting background but instead denies it entirely: embracing Catholicism strikes at everything the Solemn League and Covenant stood for. It is no surprise, then, that Effie can only be Catholic *outside* of Scotland, for her decision simultaneously rejects the past (the Covenanting heritage), the present (the move toward a moderated, establishment Presbyterianism), and, implicitly, the future (a nonpersecuting nation maintained by domestic tranquility).

Barnaby Rudge has no Covenanters, but its evangelical agitators are similarly committed to the past. During our first encounter with Lord George Gordon, the convert Gashford reads current events as a ghastly resurrection of the past: "At a crisis like the present, when Queen Elizabeth, that maiden monarch, weeps within her tomb, and Bloody Mary, with a brow of gloom and shadow, stalks triumphant—"[6] Lord John's servant, John Grueby, promptly undercuts Gashford's invocation of Bloody Mary by grumbling that Mary has "done a deal more harm in her grave than she ever did in her lifetime, I believe" (333). Later, he prophesizes (accurately) that "[o]ne of these evenings, when the weather gets warmer and Protestants are thirsty, they'll be pulling London down—and I never heard that Bloody Mary went as far as *that*" (342; emphasis in the original). This contrast between Gashford and Grueby reworks the relationship between anti-Catholic rhetoric and history on a number of levels. For the moment, at least, Gashford adheres to the Gothic reading of history discussed earlier in this volume: he interprets the present as a horrific repetition of a past conflict and, in so doing, upends the historical order of the monarchs and their respective faiths. Catholic toleration repeats history in a perverted key. But if Queen Elizabeth sits consigned to her tomb, then Protestantism itself has already "died" (or become undead?), turning this battle of faiths into something resembling a clash of the vampires. Gashford's anti-Catholic language turns around on itself, inadvertently rendering Protestantism as deathly as the Catholicism that "stalks" through the land. Grueby, however, embodies the kind of "goodwill based on reason and common sense" that Dennis Walder identifies as this novel's moral ideal.[7] His tart response reburies Queen Mary, as it were; by translating Gashford's metonymic queen into the literal body, Grueby plants Mary in the grave while calling the source of her purported agency into question. Where Gashford asserts that the sixteenth century has returned to haunt the English landscape, the impatient Grueby insists on the bodily needs of the present (his lordship needs dry clothes) and argues that the past might as well remain dead. Grueby's dour assessment of Protestantism's potential for mob action suggests that Protestants indict Catholics for their own dangerous moral failings, while he uses Mary as an ironic historical limit point: the most important thing to know about the queen is not what she did, but what she did *not* do, a lesson the Protestants apparently do not care to learn.

If, as Jason B. Jones argues, *Barnaby Rudge* "represents history as a generalized haunting," then Grueby's disinclination to see Queen Mary anywhere else than in her grave constitutes what should be a powerful alternative: in refusing to recast the present in terms of an undead past, Grueby also rejects the notion that the past provides a sufficient narrative template for the present.[8] And yet, Gashford's quasi-apocalyptic rhetoric—which casts history in terms of conflict between Protestant and Catholic, virgin queen and bloody queen— adheres remarkably well to the novel's structure. As more than one critic has noted, *Barnaby Rudge* unfolds as a series of complex doublings (for example, the elder Rudge and Chester observing their previously unrecognized sons while they sleep) and binary differences (for example, Haredale vs. Chester), which are in turn echoed by the novel's own split into halves.[9] Gashford's vision of Protestant good vs. Catholic evil is, in terms of its overall conception, no different than the line Dickens chooses to draw between, say, the elder Rudge and Gabriel Varden. The problem becomes more clear if we look at two dialogue exchanges, one famous and one not:

> "No Popery, brother!" cried the hangman.
> "No Property, brother!" responded Hugh. (359)

> "Times are changed, Mr Haredale, and times have come when we ought to know friends from enemies, and make no confusion of names." (612)

Hugh's famous slip of the tongue prophetically identifies an attack on one segment of the populace with an attack on the entire concept of private property; "no Popery" promises to create an evenly distributed Protestant nation, but "no Property" suggests a threatening world of total, devalued liquidity. Ned Dennis, the hangman, responds ominously but offhandedly to Hugh's error that "It's all the same! . . . It's all right" (359). Like Gashford, who (at least for momentary rhetorical purposes) presumes that the sixteenth century has been translated wholesale into the late eighteenth, Dennis denies the existence of any significant difference between two very different things. In both cases the reader understands that some things are not supposed to be inter-changeable, whether past and present or religion and property. At the same time, though, both Gashford and Dennis do maintain at least the *fiction* of a binary opposition between Roman Catholicism (bad) and Protestantism (good). Hugh's mistake of two letters is, in fact, a "con-fusion of names," an inability to keep things distinct and in their proper place, exactly the thing that Joe Willett warns Mr. Haredale against in the second quotation. Joe Willett, the long-lost son finally returned from America, insists that there are, after all, absolute and knowable differences between "friends" and "enemies," and indeed his reappear-ance in the plot signals the beginning of its movement toward consoli-dating friends (through marriage, among other things) and ejecting foes. Given that anti-Catholic agitation itself promises to tell friend from foe, though, what makes *its* stark distinction between Protestant England and Catholic Other so wrong?

NAMING NAMES

Paradoxically, the first part of the problem lies in anti-Catholi-cism's inability to be binary *enough*. That is to say, the novel repre-sents the entire anti-Catholic project as a confusion of names. We see this in the novel's first half: the Protestant Sir John Chester's feud with the Catholic Mr. Haredale raises the problem of religious difference, only to suggest the extent to which that difference is interchangeable with other, more pressing questions. Sir John enters his religious ob-jections to the possibility of his son marrying Haredale's niece, but he does so only in a dependent clause: "But the thing is, Haredale—for I'll be very frank, as I told you I would at first—independently of any dislike that you and I might have to being related to each other, and in-dependently of the religious differences between us—and damn it, that's important—I couldn't afford a match of this description" (145). The real meat of the objection is economic, given that Sir John's fi-nances do not coincide with his standard of living. In this sentence "religious difference" carries no more or less weight than "dislike" and counts for less than cash. For Sir John, this very local instance of "no Popery" really *is* an example of "no Property"—only, in this instance, "no Property" stands for Chester's lack thereof, not his desire to eradicate same. Given that Hugh is also Sir John's illegitimate son, Hugh's Popery/Property slip becomes an example of the son's parodic inversion of the father's priorities. If Sir John measures his language and Hugh falters in his (although, by novel's end, Hugh will burst out in prophetic eloquence), both confuse religious belief with economics. In fact, Sir John believes thoroughly in the liquidity of religion; as he later says to his son Edward, "In a religious point of view alone, how could you ever think of uniting yourself to a Catholic, unless she was amazingly rich?" (176). For Sir John, Protestantism signifies no more and no less than the dominant social grouping, to which Catholics *may* be admitted by marriage if they come equipped with the right amount of cash. Given the choice between God and Mammon, Sir John comes down in favor of the latter. From the "religious point of view," Sir John believes in nothing in particular—not because he is too tolerant but because his Protestantism shifts about to accommodate any convenient signification necessary. Even though he introduces the novel's anti-Catholic theme during his conversation with Haredale, Sir John merely deploys *Protestant* as a cover for various nefarious ends; as we see in his theological seduction of Mrs. Varden, keeping other characters in the dark about "friends" and "enemies" is the very basis of his *modus operandi*. It is in his personal and political interest to keep the names of things confused.

For Dickens, then, anti-Catholic agitation becomes problematic because it is never *about* Catholicism; it is always about something else—whether money (Sir John), general mayhem (Hugh), the good old days of capital punishment (Ned Dennis), or the apprentices' utopia (Sim Tappertit). "No Popery" is just one more empty sign, deployed to cover up for some decidedly unsavory signifiers. As constructed by Protestants, the distinction between Protestantism and Popery never makes it beyond the level of illusion and self-delusion—epitomized in the increasingly obvious madness of Lord George himself, who speaks with an undertone of "something wild and ungovernable which broke through all restraint" (340). Fittingly, Lord George fears to be called by the right name. Confronted with Barnaby Rudge for the first time, Lord George twice blushes at the possibility of eccentricity being equated with insanity, even by accident; he writes off Barnaby's mental state as a "trifling peculiarity" because "'[w]hich of us'—and here he turned red again—'would be safe, if that were made the law?'" (444). This time, Gashford unctuously reassures Lord George about Barnaby and, by extension, about himself. The next time, though, Lord George makes the mistake of asking Grueby if "'because one man dresses unlike another,' returned his angry master, glancing at himself, 'and happens to differ from other men in his carriage and manner, and to advocate a great cause which the corrupt and irreligious desert, he is to be accounted mad, is he?'" Grueby, not one to mince words, replies, "Stark, staring, raving, roaring mad, my lord" (520). In both cases Lord George tries to rationalize madness away by translating it into some other, less threatening characteristic, whether a "peculiarity" or simply a state of unlikeness. His linguistic sleight-of-hand with madness resembles the rhetorical tricks at work in anti-Catholic agitation more generally, in which "no Popery" always means something other than it says—only, in this instance, Lord George accidentally manifests his insanity by willfully rejecting what he knows to be true, namely, his (genteel) resemblance to Barnaby. Grueby, by contrast, presumes that external signs (Barnaby's physicality) accurately represent internal states and refuses to allow any slippage into this system of reference. The one man around Lord George who can tell past from present is, not coincidentally, also the one man who believes that representation works in commonsensical, even organic, terms. Lord George's system requires its practitioners to confuse their words; even Lord George's ongoing sense of self requires confusion in order to maintain itself. Grueby, of course, must be temporarily ejected from Lord George's orbit, lest his ability to tell any sort of difference bring the entire project crashing to a halt.

Dickens not only turns anti-Catholic agitation into an apparently infinite chain of wrongly interchangeable links, but he also performs the same operation on conversions from Catholicism to Protestantism.

From the beginning, as we have seen, evangelical and Catholic novels alike associated conversion with historical process; individual conversions foretold the ultimate transformation of the nation into a unified Protestant or Catholic polity. But as Gauri Viswanathan notes, *Barnaby Rudge* totally lacks "surprise conversions."[10] Even before we take explicitly religious conversion into account, it's worth noting that almost *nobody* in this novel changes their mind about *anything*: the only notable examples are Haredale, who allows Edward to marry his niece, and Mrs. Varden, who abandons both anti-popery and her poor treatment of her husband. (It is difficult to classify John Willet's later attitude to his son Joe as a "change of mind," since John reunites with Joe only after his permanent mental collapse.) By contrast, we know that Gashford is a villain in part because he *has* converted from Catholicism to Protestantism, while Miggs's attempt to convert Emma Haredale rapidly makes Miggs "rather a nuisance than a comfort" (639). While Dickens casts Miggs's evangelical project as a comical exercise in egotism, he makes Gashford's religious mobility a sign of his untrustworthiness:

> —"Dreamed he was a Jew," he said thoughtfully, as he closed the bedroom door. "He may come to that before he dies. It's like enough. Well! After a time, and provided I lost nothing by it, I don't see why that religion shouldn't suit me as well as any other. There are rich men among the Jews; shaving is very troublesome;—yes, it would suit me well enough. For the present, though, we must be Christian to the core. Our prophetic motto will suit all creeds in their turn, that's a comfort." (350)

Dickens deconstructs the classic evangelical conversion narrative, in which the convert first becomes convinced of his sinful nature, then fully accepts Christ as his savior. By contrast, Gashford, who claims to have been converted by the "magic" of Lord George's "eloquence" (340), changes faith as a matter of enlightened self-interest; even the terms of his conversion, spurred by Lord George's language, substitute man's influence for God's. Like Chester, Gashford finds religion interchangeable with cash ("rich men"), when he doesn't reduce it to an absolutely trivial exercise, equivalent to shaving or not shaving. Indifferent to any religion in particular, Gashford dons the clothes of any religion suitable to his immediate purposes. In fact, given that Gashford's attitude to religion is identical to Chester's, the narrative presents us with a difference that is not one: Gashford converts the better to remain in the same place. Despite his ironic claim to being "Christian to the core," Gashford not only has no core, but more to the point, his conversion singularly fails to do its duty; there has been no drastic reorientation of self toward God here. For that matter, Gashford's willingness to entertain converting to Judaism, as Lord George really would near the end of his life, indicates an indifference that, from the mainstream nineteenth-century Christian point of view, threatens to reverse history's trajectory altogether: to become Jewish would mean reinstituting the Law superseded by Christ's coming. Gashford's initially startled reaction to the dream—"Heaven forbid, my lord! We might as well be Papists" (349)—draws on the polemical link between Judaism and Catholicism that had been established during the Reformation and remained current throughout the nineteenth century. Far from equating non-Christian and Christian, the Judaism-Catholicism analogy actually presumes that Catholicism is as non-Christian as Judaism; Gashford is on solid Protestant ground in his initial retort. Gashford's willingness to convert to Judaism, given the right financial terms, only becomes shocking because he equates it with the "scriptural" religion, Protestantism.[11]

To put it differently: far from experiencing conversion as a new consciousness of his place in the grand biblical narrative of salvation and damnation, Gashford interprets it as a purely local tactic for self-aggrandizement. Even more, Gashford's conversion is a failed attempt to escape his own personal history as, in Haredale's terms, a "servile, false, and truckling knave" (406). Haredale's indignant "Do you know this man?" (406) anticipates Joe Willett's insistence that Haredale himself needs to "know friends from enemies"; in a novel that insists on putting characters into clearly defined boxes, religious conversion threatens the possibility of such definitive knowledge. If anything, changing religion (or, in Miggs's case, changing to the explicitly evangelical form of religion) signals the convert's *lack* of interior conviction. Both Gashford and Miggs practice religion as an antisocial and antihistorical art, Gashford on the grand scale (by using it to facilitate the riots) and Miggs on the small (by disrupting both the Varden household and the equanimity of Dolly and Emma). By contrast, when Haredale changes his mind about Edward or Mrs. Varden abandons her anti-popery, the results explicitly restore harmony—albeit, and perhaps pointedly, on a very small scale. Moreover, both Haredale and Mrs. Varden associate their change of mind with an increased self-consciousness that is accompanied by shame: Haredale confesses to Edward that "I have done you wrong, and I ask your forgiveness" (707), while Mrs. Varden, who earlier had become "impressed with a secret misgiving that she had done wrong" (473), more comically learns to "joi[n] the laugh against herself" (715). In both instances, the characters experience a more authentic, even more orthodox, *religious* conversion than Gashford or Miggs, despite the fact that neither conversion resorts to the expected theological terminologies or narratives—and despite the fact that Haredale remains Catholic and Mrs. Varden apparently abandons her evangelicalism. This Dickensian model of conversion takes as its immediate object not the convert's personal salvation but his or her relationship to the domestic circle. The novel praises these conversions because they are *other*-directed, moments in which the characters realize how their behavior has undermined the happiness of their friends and family. As a result, the sign of a true conversion is the spread of pleasure in the household, not the visible godliness of the convert.[12]

As should be clear by now, Dickens turns the tropes of anti-Catholic, antitolerationist rhetoric against their users. In *Barnaby Rudge* the advocates for absolute interchangeability are all in the anti-Catholic camp. Anti-Catholic agitation, combined with evangelical propaganda tactics, leads to the apocalyptic social collapse of the riots. Meanwhile, the illusory attachment to history associated with Gashford and Lord George parodies the evangelical call to remember (and possibly reenact) the lessons of the sixteenth century, even as it also

sends up the Covenanting obsession with a bygone warrior faith featured in *The Heart of Midlothian*. But we must be careful here, for
Dickens's cannon fires wildly. Mr. Haredale, who offers the novel's
most extended critiques of a Protestant system that disadvantages
Catholics, nevertheless shares not only the Protestant fixation on the
past but also the elder Rudge's extensive associations with death. The
intergenerational conflicts of *The Heart of Midlothian* (and the Reformation duology, for that matter) multiply rapidly in this novel,
and Protestant agitators are not the only characters to be trapped by
a deadly yearning for history. *Barnaby Rudge*'s narrator tells us that
Dolly Varden has always "associated with this gentleman the idea
of something grim and ghostly" (214), and while we might put this
down to Dolly's personality, her sentiments are frequently echoed
elsewhere—not least by Haredale himself. When it comes to the past,
Haredale's objection to Edward Chester rests entirely on the evil character of Edward's father, Sir John. Similarly, he is obsessed with his
brother's murder. He admits to Gabriel Varden that he has "brooded
on that subject [the murder] so long, that every breath of suspicion
carries me back to it" (261), and later goes on to confess that he is
"haunted" by it (394), echoing the elder Rudge's own haunting by the
murder victim (560). Even though Haredale "converts," in the sense of
allowing Edward Chester's love for Emma to trump Haredale's obsession with Sir John, this conversion does not free him from the
past; instead, it sends him hurtling toward the final confrontation with
Sir John—prophesied since their very first meeting in the novel—
in which the two men duel to the death. Far from being liberating,
Sir John's death only solidifies Haredale's decision to leave for the
Continent, where, like Effie, he dies a few years later in a monastery
known for the "merciless penitence" required of its inmates (731).

Dying to the World

In yoking Haredale's figurative death (to the world) to Sir John's
literal death, Dickens consigns *both* men to a past that needs forgetting.

Where Mrs. Varden's conversion results in rejuvenated domesticity—a life of communal pleasure with her husband, daughter, and soon-to-be son-in-law—Haredale's entombs him in his own religion: he takes "the vows which thenceforth shut him out from nature and his kind," and his short life of self-discipline ends with burial "in its [the monastery's] gloomy cloisters" (731). By fleeing to the monastery in an attempt to atone for the past, Haredale embodies Catholic difference in all its stereotypical Protestant glory; first figuratively and then literally entombed within the monastery, Haredale embraces the threatening, homosocial, and apparently quite deadly counterpoint to the comforting, heterosocial, and equally quite lively world of the liberal Protestant family. And, like Effie (along with Magdalen Graeme, whose fate he shares even more explicitly), he does so away from England. Earlier, Haredale had reminded Gashford and Sir John that "thousands of us enter your service every year, and to preserve the freedom of which [England], we die in bloody battles abroad, in heaps" (403), arguing for Catholic equality on the basis of civic engagement even as the pronouns maintain an ineradicable difference. On the novel's terms, by retreating to a foreign cloister and asserting his otherness to both Protestantism and the world, Haredale accidentally undermines his own claim to toleration: if Catholics can best make a claim for equality by dying for the state like any other (man), then Haredale's decision to disengage from the state entirely marks the limit to the novel's brief for toleration. As Myron Magnet correctly notes, from Dickens's point of view, Haredale chooses "a community which is no community."[13] In retreating to an entirely Catholic (and male) space, Haredale chooses an otherness that cannot be reintegrated into Dickens's moderately optimistic vision of Englishness after the riots. At the same time, Dickens is more willing than Scott to imagine that Catholicism could be integrated into English space. The Catholic "purple-faced vintner" who stands with Haredale during the riots ends the novel fully embedded in the community at the Maypole, "to all appearance as much at home in the best room, as if he lived there" (736). Like Mrs. Varden, the vintner chooses the route of communal pleasures instead of what most Victorians would have denounced as antisocial suffering. If the novel insists that Protestants must extend the hand of fellowship to their Catholic fellow citizens, it also insists that Catholics must willingly integrate themselves into the community at large.

In effect, the novel is willing to tolerate "embedded" Christians, Protestant or Catholic, but it denies legitimacy to anything resembling what we would now call *identity politics*. Hence the symbolic appearance of the blind magistrate Sir John Fielding (556). While Sir John Fielding makes only a flitting appearance, he counterpoints the novel's far more prominent blind man, Stagg, who is himself the lower-class version of Gashford. Although Rosemary Bodenheimer correctly notes that here and elsewhere in early Dickens, "[l]ong gazes always point to secrets, intuited but inaccessible," *Barnaby Rudge* links blindness to insight.[14] Apparently a truckling servitor to Sim Tappertit and a friend to the elder Rudge, Stagg specializes in hypocritical performances that conceal his own interests while provoking others to inadvertently reveal their worst natures. Dickens deploys both Stagg's and Sir John Fielding's literal blindness in service of a figurative point about the right and wrong way of being "blind" to others: whereas Stagg rejects Mrs. Rudge's plea to "let your heart be softened by your own affliction, friend, and have some sympathy with mine" (424), on the grounds that such appeals are themselves hypocritical, the magistrate willingly listens to Haredale's case and consigns Rudge to Newgate. While Dickens may well sympathize with Stagg in general—Stagg's point, after all, is that it's an exercise in unwitting privilege for the healthy to assume that the afflicted will magically have superior morals—in this local instance, Stagg is helping a murderer further victimize his wife. By associating Stagg's blindness with a lack of *sympathy*, Dickens ranges Stagg with Sir John Chester, Gashford, and even Haredale in his refusal to take the first emotional and imaginative step toward a shared sense of community. Morally blind to the needs of others, Stagg objectifies human beings as a means to his own individual ends. By contrast, the upright Sir John Fielding exemplifies the traditional figure of blind justice in action. Unlike the Lord Mayor, who exclaims "what a pity it is you're a Catholic!" (554), the magistrate makes no difference between Catholic and Protestant when it comes to prosecuting crime. In this case, blindness *produces* community. Yet this is not be-cause there is no difference between Catholicism and Protestantism; rather, it is because, as the vintner indignantly asks the Lord Mayor, "Am I a citizen of England? Am I to have the benefit of the laws? Am I to have any return for the King's taxes?" (554). That is, Haredale and the vintner deserve equal treatment because in the court of law, they are rightly identified as *citizens* and not as *either* Catholics or Protestants; under the laws against murder and the destruction of property, the two men deserve protection solely because they are English taxpayers in good standing. For this purpose alone, religion no longer counts.

At the same time, Sir John Fielding figures *what is to come*, for Haredale's attacks on anti-Catholic legislation prophesy the com-ing of Catholic Emancipation in 1829 and the disappearance of other anti-Catholic Penal Laws such as those regarding property owner-ship. From the point of view of Dickens's present, that is, Haredale's troubles historicize a specific moment in English anti-Catholicism, and Haredale's complaints therefore take on a note of historical irony: leg-islation will take care of (some of) these problems. Given, however, that the narrative offers itself up as a warning against anti-Catholic agitation in its own present—a warning much in line with Grueby's wry thoughts about learning from what "Bloody Mary" *didn't* do—this historicizing moment fails to do much in the way of argumentative work. Having contextualized the Penal Laws, the novel nevertheless goes on to collapse eighteenth-century anti-Catholic rhetoric into the mid-Victorian variety: the "no Popery" cry, Gashford's allusions to Queen Mary, and so forth cannot be distinguished, in either content or intent, from their nineteenth-century versions. Solving Haredale's problems does not solve the problem of anti-Catholicism, which sug-gests that reducing anti-Catholic sentiment to specifically anti-Catholic *laws* misreads the situation. And in fact, if, as we have seen, this novel represents anti-Catholicism as a stand-in for entirely different (and non-religious) discourses, then of course Haredale's strategy must fail—not because repealing the Penal Laws is a bad thing but because anti-Catholicism manifests itself as the visible symptom of *other*, irrecon-cilable hatreds and desires, whether financial or political. There cannot be a history of anti-Catholicism per se if anti-Catholicism's meaning is always elsewhere, and never truly a conflict between opposing theologies. In this reading historicizing the Penal Laws misses the proverbial forest for the trees: the reader who identifies such legislation as an anachronism, a relic of an earlier period in Protestant-Catholic relations, neglects to notice that such a historical reading does not and cannot account for the protean quality of anti-Catholic signifiers, which acquire and discard their signifieds with terrifying ease. Sir John Fielding's blindness may prefigure post-Emancipation England, but it is a solution that addresses the symptoms of an ever-shifting root cause.

CONCLUSION

If we go back to Alison Case's point about the vision of an "ahistorical family" that concludes the novel, with Edward's and Emma's interfaith marriage resolving the family feud but *not* the rift between Protestants and Catholics, then Dickens here undoes the symbolic value of Jeanie's marriage to Reuben Butler, and goes even beyond the emptied-out symbolism of Roland Graeme's marriage at the end of *The Abbot*. For in Dickens, interfaith marriage requires the past to be not merely negotiated but *dead*. If Dickensian "memory" is, in Robert Mighall's turn of phrase, "the repository of retributional impulses," then marital harmony requires cutting all those concerned loose from their potentially devastating pasts.[15] Jeanie's domestic work, we recall, helped integrate the anti-establishment Davie into the state church, defanging him without denaturing him; the past does not vanish so much as it (un)willingly agrees to moderate its influence in the present. The split between Jeanie's and Effie's fates sends the disparity between Protestant and Catholic veering off into two wildly different directions, one domestic and productive, the other foreign and sterile. Catholic spaces—homosocial, self-enclosed, Continental—make no contribution to national modernization, precisely because they resist the domesticity on which the newly moderate Presbyterian nation is founded. Roland Graeme, by contrast, serves as a linchpin between Catholic and

Protestant cultures, but only insofar as Catholics cede any right to cultural or political influence.

In some ways Dickens appears to be continuing the theme. Edward's and Emma's fertile marriage suggests that Catholics can "project" themselves into the Protestant future if they opt for Protestant domesticity as well; pointedly, Dickens refrains from telling us whether the children will be raised Protestant or Catholic. But the past self-destructs before it can be folded into the next generation. Haredale murders Sir John before Edward and Emma marry, then disappears to the Continent, and, apparently, has no further contact with his relations. Whereas Scott casts the relationship between old and new Presbyterianism as an ongoing theological negotiation apparently carried out between men but actually facilitated by women, and that between Protestantism and Catholicism as one cemented by marriage in which the feminized Catholic Church remains safely subordinate, Dickens imagines the interfaith ideal in terms of marital bliss and jovial friendship. But by the same token, he also removes the very *possibility* of theological encounter from the social equation. It is not that all religions have become interchangeable—merely that all believers have agreed, apparently, to remain silent. Far from grounding the nation in even a moderated form of the religious past, *Barnaby Rudge* denies that either Protestant or Catholic historical narratives can keep the nation from fragmentation. Quite the contrary, as it turns out: the only hope for a stable future lies in forgetting about the legacy of the Reformation past. England may remain peaceful only as long as it opts to stop telling itself stories about the religious struggles that shape its present—to bury Bloody Mary and Queen Elizabeth alike. And in thus choosing to forget the history of religious struggle altogether, Dickens rejects the historical position that, paradoxically enough, united tolerationists and antitolerationists, Protestants and Catholics.

CODA

Savonarola's Reformation Fails

In this volume we have seen Protestants celebrating the triumph of the Reformation while warning against the ever-present possibility of its present-day failure, and Catholics arguing that failure lurked at the heart of the Reformation project from its very beginning. I want to conclude with Protestant attempts in the second half of the century to wrestle with a nation whose history appeared to contradict narratives about the inevitability of religious reform—a nation that, in fact, had successfully resisted the Reformation and its call for a return to "pure" scriptural religion. This time, the nation wasn't Ireland (itself the site of "second Reformation" evangelization earlier in the century). It was Italy. In his influential *History of the Progress and Suppression of the Reformation in Italy during the Sixteenth Century*, first published in 1827 and reprinted frequently over the next several decades, Thomas M'Crie the Elder argued of the Inquisition that "[t]he ease with which it was introduced into Italy, showed that, whatever illumination there was among the Italians, and however desirous they might be to share in those blessings which other nations had secured to themselves, they were destitute of that public spirit and energy of principle which would have enabled them to shake off the degrading yoke by which they were oppressed."[1] In this reading the Italians were doomed by national character to constantly embrace their own subjugation to the papal yoke. Any attempted Reformation would necessarily rot from within, barring some sea change to the population's nature. Was it truly possible that Italy could refuse Protestantism with that much determination?

As we have seen over and over again, many Protestants saw the Reformation as a crucial phase in the battle between Christ and Antichrist, and successive historical events were but one more part of this cosmological battle. British missionaries were conducting active campaigns across Italy from the early 1860s onward.[2] The 1860s were the years in which British Protestants began to wonder if, after all, the Italians were not quite so unregenerate as they had initially appeared. This renewed interest in the possibility of another try at an Italian Reformation was sparked by the *Risorgimento*, the political and cultural movement to unify the disparate Italian states under a single national banner. Because the nationalist program ultimately required the pope to relinquish the use of his temporal powers, Protestants regarded it as a positive sign of Protestant rebirth—not realizing, of course, that anticlericalism and Roman Catholicism could still go hand in hand. The great heroes of the Risorgimento, like Garibaldi and Mazzini, were feted during their visits to or exiles in England, even if some of their political projects—like Mazzini's republicanism—garnered less enthusiasm.[3] As C. T. McIntire points out, the British government found itself supporting the antipapal nationalists because "English concerns in commerce, finance, industry, naval affairs, social class, the church and religion all easily conjoined to promote the moral and material progress of Italy and to overcome the moral and material contagion of the papacy."[4] Protestant authors were eager to seize on the nationalist uprisings in order to revisit the possibility that success might emerge, after all, from the ashes of prior failures and to construct newly successful narratives from the rubble of the Italian Reformation's beginnings. They did not, however, always succeed.

Protestants had been interested in the Risorgimento's religious implications from the beginning. Although Pope Pius IX initially professed tepid support for the nationalists, which was misread as enthusiasm both inside and outside Italy,[5] he decried them once they sought to move against the Austrians in 1848. As a result, both the nationalists and their international supporters adopted an anticlerical rhetoric that frequently escalated into full-blown anti-Catholicism, while the Jesuits attacked the nationalists for being fundamentally Protestant.[6] In Britain such views were encouraged by Italian exiles like Ferdinando Dal Pozzo and Ugo Foscolo, whose English-language political writings often shared conventional British attitudes to Catholicism's socioeconomic effects.[7] British and American observers argued that Italian nationalists were rapidly trending toward Protestantism and were therefore worth supporting for theological as well as political reasons.[8] Nevertheless, the more cautious among them questioned the extent to which the Catholic countryside was really willing to divest itself of its loyalty to both Catholicism and the pope. Thus, the journal *Evangelical Christendom*, contemplating Garibaldi's failed attempt to take the papal territories in 1867, noted that the peasants offered nothing but "bigotry" and concluded that they were fatally weakened by "[c]enturies of oppression and priestcraft."[9] Perhaps another Reformation was *not* in the offing.

The problem of the Italian peasantry thus led polemicists and novelists back to the Italian Reformation, an event defined by failure from the beginning. In turning to the fiery fifteenth-century Dominican reformer Girolamo Savonarola (now best remembered for his "Bonfire of the Vanities") as an idealized icon of religious leadership, authors recruited him as a type of full-blown Protestantism, prefiguring its rise even as he himself fell. But there were difficulties. As discussed in the early chapters of this volume, proto-Protestant narratives on explicitly *British* topics enabled authors to theorize that Protestant modernity originated in England: John de Wycliffe, located at the beginning of the true reforming impulse, demonstrated that Protestantism had been no German foreign import but instead an entirely native growth. And because Victorian evangelicals and traditional High Churchmen identified Protestantism with political liberty, the reign of interiorized virtue, and authentic respect for both women and children, making Protestantism British naturalized those cultural values. The Reformation thus restored the status quo after the long interregnum of Roman Catholicism. Moreover, insofar as *Protestantism* was another name for the modern return to primitive Christianity, insisting on its Britishness globalized and localized it all at once: Protestantism was universal insofar as it was scriptural, but it was national because it had achieved its highest expression in the modern British isles.

But attempts to transpose such a narrative to Italy went awry, even before the Risorgimento renewed interest in the possibilities of a revived Italian Protestantism. From a Victorian point of view, the equivalent to Wycliffe was Savonarola, who—like Wycliffe—enjoyed renewed cult status during the nineteenth century. But recovering Wycliffe had been a Protestant undertaking, one almost entirely identified with the evangelical wing. Catholics occasionally scoffed at proto-Protestant interpretations of Wycliffe, but they neither felt threatened by the proto-Protestant interpretation nor desired to reclaim the heretical Wycliffe for their own historical narrative.[10] Protestants trying to recover Savonarola for their own uses had a different set of problems. To begin with, Savonarola's initial revival on the Continent was a *Catholic* project. In Italy, the Dominicans established a scholarly archive of Savonarola's life and works while insisting that he "was a saint and a prophet, his example and his teaching as valid for the nineteenth century as for the fifteenth."[11] At the same time, the French art critic Alexis-François Rio popularized the myth of Savonarola as a crusader against the increasingly "pagan" nature of Renaissance art, a position that had found its way to England by the mid-1840s.[12] Savonarola's Catholic supporters in general and his Italian Catholic supporters in particular found in him a model Christian leader whose failed reforms presaged not the Reformation but the Risorgimento; his Florentine reforms were "the last manifestation of an Italian spirit of independence before 'Italia' was enslaved by the foreign oppressor," making the friar a figure who could usefully "instruct and admonish the present."[13]

Savonarola's importance to both Continental and English Catholics turned Protestants' attempts to appropriate him for their own purposes into a prickly business, but his role as an Italian *political* hero caused its own problems. Proto-Protestant history ultimately subsumes national differences into an overarching narrative about *global* Christianity; Savonarola, by contrast, was not as easily extracted from his local context as Wycliffe could be (even though Wycliffe himself had hardly been apolitical). Prior to the nineteenth century Savonarola's reception history in England had moved in fits and starts. Bruce Gordon indicates that English Protestants incorporated two of Savonarola's meditations into their versions of the Primer, but that ended with the publication of Henry VIII's Primer in 1545.[14] Nor did Savonarola loom large in Foxe's *Book of Martyrs*. Foxe represents Savonarola as a straightforward antipapal clergyman, skipping over not only the details of his political involvement with the Florentine government but also the potentially most colorful details of his career, like Lorenzo de Medici's deathbed, the Bonfire of the Vanities, and his (averted) trial by fire. He is neither the protonationalist leader celebrated by proponents of the Risorgimento nor the tainted religious hero pondered by evangelicals.

For that matter, even in the nineteenth century, English Catholics were initially unenthusiastic about Savonarola. Thus, in 1826, William Eusebius Andrews published a description of Savonarola as "a learned man, and held for virtuous in those days; but of a hot and choleric nature, and living in the time of great political excitement, when Florence was divided into factions, he outstepped the bounds of prudence, and made the pulpit the vehicle of his *political* feelings"; by contrast, nearly seventy years and much spilt ink later, the Very Rev. John Procter, O.P., celebrated Savonarola as "a Catholic, Catholic to the heart's core, Catholic to the very marrow of his bones; Catholic in life, Catholic in death."[15] Both men were refuting proto-Protestant readings of Savonarola and his teachings, but for Andrews, publishing prior to Catholic Emancipation, Savonarola is a minor, ever-so-slightly reprehensible figure. The politicized Savonarola represents a now-outdated clerical ideal, to be shunned in favor of a rational spirituality and a strict separation between pulpit and state. By problematizing Savonarola—as an orthodox Catholic but not fit for modern emulation—Andrews implies that the nineteenth-century Catholic priest eschews precisely the politicking that contemporary Protestants would find threatening.

But for Procter, writing after several decades of social and civil advances for Catholics, Savonarola is a heroic, exemplary Dominican, the very model of Catholic devotion. Instead of castigating Savonarola for mixing politics with churchmanship, Procter celebrates Savonarola's understanding of reform—a "reformer of the evil ways of men" (90), not of the untouchable Catholic Church itself—and contrasts Savonarola's pre-Reformation world of the faithful with post-Reformation, dangerously liberalized England, where "leaders and led have fallen into the pit of ignorance of Divine truth" (92). Andrews's Savonarola is an agent of social unrest; Procter's is, perhaps, a solution to it.

This transformation in Catholic opinion was well under way by the 1850s, but as Eleanor McNees has recently demonstrated, authors writing from wildly different theological perspectives frequently offered overlapping assessments of the friar's career and fate.[16] Prior to the nineteenth century Savonarola had been noted favorably by such authors as J. L. Mosheim and Erasmus Middleton, but Middleton also acknowledged that Savonarola was popular with *both* sides of the question, not just the Protestant one.[17] Notably, it took some time before full-length popularizing or scholarly biographies of Savonarola made much headway in the English market. Although English-language publications reviewed and referenced such influential Continental biographies as A. G. Rudelbach's Protestantizing *Hieronymus Savonarola und Seine Zeit* (1835) and F.-T. Perrens's Catholic *Jérome Savonarola* (1854), neither was ever translated into English. The most significant biography to appear in English before George Eliot's *Romola*, the translation of Pasquale Villari's soon-to-be-standard *Life and Times of Girolamo Savonarola* (1859–61), also known in England as *The History of Girolamo Savonarola and His Times*, insisted that Savonarola was "essentially Catholic" and chastised English historians in particular for attempting "to place the Friar of St. Mark among the Martyrs of the Reformation."[18] Of the three others to appear between 1843 and 1860, John Abraham Heraud's *The Life and Times of Girolamo Savonarola, Illustrating the Progress of the Reformation in Italy During the Fifteenth Century* (1843), targeted against both the Oxford Movement and evangelicalism, treated Savonarola as Luther's progenitor; Richard Robert Madden's *The Life and Martyrdom of Savonarola* (1853) not only insisted that Savonarola was Catholic but also suggested that he might be worthy of canonization; and William Harris Rule's *The Dawn of the Reformation* (1855) located Savonarola in a spiritual limbo between Catholic degeneracy and Protestant enlightenment, heralding the arrival of the former but bearing all the scars of the latter.[19] To complicate matters further, the ecclesiastical historian Henry Hart Milman's influential review of Perrens, first published in the *Quarterly Review* (1856), ejected Savonarola altogether from both Protestant and Catholic narratives, painting him as a deeply confused, tragic figure who was, at best, an accidental Reformer.

The discourse on Savonarola tended to leave him in a theologically and politically liminal space. The author most enthusiastic about reclaiming Savonarola for Protestantism, Heraud, was his least significant biographer, while Rule's ambiguity about Savonarola coincided with Henry Hart Milman's warning that if Savonarola had "foreseen" Luther's Reformation, "he had hid his face in sorrow."[20] As they struggled to ground Savonarola at the beginning of *any* historical narrative, these four authors found themselves simultaneously seeking the roots of his collapse. Was he a deluded fanatic? Heraud and Madden both insist that Savonarola was a divinely inspired prophet; Rule and Villari, by contrast, believe that the prophetic visions were artifacts of Savonarola's time and education, terrible illusions that nevertheless contained a real core of insight. Heraud and Madden ground Savonarola in a very particular epoch, one that calls out for divine warnings in order to avert impending damnation, and transforms him into the locus of a voice that entirely transcends mere human history. Savonarola is not just a transformative historical agent but also the fragile site of the All-Powerful's momentarily audible entrance into man's affairs. In this aspect of his character, Savonarola himself only matters insofar as his historical conditioning enables him to decode and articulate his divinely inspired visions. His work fails, then, not because of any innate flaw in his prophetic character but because the people are too attached to their own corruption. By contrast, Rule's and Villari's position certainly allows for divine *providence* to work itself out in Savonarola's career, but it also leaves Savonarola offering up a "blind faith" to his "visions," even "becom[ing] their slave," as Villari puts it (1:306). In both Rule's and Villari's narratives, the visions are the detritus of medieval philosophy and theology—the virulent symptoms of the very culture that Savonarola seeks to reform. As a result, Savonarola is crucially blind to his own fatal involvement in late-medieval Catholicism and therefore lacks the requisite intellectual equipment to understand just how much of the system needs to be dismantled. At best, Rule suggests, his prophecies should be understood as culturally convenient fictions, "merely the garb and vehicle of the predictions."[21]

But while Rule and Villari argue that Savonarola was doomed to failure by the very historical conjunction to which he belonged, they abruptly part ways on the meaning of that failure. Now the Catholic Madden and the anti-Catholic Rule find themselves agreeing that Savonarola's case indicates the dangers of conflating politics and theology. By contrast, Heraud celebrates Savonarola's attempt to found a "theocracy"[22] (a project Heraud believes he has in common with contemporary Victorian theology), and Villari, of course, believes that Savonarola "desire[d] that reason and faith, religion and liberty, might meet in harmonious union," (2.374), anticipating the cultural and political revival of the nineteenth century. But Madden holds that any combination of church and state inexorably leads to rampant corruption, and he goes so far as to argue that the current condition of Italy disqualifies it as the site of the holy see.[23] Assessing Savonarola's own possibly problematic behavior, Madden compares some of his less-salubrious political suggestions to those of St. Bernard and concludes that "holy men" who involve themselves in "temporal affairs" soon "show abundantly by their acts that they are subject to human frailties, liable to be misled in their judgments, and to be inconsistent in their conduct"—although without losing their essentially holy character (2:124). In Madden's case this anxiety about priestly interference in secular affairs reflects both the pope's increasingly unstable position in Italy and, nearer home, the Irish hierarchy's somewhat frustrated attempts to prevent Catholic clergy from politicking in the pulpit.[24] In Rule's, though, it derives from a combination of Dissenting skepticism about any established church and heavy-handed anti-Romanist sentiment. As far as Rule is concerned, Savonarola participates in a thoroughly degenerate system whose theological foundations he never rejects. Madden's narrative works through Savonarola's failure to suggest the possibility of a thoroughly depoliticized, and therefore truly global, Catholic Church; Rule's uses that same failure to insist that the Roman Catholic Church cannot be reformed from within and can only be abandoned. In fact, for Rule, Savonarola's ultimate relevance to the nineteenth century lies in his unintentional *anti*-Catholicism, thanks to his "exposure" of the church's "corruption" and "tyranny" (259). Alone of the four, Rule appropriates Savonarola for modern use by reading the friar against himself.

Only Heraud maps Savonarola onto Luther. *The Life and Times of Girolamo Savonarola* opens with a popular set-piece in Savonarola mythology, made famous by J. H. Merle D'Aubigné: a priest invites Martin Luther to contemplate a painting of Savonarola that functions simultaneously as exemplar and warning; Luther, nothing daunted, "conceived rather courage than fear from the lesson it presented."[25] This moment simultaneously establishes Savonarola as both Luther's consciously chosen precursor and as the embodiment of the threat facing all Reformers—namely, martyrdom. Heraud need not argue for Savonarola's "Protestantism," for in that moment of recognition Luther has already done it for him.[26] But the link between Savonarola and Luther works backwards as well as forwards. Luther's followers dub Savonarola "the Luther of Italy" (vi); Savonarola seems to surpass Luther in humility when he yearns to remain a mere "servant" in the monastery (66); he is the "St. John" to Luther's "St. Paul" (387). Although Heraud ultimately judges that Savonarola's practice and theology were badly flawed, he nevertheless makes the earlier figure both anticipate *and* complete the later. Contemplating an alternative history in which Savonarola's project succeeded, Heraud speculates that the newly reformed church "would have had less of faith and more of love. It would have retained less of ceremony, and recognized more of spiritualism. It would have been less Protestant, and more Catholic. Mystic sentiment would have been encouraged, not discarded" (389). For

Heraud, Savonarola's failure identifies a lack in the current Protestant church's structure, one that points to the Reformation's status as an ongoing *process* rather than a completed event. This brief counterfactual insists that the Reformation (as Heraud understands it) contains "Catholicity" *within* itself, rather than expels it, which simultaneously undermines the positions of both the Oxford Movement and the evangelicals; by returning to Luther's precursor, rather than to Luther, the modern Protestant can revitalize his faith by activating the possibilities only suppressed, not erased from it.

These ambiguities surrounding Savonarola's proto-Protestantism, or not, characterize fictional attempts to turn him into a founding Reformer—with matters further complicated, of course, by the difficulties involved in identifying Savonarola with Bible reading in the manner discussed in chapters 2 and 3. Instead, novelists were forced to fall back on Savonarola as a charismatic innovator from above, perhaps even an equivalent to contemporary heroes like Garibaldi.[27] Of the three nineteenth-century historical novels set in and around Savonarola's ministry, only the first, Harriet Beecher Stowe's *Agnes of Sorrento* (1861), fully endorses a Protestant reading of his career. (*Agnes of Sorrento* was initially published in England in the *Cornhill Magazine*, just before George Eliot's *Romola*.) Stowe's title character, the dismayingly innocent (and heavy-handedly named) Agnes, vows that she will undertake a "pilgrimage" to Rome, where she will "seek the house of our dear father, the Pope, and entreat his forgiveness for this poor soul"—the soul in question belonging to Agostino Sarelli, a young man whose family has been brutally wronged by Caesar Borgia.[28] This pilgrimage rapidly turns into parody. In good stereotypical fashion, Agnes's father confessor is consumed with lust for his naïve penitent, but he is also open-eyed enough about his church to inwardly scoff at the notion that Alexander the Sixth might be a man with "all the meekness and gentleness of Christ" (158). Nevertheless, the confessor's repressed sexual tumults foreshadow what Agnes eventually encounters in Rome itself, where the Borgias "entic[e] her into their impure den" (393). Seeking redemption, virginal innocence instead faces threatened rape. Not surprisingly, the pilgrimage turns out to be a fortunate fall of sorts, revealing the hollowness at Catholicism's core. Although the conclusion does not result in Agnes precisely converting to Protestantism, she and Agostino nevertheless achieve a romantic union that, according to a beloved priest, signifies a "vocation unto marriage" (411). The Catholic pilgrimage thus finds itself waylaid by a proto-Protestant marriage plot, which disentangles virtue from vowed virginity.

As Agnes journeys toward Rome and ultimately away from Catholicism, Savonarola seeks to reform the church from within. Savonarola, the narrator informs us, is an "Italian Luther" (98), or, alternately, the author of hymns that combine "the Moravian quaintness and energy with the Wesleyan purity and tenderness" (247). Similarly, his preaching constitutes the equivalent of a nineteenth-century "revival" (41). Stowe's quite unapologetic anachronism, which locates Savonarola's pastoral practice everywhere from the sixteenth century to the nineteenth, both modernizes him and reclaims him for an ecumenically generic Protestant history; far from being shaped by the exigencies of his own moment, he embodies all modes of Protestant spirituality and practice at once. This is the ideal Protestantism imagined by more strictly evangelical novelists, transcending denominational differences in its allegiance to purely scriptural principles. Overall, as Robin Sheets suggests, this Savonarola exemplifies a "liberal religion based on a meek and loving Christ"—very far from George Eliot's much more hardheaded leader, as we shall see in a moment.[29] But this preaching is not apolitical. In the words of young Agostino, "All Italy, all Christendom, is groaning and stretching out the hand to him to free them from these abominations" (174). Savonarola's moral reforms encompass unifying political reforms as well, transforming the country (and, indeed, the world) into an organic whole dead set against the evils of Rome—possibly promising the beginnings of Christ's kingdom on earth.

Yet even as Stowe seeks to integrate the Catholic Savonarola into Protestant modes of thinking about history, she also shadows him with anticipations of his death as a "martyr" (118), destroyed by the corrupt culture of his birth. Unlike Agnes, whose "devotional femininity" may embody the successful continuity of Christianity's essence across the

Catholic-Protestant divide, Savonarola suggests the far more fraught historical career of the masculine reformer.[30] He properly belongs to the sweep of providential history, but political history drags him back. Instead, Savonarola truly belongs to modernity: he offers a momentary gleam of divine truth that is indeed invisible to his contemporaries but not to those in a post-Reformation world. Much like the Lollard novels, *Agnes of Sorrento* imagines the grand sweep of Christian history in terms of nascent Protestantism, a *telos* visible only from the point of a view of a reader properly grounded in the scriptures. In the chaos of a merely human history, marred by the fall, the workings of God's will prove difficult to discern; but inasmuch as he models the possibility of a virtuous Florentine republic, founded on scriptural truth instead of human fictions, Savonarola prefigures what Stowe imagines to be a post-Risorgimento new Italy.

In *Romola*, however, George Eliot's Savonarola inhabits a far more problematic narrative, one that in its emphasis on unpredictability harkens back to the eighteenth-century fictions of the Reformation discussed in chapter 1. In part, this is because Eliot tends to distrust activists like Savonarola, who are never as effective as those working silently behind the scenes.[31] It is also because Eliot draws heavily on Villari, who argued sternly against English attempts to hijack Savonarola for proto-Protestant historiography; expanding Villari's historicist interpretation of Savonarola's mindset, Eliot finds that Savonarola is "trapped within his own epoch, not realizing that his religious beliefs are a mythical hypothesis which will inevitably be superseded."[32] Far from prefiguring Protestant reform, Eliot's Savonarola suggests its tentativeness, its potential collapse into incoherent confusion.[33] The novel does not, I would argue, find that Savonarola can be easily assimilated into the more cookie-cutter evangelical narratives of Protestantism's victory against the Antichrist, or even of proto-Protestantism, precisely because Savonarola himself inadvertently shatters his own saintly image in the act of constructing it. Stowe's Savonarola morphs into Martin Luther; Eliot's subsides into something resembling a museum piece.

Repeatedly associated with the power of *voice*, of a speech so intense that it seems to invade and transform the mind of its auditors,

Eliot's Savonarola at once grips and is gripped by his own vocal performances.[34] In Savonarola's first significant appearance in the novel, nearly halfway through, he delivers a powerful and moving sermon in which he volunteers to martyr himself, emulating Christ ("let the thorns press upon my brow") in order to regenerate a degenerate Florence.[35] The intensity of this movement moves both him and his audience to a moment of shared anguish: his "sob" returns in the "loud responding sob" of the audience (294). As language breaks down under the force of religious passion, Savonarola undergoes a momentary apotheosis, feeling "the rapture and glory of martyrdom without its agony" (294). In effect, this emotional climax momentarily spills Savonarola's narrative of future, conditional self-sacrifice into a completed hagiography—but one that conveniently erases the extreme corporeal pain associated with real-life martyrdoms in favor of spiritual ecstasy. Savonarola's temporary fantasy of martyrdom ironically anticipates his much later experience of actual physical suffering, which leaves him "crying out in his agony, 'I will confess!'" (639) Romola, reading his confessions, detects a very human "doubleness" between the lines, a split between ideal intentions and their encounter with brutal reality (665). And yet this doubleness was already present in the sermon scene. The apparently cohesive moment of religious sympathy turns out to be fundamentally unstable: Baldassare, the badly betrayed stepfather of Romola's husband Tito Melema, rejoices in the preaching, not because he yearns for salvation but because he hears in it "the idea of perpetual vengeance" (295).[36] At the very moment when Savonarola appears to have shaped his own future as reforming saint, his influence shunts off into an entirely unanticipated, and dangerously uncontrollable, direction.

Instead of unambiguously serving as a proto-Protestant Great Man, Eliot's Savonarola suggests instead that self-contradictions, frustrations, and downright equivocations characterize the march of religious reform through history. Precisely because he situates himself as the movement's point of origin, the tension between his "never-silent hunger after purity and simplicity" and the opposing "tangle of egoistic demands, false ideas, and difficult outward conditions" (576) that jangle awkwardly through his mind inescapably manifests itself in his work in the world. To chart "Reform" from one half of Savonarola's mind, as it were, falsely streamlines the chaos of what he actually accomplishes. In fact, this is precisely what Savonarola himself attempts to do, embroiled as he is in the messiness of secular and religious reform: as he explains to an increasingly enraged Romola, he cannot secure the pardon of her godfather, Bernardo del Nero, because of the many "action[s]" available to him, "I have to choose that which will further the work intrusted to me. The end I seek is one to which minor respects must be sacrificed" (577). Above all, Savonarola the politician entertains a fantasy of perfect control over his outcomes.[37] Seeking a truly unitary and straightforward course from one religious state of affairs to another, Savonarola inadvertently suggests that cruelty informs the reformer's understanding of a future that will one day be a renewed religion's past. In aspiring to theocracy, which will unite the sacred and profane spheres of life into a perfect whole, Savonarola refuses to grant that a sacralized politics is still as morally muddy as any other. There is no "world of transparent and comprehensive meaning" here.[38] Far from achieving that end, Savonarola becomes Romola's personalized moral exemplar, a purely private saint who embodies "the greatness which belongs to a life spent in struggling against powerful wrong, and in trying to raise men to the highest deeds they are capable of" (675)—an ideal that has its place in the Positivist calendar of saints but that excludes much that Savonarola would deem important.[39] As a martyr, Savonarola winds up testifying to something that he would not recognize as the essential truth.

But even some orthodox Christians felt that Savonarola did not, after all, herald the coming of even a belated Italian Reformation. We see this skepticism emerging in a much later novel about Savonarola, the anonymously authored *The Martyr of Florence*, initially published around 1880. Despite the conspicuous lack of a new Italian Reformation by that point, British Protestants nevertheless still found much to be optimistic about, such as the expansion of the Free Christian Church of Italy, founded in 1870.[40] *The Martyr of Florence*, though, urges caution. Although it was published by a strict evangelical press, John F. Shaw, it accepts Villari's position that Savonarola was Catholic, albeit with the rider that the essential truths of Savonarola's preaching were fundamentally Protestant. However, *The Martyr of Florence* also revises both *Agnes of Sorrento* and *Romola* by linking Savonarola's failure to an explicitly Protestant failure: that of modern revivalism, by then associated with such traveling Americans as D. W. Moody and Ira Sankey. In *The Martyr of Florence* Savonarola preaches the same sermon that elicits sobs from the audience in *Romola* but with not quite the same result: "At these words a sob broke from that great multitude; cries and groans were heard on every side; the writer who took down notes of the sermon dropped his tablets, overcome with the force of his emotion; and the preacher himself paused, troubled at the effect of his own words."[41] This sermon converts one of the novel's main characters, but that ambiguous fourth clause, in which the preacher draws back from the effect of his language instead of being elevated by it, renders such crowd appeal suspect. Far from achieving the illusory apotheosis that Eliot's Savonarola does, this Savonarola suddenly finds himself divided against both himself and the crowd, excluded from their passion in the moment that he elicits it. After all, many of those who "sob" at this very moment will abandon him several chapters later, thus warning the reader about the difference between the momentary rush occasioned by highly wrought rhetoric and genuine conviction.

For the anonymous author, Savonarola's moral influence is fleeting exactly because it is so affective, so calculated to woo a crowd that lacks his own self-discipline. Near the end of the novel the skeptical Mariotto Albertinelli tells the saintly heroine Annunziata that "sooner or later all revivals come to this. Men cannot keep long at such a high tension as the Frate required" (249). The fault, replies Annunziata, echoing Thomas M'Crie, lies in Florence's "unworthy" nature. And yet, both points appear to be correct: both the method and the goal appear to be useless in Italy. Without a populace itself intent on reform, the cult of the great religious leader must necessarily come to nothing. No wonder that the *Sunday Magazine*, reporting on Italy in 1886, sadly concluded that the effect of the Risorgimento had only been a spread of "infidelity" among the peasantry.[42] Reformations could, after all, come to naught.

Notes

Introduction

1. Edward Bickersteth, *The Present Duties of the Protestant Churches. A Sermon Preached Before the British Society for Promoting the Religious Principles of the Reformation, on Friday Evening, May 5, 1837, at Percy Chapel, London* (London: G. Norman, 1837), 37. Bickersteth (1786–1850) was lawyer-turned-evangelical and missionary and father of Edward Henry Bickersteth (1825–1906), bishop of Exeter and hymnodist.

2. E. G. Rupp, "The Influence of Victorian Nonconformity," *The Listener* 1359 (March 17, 1955): 469.

3. One of the reasons so much work on literature and religion focuses on canonical texts, I would argue, is simply that such texts mesh well with the expectations of contemporary professional criticism. They are "difficult," "complex," or "subtle"; they must be carefully "unpacked."

4. The locus classicus for such discussions is perhaps Olive Anderson, "The Political Uses of History in Mid-Nineteenth Century England," *Past and Present* 36 (April 1967): 87–105. More recently and most famously, see the essays collected in Eric Hobsbawm and Terence Ranger, eds., *The Invention of Tradition* (Cambridge: Cambridge University Press, 1983).

5. George Levine, *Realism, Ethics, and Secularism: Essays on Victorian Literature and Science* (Cambridge: Cambridge University Press, 2009), 210, 214.

6. I use *evangelicalism* as defined by David Bebbington to describe those Protestants across all denominations who took "[c]onversionism, activism, biblicism, and crucicentrism" to be fundamental to their beliefs (*Evangelicalism in Modern Britain: A History from the 1730s to the Present* [1989; repr., Grand Rapids, MI: Baker Book House, 1992], 4).

7. Elizabeth Deeds Ermarth, *The English Novel in History, 1840–1895* (New York: Routledge, 1997), 72. The best study of fictional conversion

narratives is Michael Ragussis, *Figures of Conversion: "The Jewish Question" and English National Identity* (Durham, NC: Duke University Press, 1995); see also Elisabeth Jay, *The Religion of the Heart: Anglican Evangelicalism and the Nineteenth-Century Novel* (Oxford: Clarendon Press, 1979), 59–65. On nonfiction evangelical conversion narratives in the Victorian period, see Callum G. Brown, *The Death of Christian Britain: Understanding Secularization, 1800–2000* (London: Routledge, 2001), 59–85.

8. Maureen Moran, "Pater's 'Great Change': *Marius the Epicurean* as Historical Conversion Romance," in *Walter Pater: Transparencies of Desire*, ed. Laurel Brake, Leslie Higgins, and Carolyn Williams (Greensboro, NC: ELT Press, 2002), 173.

9. As it happens, the scant handful of novels about the Irish Reformation do not fit this pattern at all: authors subordinate or virtually eliminate representations of religious conflict in favor of the problems of warfare and the possibility of sustaining Irish national identity under English oppression. This is true even when the author normally writes controversial fiction, like Selina Bunbury. For that reason, these novels do not appear in this book, although I hope to pursue the questions they raise in another venue.

10. J. Russell Perkin, *Theology and the Victorian Novel* (Montreal: McGill-Queen's University Press, 2009), 69.

11. Grace Kennedy, *Father Clement: A Roman Catholic Tale* (1823; repr., Edinburgh: William Oliphant and Son, 1838), 344.

12. Notable responses included the Italian-American Charles Constantine Pise's *Father Rowland: A North American Tale* (1829), Mrs. Robertson's *Florence; Or, the Aspirant* (1829), the anonymous *The Biblicals; Or, Glenmoyle Castle, A Tale of Modern Times* (1831), E. C. Agnew's *Geraldine: A Tale of Conscience* (1837–39), the anonymous *The Converts: A Tale of the Nineteenth Century* (1837), and the anonymous *Father Oswald* (1842).

13. See Samuel Pickering Jr., *The Moral Tradition in English Fiction, 1785–1850* (Hanover, NH: University Press of New England, 1976), 96–105.

14. Hutcheon defines the term in *A Poetics of Postmodernism: History, Theory, Fiction* (London: Routledge, 1988), 105–23.

15. Georg Lukács, *The Historical Novel*, trans. Hannah and Stanley Mitchell (Lincoln: University of Nebraska Press, 1983), 21.

16. Harry Shaw identifies Scott as "the greatest historical novelist" (148) but only in the course of pointing out that Scott's approach to the historical novel is hardly the only one; see *The Forms of Historical Fiction: Sir Walter Scott and His Successors* (Ithaca, NY: Cornell University Press, 1983).

17. Fiona Price, "Resisting 'The Spirit of Innovation': The Other Historical Novel and Jane Porter," *Modern Language Review* 101 (2006): 640.

18. A. Dwight Culler is on point when he argues of John Henry Newman's *Callista* that "[i]n third-century Africa there had occurred the same life-

and-death struggle between Christianity and paganism which Newman believed was still taking place in his own day, but through the perspective of sixteen hundred years and through the clear air and vivid colors of the Mediterranean world one could see its shape and meaning more clearly" (*The Victorian Mirror of History* [New Haven, CT: Yale University Press, 1985], 115).

19. [Elizabeth Rundle Charles], *The Draytons and the Davenants: A Story of the Civil Wars* (New York: Dodd and Mead, 1877), 247.

20. Thus, Thomas Vargish comments that "straightforward providential fiction" (he cites *Jane Eyre* and *David Copperfield* as examples) ebbs at mid-century, and its later, more complex substitutes enter into "decline" with George Eliot (*The Providential Aesthetic in Victorian Fiction* [Charlottesville: University Press of Virginia, 1985], 23). Cf. David S. Katz, *God's Last Words: Reading the English Bible from the Reformation to Fundamentalism* (New Haven, CT: Yale University Press, 2004), 216.

21. Peter Hinchliff, *God and History: Aspects of British Theology, 1875–1914* (Oxford: Clarendon Press, 1992), 8.

22. As Michael Ledger-Lomas wryly notes, we still have no evidence that the outpouring of popular religious texts led to the mass conversion of Catholics (and, I would add, Jews); see "Mass Markets: Religion," in *The Cambridge History of the Book in Britain, Vol. 6: 1830–1914*, ed. David McKitterick (Cambridge: Cambridge University Press, 2009), 339–40. On the same note, Kimberley Reynolds argues that the survival of a Victorian prize book almost certainly means that it was *never* read (or, at least, not read very much) ("Rewarding Reads? Giving, Receiving, and Resisting Evangelical Reward and Prize Books," in *Popular Children's Literature in Britain*, ed. Julia Briggs, Dennis Butts, and M. O. Grenby ([Aldershot: Ashgate, 2008], 192).

23. For Gosse, see Edmund Gosse, *The Life of Philip Henry Gosse, F.R.S.* (London: Kegan Paul, Trench, Trübner, 1893), 19; for Lady Georgiana, see Mrs. Augustus Craven, *The Life of Lady Georgiana Fullerton*, trans. Henry James Coleridge (London: Richard Bentley and Son, 1888), 28–30.

24. Cf. Michael Wheeler, who notes Lingard's influence on W. H. Ainsworth's *The Tower of London* (1840) in *The Old Enemies: Catholic and Protestant in Nineteenth-Century England* (Cambridge: Cambridge University Press, 2006), 86. Valerie Chancellor points out that children's history books were often sympathetic to figures like Thomas More, if not to their policies; see *History for Their Masters: Opinion in the English History Textbook, 1800–1914* (Bath: Adams and Dart, 1970), 104–5.

25. Jay, *The Religion of the Heart*, 69.

26. See, for example, *Confessions of a Convert, from Baptism in Water to Baptism with Water* (London: John Snow, 1845).

27. Emily Sarah Holt, *Out in the Forty-Five: Or, Duncan Keith's Vow. A Tale of the Last Century* (London: John F. Shaw, n.d.), 343.

28. Linda Colley, *Britons: Forging the Nation, 1707–1837* (New Haven, CT: Yale University Press, 1992), 53.

29. Sarah C. Williams, "Is There a Bible in the House? Gender, Religion, and Family Culture," in *Women, Gender, and Religious Cultures in Britain, 1800–1940*, ed. Sue Morgan and Jacqueline de Vries (London: Routledge, 2010), 17.

30. Leslie Howsam, *Cheap Bibles: Nineteenth-Century Publishing and the British and Foreign Bible Society* (Cambridge: Cambridge University Press, 1991), 16–17, 33. The society was always beset by internal controversies; introducing prayers eventually undermined its stability as an interdenominational organization (196–97).

31. On the increasingly specialized nature of religious publishing, see Patrick Scott, "The Business of Belief: The Emergence of Religious Publishing," in *Sanctity and Secularity: The Church and the World*, ed. Derek Baker (Oxford: Basil Blackwell, 1973), 220–22 ; and on the actual practice of writing for the Religious Tract Society, see Aileen Fyfe, *Science and Salvation: Evangelical Popular Science Publishing in Victorian Britain* (Chicago: University of Chicago Press, 2004), 184–223. The gender imbalance Fyfe found in Christian science writers (194) did not repeat itself in this study. The RTS started publishing fiction in earnest around midcentury, as part of its larger expansion into still Christian but less overtly dogmatic projects; see Fyfe, "A Short History of the Religious Tract Society," in *From the Dairyman's Daughter to Worrals of the WAAF: The Religious Tract Society, Lutterworth Press, and Children's Literature*, ed. Dennis Butts and Pat Garrett (Cambridge: Lutterworth Press, 2006), 23–28.

32. On the problematic status of children's literature in particular within circulating libraries, see M. O. Grenby, "Adults Only? Children and Children's Books in British Circulating Libraries, 1748–1848," *Book History* 5, no. 1 (2002): 19–38. For a discussion of James Nisbet, a religious publisher whose own circulating library included at least some Christian children's and adult fiction, see J. S. Bratton, *The Impact of Victorian Children's Fiction* (London: Croom Helm, 1981), 57–59.

33. Christopher Haigh, "The Recent Historiography of the English Reformation," in *The English Reformation Revised*, ed. Christopher Haigh (Cambridge: Cambridge University Press, 1987), 30. One of the first major overviews was offered by John Stockton Littell, *The Historian and the Reformation* (New York: Young Churchman, 1910); more recent accounts include A. G. Dickens and John M. Tonkin with Kenneth Powell, *The Reformation in Historical Thought* (Cambridge, MA: Harvard University Press, 1985); Rosemary O'Day, *The Debate on the English Reformation* (London: Methuen, 1986); and John Vidmar, *English Catholic Historians and the English Reformation, 1585–1954*

(Sussex: Sussex Academic Press, 2005). For the Reformation in Britain during the mid-nineteenth century, see Wheeler, *The Old Enemies*, 77–110.

34. James Augustus Page, "The Bill of Twenty-Nine," in *Protestant Ballads* (London: Whittaker and Company, 1852), 5.

35. This is a very old theme in anti-Catholic and anti-Protestant polemic; see Alexandra Walsham, *Charitable Hatred: Tolerance and Intolerance in England, 1500–1700* (Manchester: Manchester University Press, 2006), 46; and Andrew Murphy, *Conscience and Community: Revisiting Toleration and Religious Dissent in Early Modern England and America* (University Park: Pennsylvania State University Press, 2001), 48, 54.

36. On the population increase—from "80,000 Catholics in England in 1770" to "three-quarters of a million in 1850"—and its underlying causes, see John Bossy, *The English Catholic Community, 1570–1850* (New York: Oxford University Press, 1976), 298–316, statistics on 298. See also Bossy's discussion of the movement to convert England to Catholicism (387–90).

37. On the surge in English millennialism immediately pre- and post-Emancipation, see Grayson Carter, *Anglican Evangelicals: Secessions from the Via Media, c. 1800–1850* (Oxford: Clarendon Press, 2001), 152–94; D. G. Paz, *Popular Anti-Catholicism in Mid-Victorian Britain* (Stanford, CA: Stanford University Press, 1992), 107–9; and John Wolffe, *The Protestant Crusade in Great Britain, 1829–1860* (Oxford: Clarendon Press, 1991), 113–16.

38. James Pereiro, *"Ethos" and the Oxford Movement: At the Heart of Tractarianism* (Oxford: Oxford University Press, 2008), 188.

39. C. Brad Faught, *The Oxford Movement: A Thematic History of the Tractarians and Their Times* (University Park: Pennsylvania State University Press, 2003), 38, 46.

40. Mark Chapman, "John Keble, National Apostasy, and the Myths of 14 July," in *John Keble in Context*, ed. Kirstie Blair (London: Anthem Press, 2004), 48, 51.

41. Bebbington points out that many evangelicals were adopting proto-Tractarian positions in the 1820s, only to abandon them later (*Evangelicalism in Modern Britain*, 96–97).

42. [John Henry Newman and James Mozley, eds.], *Remains of the Late Reverend Richard Hurrell Froude*, 2 vols. (London: J. G. and F. Rivington, 1838), 1:433, 336.

43. On the seventeenth-century antecedents, see Nigel Yates, *Anglican Ritualism in Victorian Britain, 1830–1910* (Oxford: Oxford University Press, 1999), 10–25; and on Anglo-Catholic arguments for the morality of beauty in worship, see Dominic Janes, *Victorian Reformation: The Fight over Idolatry in the Church of England, 1840–1860* (Oxford: Oxford University Press, 2009), 38–42.

44. Nigel Yates, *Buildings, Faith and Worship: The Liturgical Arrangement of Anglican Churches, 1600–1900*, rev. ed. (Oxford: Oxford University Press, 2000), 145. Such confusions are satirized in Henry Patrick Russell, *Cyril Westward: The Story of a Grave Decision* (London: Art and Book Company, 1899), 74. On internal debates over the Anglican revival of interest in the Virgin Mary, see Carol Engelhardt Herringer, *Victorians and the Virgin Mary: Religion and Gender in England, 1830–85* (Manchester: Manchester University Press, 2008), 60–63.

45. See, for example, Diarmaid MacCulloch, "The Myth of the English Reformation," *Journal of British Studies* 30, no. 1 (1991): esp. 3–8.

46. Susan Mumm, *Stolen Daughters, Virgin Mothers: Anglican Sisterhoods in Victorian Britain* (London: Leicester University Press, 1999), 211–13.

47. See John Shelton Reed, *Glorious Battle: The Cultural Politics of Victorian Anglo-Catholicism* (Nashville, TN: Vanderbilt University Press, 1996), 57–59; and James Whisenant, *A Fragile Unity: Anti-Ritualism and the Division of Anglican Evangelicalism in the Nineteenth Century* (Milton Keynes: Paternoster, 2003), 27–30.

48. "Devout pugnacity" is from James Bentley, *Ritualism and Politics in Victorian Britain: The Attempt to Legislate for Belief* (Oxford: Oxford University Press, 1978), 13; see also Yates, *Anglican Ritualism*, 213–77. On the bad press for evangelicals, see Reed, *Glorious Battle*, 247.

49. Lord John Russell, *Papal Aggression. Speech of the Right Honourable Lord John Russell, Delivered in the House of Commons, February 7, 1851* (London: Longman, Brown, Green, and Longman, 1851), 23.

50. Richard J. Schiefen, *Nicholas Wiseman and the Transformation of English Catholicism* (Shepherdstown: Patmos Press, 1984), 189.

51. See, for example, J. B. Conacher, "The Politics of the 'Papal Aggression' Crisis, 1850–51," *Canadian Catholic Historical Association* 25 (1959): 17. See also Donal A. Kerr, *'A Nation of Beggars'? Priests, People, and Politics in Famine Ireland, 1846–1852* (Oxford: Clarendon Press, 1994), 241–81; Paz, *Popular Anti-Catholicism*, 8–12; Walter Ralls, "The Papal Aggression of 1850: A Study in Victorian Anti-Catholicism," in *Religion in Victorian Britain: Interpretations*, ed. Gerald Parsons (Manchester: Manchester University Press, 1988), 115–34; and Wolffe, *Protestant Crusade*, 243–49.

52. On the ebb and flow of anti-Catholicism's effect on the ballot box, see Paz, *Anti-Catholicism*, 197–224, and Wolffe, *Protestant Crusade*, esp. 266–89.

53. "The Present Crisis," *London-Scottish Reformed Presbyterian Magazine* 1 (January 1, 1869): 484.

54. See, for example, Steven M. Nolt, *Foreigners in Their Own Land: Pennsylvania Germans in the Early Republic* (University Park: Pennsylvania

State University Press, 2002), 110–15. On the English commemorations, see Wolffe, *Protestant Crusade*, 90–91, 111.

55. For Horne's public and private correspondence on the topic, see Thomas Hartwell Horne, *Reminiscences, Personal and Bibliographical, of Thomas Hartwell Horne*, ed. Sarah Anne Cheyne (London: Longman, Green, Longman, and Roberts, 1862), 99–115.

56. Thomas Hartwell Horne, *A Protestant Memorial, for the Commemoration, on the Fourth Day of October, MDCCCXXXV, of the Third Centenary of the Reformation, and of the Publication of the First Entire Protestant English Version of the Bible, Oct. IV, MDXXXV*, 2nd ed. (London: T. Cadell et al., 1835), 4. Hereafter cited parenthetically in the text.

57. Andrew Atherstone, *Oxford's Protestant Spy: The Controversial Career of Charles Golightly* (Bletchley: Paternoster Press, 2007), 60–61.

58. On evangelical arguments (across denominations) that their theological outlook descended directly from the Reformation, see Ian Shaw, "The Evangelical Revival through the Eyes of the 'Evangelical Century': Nineteenth-Century Perceptions of the Origins of Evangelicalism," in *The Advent of Evangelicalism: Exploring Historical Continuities*, ed. Michael A. G. Haykin and Kenneth J. Stewart (Nashville, TN: B and H Academic, 2008), 302–23; Dickens and Tonkin, *The Reformation in Historical Thought*, 190. For Protestantism as the historical source of modern domestic and gender relationships, see Lenore Davidoff and Catherine Hall, *Family Fortunes: Men and Women of the English Middle Class, 1780–1850* (Chicago: University of Chicago Press, 1991), 115.

59. Horton Davies notes that "family prayers" were key to evangelical practice, arguing that whereas High Church family prayers were "liturgical" in nature, the evangelical version emphasized "extemporary prayer, with either the exposition of Scripture or the reading from an edifying book" (*Worship and Theology in England: From Watts and Wesley to Martineau, 1690–1900* [1961–62; repr., Grand Rapids, MI: William B. Eerdmans, 1996], 219–20). See also Davidoff and Hall, *Family Fortunes*, 89, 109; Jay, *Religion of the Heart*, 131–48.

60. On the relative absence of women from such activism, see Paz, *Popular Anti-Catholicism*, 274–80. However, as Colley points out, this didn't mean that they didn't participate in other forms of political agitation, such as signing petitions; see *Britons*, 23.

61. Kevin L. Morris, "John Bull and the Scarlet Woman: Charles Kingsley and Anti-Catholicism in Victorian Literature," *Recusant History* 23, no. 2 (October 1996): 207.

62. W. H. G. Kingston, *The Last Look: A Tale of the Spanish Inquisition* (London: S. W. Partridge, 1869), 91.

63. Hugh M'Neile, *The English Reformation, a Re-Assertion of Primitive Christianity. A Sermon, Preached in Christ Church, Newgate Street, on the 17th of November, 1858, the Tercentenary Commemoration of the Accession of Queen Elizabeth*, 2nd ed. (Liverpool: Adam Holden; London: Longman, Green, Longman, and Roberts, 1858), 39.

64. Grant A. Wacker, *Augustus H. Strong and the Dilemma of Historical Consciousness* (Macon, GA: Mercer University Press, 1985), 11.

65. Margaret Nancy Cutt, *Ministering Angels: A Study of Nineteenth-Century Evangelical Writing for Children* (Wormley: Five Owls Press, 1979), 91.

66. Useful accounts of the proto-Protestant trend in English theology include S. J. Barnett, "Where Was Your Church Before Luther? Claims for the Antiquity of Protestantism Examined," *Church History* 68 (1999): 14–41; Anthony Milton, *Catholic and Reformed: The Roman and Protestant Churches in English Protestant Thought, 1600–1640* (Cambridge: Cambridge University Press, 1995), esp. 270–310; O'Day, *The Debate on the English Reformation*, 5–30. On John Bale's popularization of Joachim de Fiore, see John N. King, *English Reformation Literature: The Tudor Origins of the Protestant Tradition* (Princeton, NJ: Princeton University Press, 1982), 61–64.

67. Rosemary Mitchell, *Picturing the Past: English History in Text and Image, 1830–1870* (Oxford: Clarendon Press, 2000), 177. For a brief overview of evangelical reading in this area, including Milner and D'Aubigné, see Wolffe, *Protestant Crusade*, 111–13.

68. There is still much to explore in the fields of painting, sculpture, architecture, and material culture more generally. See, for example, Ann V. Gunn, "Sir George Hayter, Victorian History Painting, and a Religious Controversy," *Record of the Art Museum, Princeton University* 53, no. 1 (1994): 2–32; Janes, *Victorian Reformation*.

CHAPTER ONE. SCOTT'S REFORMATIONS

1. Sir Walter Scott, *The Monastery*, ed. Penny Fielding (Edinburgh: Edinburgh University Press, 2000), 302–3. Hereafter cited parenthetically in the text as *TM*.

2. Christopher Johnson, "The Relationship between *The Monastery* and *The Abbot*," *Scottish Literary Journal* 20, no. 2 (1993): 38; Lionel Lackey, "*The Monastery* and *The Abbot*: Scott's Religious Dialectics," *Studies in the Novel* 19, no. 1 (1987): 57.

3. Michael Schiefelbein, *The Lure of Babylon: Seven Protestant Novelists and Britain's Roman Catholic Revival* (Macon, GA: Mercer University Press, 2001), 22.

4. On Scott's evangelical readership, see Sam Pickering Jr., "Evangelical Readers and the Phenomenal Success of Walter Scott's First Novels," *Christian Scholar's Review* 3 (1974): 345–59; Doreen Rosman, *Evangelicals and Culture*, 2nd ed. (Eugene, OR: Pickwick Press, 2011), 138–40. And on the rather contradictory run of religious responses to his work, see William McKelvy, *The English Cult of Literature: Devoted Readers, 1774–1880* (Charlottesville: University Press of Virginia, 2007), 193–94.

5. Judith Wilt, *Secret Leaves: The Novels of Walter Scott* (Chicago: University of Chicago Press, 1985), 107.

6. G. I. T. Machin, *The Catholic Question in English Politics, 1820 to 1830* (Oxford: Clarendon Press, 1964), 21.

7. Walter Scott, *The Journal of Sir Walter Scott*, ed. W. E. K. Anderson (1972; repr., Edinburgh: Canongate, 1998), 590.

8. Gilbert Stuart, *The History of the Establishment of the Reformation of Religion in Scotland* (London: J. Murray, 1780), 28, 125. On the history of such ambivalent responses to Reformation iconoclasm, see Margaret Aston, *Lollards and Reformers: Imagery and Literacy in Late Medieval Religion* (London: Hambledon Press, 1984), chap. 10, "English Ruins and English History: The Dissolution and the Sense of the Past," esp. 316–18; Alexandra Walsham, *The Reformation of the Landscape: Religion, Identity, and Memory in Early Modern Britain and Ireland* (Oxford: Oxford University Press, 2011), 274–96, and for Scotland specifically, 100–103.

9. Sophia Lee, *The Recess; Or, a Tale of Other Times*, ed. April Alliston (Lexington: University Press of Kentucky, 2000), 155. Hereafter cited parenthetically in the text.

10. E.g., Janina Nordius, "A Tale of Other Places: Sophia Lee's *The Recess* and Colonial Gothic," *Studies in the Novel* 34, no. 2 (2002): 165; Anne H. Stevens, *British Historical Fiction before Scott* (Houndmills: Palgrave Macmillan, 2010), 47.

11. April Alliston, "The Value of a Literary Legacy: Retracing the Transmission of Value through Female Lines," *Yale Journal of Criticism* 4, no. 1 (1990): 122.

12. Diane Long Hoeveler, *Gothic Riffs: Secularizing the Uncanny in the European Imaginary, 1780–1820* (Columbus: Ohio State University Press, 2010), 86.

13. Charles Taylor, *A Secular Age* (Cambridge, MA: Belknap Press of Harvard University Press, 2007), 39.

14. Walter Scott, *The Abbot*, ed. Christopher Johnson (1820; repr., Edinburgh: Edinburgh University Press, 2000), 374–75. Hereafter cited parenthetically in the text as *TA*.

15. Donald Cameron, "History, Religion, and the Supernatural: The Failure of *The Monastery*," *Studies in Scottish Literature* 6 (1969): 77.

16. Andrew Lincoln points out that *The Abbot* casts Catholic carnival as "an insolent threat that both Catholic and Protestant authorities seek to repress"—in effect, that both sides unite against what is perceived as the modern mob (*Walter Scott and Modernity* [Edinburgh: Edinburgh University Press, 2007], 11).

17. Fiona Robertson, *Legitimate Histories: Scott, Gothic, and the Authorities of Fiction* (Oxford: Clarendon Press, 1994), 134.

18. Caroline McCracken-Flesher, *Possible Scotlands: Walter Scott and the Story of Tomorrow* (Oxford: Oxford University Press, 2005), 45–46. Cf. Patricia S. Gaston on the core "dilemma" of subjective "human witness" in the Waverley prefaces: "What the personae most frequently do in the face of this dilemma is to include as many versions as possible of accounts of any given event; but what this strategy amounts to within the text is an undermining of traditional narrative authority, because all of the versions are flawed and because together, they still cannot recreate [a] past event" (*Prefacing the Waverley Prefaces: A Reading of Sir Walter Scott's Prefaces to the Waverley Novels* [New York: Peter Lang, 1991], 76).

19. In that sense, intentionally or not, Scott inherits the seventeenth-century polemical tradition that equated Protestantism with reason. As Raymond Tumbleson argues, Catholicism must "become unthinkable in order for the Protestant to become thinkable. Protestantism, the scientific site of the rational subject, figures as the prototype of the modern" (*Catholicism in the English Protestant Imagination: Nationalism, Religion, and Literature, 1660–1745* [1998; repr., Cambridge: Cambridge University Press, 2008], 101).

20. Jerome McGann, "Walter Scott's Romantic Postmodernity," in *Scotland and the Borders of Romanticism*, ed. Leith Davis, Ian Duncan, and Janet Sorensen (Cambridge: Cambridge University Press, 2004), 127.

21. See, for example, Daniel Cottom, "The Waverley Novels: Superstition and the Enchanted Reader," *English Literary History* 47, no. 1 (1980): 101; Ian Duncan, *Scott's Shadow: The Novel in Romantic Edinburgh* (Princeton, NJ: Princeton University Press, 2007), 194; and Francis Hart, *Scott's Novels: The Plotting of Historic Survival* (Charlottesville: University of Virginia Press, 1966), 190.

22. Lackey, "*The Monastery* and *The Abbot*," 53; Patricia Harkin, "The Fop, the Fairy, and the Genres of Scott's *The Monastery*," *Studies in Scottish Literature* 19, no. 1 (1984): 179.

23. See Alison Shell, *Oral Culture and Catholicism in Early Modern England* (Cambridge: Cambridge University Press, 2007), 68–69.

24. Horace Walpole, *The Castle of Otranto: A Gothic Story*, ed. W. S. Lewis and E. J. Clery (Oxford: Oxford University Press, 2008), 6.

25. E. J. Clery, *The Rise of Supernatural Fiction, 1762–1800* (1995; repr., Cambridge: Cambridge University Press, 1999), 54.

26. A. B., "Remarks on 'The Monastery,'" *Gentleman's Magazine* 128 (October 1820): 320; Lackey, "*The Monastery* and *The Abbot*," 53.

27. Jane Shaw, *Miracles in Enlightenment England* (New Haven, CT: Yale University Press, 2006), 33; see also Alexandra Walsham, *Providence in Early Modern England* (Oxford: Oxford University Press, 1999), 225–80.

28. Euan Cameron, *Enchanted Europe: Superstition, Reason, and Religion, 1250–1750* (2010; repr., Oxford: Oxford University Press, 2011), 207. Cameron is addressing the problem of exorcism.

29. James Kerr, *Fiction against History: Scott as Storyteller* (Cambridge: Cambridge University Press, 1989), 90.

30. Michael Gamer, *Romanticism and the Gothic: Genre, Reception, and Canon Formation* (Cambridge: Cambridge University Press, 2009), 180. Cf. Kerr, *Fiction against History*, 7–8, 38.

31. James Kearney, *The Incarnate Text: Imagining the Book in Reformation England* (Philadelphia: University of Pennsylvania Press, 2009), 22.

32. Wesley A. Kort, *"Take, Read": Scripture, Textuality, and Cultural Practice* (University Park: Pennsylvania State University Press, 1996), 14.

33. Hart, *Scott's Novels*, 194.

34. Hoeveler comments that "within the gothic imaginary there is a fair amount of slippage between the primitive and infantile 'Catholic' past that the European imaginary would like to repress or 'surmount' and the modern, secular tropes of Protestantism that appear as liberatory and rational" (*Gothic Riffs*, 30).

35. Cf. Beth Newman's argument that "[b]y eliminating women from the 'birth' of *The Heart of Midlothian* and having men only preside over the transmission of the narrative, Scott consolidates male narrative power in order to solve the problem of masculinity inhabiting the novel as a genre" ("*The Heart of Midlothian* and the Masculinization of Fiction," *Criticism* 36, no. 4 [Fall 1994]: 529).

36. See, for example, Jacqueline Pearson, *Women's Reading in Britain, 1750–1835: A Dangerous Recreation* (Cambridge: Cambridge University Press, 1999), 43–44.

37. Edith Snook, *Women, Reading, and the Cultural Politics of Early Modern England* (Aldershot: Ashgate, 2005), 35.

38. Ina Ferris, *The Achievement of Literary Authority: Gender, History, and the Waverley Novels* (Ithaca, NY: Cornell University Press, 1991), 99; emphasis in the original. Cf. James Watt, who points out Scott's habit of mocking female readers and their desire for conventional plots: *Contesting the Gothic: Fiction, Genre and Cultural Conflict, 1764–1832* (Cambridge: Cambridge University Press, 1999), 137–38.

39. On the novel's debt to the Gothic, see Robertson, *Legitimate Histories*, 6–7.

40. Michael Tomko, *British Romanticism and the Catholic Question: Religion, History, and National Identity, 1778–1829* (Houndmills: Palgrave Macmillan, 2011), 159.

41. Jayne Lewis, *Mary Queen of Scots: Romance and Nation* (London: Routledge, 1998), 166.

42. This absolutist mode is a general bugbear of Scott's, and one that also crops up in his critiques of the Covenanters; for example, see Ferris's analysis of *Old Mortality* in *Achievement of Literary Authority*, 175.

43. Tomko, *British Romanticism*, 173.

44. Alison Shell, *Shakespeare and Religion* (London: Methuen Drama, 2010), 116.

CHAPTER TWO. THE "MORNING STAR" OF THE REFORMATION

1. See, for example, Alison A. Chapman's argument that John Foxe's calendar prefaced to the Book of Martyrs delineates a shift from Catholic "liturgical" time to Protestant "historical" time: "Now and Then: Sequencing the Sacred in Two Protestant Calendars," *Journal of Medieval and Early Modern Studies* 33, no. 1 (Winter 2003): 100.

2. In the argument that follows, I do not discount the actual (if still hotly debated) relationship between those groups lumped together under the term *Lollard* and the theologians of the English Reformation; as Diarmaid MacCulloch reminds us, there were distinct continuities between Lollard and Elizabethan establishment priorities, even though he warns against reading the English Reformation as "nothing but Lollardy writ large." The Victorian popularized and fictionalized version of this history, however, generally ignores both the subtleties and qualifications involved in the contemporary scholarship. MacCulloch, "Putting the English Reformation on the Map: The Prothero Lecture," *Transactions of the Royal Historical Society*, 6th ser., 15 (2005): 80–81.

3. [George Stokes], *The Lollards; Or, Some Account of the Witnesses for the Truth in Great Britain, from A.D. 1400 to A.D. 1546; With a Brief Notice of Events Connected with the History of the Early Reformation* (London: Religious Tract Society, 1838), 4.

4. Norman W. Jones, *Gay and Lesbian Historical Fiction: Sexual Mystery and Post-Secular Narrative* (Houndmills: Palgrave Macmillan, 2007), 79.

5. Anna Vaninskaya summarizes the wild range of Victorian interpretations of the Peasants' Revolt (ranging from celebration of liberty to conservative denunciation) in "Dreams of John Ball: Reading the Peasants' Revolt in the Nineteenth Century," *Nineteenth-Century Contexts* 31, no. 1 (March 2009): 46–47.

6. Alexandra Walsham, "Inventing the Lollard Past: The Afterlife of a Medieval Sermon in Early Modern England," *Journal of Ecclesiastical History* 58, no. 4 (October 2007): 646. See also Aston, *Lollards and Reformers*, chap. 8, "John Wycliffe's Reformation Reputation," esp. 250–62; and James Crompton, "John Wyclif: A Study in Mythology," *Transactions of the Leicester Archaeological and Historical Society* 42 (1966–67): 6–34. Christina von Nolcken maps the links between biographers' and historians' own intellectual contexts and the assessments of the Lollards they produce in "Wyclif, the Wycliffites, and the *Oxford Dictionary of National Biography*," *Medieval Prosopography* 25 (2004): 223–25.

7. [Charlotte Mary Yonge?], "A Conversation on Books: Historical Tales," *The Monthly Packet* 31 (March 1881): 230.

8. Andrew Atherstone, "The Founding of Wycliffe Hall, Oxford," *Anglican and Episcopal History* 73, no. 1 (2004): 86. Compare Wycliffe College in Canada, noted by Crompton, "John Wyclif," 6.

9. The Nonconformist enthusiasm for Wycliffe had been well established since at least the eighteenth century; see John Seed, *Dissenting Histories: Religious Division and the Politics of Memory in Eighteenth-Century England* (Edinburgh: Edinburgh University Press, 2008), 42, 139; and Crompton, "John Wyclif," 15–16.

10. John Foxe, *The Unabridged Acts and Monuments Online* (Sheffield: HRI Online Publications, 2011), 5:445. www.johnfoxe.org.

11. Anna Maria Sargeant, *Tales of the Reformation* (London: Dean and Company, 1846), 20.

12. Anthony Kenny, "The Accursed Memory: The Counter-Reformation Reputation of John Wyclif," in *Wyclif and His Times*, ed. Anthony Kenny (Oxford: Clarendon Press, 1986), 159–60.

13. On the theological problems this had begun to pose by the seventeenth century, see Milton, *Catholic and Reformed*, 300–310. For an example of Anglican anxiety on this point, see Charles Webb Le Bas, *The Life of Wiclif* (London: J. G. and F. Rivington, 1832), 31–33.

14. G. R. Evans, *John Wyclif: Myth and Reality* (Downers Grove, IL: IVP Press, 2006), 146.

15. David Hume, *The History of England from the Invasion of Julius Caesar to the Revolution of 1688*, 6 vols. (1778; repr., Indianapolis: Liberty Classics, 1983), 2:322; John Lingard, *The History of England, from the First Invasion by the Romans to the Accession of William and Mary in 1688*, 6th ed., rev., 10 vols. (London: Charles Dolman, 1855), 3:133, 134, 150. Vaughan grumbles of Hume and Lingard that "[i]t is to the men who have most corrupted Christianity, and to those who treat it as a lie, that the rumours opposed to the reputation of the christian [*sic*] reformers have always been most acceptable" (*The Life and Opinions of John de Wycliffe: Illustrated Principally from His Unpublished*

Manuscripts; with a Preliminary View of the Papal System, and of the State of the Protestant Doctrine in Europe to the Commencement of the Fourteenth Century, 2 vols. [1828; repr., New York: AMS Press, 1971], 2:377n30).

16. Rudolf Buddensieg, "Wyclif Literature: Communication on the History and the Work of the Wyclif Society," *Critical Review of Theological and Philosophical Literature* 3, no. 3 (1893): 280.

17. In an otherwise unintentionally comical review essay, indicating a somewhat bruised ego, Robert Vaughan praises the superiority of German scholarship on Wycliffe; see "Wycliffe—His Biographers and Critics," *British Quarterly Review* 10 (1858): 399.

18. Mary Dove argues that Wycliffe believed that the church *should have been* responsible for authoritatively transmitting the scripture's meanings but currently *wasn't*, so that what he insisted on was "[n]ot *sola scriptura*, then, but a renewal of the authentic tradition of biblical interpretation" ("Wyclif and the English Bible," in *A Companion to John Wyclif: Late Medieval Theologian*, ed. Ian Christopher Levy [Leiden: Brill, 2006], 378). Cf. Henning Graf Reventlow, who warns that Wycliffe's *sola scriptura* is not Martin Luther's (*The Authority of the Bible and the Rise of the Modern World*, trans. John Bowden [Philadelphia: Fortress Press, 1985], 32, 37).

19. Vaughan, *Life*, 2:340; Rudolf Buddensieg, *John Wiclif: Patriot and Reformer, Life and Writings* (London: T. Fisher Unwin, 1884), 10–11; Johann Loserth, *Wiclif and Hus*, trans. M. J. Evans (London: Hodder and Stoughton, 1884). Loserth's thesis is that much of Hus's work is identical to or otherwise derives from Wycliffe's. On the paradoxically nationalist politics of this German position, however, see Crompton, "John Wiclif," 19–20.

20. [Anne Manning], *The Cottage History of England* (London: Arthur Hall, 1861), 79, 80.

21. On the problems with Wycliffe as Bible translator, see Anne Hudson, *The Premature Reformation: Wycliffite Texts and Lollard History* (Oxford: Clarendon Press, 1988), 238–47; and on the problems with Wycliffe as author of the *Wycket* (or *Wicket*), see Aston, *Lollards and Reformers*, 257–58. In 1895 Francis Aidan Cardinal Gasquet suggested that what Forshall and Madden had reprinted was really an orthodox *Catholic* translation; see "The Pre-Reformation Bible (I)," in *The Old English Bible and Other Essays*, new ed. (London: George Bell and Sons, 1908), 87–134. It's perhaps symptomatic of late-Victorian doubts that C. E. Sayle simply avoids the subject altogether in *Wiclif: An Historical Drama* (Oxford: James Thornton, 1887).

22. Velma Bourgeois Richmond argues of this and other examples of Brown's "Protestant medievalism" that it represents "events in the lives of Protestant English heroes of the Middle Ages, men whose development of the English language was crucial to breaking the hold of the Catholic church by

the clergy and to the formation of national identity" ("Ford Madox Brown's Protestant Medievalism: Chaucer and Wycliffe," *Christianity and Literature* 54, no. 3 [Spring 2005]: 366).

23. Frederic G[eorge] Kenyon, *Our Bible and the Ancient Manuscripts: Being a History of the Text and Its Translations*, 3rd ed. (London: Eyre and Spottiswode, 1898), 200.

24. As Jennifer Bryan reminds us, objections to Lollardy rested as much with "context (especially social class) as with theological content"; thus, the Bibles "were approved for the use of the wealthy and powerful, while even the most innocuous vernacular text in the hands of a laborer was cause for concern" (*Looking Inward: Devotional Reading and the Private Self in Late Medieval England* [Philadelphia: University of Pennsylvania Press, 2008], 31).

25. Frances Eastwood, *Geoffrey the Lollard* (New York: Dodd and Mead, 1870), 48. The book was reprinted in the United Kingdom in 1873.

26. Apropos of Ford Madox Brown's John Wycliffe, Michaela Giebelhausen makes the telling point that the most passionate response in the painting comes from the female auditor (*Painting the Bible: Representation and Belief in Mid-Victorian Britain* [Aldershot: Ashgate, 2006], 3).

27. Henry P. Cameron, *History of the English Bible* (London: Alexander Gardner, 1885), 52.

28. Christopher Anderson, *The Annals of the English Bible*, 2 vols. (London: William Pickering, 1845), 1:xxxvii.

29. John Stoughton, *Our English Bible: Its Translations and Translators* ([London]: Religious Tract Society, n.d.), 41.

30. Francis Charles Massingberd, *The English Reformation*, 3rd ed., rev. and enl. (London: John W. Parker and Son, 1857), for example, 136–37, 156–57; Anon., "Wycliffe and His Relation to the Reformation," *British Quarterly Review* 4 (1879): 334–68.

31. Robert Southey, *The Book of the Church*, from the 5th London ed. (Flemington, NJ: J. R. Dunham, 1844), 94.

32. [Thomas Gaspey], *The Lollards: A Tale, Founded on the Persecutions which Marked the Early Part of the Fifteenth Century*, 2 vols. (New York: James and John Harper, 1822). Originally published in Britain the same year.

33. James Eli Adams, *Dandies and Desert Saints: Styles of Victorian Manhood* (Ithaca, NY: Cornell University Press, 1995), 51; emphasis in the original.

34. Vaughan, *Life*, 2:49–50.

35. [Elizabeth Rundle Charles], "A Story of the Lollards," in *The Early Dawn; Or, Sketches of Christian Life in England in the Olden Time*, intro. Henry B. Smith (New York: M. W. Dodd, 1864), 390. Originally published in England the same year as *Sketches of Life in England in the Olden Time*. Hereafter cited parenthetically in the text as "Story." Elizabeth Rundle Charles

(1828–96) was a Quaker-turned-Anglican novelist, theologian, and hymnodist (*Dictionary of National Biography*).

36. For example, see Agnes Giberne, *Coulyng Castle; Or, a Knight of the Olden Days* (London: Seeley, Jackson, and Halliday, 1875), 14–15, 44, 82, 96–98.

37. For a documentary overview, see R. B. Dobson, ed., *The Peasants' Revolt of 1381* (London: Macmillan, 1970). Henry Hallam got as close as any nineteenth-century Protestant did to suggesting that Wycliffe might be at least remotely responsible for the revolt; see *View of the State of Europe in the Middle Ages*, 2 vols. (1818; repr., New York: Thomas Y. Crowell, 1880), 2:379. Emily Sarah Holt, who noted that "Wycliffe was himself one of the parish priests doomed to extermination, and that all his principal friends and supporters would likewise have been put to death," represents received opinion (*John de Wycliffe and What He Did for England* [London: John F. Shaw, n.d.], 106–7).

38. [G. V.] Lechler, *John Wycliffe and His English Precursors*, trans. with add. notes by [Peter] Lorimer, new rev. ed. (London: Religious Tract Society, n.d.), 202.

39. Emma Leslie, *Conrad: A Tale of Wiclif and Bohemia* (1880; repr., New York: Phillips and Hunt; Cincinnati, OH: Walden and Stowe, 1881). Earlier published by the Religious Tract Society as *Before the Dawn: A Tale of Wycliffe and Bohemia*. Hereafter cited parenthetically in the text as *Conrad*. Emma Leslie (1837–1909), actually Emma Dixon, was the author of several dozen novels. My thanks to Daniel Mills for Leslie's birth and death dates.

40. For an interesting discussion of later nineteenth-century attempts to rebel against this interpretation of suffering, see Lucy Bending, *The Representation of Bodily Pain in Late Nineteenth-Century English Culture* (Oxford: Oxford University Press, 2000).

41. Charlotte Brontë, *Jane Eyre*, ed. Richard J. Dunn, 3rd ed. (New York: W. W. Norton, 2001), 320.

42. On the importance of Matthew 10:37 in evangelical anti-Catholic polemic, see my "Protestants, Convents, and Seduction by Matthew 10:37," *Victorian Review* 37, no. 2 (Fall 2011): 16–20.

43. For a more detailed account of Holt's interest in the Lollards, see my "Emily Sarah Holt and the Evangelical Historical Novel: Undoing Sir Walter Scott," in *Clio's Daughters: British Women Making History, 1790–1899*, ed. Lynette Felber (Newark, NJ: University of Delaware Press, 2007), 167–73.

44. Emily Sarah Holt, *The Lord Mayor: A Tale of London in 1384* (London: John F. Shaw, 1885), 56. Hereafter cited parenthetically in the text.

45. W. Oak Rhind, *Hubert Ellerdale: A Tale of the Days of Wycliffe* (1881; repr., London: S. W. Partridge, n.d.), 18. Hereafter cited parenthetically in the text as *Hubert*. Nothing else about the author is known, and the novel was last reprinted in 1906.

46. David Rosen, "The Volcano and the Cathedral: Muscular Christianity and the Origins of Primal Manliness," in *Muscular Christianity: Embodying the Victorian Age*, ed. Donald E. Hall (Cambridge: Cambridge University Press, 1994), 26.

47. Charles Edmund Maurice, *Richard de Lacy. A Tale of the Later Lollards* (1892; repr., London: British Library, n.d.), 240. Hereafter cited parenthetically in the text.

48. Henry Cadwallader Adams, *Mark's Wedding, or Lollardy*, in *Tales Illustrating Church History. England, Vol. III, Mediæval Period* (Oxford: James Parker, 1877), 281–82.

49. Adams, *Dandies and Desert Saints*, 29.

50. David Vallins, "The Feeling of Knowledge: Insight and Delusion in Coleridge," *English Literary History* 64, no. 7 (1997): 168.

51. Arthur Brown, *The Knight of Dilham: A Story of the Lollards* (London: S. W. Partridge, [1875?]), 30.

52. Emily Sarah Holt, *Mistress Margery: A Tale of the Lollards* (1868; repr., London: John F. Shaw, n.d.), 26.

Chapter Three. "The Word of Life lies open before us"

1. Alexander Duff, "On the External Homage and Private Neglect of the Bible,—And Its Paramount Claims on the Attention of Man," *Scottish Christian Herald* 2 (February 18, 1837): 105–6.

2. Mary Wilson Carpenter, *Imperial Bibles, Domestic Bodies: Women, Sexuality, and Religion in the Victorian Market* (Columbus: Ohio University Press, 2003), 5. Carpenter examines the dissemination of elaborately printed and bound Bibles, aimed primarily at women, on 54–64.

3. Ledger-Lomas, "Mass Markets: Religion," 340. On the popular perception among even lower- and working-class Protestants that literacy and access to the Bible set them apart from Catholics, see Colley, *Britons*, 42–43.

4. Patrick Brantlinger, *The Reading Lesson: The Threat of Mass Literacy in Nineteenth-Century British Fiction* (Bloomington: Indiana University Press, 1998), 206.

5. In a striking example of the Bible exerting "drag" on an argument, as it were, Frederick Somner Merryweather's Lollard novel *Gilbert Wright, the Gospeller* (London: S. W. Partridge, 1877) acknowledges that transubstantiation was "*the* subject of the controversial battle of the Reformation" (88) and features it prominently during trial scenes—but nevertheless makes most of the drama hinge on owning and reading the vernacular Bible.

6. In Elaine Freedgood's terms, one might say that Duff's Bible has stopped being a "thing," which is still imbued with the "social relations of [its] production," and become a "commodity," which is "fetishized" and

experienced as outside those networks that origianlly granted it meaning. In Duff's imagination, the Bible has turned into pure decoration. See *The Ideas in Things: Fugitive Meaning in the Victorian Novel* (Chicago: University of Chicago Press, 2006), 75.

7. Scott Schofield, "Cain's Crime of Secrecy and the Unknowable Book of Life: The Complexities of Biblical Referencing in *Richard II*," in *Shakespeare, the Bible, and the Form of the Book: Contested Scriptures*, ed. Travis DeCook and Alan Galey (London: Routledge, 2012), 43. For an extensive discussion of what aids were available, see Ian Green, *Print and Protestantism in Early Modern England* (Oxford: Oxford University Press, 2000), 101–66.

8. Ruth B. Bottigheimer, *The Bible for Children: From the Age of Gutenberg to the Present* (New Haven, CT: Yale University Press, 1996), 21.

9. Kate Flint, *The Woman Reader, 1837–1914* (Oxford: Clarendon Press, 1993), 80.

10. As noted by Pearson in *Women's Reading in Britain*, 45.

11. Peter J. Thuesen, *In Discordance with the Scriptures: American Protestant Battles over Translating the Bible* (New York: Oxford University Press, 1999), 32, 35, 37, 39.

12. Brooke Foss Westcott, *A General View of the History of the English Bible* (London: Macmillan, 1868), 3.

13. Brian Cummings, *The Literary Culture of the Reformation: Grammar and Grace* (Oxford: Oxford University Press, 2002), 199–200.

14. For an introductory overview, including the work of Westcott and Moulton, see Owen Chadwick, *The Victorian Church*, vol. 2 (London: Adam and Charles Black, 1970), 39–57; cf. Thuesen, *Discordance*, 17–41.

15. John Stoughton, *Our English Bible*, 280–81. John Stoughton (1807–97) was a Congregationalist minister, prolific popular historian and biographer, and editor (*Dictionary of National Biography*).

16. Mrs. H[annah] C[haplin] Conant, *The English Bible. History of the Translation of the Holy Scriptures into the English Tongue. With Specimens of the Old English Versions* (New York: Sheldon, Blakeman, and Company, 1856), 99. Hannah Chaplin Conant (1809–65) was a Baptist biblical scholar, biographer, and translator and editor of the *Mother's Journal*.

17. Ibid., 129.

18. Candy Gunther Brown, *The Word in the World: Evangelical Writing, Publishing, and Reading in America, 1789–1880* (Chapel Hill: University of North Carolina Press, 2004), 32.

19. Selina A. Bower, *"Let There Be Light"; Or, the Story of the Reformation* (London: James Nisbet, 1883), 27. Hereafter cited parenthetically in the text. Selina A. Bower, fl. 1880s, was a poet and educational writer.

20. James Simpson, *Burning to Read: English Fundamentalism and Its Reformation Opponents* (Cambridge, MA: Belknap Press of Harvard Uni-

versity Press, 2007). For example: "God's law is found in Scripture and Scripture alone; however, the point of that written law is to insist on the reader's inability to fulfill it. Because human will and reason are irredeemably abject, in a Lutheran scheme, Biblical injunction hovers over an abyss: apparently it says 'do this,' but in reality it says 'know that this cannot be done'" (4–5).

21. Colleen McDannell, *The Christian Home in Victorian America, 1840–1900* (1986; repr., Bloomington: Indiana University Press, 1994), 85.

22. Sarah Robbins, *Managing Literacy, Mothering America: Women's Narratives on Reading and Writing in the Nineteenth Century* (Pittsburgh: University of Pittsburgh Press, 2004), 157.

23. This emphasis on feminine Bible reading is actually ironic; as Michael Ledger-Lomas reminds us, Victorian biblical commentaries (which go virtually unmentioned in these novels) generally "involve men assisting men in hammering the Bible's message into an endorsement of their authority" ("Caroline and Paul: Biblical Commentaries as Evidence of Reading in Victorian Britain," in *The History of Reading, Volume 2: Evidence from the British Isles, c. 1750–1950*, ed. Katie Halsey and W. R. Owens [Houndmills: Palgrave Macmillan, 2011], 34).

24. Michael Simpson, "Telling Lives to Children: Young Versus New Historicism in *Little Arthur's History of England*," in *Romanticism, History, Historicism: Essays on an Orthodoxy*, ed. Damian Walford Davies (New York: Routledge, 2009), 64.

25. Emma Marshall, *Dayspring: A Story of the Time of William Tyndale, Reformer, Scholar, and Martyr*, 2nd ed. (London: "Home Words" Publishing Office, n.d.), 146–47. Emma Marshall (1830–98), an Anglican originally brought up in the Society of Friends, was the author of dozens of novels for adults and children, many historical. See Beatrice Marshall, *Emma Marshall: A Biographical Sketch* (London: Seeley and Co., 1901).

26. For an attack on the book's overtly "Protestant" attitude, see "Children's Books," *Literary Churchman: A Critical Record of Religious Publications* 5, no. 5 (March 1, 1859): 89. By contrast, in 1865 a Protestant clergyman in Lancashire identified *Historical Tales* as one of the books he was using to evangelize the locals ("Correspondence and Publications," *Protestant Magazine* 27 [July 1, 1865]: 78). The Catholic journalist James Britten was still complaining about the book as late as 1896 ("'Pure Literature': A Postscript to 'Protestant Fiction,'" *The Month* 87 [June 1896]: 255). At least one story may have been written by the Baptist novelist Esther Beuzeville Hewlett Copley; see J. Gilbert Wiblin, "A Quiet By-Lane of Huguenot Story (A Refugee Family of Roussel)," *Proceedings of the Hugenot Society of London* 14, no. 2 (1931): 192. My thanks to Ralph Byles, one of Copley's descendants, for calling this to my attention. The British Library's attribution to J. H. Crosse should be to John Henry Cross, children's editor at the Religious Tract Society, who appears to

have edited the book (but is unlikely to be the author); see "John Henry Cross," *Child's Companion* 89 (May 1, 1876): 76. *Historical Tales for Young Protestants*, first published in 1857, remained in print in the United States and United Kingdom throughout the nineteenth century; it was last reprinted as late as 1950.

27. Advertisement for *Historical Tales for Young Protestants* in the *Religious Tract Society Reporter* 5 (September 16, 1857): 79.

28. *Historical Tales for Young Protestants*, ed. [John Henry Cross] (1857; repr., Philadelphia: American Sunday-School Union, n.d.), 5.

29. John Foxe, *The Unabridged Acts and Monuments Online* [*Book of Martyrs*], 1570 ed. (Sheffield: HRI Online Publications, 2011), 17. Unless noted, all further references are to this edition and will be given parenthetically in the text.

30. "The Youthful Martyr," in *Historical Tales for Young Protestants*, 67. Hereafter cited parenthetically in the text.

31. "Literary Notices," *Bradford Observer* 7, no. 1558 (December 17, 1863): 7.

32. For a convenient overview of Charles's life and work from the point of view of her interest in the Bible, see Marion Ann Taylor, "Elizabeth Rundle Charles: Translating the Letter of Scripture into Life," in *Recovering Nineteenth-Century Women Interpreters of the Bible*, ed. Christiana de Groot and Marion Ann Taylor (Atlanta, GA: Society of Biblical Literature, 2007), 149–64; for Charles's broad religious sympathies specifically, see 152.

33. [Elizabeth Rundle Charles], *Chronicles of the Schönberg-Cotta Family. By Two of Themselves* (New York: M.W. Dodd, 1864), 103. Hereafter cited parenthetically in the text.

34. The outcome of this plot exasperated the Catholic reviewer from *The Month*, who noted that a man who "has been saying the canonical hours for more than seven years, and has been six months a novice in Luther's monastery" ought not to have taken *quite* so long to recognize the quotation. See "Our Library Table," *The Month: A Magazine and Review* 5 (1866): 541.

35. Brian Cummings argues of Luther's own account that he "offers to replicate in his readers the reformatory powers he attributes to his own experience of reading. He presents a history of reading which demands of the reader a corresponding energy and power in interpretation" (Cummings, *The Literary Culture of the Reformation*, 63).

36. [Mary Atkinson Maurice], *Isabella Hamilton: A Tale of the Sixteenth Century* (London: John Farquar Shaw, 1852), 31. Mary Atkinson Maurice (1797–1858), sister of the theologian Frederic Denison Maurice, was a pedagogical theorist and children's author.

37. Cheryl A. Wilson, "Female Reading Communities in *Jane Eyre*," *Brontë Studies* 30, no. 2 (July 2005): 138.

38. Deborah Alcock, *No Cross, No Crown: A Tale of the Scottish Reformation* (London: T. Nelson and Sons, 1887), 90. The novel was first published, with identical pagination, as *The Dark Year of Dundee: A Tale of the Scottish Reformation* in 1867. Deborah Alcock (1825–1913) was an Irish novelist and popular historian and daughter of the archdeacon of Waterford (*Dictionary of National Biography*; Rolf Loeber and Magda Stouthamer-Loeber, eds., with Anne Mullin Burham, *A Guide to Irish Fiction, 1650–1900* [Dublin: Four Courts Press, 2006]).

39. In some apparent irritation, John Read Dore tartly commented that "We must remember that the universal desire for a Bible in England, we read so much of in most works on the subject, existed only in the minds of the writers" (*Old Bibles: An Account of the Early Versions of the English Bible*, 2nd ed. [London: Eyre and Spottiswode, 1888], 13).

40. Ayşe Çelikkol, "Free Trade and Disloyal Smugglers in Scott's *Guy Mannering* and *Redgauntlet*," *English Literary History* 74, no. 4 (2007): 760.

41. Charles Bruce, *The Story of John Heywood: A Historical Tale of the Time of Harry VIII* (Edinburgh: W. P. Nimmo, [1873?]), 44–45. A children's author and biographer, Bruce published at least twenty books in the 1870s and 1880s. *The Story of John Heywood* was reprinted in 1878 (Samuel Austin Allibone, *A Critical Dictionary of English Literature and British and American Authors, Living and Deceased, from the Earliest Account to the Latter Half of the Nineteenth Century*, 3 vols. [Philadelphia: J. B. Lippincott, 1891–1908]).

42. Deborah Alcock, *The Spanish Brothers: A Tale of the Sixteenth Century* (1870; repr., London: T. Nelson and Sons, 1895), 69. One of Alcock's most popular novels, it was translated into Dutch, French, and German and last reprinted in the 1960s by the Bethany Fellowship.

43. Kingston, *The Last Look*, 123. William Henry Giles Kingston (1814–80) was a popular historical novelist for boys (*Dictionary National Biography*).

44. Emma Leslie, *Soldier Fritz and the Enemies He Fought: A Story of the Reformation* (London: Religious Tract Society, [1871?]), 14.

45. H. S., "Missionary Records. No. XXVII," *Church of England Magazine* 23 (October 1847): 235.

46. David Paul Nord, *Faith in Reading: Religious Publishing and the Birth of Mass Media in America* (New York: Oxford University Press, 2004), 98.

47. J[ohn] A[ngell] James, "On Reading the Scriptures," *Tract Magazine and Christian Miscellany* (London: Religious Tract Society, 1869): 72. Leslie Howsam suggests that "[t]his particular piece of print was the means of everlasting salvation; at the same time it was also a marketplace commodity, a physical object bearing an identifiable commercial resale value. Because it embodied the sacred text, the material book was too valuable to be given as a free

gift, no matter how cheap to produce, nor how much wealthier the donor than the recipient" ("The Nineteenth-Century Bible Society and 'The Evil of Gratuitous Distribution,'" in *Free Print and Non-Commercial Publishing since 1700*, ed. James Raven [Aldershot: Ashgate, 2000], 131).

48. Howsam, "Nineteenth-Century Bible Society," 129.

49. Alice Lang, *The Adventures of Hans Müller* (London: Religious Tract Society, [1894?]), 26, 197. Hereafter cited parenthetically in the text.

50. Harriet Warner Ellis, *The Melvill Family and Their Bible Readings* (1871; repr., London: Hodder and Stoughton, 1885), 13.

51. Emma Leslie, *Daybreak in Italy* (London: Religious Tract Society, 1870), 129. Leslie probably got the story from J. H. Merle d'Aubigné's *History of the Reformation in Europe in the Time of Calvin*, 8 vols. (New York: Robert Carter and Brothers, 1863–68), 4:417.

52. Anne Stott, *Hannah More* (Oxford: Oxford University Press, 2003), 124. Stott points out that More's best-known statement of her educational policy was made in the context of an appeal to the "extreme conservative Dr John Bowdler" (120), and thus needs to be taken with a grain or two of salt in light of her statements elsewhere.

53. Antoinina Bevan Zlatar, *Reformation Fictions: Protestant Polemical Dialogues in Elizabethan England* (Oxford: Oxford University Press, 2011), 50.

54. E[lizabeth] H[ely] Walshe, *From Dawn to Dark in Italy: A Tale of the Reformation in the Sixteenth Century* (1864; repr., Boston: American Tract Society, [1865?]), 11–12. Elizabeth Hely Walshe (1835–68) was an Irish evangelical novelist (Loeber et al., *A Guide to Irish Fiction*).

55. Emily Sarah Holt, *Robin Tremayne: A Tale of the Marian Persecution* (1872; repr., New York: Robert Carter and Brothers, 1876), 289, 291–92. Hereafter cited parenthetically in the text.

56. Dora M. Jones, *At the Gates of the Morning: A Story of the Reformation in Kent* (London: Charles H. Kelly, 1898), 40. The novel had earlier been serialized as *The Rose of Dawn* in the *Wesleyan Methodist Magazine*. Jones appears to conflate the Six Articles with the Act for Advancement of True Religion (1543), which did indeed forbid those like Margery from reading the scriptures themselves. Jones was a novelist and literary critic active into the twentieth century.

57. It is also worth noting that any claims for the feminism of this scripture-for-all mode—the "liberating potential of Scripture," in Christine Krueger's phrasing (*The Reader's Repentance: Women Preachers, Women Writers, and Nineteenth-Century Social Discourse* [Chicago: University of Chicago Press, 1992], 149)—must take into account that it implicitly subordinates or strips of agency Catholic women (usually figured as biblically illiterate) as well as non-Christians.

58. Leslie also harnessed Anne Boleyn for evangelical purposes in *At the Sign of the Golden Fleece: A Story of Reformation Days* (London: Gall and Inglis, 1900), for example, at 301; and *Peter the Apprentice: A Tale of the Reformation in England* (London: Religious Tract Society, n.d.), for example, 51–57, 126. A more sensationalized version of the same evangelical Anne appears in the anonymous *Anne Boleyn: Or, the Suppression of the Religious Houses* (London: Saunders and Otley, 1854). Although Michael Wheeler notes that "[i]t was also difficult to present Anne Boleyn as a Protestant martyr" (Wheeler, *The Old Enemies*, 105), nineteenth-century interest in Anne as a proto-evangelical goes back to Elizabeth Benger's *Memoirs of the Life of Anne Boleyn, Queen of Henry VIII* (1822).

59. Emma Leslie, *The Chained Book* (London: George Cauldwell, [1878?]), 56. Hereafter cited parenthetically in the text. Initially serialized in 1874 in the Sunday School Union magazine *Kind Words*.

60. On the importance of women reading aloud, see Suzanne M. Ashworth, "Susan Warner's *The Wide, Wide World*, Conduct Literature, and Protocols of Female Reading in Mid-Nineteenth-Century America," *Legacy* 17, no. 2 (2000): 153.

61. [George Eliel Sargent], *Lilian: A Tale of Three Hundred Years Ago* (1864; repr., New York: American Tract Society, [1865?]), 111. The book was first published in the United Kingdom by the Religious Tract Society and was still in print as late as 1902. George Eliel Sargent (1809–83), Baptist children's novelist, was related by marriage to Esther Copley, author of one of the tales in *Historical Tales for Young Protestants*. See Marion Sargent, "George Eliel Sargent and Emma Hewlett," in *Sargent Family History*, November 28, 1998. http://www.angelfire.com/ms/mysargentfamily/eliel.html.

62. Helen Parish, *Monks, Miracles, and Magic: Reformation Representations of the Medieval Church* (New York: Routledge, 2005), 23.

CHAPTER FOUR. REINVENTING THE MARIAN PERSECUTIONS IN VICTORIAN ENGLAND

1. For both the comic and the serious permutations of *martyrdom* in Victorian culture, see Dominic Janes, "The 'Modern Martyrdom' of Anglo-Catholics in Victorian England," *Journal of Religion and Society* 13 (2011), http://moses.creighton.edu/jrs/2011/2011-16.pdf.

2. Charlotte Elizabeth [Phelan Tonna], *Alice Benden; Or, the Bowed Shilling, and Other Tales* (New York: Baker and Scribner, 1846), 68. Tonna (1790–1846) was a poet, novelist, and tract-writer and editor of multiple religious periodicals, including the *Protestant Magazine*.

3. Thomas S. Freeman, "Inventing Bloody Mary: Perceptions of Mary Tudor from the Restoration to the Twentieth Century," in *Mary Tudor: Old and New Perspectives*, ed. Susan Doran and Thomas S. Freeman (Houndmills: Palgrave Macmillan, 2011), 81. More generally, see John Miller, *Popery and Politics in England, 1660–1688* (Cambridge: Cambridge University Press, 1973), 67–90; and Jack Lynch, *The Age of Elizabeth in the Age of Johnson* (Cambridge: Cambridge University Press, 2003), 78–96.

4. Wheeler, *The Old Enemies*, 77.

5. Billie Melman, "The Pleasures of Tudor Horror: Popular Histories, Modernity and Sensationalism in the Long Nineteenth Century," in *Tudorism: Historical Imagination and the Appropriation of the Sixteenth Century*, ed. Tatiana C. String and Marcus Bull (Oxford: Oxford University Press, 2011), 49.

6. Patrick Collinson, "The Persecution in Kent," in *The Church of Mary Tudor: Catholic Christendom, 1300–1700*, ed. Eamon Duffy and David Loades (Aldershot: Ashgate, 2006), 311.

7. I am more skeptical than Billie Melman that the figure of the imprisoned Christian woman and her ability to argue religious topics "erodes the Victorian notion of female pietism" that emphasizes private faith; despite prejudices against women *doing* theology, a woman's ability to *defend* a Protestant (or, for that matter, Catholic) theological position is considered a standard part of her armory in these texts. See *The Culture of History: English Uses of the Past, 1800–1953* (Oxford: Oxford University Press, 2006), 177.

8. Brad Gregory, *Salvation at Stake: Christian Martyrdom in Early Modern Europe* (Cambridge, MA: Harvard University Press, 1999), 119. On the history of debates over pseudomartyrdom, still going strong in the nineteenth century, see 315–41; and, focusing on Catholic arguments, see Anne Dillon, *The Construction of Martyrdom in the English Catholic Community, 1535–1603* (Aldershot: Ashgate, 2002), 18–71.

9. I earlier offered a very brief discussion of these two novelists in "Reviving the Reformation: Victorian Women Writers and the Protestant Historical Novel," *Women's Writing* 12, no. 1 (2005): 77–78.

10. David Loades, "Introduction: The Personal Religion of Mary I," in *The Church of Mary Tudor: Catholic Christendom, 1300–1700*, ed. Eamon Duffy and David M. Loades (Aldershot: Ashgate, 2006), 18; see also Lucy Wooding, *Rethinking Catholicism in Reformation England* (Oxford: Oxford University Press, 2000), 118.

11. For an overview of the debate, see John Edwards, *Mary I: England's Catholic Queen* (New Haven, CT: Yale University Press, 2011), 259–65. Loades concludes point-blank that Mary bears most of the onus ("Personal Religion," 28), as does Thomas Freeman in "Burning Zeal: Mary Tudor and the Marian

Persecution," in *Mary Tudor: Old and New Perspectives*, ed. Susan Doran and Thomas S. Freeman (Houndmills: Palgrave Macmillan, 2011), 172–73.

12. For an assessment of the conflict, focusing on Reginald Cardinal Pole, see D. M. Loades, *The Reign of Mary Tudor: Politics, Government, and Religion in England, 1553–1558* (New York: St. Martin's Press, 1979), 428–37.

13. Wooding, *Rethinking Catholicism*, esp. 117–23.

14. See, for example, William Wizeman, S.J., "The Religious Policy of Mary I," in *Mary Tudor: Old and New Perspectives*, ed. Susan Doran and Thomas S. Freeman (Houndmills: Palgrave Macmillan, 2011), 169–70. For a more skeptical reading, see Loades, *Reign of Mary*, 464–66.

15. On the inaccessibility of Reformation primary texts, Luther included, see Kenneth J. Stewart (citing Gordon Rupp), *Restoring the Reformation: British Evangelicalism and the Francophone 'Réveil,' 1816–1849* (Milton Keynes, UK: Paternoster, 2006), 206n13; and on Victorian reprints of relevant primary and secondary texts, see John Edward Drabble, "The Historians of the English Reformation: 1780–1850" (PhD diss., New York University, 1975), 259–66.

16. John Stock, *A Sermon Preached in the Parish Churches of St. Mary Stratford Bow, and of All Saints, Poplar, Middlesex, on Sunday, October 4th, 1835, in Commemoration of the Third Centenary of the Reformation, and of the Publication of the First Entire Protestant English Version of the Bible, October 4th, 1835 [sic]* (London: A. and S. Alston, 1835), 11.

17. There's some controversy about attitudes toward Catholicism in these abridgements: Devorah Greenberg finds that they tone down Foxe's vitriol, whereas Thomas S. Freeman argues that they actually exacerbated the "Bloody Mary" myth. See Greenberg, "Eighteenth-Century 'Foxe': History, Historiography, and Historical Consciousness," in *John Foxe's The Acts and Monuments Online* (Sheffield: HRI Online Publications, 2011); Freeman, "Inventing Bloody Mary," 86.

18. For Maitland's long-running jeremiad against the Cattley-Townsend edition, see D. Andrew Penny, "John Foxe's Historical Reception," *Historical Journal* 40, no. 1 (1997): 111–42; Patrick Collinson, "Through Several Glasses Darkly: Historical and Sectarian Perceptions of the Tudor Church," in *Tudorism: Historical Imagination and the Appropriation of the Sixteenth Century*, ed. Tatiana C. String and Marcus Bull (Oxford: Oxford University Press, 2011), 104–5. In addition to discussing Maitland, Penny offers a more thorough overview of Cattley's and Townsend's editorial practice in "John Foxe, Evangelicalism, and the Oxford Movement," in *John Foxe: An Historical Perspective*, ed. David Loades (Aldershot: Ashgate, 1999), 195–217. Thomas S. Freeman has offered a scathing assessment of both Cattley-Townsend (editorial practices, silent alterations to the text, censorship, and so forth) and the perils

of relying on it in "Text, Lies, and Microfilm: Reading and Misreading Foxe's 'Book of Martyrs,'" *Sixteenth Century Journal* 30, no. 1 (Spring 1999): 23–46.

19. Jonathan Rose, *The Intellectual Life of the British Working Classes* (New Haven, CT: Yale University Press, 2001), 152.

20. Devorah Greenberg, "Reflexive Foxe: The *Book of Martyrs* Transformed, 'Foxe' Reinterpreted—Sixteenth through Twenty-First Centuries" (PhD diss., Simon Fraser University, 2002), 318.

21. Peter Nockles, "The Nineteenth-Century Reception," in *The Unabridged Acts and Monuments Online* (Sheffield: HRI Online Publications, 2011).

22. M. Hobart Seymour, "Danger to England from Treacherous Popery and Unwatchful Protestantism. Preached at St. Ann's Church, Blackfriars, on Sunday Afternoon, Nov. 3, 1839," *The Pulpit* 36, no. 909 (1839): 231. Michael Hobart Seymour (1800–74) made a name for himself through his anti-convent crusading in the early 1850s and, in particular, his attacks on both Jesuits and Catholics more generally in *A Pilgrimage to Rome* (1848), *Mornings among the Jesuits at Rome* (1849), and *Evenings with the Romanists* (1854). He was the brother of hymnodist, biographer, and popular theologian Aaron Crossley Hobart Seymour (Allibone, *Critical Dictionary of English Literature*; *Dictionary of National Biography*).

23. W. Jay Bolton, *The Stratford Martyrs of the Reformation. A Sermon Preached at St. John's, Stratford, E., on Sunday, July 12th, 1868* (London: Hamilton, Adams, and Company, 1868), 6. William Jay Bolton (1816–84), initially a successful designer of stained glass windows, entered the church in his late thirties. See Jonathan P. Harding, "William Jay Bolton," *Paintings and Sculpture in the Collection of the National Academy of Design*, ed. David Bernard Dearinger (Manchester, VT: Hudson Hills Press, 2004), 56.

24. John Cunningham Geikie, *The English Reformation: How It Came About, and Why We Should Uphold It* (New York: D. Appleton, 1879), 482.

25. "Popish Tortures, Massacres, and Persecutions," *Bulwark or Reformation Journal* 1 (1852): 295.

26. "The Reign of Bloody Mary," *Bulwark or Reformation Journal* 8 (January 1859): 182.

27. For a detailed account of Lingard's revisionist approach to conventional Protestant historiography, see Rosemary Mitchell, "Every Picture Tells a Catholic Story: Lingard's *History of England* Illustrated and the Transition in Catholic Historiography," in *Lingard Remembered: Essays to Mark the Sesquicentenary of John Lingard's Death*, ed. Peter Phillips (London: Catholic Record Society, 2004), 125–42. Sabine Müller notes that Mary's reputation in the nineteenth century rose as Elizabeth's sank; "Romancing the (Unhappy) Queen: Emplotment Frühneuzeitlichen Weiblichen Königtums

am Beispiel Mary Tudors (1553–1558)," *Zeitsprünge Forschungen zur Frühen Neuzeit* 10, nos. 3–4 (2006): 361.

28. John Drabble, "Mary's Protestant Martyrs and Elizabeth's Catholic Traitors in the Age of Catholic Emancipation," *Church History* 51 (1982): 172–85; O'Day, *The Debate on the English Reformation*, 65; Wheeler, *The Old Enemies*, 77–110.

29. Müller, "Romancing the (Unhappy) Queen," 343: "oszilliert zwischen verschiedenen Polen"—"bespielsweise ihrer Darstellung als Königin von Gottes Gnaden und als Verkörperung der Monstrosität weiblicher Herrschaft[,] als Königin von England und als Gattin Philips I., des titulären Königs von England, oder eben zwischen ihrer Darstellung als *victimizer* und *victimized* (*bloody/unhappy*)" (translated by the author).

30. John Lingard, *The History of England*, 5:227. Hereafter cited parenthetically in the text.

31. In martyrological and pseudomartyrological discourse, *persecution* signifies an unjust act; as Gregory points out, sixteenth-century Protestants and Catholics distinguished between righteous *prosecution* and unrighteous *persecution* (*Salvation at Stake*, 74–96). This distinction remained operational in the nineteenth century, as the Catholic polemicist C. W. Russell illustrates: "we must avow our opinion that Mary's sanguinary acts were indefensible, and deserve the name of persecution" ("Mary Tudor," *Dublin Review* 25, n.s. [1875]: 446).

32. Donald F. Shea, *The English Ranke: John Lingard* (New York: Humanities Press, 1969), 66–67.

33. Mary Spongberg, "*La Reine Malheureuse*: Stuart History, Sympathetic History, and the Stricklands' History of Henrietta Maria," *Women's History Review* 20, no. 5 (2011): 753.

34. Agnes Strickland [and Elizabeth Strickland], *Lives of the Queens of England, from the Norman Conquest; With Anecdotes of Their Courts, Now First Published from Official Records and Other Authentic Documents, Private as Well as Public*, new ed., corr., 9 vols. (London: Henry Colburn, 1844), 5:280. Hereafter cited parenthetically in the text.

35. Thomas Betteridge, *Tudor Histories of the English Reformations, 1530–1583* (Aldershot: Ashgate, 1999), 169–71, 179–81; cf. Frances Dolan, *Whores of Babylon: Catholicism, Gender, and Seventeenth-Century Print Culture* (Ithaca, NY: Cornell University Press, 1999), 39–41; Glyn Redworth, "'Matters Impertinent to Women': Male and Female Monarchy under Philip and Mary," *English Historical Review* 112, no. 47 (June 1997): 603–4. Judith M. Richards points out that false pregnancy would have been a relatively well-known problem at the time, and that we have no actual evidence that it badly destabilized the queen; see "Reassessing Mary Tudor: Some Concluding

Points," in *Mary Tudor: Old and New Perspectives*, ed. Susan Doran and Thomas S. Freeman (Houndmills: Palgrave Macmillan, 2011), 214–15. John Edwards offers a slightly different reading, focusing on psychological factors, in *Mary I*, 269.

36. Hume, *The History of England*, 3:444.

37. Cf. Maureen Moran, who notes that "[r]epresentations of the sixteenth-century Marian persecutions . . . vilify sovereigns who sacrifice the interests of their subjects for reasons of their own personal prejudices and predispositions" (*Catholic Sensationalism and Victorian Literature* [Liverpool: Liverpool University Press, 2007], 136). As we see in Strickland and elsewhere, however, writers who wanted to complicate the portrait of Mary herself often gendered such bad sovereigns as male.

38. Charles Butler, *Historical Memoirs Respecting the English, Irish, and Scottish Catholics, from the Reformation, to the Present Time*, 2nd ed., 2 vols. (London: John Murray, 1819), 1:137–38. From a conservative, anti-Catholic point of view, Robert Southey conceded much the same thing, suggesting that Mary had the seeds of "a good and beneficent, as well as conscientious queen," but thanks to contemporary religious upheaval, she "delivered her conscience to the direction of cruel men" and became viciously intolerant (*The Book of the Church*, 144).

39. The historian J. A. Froude offered a slightly different interpretation of this point, blaming the persecutions on the influence of the usually celebrated Cardinal Pole: "Mary was driven to madness by the disappointment of the grotesque imaginations with which he had inflated her; and where two such persons were invested by the circumstances of the time with irresponsible power, there is no occasion to look further for the explanation of the dreadful events of the three ensuing years." Note how the imagery suggests false pregnancy, as though the persecutions are the unnatural result of an equally unnatural relationship. *The Reign of Mary Tudor* (London: J. M. Dent; New York: E. P. Dutton, 1913), 223–24. For Froude's interest in the false pregnancy more generally, see Eamon Duffy, Introduction to *J. A. Froude's The Reign of Mary Tudor*, ed. Eamon Duffy (London: Continuum, 2009), 15, 17–18.

40. [Miss] L. Pocklington, *The Secret Room: A Story of Tudor Times* (1884; repr., London: Religious Tract Society, n.d.), 186. Hereafter cited parenthetically in the text.

41. Ramona Garcia, "'Most wicked superstition and idolatry': John Foxe, His Predecessors and the Development of an Anti-Catholic Polemic in the Sixteenth-Century Accounts of the Reign of Mary I," in *John Foxe at Home and Abroad*, ed. David Loades (Aldershot: Ashgate, 2004), 80. Even Catholic writers occasionally agreed on this point, for example, the author of the oft-reprinted *A Popular Manual of Church History* (1857; repr., Baltimore,

MD: Kelly, Piet, and Company, 1876), 202. Originally published in the United Kingdom in 1857, the manual was still in print as late as 1921.

42. Müller, "Romancing the (Unhappy) Queen," 356; Körper und Geist als essentiell spanisch . . . (translated by the author).

43. On the Black Legend, which emphasized the moral perils of Spain's Catholic identity, see, for example, Robert E. Scully, S.J., " 'In the Confident Hopes of a Miracle': The Spanish Armada and Religious Mentalities in the Late Sixteenth Century," *Catholic Historical Review* 89, no. 4 (2003): 663–65.

44. Sir Aubrey de Vere, *Mary Tudor. A Tragedy. Part the Second*, in *Mary Tudor: An Historical Drama, the Lamentation of Ireland, and Other Poems* (London: William Pickering, 1847). Hereafter cited parenthetically in the text. It was reprinted in 1858, 1875, and 1884; according to his son, also Aubrey de Vere, the poem's reputation revived with the appearance of Lord Tennyson's verse tragedy on the same topic. See *Recollections of Aubrey de Vere*, 3rd ed. (London: Edward Arnold, 1897), 216.

45. Dolan, *Whores of Babylon*, 36–37.

46. Alfred, Lord Tennyson, *Queen Mary: A Drama*, in *Tennyson: Poems and Plays* (London: Oxford University Press, 1968), 538–606. Hereafter cited parenthetically in the text. Dennis Taylor suggests that in the play, Mary I stands "at the crossroads of the dark and light Catholicism," between genuinely spiritual Catholic virtue and a far more brutal, dangerous form ("Tennyson's Catholic Years: A Point of Contact," *Victorian Poetry* 47, no. 1 [2009]: 303).

47. On the play's perceived topicality at the time, see Robert Bernard Martin, *Tennyson: The Unquiet Heart* (London: Faber and Faber, 1980), 513.

48. Respectively, Margaret Homans, *Royal Representations: Queen Victoria and British Culture, 1837–1876* (Chicago: University of Chicago Press, 1998), 156; Elizabeth Langland, "Nation and Nationality: Queen Victoria in the Developing Narrative of Englishness," in *Remaking Queen Victoria*, ed. Margaret Homans and Adrienne Munich (Cambridge: Cambridge University Press, 1997), 21; Alison Booth, *How to Make It as a Woman: Collective Biographical History from Victoria to the Present* (Chicago: University of Chicago Press, 2004), 263.

49. Emma Leslie, *Cecily: A Tale of the English Reformation* (London: Wesleyan Conference Office, 1881), 70. Hereafter cited parenthetically in the text.

50. In fact, although there were some naysayers, Mary's self-deconstructing eulogy runs counter to most Victorian representations of Catherine, which increasingly emphasized her positive virtues as the century wore on; see Georgianna Ziegler, "Reimagining a Renaissance Queen: Catherine of Aragon Among the Victorians," in *"High and Mighty Queens" of Early Modern England: Realities and Representations*, ed. Carole Levin, Jo Eldridge Carney, and Debra Barrett-Graves (Houndmills: Palgrave Macmillan, 2003), 203–22.

51. Although, as Glyn Redworth notes, all Philip appeared to be doing in reality was "exercise[ing] a temporary political dominance through being the husband of the Queen," as opposed to absorbing England wholesale ("'Matters Impertinent,'" 607).

52. Cristina Mazzoni, *Maternal Impressions: Pregnancy and Childbirth in Literature and Theory* (Ithaca, NY: Cornell University Press, 2002), 68.

53. Edith Dolnikowski, "Feminine Exemplars for Reform: Women's Voices in John Foxe's *Acts and Monuments*," in *Women Preachers and Prophets through Two Millennia of Christianity*, ed. Beverly Mayne Kienzle and Pamela J. Walker (Berkeley: University of California Press, 1998), 207.

54. Edith Snook, *Women, Reading, and the Cultural Politics*, 43.

55. John Foxe, *Book of Martyrs*, 1570, 12.2239–40. Some readers were skeptical about the story of Allin's burning, for example, Richard Watson Dixon, in *History of the Church of England from the Abolition of the Roman Jurisdiction*, 4 vols. (London: George Routledge and Sons, 1891), 4:n.†. William Eusebius Andrews completely omits the burning from his review of Foxe's account of the Mounts' martyrdom; see *An Examination of Fox's Calendar of Protestant Saints, Martyrs, &c., &c., Contrasted with a Biographical Sketch of Catholic Missionary Priests . . .* , 3 vols. (London: W. E. Andrews, 1826), 3:351–52.

56. Joseph Glass, *Reminiscences of Manningtree and Its Vicinity, with Some Reference to the Past and Present History of the Town and Neighborhood* (London: Judd and Glass, 1855), 24.

57. Foxe initially invoked Mucius Scaevola in his discussion of Thomas Tomkins, who was also burnt in the hand (*Book of Martyrs*, 1563, 5.1171); he extended the moral to Rose Allin in 1570, 12.2240.

58. Thomas Fuller, *The History of the Worthies of England*, ed. John Nichols, 2 vols. (London: F. C. and J. Rivington, 1811), 1:343; John Milner [Francis William Blagdon], *An Universal History of Christian Martyrdom, Being a Complete and Authentic Account of the Lives, Sufferings, and Triumphant Deaths of the Primitive as Well as Protestant Martyrs, in All Parts of the World, from the Birth of the Blessed Saviour to the Latest Periods of Pagan and Catholic Persecution* (London: J. G. Barnard, 1807), 948.

59. A Father [pseudo.], *Rose Allen, a Martyr Story; And Other Poems, Chiefly Sacred* (London: James Nisbet, 1851), 5.

60. Maria LaMonaca, *Masked Atheism: Catholicism and the Secular Victorian Home* (Columbus: Ohio State University Press, 2008), 111.

61. Dolan, *Whore of Babylon*, 180. On the Victorian antagonism to women's "vowed virginity," see Susan P. Casteras, "Virgin Vows: The Early Victorian Artists' Portrayal of Nuns and Novices," in *Religion in the Lives of English Women, 1760–1930*, ed. Gail Malmgreen (London: Croom Helm, 1986), 129–60.

62. I realized what Bray was doing only after reading Janel Mueller, "Pain, Persecution, and the Construction of Selfhood in Foxe's *Acts and Monuments*," in *Religion and Culture in Renaissance England*, ed. Claire McEachern and Debra Shuger (Cambridge: Cambridge University Press, 2006), 166.

63. Megan L. Hickerson, *Making Women Martyrs in Tudor England* (Houndmills: Palgrave Macmillan, 2005), 89. On female martyrs and torture as a form of sexualization or rape, see James C. W. Truman, "John Foxe and the Desires of Reformation Martyrology," *English Literary History* 70, no. 1 (2003): 40–43. Some of the obscenity derives from what Daryl Parker notes is the "discordant domesticity of what ought to be a public scene"; indeed, Bray's insertion of a witness suggests that she felt that Rose Allin's torture needed to become *spectacle*. Parker, "Histories of Violence and the Writer's Hand: Foxe's *Acts and Monuments* and *Titus Andronicus*," in *Reading and Writing in Shakespeare*, ed. David Moore Bergeron (Newark, NJ: University of Delaware Press, 1996), 93.

64. Irene Bostrom, "The Novel and Catholic Emancipation," *Studies in Romanticism* 2, no. 3 (1963): 165. Bray complained that "[a]ny one would have supposed by the rancor and the abuse aimed at me, that the whole Catholic question was dependent on discrediting or extinguishing a tale grounded on *historical record*, and written in illustration of the principles which led so many martyrs to the stake during the sanguinary reign of Mary" (*Autobiography of Anna Eliza Bray (Born 1789; died 1883)*, ed. John A. Kempe [London: Chapman and Hall, 1884], 203–4). The novel was reprinted by Smith, Elder in 1833 and again in single-volume form as part of Bray's collected works in 1845 and 1856; it was last reprinted by Chapman and Hall in 1884.

65. Anna Eliza Bray, *The Protestant: A Tale of the Reign of Queen Mary*, 3 vols. (London: Henry Colburn, 1828), 2:107, 110. Hereafter cited parenthetically in the text.

66. On the beginnings of the Church Association, founded in 1866, see Whisenant, *A Fragile Unity*, 81–85.

67. Emily Sarah Holt, *Margery's Son; Or, "Until He Find It." A Fifteenth-Century Tale of the Court of Scotland* (London: John F. Shaw, n.d.), v.

68. Emily Sarah Holt, *The King's Daughters: How Two Girls Kept the Faith*, new ed. (London: John F. Shaw, n.d.), 146. Hereafter cited parenthetically in the text. The novel had previously been serialized in John F. Shaw's magazine *Our Darlings*.

69. John R. Knott, *Discourses of Martyrdom in English Literature, 1563–1694* (Cambridge: Cambridge University Press, 1993), 59. Also apropos here is Alice A. Dailey's observation that one of Foxe's innovations in martyrological literature was "the simultaneous representation of the martyr as a specific human being and as an archetypal soldier and sufferer for Christ";

see "Typology and History in Foxe's *Acts and Monuments,*" *Prose Studies* 25, no. 3 (2002): 13.

70. Dailey, "Typology and History," 23. Cf. Maureen Moran, who argues that "Victorian martyrdom narratives are as much texts about how to look at and make sense of spectacles of the unimaginable, of violent, profane physical excess, as texts about how to gain spiritual victory"; ultimately, "[t]he reader cannot forget the process of bodily destruction but the impact of the description underlines the point that 'celestial vision' is achieved because of bodily anguish, not despite it" ("The Art of Looking Dangerously: Victorian Images of Martyrdom," *Victorian Literature and Culture* 32, no. 2 [2004]: 478, 485).

71. Alice Lang, *From Prison to Paradise: A Story of English Peasant Life in 1557* (London: Religious Tract Society, n.d.), 241.

72. On the "comedic" nature of Foxe's plotting, see King, *English Reformation Literature*, 443.

73. Foxe, *Book of Martyrs*, 2002.

74. Lady Charlotte Maria Pepys, *The Diary and Houres of the Ladye Adolie, A Faythfulle Childe, 1552* (London: Addey and Company, 1853), 181–85. Hereafter cited parenthetically in the text.

CHAPTER FIVE. UNNOTICED PERSECUTIONS

1. Paul Peppergrass [Father John Boyce], *The Spaewife; Or, the Queen's Secret. A Story of the Reign of Elizabeth*, new ed. (Boston: Patrick Donahoe, 1876), 251.

2. Emer Nolan has argued that for Irish Catholic novelists, Scott's focus on "the viewpoint of the historically victorious" was hardly appealing, especially given their interest in "Catholic *recovery.*" However, as I argue here, there is a difference between the Protestant viewpoint and the strategies used to represent same—and that is where Scott's Reformation, ironically enough, proved appealing. See Emer Nolan, *Catholic Emancipations: Irish Fiction from Thomas Moore to James Joyce* (Syracuse, NY: Syracuse University Press, 2007), 79; emphasis in the original.

3. Mrs. Robertson, *Florence; Or, the Aspirant*, 3 vols. (London: Whittaker Treacher, 1829), 3:201–2; emphasis in the original.

4. Gary Kuchar, *Divine Subjection: The Rhetoric of Sacramental Devotion in Early Modern England* (Pittsburgh, PA: Duquesne University Press, 2005), 77.

5. John Henry Newman, *An Essay on the Development of Christian Doctrine*, fwd. Ian Ker (Notre Dame, IN: University of Notre Dame Press, 1989), 8.

6. Corinna M. Wagner, "'Standing Proof of the Degeneracy of Modern Times': Architecture, Society, and the Medievalism of A. W. N. Pugin," in *Beyond Arthurian Romances: The Reach of Victorian Medievalism*, ed. Jennifer A. Palmgren and Lorretta M. Holloway (Houndmills: Palgrave Macmillan, 2005), 24. According to Rosemary Hill, writing about the "nightmare images" of the Reformation appears to have once led Pugin to the point of a nervous breakdown (*God's Architect: Pugin and the Building of Romantic Britain* [London: Penguin, 2007], 266).

7. C. J. M[ason], *Alice Sherwin: A Tale of the Days of Sir Thomas More* (New York: D. and J. Sadlier, n.d.), 362–63. First issued in 1857 as part of the Catholic Popular Library, the novel was reprinted at least once in the United Kingdom in 1895; Sadlier advertised it in the United States as late as 1911. It was also translated into French and German. Depending on the edition and publisher, *Alice Sherwin* is sometimes found with the subtitles *A Historical Tale* and *A Tale of the Days of Henry VIII*.

8. Vidmar, *English Catholic Historians*, for example, 29, 42, 57; Rosemary O'Day, "John Lingard, Historians, and Contemporary Politics, 1780–1850," in *Lingard Remembered: Essays to Mark the Sesquicentenary of John Lingard's Death*, ed. Peter Phillips (London: Catholic Record Society, 2004), 85; Drabble, "The Historians of the English Reformation," for example, 54–55.

9. Lingard, *The History of England*, 6:166. Hereafter cited parenthetically in the text.

10. Thomas Flanagan, *A History of the Church in England, From the Earliest Period, to the Re-Establishment of the Hierarchy in 1850*, 2 vols. (London: Charles Dolman, 1857), 2:1. Hereafter cited parenthetically in the text.

11. [Frances Taylor], *Tyborne: And "Who Went Thither in the Days of Queen Elizabeth." A Sketch* (London: Catholic Publishing and Bookselling Company, Limited, 1859), ix–x. Hereafter cited parenthetically in the text.

12. There are a number of helpful recent studies about this figuring of Elizabeth, including Michael Dobson and Nicola J. Watson, *England's Elizabeth: An Afterlife in Fame and Fantasy* (Oxford: Oxford University Press, 2002); Rohan Maitzen, "Plotting Women: Froude and Strickland on Elizabeth I and Mary Queen of Scots," in *Clio's Daughters: British Women Making History, 1790–1899*, ed. Lynette Felber (Newark, NJ: University of Delaware Press, 2007), 123–50; Julia M. Walker, *The Elizabeth Icon, 1603–2003* (Houndmills: Palgrave Macmillan, 2004); Nicola Watson, "Gloriana Victoriana: Victoria and the Cultural Memory of Elizabeth I," in *Remaking Queen Victoria*, ed. Margaret Homans and Adrienne Munich (Cambridge: Cambridge University Press, 1997), 79–104.

13. Thomas S. Freeman, "Providence and Prescription: The Account of Elizabeth in Foxe's 'Book of Martyrs,'" in *The Myth of Elizabeth*, ed.

Susan Doran and Thomas S. Freeman (Houndmills: Palgrave Macmillan, 2002), 27–55; Alexandra Walsham, "'A Very Deborah?' The Myth of Elizabeth I as a Providential Monarch," in *The Myth of Elizabeth*, ed. Susan Doran and Thomas S. Freeman (Houndmills: Palgrave Macmillan, 2002), 143–68.

14. Mary Howitt, ed., *Biographical Sketches of the Queens of Great Britain. From the Norman Conquest to the Reign of Victoria. Or, Royal Book of Beauty* (London: Henry G. Bohn, 1851), 389.

15. Drabble, "The Historians of the English Reformation," 238.

16. See, for example, Emily Sarah Holt, *Sister Rose: Or Saint Bartholomew's Eve* (London: John F. Shaw, n.d.), 271–78.

17. Kevin L. Morris, "Rescuing the Scarlet Woman: The Promotion of Catholicism in English Literature, 1829–1850," *Recusant History* 22, no. 1 (May 1994): 81. In fact, as Mary Heimann notes of the mid-Victorian Catholic spiritual revival, Victorian English Catholicism exhibited more continuity with its own "recusant tradition" than with its Continental counterparts and tended to resist or otherwise moderate Continental modes of devotion: *Catholic Devotion in Victorian England* (Oxford: Clarendon Press, 1995), 138. On conflicts between the "Old Catholics" and advocates of more Italianate practices, see Edward Norman, *The English Catholic Church in the Nineteenth Century* (1984; repr., Oxford: Clarendon Press, 1985), 231–32, 234–38.

18. Alison Shell, *Catholicism, Controversy, and the English Literary Imagination, 1558–1660* (Cambridge: Cambridge University Press, 1999), 195.

19. Alice O'Hanlon, *Erleston Glen: A Story of Lancashire in the Sixteenth Century* (London: Burns and Oates, 1878), 2–3. Hereafter cited parenthetically in the text.

20. Wagner, "'Standing Proof,'" 29. Cf. Michael Alexander, *Medievalism: The Middle Ages in Modern England* (New Haven, CT: Yale University Press, 2007), 76.

21. Herringer, *Victorians and the Virgin Mary*, 16–17.

22. Devon Fisher, *Roman Catholic Saints and Early Victorian Literature: Conservatism, Liberalism, and the Emergence of Secular Culture* (Aldershot: Ashgate, 2012), 78. In its most liberal version, as Duncan Forbes summarizes it, the argument was that in the earliest ages, "God could not appeal to man's reason, when there was no reason" (*The Liberal Anglican Idea of History* [1952; repr., Cambridge: Cambridge University Press, 2006], 73).

23. For William Gresley's career, See S. A. Skinner, *Tractarians and the 'Condition of England': The Social and Political Thought of the Oxford Movement* (Oxford: Clarendon Press, 2004), esp. 65–83.

24. A. D. Crake, *The Last Abbot of Glastonbury: A Tale of the Dissolution of the Monasteries* (1884; repr., London: A. R. Mowbray, n.d.), iv. Hereafter cited parenthetically in the text as *Glastonbury*.

25. Peter Nockles, "A Disputed Legacy: Anglican Historiographies of the Reformation from the Era of the Caroline Divines to That of the Oxford Movement," *Bulletin of the John Rylands University Library of Manchester* 83, no. 1 (2001): 122.

26. Faught, *The Oxford Movement*, 36.

27. See Pereiro, *"Ethos" and the Oxford Movement*, 74–75.

28. William Gresley, *The Forest of Arden: A Tale Illustrative of the English Reformation*, 2nd ed. (London: James Burns, 1852), viii. Hereafter cited parenthetically in the text. The novel was reprinted at least six times.

29. On the ongoing presence of this theme in Anglo-Catholic Reformation historiography in the later nineteenth century, see Dickens and Tonkin, *The Reformation in Historical Thought*, 195.

30. A. D. Crake, *The Heir of Treherne: A Tale of the Reformation in Devonshire and of the Western Rebellion* (London: A. R. Mowbray and the Young Churchman, 1912), 236. Hereafter cited parenthetically in the text as *Treherne*.

31. Thomas Woodhouse, *Faithful Fictions: The Catholic Novel in British Literature* (Milton Keynes: Open University Press, 1991), 54. For a discussion of how early modern Catholic martyrologies also deployed the martyr as a way of thinking about Catholicism and English national continuity, see Catherine Sanok, *"The Lives of Women Saints of Our Contrie of England*: Gender and Nationalism in Recusant Hagiography," in *Catholic Culture in Early Modern England*, ed. Ronald Corthell et al. (Notre Dame, IN: University of Notre Dame Press, 2007), 261–80.

32. The novel was occasionally ascribed to Taylor's contemporary, the Irish novelist and biographer Cecilia Mary Caddell (1814–77), who later published a similar novel, *Wild Times* (1872).

33. There is no detailed recent account of Taylor's editorial career. See Ruth Gilpin Wells, *A Woman of Her Time and Ours: Mother Mary Magdalen Taylor, SMG* (Charlotte, NC: Laney-Smith, 1988), 81–84.

34. Bishop [Richard] Challoner, *Memoirs of Missionary Priests, and Other Catholics of Both Sexes, That Have Suffered Death in England on Religious Accounts, from the Year 1577, to 1684*, 2 vols. (Philadelphia: John T. Green, 1839), 1:55.

35. A point made by Thomas J. Heffernan, *Sacred Biography: Saints and Their Biographers in the Middle Ages* (Oxford: Oxford University Press, 1988), 6. There appears to have been some confusion about the novel's classification, as its *Publisher's Circular* entry lists it under "History and Biography" (*Publisher's Circular* 22 [July 1, 1859]: 306).

36. "Tyborne," *Dublin Review* 48 (August 1860): 539.

37. Moran, *Catholic Sensationalism*, 135.

38. Christopher Highley, *Catholics Writing the Nation in Early Modern Britain and Ireland* (Oxford: Oxford University Press, 2008), 15.

39. Tonya Moutray McArthur, "Through the Grate; Or, English Convents and the Transmission and Preservation of Female Catholic Recusant History," in *The Catholic Church and Unruly Women Writers: Critical Essays*, ed. Jeana DelRosso, Leigh Eicke, and Ana Kothe (Houndmills: Palgrave Macmillan, 2007), 119. Discussing Georgiana Fullerton's *Lady-Bird*, Maria LaMonaca notes the potentially "radical" nature of such reworkings of the marriage plot, in which Catholic women can discover "their true vocation outside of marriage and traditional domesticity" (*Masked Atheism*, 66).

40. Troy J. Bassett, "Living on the Margin: George Bentley and the Economics of the Three-Volume Novel, 1865–70," *Book History* 13, no. 1 (2010): 61.

41. Rev. of *Constance Sherwood*, *Spectator* no. 1951 (November 18, 1865): 1292.

42. On Taylor's role, see Kathleen Grant Jaeger, "Martyrs or Malignants? Some Nineteenth-Century Portrayals of Elizabethan Catholics," *Early Modern Literary Studies* Special Issue 7 (May 2001): 16.41. As Jaeger notes elsewhere, *Constance Sherwood* was one of the books written at the advice of Lady Georgiana's confessor, Peter Gallwey, who believed that for someone like herself, "the ideal apostolate was as a proselytizer amongst persons of rank and fortune," with fiction an important part of that role. See Kathleen Jaeger, "A Writer or a Religious? Lady Georgiana Fullerton's Dilemma," in *The Church and Literature*, ed. Peter Clarke and Charlotte Methuen (Woodbridge, Suffolk, UK: Boydell Press, 2012), 278.

43. Christine d'Haussy, "Les Récusants dans *Constance Sherwood*: Confesseurs et Martyrs in Ecrivains catholiques anglo-saxons," *Caliban* 24 (1987): 53.

44. For a detailed assessment of how Fullerton manipulates her sources, especially Challoner (and sometimes just gets things wrong), see ibid., 55–58.

45. Lady Georgiana Fullerton, *Constance Sherwood: An Autobiography of the Sixteenth Century* (1865; repr. New York: Catholic Publication Society, 1875), 232. Hereafter cited parenthetically in the text.

46. Maureen Moran comments that "[i]n Catholic versions of the persecution plot, only a transparent disaggregation of religious and secular authority guarantees the claims of individual conscience and ensures social stability" (*Catholic Sensationalism*, 135).

47. Jaeger, "Martyrs or Malignants?," 16.49.

48. John Geninges, *The Life and Death of Mr. Edmund Geninges Priest, Crowned with Martyrdome at London, the 10. Day of Nouember, in the Yeare M.D.XCI* (S. Omers: Charles Boscard, 1614), 93.

49. Flanagan similarly argues that Bellamy permitted herself to be "tampered with" (*A History of the Church in England*, 2:247).

50. Shell, *Oral Culture and Catholicism*, 27.

51. Ibid., 42.

52. See Margaret Aston, "English Ruins and English History: The Dissolution and the Sense of the Past," *Journal of the Warburg and Courtauld Institutes* 36 (1973): esp. 244–54.

53. See Susan O'Brien, "Making Catholic Spaces: Women, Décor, and Devotion in the English Catholic Church, 1840–1900," in *The Church and the Arts: Papers Read at the 1990 Summer Meeting and the 1991 Winter Meeting of the Ecclesiastical History Society*, ed. Diana Wood (Oxford: Blackwell, 1992), 449–64.

54. See, for example, Norman, *English Catholic Church*, 234–43.

55. As Colleen McDannell points out, "Catholicism's sacramental emphasis focused on the physical space of the church, and the home remained only a reminder of that sacredness" (*The Christian Home in Victorian America*, 104).

56. Agnew's first name—Eleanor, Elizabeth, or Emily—has been the source of some debate. There are Victorian sources for both Eleanor and Elizabeth; Emily, however, seems to be more recent, and Loeber et al. (*A Guide to Irish Fiction*) suggests Eleanor.

57. Penny Edgell Becker, "'Rational Amusement and Sound Instruction': Constructing the True Catholic Woman in the *Ave Maria*, 1865–1889," *Religion and American Culture* 8, no. 1 (1998): 77.

58. John Nicholas Murphy claimed that Agnew's profession took place between the second and third volumes (*Terra Incognita, Or the Convents of the United Kingdom* [London: Longmans, Green, 1873], 168n3). Agnew's career as a nun proved checkered: although Catherine McAuley praised her "genuine meekness and humility" when she resided at the Sisters of Mercy convent on Baggot Street, she later warned of her "*extremes* in piety" after Agnew became superior of the Sisters of Mercy convent in Bermondsey. Agnew's behavior led to her removal in 1841, and she briefly became a Trappistine. By the 1860s she had become "Lady Abbess of the Convent of the Blessed Sacrament, Nice" (Mrs. Agnew, "The Merchant Prince and His Heir," *Duffy's Hibernian Magazine* 4, n.s. 19 [July 1863]: 70). But this project, too, appears to have failed. For McAuley's opinion, see *The Correspondence of Catherine McAuley, 1818–1841*, ed. Mary C. Sullivan (Dublin: Four Courts Press, 2004), letters to Sister M. Frances Warde, September 27, 1839, 205, and July 26–27, 1841, 419; and for Agnew's failure as the mother superior of the Bermondsey convent, along with her later career in the Trappistines and elsewhere, see [Mother Mary Austin Carroll], *Leaves from the Annals of the Sisters of Mercy*, 3 vols. (New York: Catholic Publication Company, 1885), 2:87–94.

59. Margaret Maison, *The Victorian Vision: Studies in the Religious Novel* (New York: Sheed and Ward, 1961), 149.

60. [John Henry Newman], rev. of *Geraldine: A Tale of Conscience*, *The British Critic, and Quarterly Theological Review* 23 (1838): 61–82.

61. The American Catholic convert Orestes Brownson, reviewing a much later reprint, complained that this was precisely how a Protestant would go about doing things: "The process through which the authoress conducts her heroine, never did and never could of itself alone have led to her conversion. It is precisely the process by which every Protestant seeks to ascertain what is the Christian church and the Christian faith; and if it could be successful in Geraldine's case, why is it not in theirs? and why do we not find them all of one mind instead of being cut up into a thousand and one conflicting sects, holding every variety of opinion, from the high-church Anglican down to the bald rationalist?" (O. A. Brownson, "Catholic Popular Literature," in *Essays on Modern Popular Literature*, ed. Henry F. Brownson [Detroit, MI: H. F. Brownson, 1888], 584).

62. E. C. Agnew, *Geraldine: A Tale of Conscience*, 14th ed. (London: Burns and Oates, n.d.), 6. Hereafter cited parenthetically in the text.

63. On the Reformation Society up until about the time Agnew would have begun writing, see Wolffe, *Protestant Crusade*, 36–61.

64. Fiorentina Straker, *Immacolata, the Catholic Flower: A Convent Tale* (London: W. Knowles, 1860), 1–2.

65. Laetitia Selwyn Oliver, *Father Placid; Or, the Custodian of the Blessed Sacrament* (London: R. Washbourne, 1884), 6. Hereafter cited parenthetically in the text. *Father Placid* was Oliver's joint debut novel, appearing with *Rose Fortescue* as part of Washbourne's one-shilling line of cheap books. It was reprinted in 1892. Laetitia (sometimes Letitia) Selwyn Oliver (1853–1926) wrote genre fiction with strong religious messages. See Allen J. Hubin, *Crime Fiction IV: A Comprehensive Bibliography, 1749–2000, Addenda to the Revised Edition* (http://www.crimefictioniv.com/Part_32.html).

66. Everard's and Gertrude's insight echoes a point made by Susannah Brietz Monta about early modern Catholic martyrologies: only Catholics can interpret the "wondrous signs" of martyrdom, leaving Protestants entrapped in "clumsy literalness." Or, in this case, clumsy genre conventions. *Martyrdom and Literature in Early Modern England* (Cambridge: Cambridge University Press, 2005), 67.

67. Ian Ker, *John Henry Newman: A Biography* (Oxford: Oxford University Press, 1988), 333.

68. For this phase in Newman's thinking, see James Patrick, "Newman, Pugin, and Gothic," *Victorian Studies* 24, no. 2 (1981): 197–205. As it happens, Pugin actually wound up agreeing with him; see Alexander, *Medievalism*, 150–51; Hill, *God's Architect*, 456–57.

69. John Henry Newman, *Loss and Gain: The Story of a Convert*, ed. Alan G. Hill (Oxford: Oxford University Press, 1986), 289–90. Hereafter cited parenthetically in the text.

70. R. J. M., "What Do We Read?," *American Catholic Quarterly Review* 22, no. 43 (October 1897): 680.

71. Nicholas Tyacke, *Aspects of English Protestantism, c. 1530–1700* (Manchester: Manchester University Press, 2001), 38. Tyacke dates this earlier phase of Catholic revisionism to the late-Victorian and Edwardian historical research of Cardinal Aidan Francis Gasquet, but as this chapter suggests, less formal versions preceded Gasquet by several decades.

CHAPTER SIX. REJECTING THE CONTROVERSIAL
HISTORICAL NOVEL

1. Alison Case, "Against Scott: The Antihistory of Dickens' *Barnaby Rudge*," *Clio* 19, no. 2 (1990): 144.

2. The quotation is from George Scott Christian, "'They lost the whole': Telling Historical (Un)truth in *Barnaby Rudge*," *Dickens Studies Annual* 32 (2002): 58; cf. Jason B. Jones, *Lost Causes: Historical Consciousness in Victorian Literature* (Columbus: Ohio State University Press, 2006), 53; and John Bowen, *Other Dickens: Pickwick to Chuzzlewit* (2000; repr., Oxford: Oxford University Press, 2003), 157–82. Catherine Robson similarly notes that "at the same time that he questions the status of the past as an incontestable site of value, Dickens' writings frequently evince doubts as to whether the past is a secure and stable site at all" ("Historicizing Dickens," in *Palgrave Advances in Charles Dickens Studies*, ed. John Bowen and Robert L. Patten [Houndmills: Palgrave Macmillan, 2006], 236).

3. Avrom Fleishman, *The English Historical Novel: Walter Scott to Virginia Woolf* (Baltimore, MD: Johns Hopkins University Press, 1971), 105.

4. D. G. Paz, *Dickens and* Barnaby Rudge: *Anti-Catholicism and Chartism* (Monmouth: Merlin Press, 2006), 146. Paz concludes that the novel's primary concern is with early Victorian anti-Catholicism, despite how the riots resonate with contemporary anxieties about Chartism (160–61).

5. Sir Walter Scott, *The Heart of Midlothian*, ed. Claire Lamont (1818; repr., Oxford: Oxford University Press, 1982), 77. Hereafter cited parenthetically in the text.

6. Charles Dickens, *Barnaby Rudge*, ed. Gordon Spence (1973; repr., London: Penguin, 1986), 333. Hereafter cited parenthetically in the text.

7. Dennis Walder, *Dickens and Religion* (1981; repr., London: Routledge, 2007), 92.

8. Jones, *Lost Causes*, 39.

9. The most detailed overview of all the doublings is Thomas Jackson Rice, "The End of Dickens' Apprenticeship: Variable Focus in *Barnaby Rudge*," *Nineteenth-Century Fiction* 30, no. 2 (1975): 172–84. On the moral dichotomies involved, see, for example, Bowen, *Other Dickens*, 174–75; and Ian Duncan, *Modern Romance and the Transformations of the Novel: The Gothic, Scott, Dickens* (Cambridge: Cambridge University Press, 1992), 228.

10. Gauri Viswanathan, *Outside the Fold: Conversion, Modernity, and Belief* (Princeton, NJ: Princeton University Press, 1998), 26.

11. I've discussed the Victorian version of this argument in "Protestants Against the Jewish and Catholic Family, c. 1829 to c. 1860," *Victorian Literature and Culture* 31 (2003): 333–57. My reading of this moment in *Barnaby Rudge* is much less optimistic than that offered by Heidi Kaufman in *English Origins, Jewish Discourse, and the Nineteenth-Century British Novel: Reflections of a Nested Nation* (University Park: Pennsylvania State University Press, 2009), 53–54.

12. My reading here departs quite far from Samuel Pickering's, who interprets Mrs. Varden's conversion in full-fledged evangelical terms; in general, I disagree strongly with Pickering's argument that *Barnaby Rudge* offers Dickens's "fullest and most sympathetic treatment" of evangelicalism. Pickering, *The Moral Tradition in English Fiction*, 135, 123.

13. Myron Magnet, *Dickens and the Social Order* (Philadelphia: University of Pennsylvania Press, 1985), 99.

14. Rosemary Bodenheimer, *Knowing Dickens* (Ithaca, NY: Cornell University Press, 2007), 107.

15. Robert Mighall, *A Geography of Victorian Gothic Fiction: Mapping History's Nightmares* (Oxford: Oxford University Press, 1999), 113.

CODA

1. Thomas M'Crie, *History of the Progress and Suppression of the Reformation in Italy during the Sixteenth Century; Including a Sketch of the History of the Reformation in the Grisons* (Edinburgh: William Blackwood, 1827), 205.

2. On the presence of British missions to Italian Catholics and anxieties about the safety thereof, see Danilo Raponi, "An 'Anti-Catholicism of Free Trade'? Religion and the Anglo-Italian Negotiations of 1863," *European History Quarterly* 39, no. 4 (2009): 634–36.

3. Alison Milbank, *Dante and the Victorians* (Manchester: Manchester University Press, 1998), 75.

4. C. T. McIntire, *England against the Papacy, 1858–1861* (1983; repr., Cambridge: Cambridge University Press, 2008), 224.

5. Dennis Mack Smith, *Victor Emanuel, Cavour, and the Risorgimento* (London: Oxford University Press, 1971), 12.

6. Ibid., 20.

7. Maurizio Isabella, *Risorgimento in Exile: Italian Emigres and the Liberal International in the Post-Napoleonic Era* (Oxford: Oxford University Press, 2009), 132–34, 203–7.

8. McIntire, *England against the Papacy*, 224.

9. "Garibaldi's Last Expedition," *Evangelical Christendom* 21 (December 2, 1867): 606.

10. For example, "[b]ut if our separate Protestant brethren pretend to be the true Church of Jesus Christ, reaching back by an uninterrupted succession in unity of faith to her divine Founder, and built up on the basis of private interpretation of the Bible, then Wycliffe does not belong to them" (L[ouis] Delplace, S.J., "Wycliffe and His Teaching Concerning the Primacy," *Dublin Review* 11, no. 1, 3rd ser. [January 1884]: 60).

11. Donald Weinstein, *Savonarola and Florence: Prophecy and Patriotism in the Renaissance* (Princeton, NJ: Princeton University Press, 1970), 3.

12. Ronald M. Steinberg, *Fra Girolamo Savonarola, Florentine Art, and Renaissance Historiography* (Athens: Ohio University Press, 1977), 29.

13. Andrew Thompson, *George Eliot and Italy: Literary, Cultural and Political Influences from Dante to the* Risorgimento (Houndmills: Macmillan, 1998), 70.

14. Bruce Gordon, "'This Worthy Witness of Christ': Protestant Uses of Savonarola in the Sixteenth Century," in *Protestant History and Identity in Sixteenth Century Europe: Volume 1, The Medieval Inheritance*, ed. Bruce Gordon (Aldershot: Ashgate, 1996), 102.

15. Andrews, *An Examination of Fox's Calendar*, 3:190; the Very Rev. J[ohn] Procter, O.P., "The Dominican Savonarola and the Reformation. A Reply to Dean Farrar," *Publications of the Catholic Truth Society*, vol. 28 (1895; repr., London: Catholic Truth Society, 1900), 81.

16. Eleanor McNees, "The Resurgence of Savonarola in Victorian England," in *The Grand Tour Lives On*, ed. Alessandra di Luzio (Bologna, Italy: CLUEB, 2006), 75–100.

17. Erasmus Middleton, "Luther," in *Biographia Evangelia: Or An Historical Account of the Lives and Deaths of the Most Eminent and Evangelical Authors and Preachers* . . . 4 vols. (London: J.W. Pasham, 1779), 1:196.

18. Pasquale Villari, *The History of Girolamo Savonarola and His Times*, trans. Leonard Horner, 2 vols. (London: Longman, Green, Longman, Roberts, and Green, 1863), 1:xxxiv, xxiv. Hereafter cited parenthetically in the text. Mary Wilson Carpenter's claim that Villari identified Savonarola as a Protestant is based on Villari's summary of *Luther's* position, which Villari offers in the process of explaining why such readings are *wrong* (1:xiv) (*George Eliot and*

the Landscape of Time: Narrative Form and Protestant Apocalyptic History [Chapel Hill: University of North Carolina Press, 1986], 70).

19. Richard Robert Madden (1798–1886) was an Irish Catholic lawyer and popular historian, best known as the author of *The United Irishmen, Their Life and Times* (1843); John Abraham Heraud (1799–1887) was an autodidactic hack, poet, dramatist, and editor of the *New Monthly Magazine*; William Harris Rule (1802–90), clergyman and popular historian, was involved with the Italian-language (later bilingual) Protestant journal *L'Eco di Savonarola*.

20. Henry Hart Milman, "Savonarola," in *Savonarola, Erasmus, and Other Essays* (London: John Murray, 1870), 74.

21. William Harris Rule, *Dawn of the Reformation. Savonarola. With Events of the Reign of Pope Alexander VI* (London: John Mason, 1855), 44. Hereafter cited parenthetically in the text.

22. John Abraham Heraud, *The Life and Times of Girolamo Savonarola, Illustrating the Progress of the Reformation in Italy During the Fifteenth Century* (London: Whittaker, 1843), 388. Hereafter cited parenthetically in the text.

23. Richard Robert Madden, *The Life and Martyrdom of Savonarola, Illustrative of the History of Church and State Connexion*, 2nd ed., 2 vols. (London: Thomas Caviley Newby, 1854), 2:235. Hereafter cited parenthetically in the text.

24. On then-archbishop Paul Cullen's crackdown on politically active priests during the early 1850s, see Emmett Larkin, *The Making of the Roman Catholic Church in Ireland, 1850–1860* (Chapel Hill: University of North Carolina Press, 1980), esp. 203–40.

25. John Abraham Heraud, *The Life and Times of Girolamo Savonarola, Illustrating the Progress of the Reformation in Italy During the Fifteenth Century* (London: Whittaker 1843), v.

26. In fact, as Bruce Gordon points out, Luther does not seem to have been particularly interested in Savonarola at all, aside from bringing out a German edition of the *Meditatio* (1523): he "neither identified himself with Savonarola nor argued that men such as the Florentine formed a chain of witnesses to the truth" ("Worthy Witness," 100, 101).

27. As Pam Morris suggests is the case with Eliot; see *Imagining Inclusive Society in 19th-Century Novels: The Code of Sincerity in the Public Sphere* (Baltimore, MD: Johns Hopkins University Press, 2004), 171.

28. Harriet Beecher Stowe, *Agnes of Sorrento* (1861; repr., Boston: Ticknor and Fields, 1865), 241. Hereafter cited parenthetically in the text.

29. Robin Sheets, "History and Romance: Harriet Beecher Stowe's *Agnes of Sorrento* and George Eliot's *Romola*," *Clio* 26, no. 3 (1997): 330.

30. Jenny Franchot, *Roads to Rome: The Antebellum Protestant Encounter with Catholicism* (Berkeley: University of California Press, 1994), 249.

31. Stefanie Markovits, "George Eliot and Action," *Studies in English Literature, 1500–1900* 41, no. 4 (Autumn 2001): 790, 792; Evan Horowitz, "George Eliot: The Conservative," *Victorian Studies* 49, no. 1 (2006): 22–23.

32. David Carroll, "George Eliot Martyrologist: The Case of Savonarola," in *From Author to Text: Re-reading George Eliot's* Romola, ed. Caroline Levine and Mark W. Turner (Aldershot: Ashgate, 1998), 118.

33. Felicia Bonaparte's suggestion that Romola enters her "Protestant period" after abandoning Savonarola is problematic, I think, because to be not dogmatically Catholic is not the same thing as being a Protestant as any of Eliot's contemporaries would have defined it—even those who liked to play fast and loose with proto-Protestant beliefs. See *The Triptych and the Cross: The Central Myths of George Eliot's Poetic Imagination* (New York: New York University Press, 1979), 206. Wilson Carpenter makes a similar claim in *George Eliot*, 70–71.

34. For a detailed analysis of voice's function in the novel, see Beryl Gray, "Power and Persuasion: Voices of Influence in *Romola*," in *From Author to Text: Re-reading George Eliot's* Romola, ed. Caroline Levine and Mark W. Turner (Aldershot: Ashgate, 1998), 124–34. I am much more skeptical about Eliot's treatment of the sermon than Gray is (126–27).

35. George Eliot, *Romola*, ed. Andrew Saunders (London: Penguin, 1980), 294. Hereafter cited parenthetically in the text.

36. Pam Morris makes an interesting case that Savonarola and Baldassare effectively share a "similar psychology of narcisstic projection" in *Imagining Inclusive Society*, 187; cf. Moran, *Catholic Sensationalism*, 164–65; Christine L. Krueger, *The Reader's Repentance*, 280–82. In a different context, Paul Yeoh observes that in Eliot, "the hagiographic script . . . can become a means of gratifying egoism at the expense of others" ("*Saints' Everlasting Rest*: The Martyrdom of Maggie Tulliver," *Studies in the Novel* 41, no. 1 [Spring 2009]: 4).

37. Gary Wihl suggests that "Savonarola cannot afford to tamper further with public opinion at a moment when the state faces so much instability, but where Machiavelli acknowledges these moments as true tests of virtue, or statecraft, in the face of imminent danger, Savonarola retreats to a much cruder model of political management grounded in sophistry" ("Republican Liberty in George Eliot's *Romola*," *Criticism* 51, no. 2 [Spring 2009]: 257). For a more detailed assessment of Savonarola's theocratic failure, see Bonaparte, *Triptych*, 212–24.

38. David Carroll, *George Eliot and the Conflict of Interpretations: A Reading of the Novels* (Cambridge: Cambridge University Press, 1992), 186.

39. T. R. Wright notes that Eliot's Savonarola accords with "Comte's analysis of the way in which the moral influence of medieval Catholicism began to decay because of its failure to preserve the separation of the spiritual from the temporal powers" but "remains worthy of Positivist veneration" (*The Religion of Humanity: The Impact of Comtean Positivism on Victorian Britain* [1986; repr., Cambridge: Cambridge University Press, 2008], 190). That being said, Gennaro Anthony Santangelo reminds us that Romola's final assessment of Savonarola is very close to Villari ("Villari's *Life and Times of Savonarola*: A Source for George Eliot's *Romola*," *Anglia* 90 [1972]: 129–30).

40. "Signor Gavazzi," *Bulwark or Reformation Journal* 10 (February 1881): 51.

41. *The Martyr of Florence; Or, the Home of Fiesole* (London: John F. Shaw, n.d.), 97. Hereafter cited parenthetically in the text.

42. G. Holden Pike, "A Century of Bible Distribution," *Sunday Magazine* (1886): 736.

Bibliography

PRIMARY SOURCES

A. B. "Remarks on 'The Monastery.'" *Gentleman's Magazine* 128 (October 1820): 320.

Adams, Henry Cadwallader. *Mark's Wedding, or Lollardy.* In *Tales Illustrating Church History. England, Vol. III, Mediæval Period*, 141–282. Oxford: James Parker, 1877. http://books.google.com.

Advertisement for *Historical Tales for Young Protestants. Religious Tract Society Reporter* 5 (September 16, 1857): 79.

A Father [pseud.]. *Rose Allen, a Martyr Story; And Other Poems, Chiefly Sacred.* London: James Nisbet, 1851. http://books.google.com.

Agnew, E. C. [E. C. A.]. *Geraldine: A Tale of Conscience.* 14th ed. London: Burns and Oates, n.d.

———. [Mrs. Agnew]. "The Merchant Prince and His Heir." *Duffy's Hibernian Magazine* 4, n.s. 19 (July 1863): 70.

Alcock, Deborah. *No Cross, No Crown: A Tale of the Scottish Reformation.* London: T. Nelson and Sons, 1887.

———. *The Spanish Brothers: A Tale of the Sixteenth Century.* 1870. Reprint, London: T. Nelson and Sons, 1895.

Anderson, Christopher. *The Annals of the English Bible.* 2 vols. London: William Pickering, 1845.

Andrews, William Eusebius. *An Examination of Fox's Calendar of Protestant Saints, Martyrs, &c., &c.; Contrasted with a Biographical Sketch of Catholic Missionary Priests and Others, Executed Under Protestant Penal Laws, from the Years 1585 to 1684, Abridged from Parson's Examen and Challoner's Memoirs, with Additional Remarks.* 3 vols. London: W. E. Andrews, 1826. http://books.google.com.

Anne Boleyn: Or, the Suppression of the Religious Houses. London: Saunders and Otley, 1854. http://books.google.com.

Bickersteth, Edward. *The Present Duties of the Protestant Churches. A Sermon Preached Before the British Society for Promoting the Religious Principles of the Reformation, on Friday Evening, May 5, 1837, at Percy Chapel, London.* London: G. Norman, 1837.

Bolton, W. Jay. *The Stratford Martyrs of the Reformation. A Sermon Preached at St. John's, Stratford, E., on Sunday, July 12th, 1868.* London: Hamilton, Adams, and Company, 1868.

Bower, Selina A. *"Let There Be Light"; Or, the Story of the Reformation.* London: James Nisbet, 1883. http://books.google.com.

Bray, Anna Eliza. *Autobiography of Anna Eliza Bray (Born 1789; died 1883).* Edited by John A. Kempe. London: Chapman and Hall, 1884.

———. *The Protestant: A Tale of the Reign of Queen Mary.* 3 vols. London: Henry Colburn, 1828.

Britten, James. "'Pure Literature': A Postscript to 'Protestant Fiction.'" *The Month* 87 (June 1896): 248–59.

Brontë, Charlotte. *Jane Eyre.* Edited by Richard J. Dunn. 3rd ed. New York: W. W. Norton, 2001.

Brown, Arthur. *The Knight of Dilham: A Story of the Lollards.* London: S. W. Partridge, [1875?].

Brownson, O[restes] A. "Catholic Popular Literature." In *Essays on Modern Popular Literature*, edited by Henry F. Brownson, 575–94. Detroit, MI: H. F. Brownson, 1888. http://books.google.com.

Bruce, Charles. *The Story of John Heywood: A Historical Tale of the Time of Harry VIII.* Edinburgh: W. P. Nimmo, [1873?]. http://books.google.com.

Buddensieg, Rudolf. *John Wiclif: Patriot and Reformer, Life and Writings.* London: T. Fisher Unwin, 1884.

———. "Wyclif Literature: Communication on the History and the Work of the Wyclif Society." *Critical Review of Theological and Philosophical Literature* 3, no. 3 (1893): 280–94. http://books.google.com.

Butler, Charles. *Historical Memoirs Respecting the English, Irish, and Scottish Catholics, from the Reformation, to the Present Time.* 2nd ed. 2 vols. London: John Murray, 1819. http://books.google.com.

Cameron, Henry P. *History of the English Bible.* London: Alexander Gardner, 1885.

[Carroll, Mother Mary Austin]. *Leaves from the Annals of the Sisters of Mercy.* 3 vols. New York: Catholic Publication Company, 1885. http://archive.org.

Challoner, [Richard]. *Memoirs of Missionary Priests, and Other Catholics of Both Sexes, That Have Suffered Death in England on Religious Accounts, from the Year 1577, to 1684.* 2 vols. Philadelphia: John T. Green, 1839. http://books.google.com.

[Charles, Elizabeth Rundle]. *Chronicles of the Schönberg–Cotta Family. By Two of Themselves.* New York: M. W. Dodd, 1864.
———. *The Draytons and the Davenants: A Story of the Civil Wars.* New York: Dodd and Mead, 1877.
———. "A Story of the Lollards." In *The Early Dawn; Or, Sketches of Christian Life in England in the Olden Time.* Introduction by Henry B. Smith. New York: M. W. Dodd, 1864.
"Children's Books." *Literary Churchman: A Critical Record of Religious Publications* 5, no. 5 (March 1, 1859): 89.
Conant, Mrs. H[annah] C[haplin]. *The English Bible. History of the Translation of the Holy Scriptures into the English Tongue. With Specimens of the Old English Versions.* New York: Sheldon, Blakeman, and Company, 1856. http://books.google.com.
Confessions of a Convert, from Baptism in Water to Baptism with Water. London: John Snow, 1845.
"Correspondence and Publications." *Protestant Magazine* 27 (July 1, 1865): 78.
Crake, A. D. *The Heir of Treherne: A Tale of the Reformation in Devonshire and of the Western Rebellion.* 1888. Reprint, London: A. R. Mowbray and the Young Churchman, 1912.
———. *The Last Abbot of Glastonbury: A Tale of the Dissolution of the Monasteries.* 1884. Reprint, London: A. R. Mowbray, n.d.
[Cross, John Henry, ed.]. *Historical Tales for Young Protestants.* 1857. Reprint, Philadelphia: American Sunday-School Union, n.d.
D'Aubigné, J. H. Merle. *History of the Reformation in Europe in the Time of Calvin.* 8 vols. New York: Robert Carter and Brothers, 1863–68.
Delplace, L[ouis], S.J. "Wycliffe and His Teaching Concerning the Primacy." *Dublin Review* 11, no. 1, 3rd ser. (January 1884): 60.
de Vere, Aubrey. *Mary Tudor. A Tragedy. Part the Second.* In *Mary Tudor: An Historical Drama, the Lamentation of Ireland, and Other Poems.* London: William Pickering, 1847.
Dickens, Charles. *Barnaby Rudge.* Edited by Gordon Spence. 1973. Reprint, London: Penguin, 1986.
Dixon, Richard Watson. *History of the Church of England from the Abolition of the Roman Jurisdiction.* 4 vols. London: George Routledge and Sons, 1891. http://books.google.com.
Dore, John Read. *Old Bibles: An Account of the Early Versions of the English Bible.* 2nd ed. London: Eyre and Spottiswode, 1888. http://books.google.com.
Duff, Alexander. "On the External Homage and Private Neglect of the Bible,— And Its Paramount Claims on the Attention of Man." *Scottish Christian Herald* 2 (February 18, 1837): 105–8.

Eastwood, Frances. *Geoffrey the Lollard*. New York: Dodd and Mead, 1870.

Eliot, George. *Romola*. Edited by Andrew Saunders. London: Penguin, 1980.

Elizabeth [Phelan Tonna], Charlotte. *Alice Benden; Or, the Bowed Shilling, and Other Tales*. New York: Baker and Scribner, 1846.

Ellis, Harriet Warner. *The Melvill Family and Their Bible Readings*. 1871. Reprint, London: Hodder and Stoughton, 1885. http://books.google.com.

Flanagan, Thomas. *A History of the Church in England, From the Earliest Period, to the Re–Establishment of the Hierarchy in 1850*. 2 vols. London: Charles Dolman, 1857.

Foxe, John. *The Unabridged Acts and Monuments Online* [*Book of Martyrs*]. Sheffield: HRI Online Publications, 2011. http://www.johnfoxe.org.

Froude, J. A. *The Reign of Mary Tudor*. London: J. M. Dent; New York: E. P. Dutton, 1913.

Fuller, Thomas. *The History of the Worthies of England*. Edited by John Nichols. 2 vols. London: F. C. and J. Rivington, 1811. http://books.google.com.

Fullerton, Georgiana. *Constance Sherwood: An Autobiography of the Sixteenth Century*. 1865. Reprint, New York: Catholic Publication Society, 1875.

"Garibaldi's Last Expedition." *Evangelical Christendom* 21 (December 2, 1867): 605–7. http://books.google.com.

[Gaspey, Thomas]. *The Lollards: A Tale, Founded on the Persecutions which Marked the Early Part of the Fifteenth Century*. 2 vols. New York: James and John Harper, 1822.

Gasquet, Francis Aidan. "The Pre–Reformation Bible (I)." In *The Old English Bible and Other Essays*, 87–134. New ed. London: George Bell and Sons, 1908.

Geikie, John Cunningham. *The English Reformation: How It Came About, and Why We Should Uphold It*. New York: D. Appleton, 1879.

Geninges, John. *The Life and Death of Mr. Edmund Geninges Priest, Crowned with Martyrdome at London, the 10. Day of Nouember, in the Yeare M.D.XCI*. S. Omers: Charles Boscard, 1614.

Giberne, Agnes. *Coulyng Castle; Or, a Knight of the Olden Days*. London: Seeley, Jackson, and Halliday, 1875. http://books.google.com.

Glass, Joseph. *Reminscences of Manningtree and Its Vicinity, with Some Reference to the Past and Present History of the Town and Neighborhood*. London: Judd and Glass, 1855. http://books.google.com.

Gresley, William. *The Forest of Arden: A Tale Illustrative of the English Reformation*. 2nd ed. London: James Burns, 1852.

Hallam, Henry. *View of the State of Europe in the Middle Ages*. 2 vols. 1818. Reprint, New York: Thomas Y. Crowell, 1880.

Heraud, John Abraham. *The Life and Times of Girolamo Savonarola, Illustrating the Progress of the Reformation in Italy during the Fifteenth Century*. London: Whittaker, 1843. http://books.google.com.

Holt, Emily Sarah. *John de Wycliffe and What He Did for England*. London: John F. Shaw, n.d.

————. *The King's Daughters: How Two Girls Kept the Faith*. New ed. London: John F. Shaw, n.d.

————. *The Lord Mayor: A Tale of London in 1384*. London: John F. Shaw, 1885.

————. *Margery's Son; Or, "Until He Find It." A Fifteenth-Century Tale of the Court of Scotland*. London: John F. Shaw, n.d.

————. *Mistress Margery: A Tale of the Lollards*. 1868. Reprint, London: John F. Shaw, n.d.

————. *Out in the Forty-Five: Or, Duncan Keith's Vow. A Tale of the Last Century*. London: John F. Shaw, n.d.

————. *Robin Tremayne: A Tale of the Marian Persecution*. 1872. Reprint, New York: Robert Carter and Brothers, 1876.

————. *Sister Rose: Or Saint Bartholomew's Eve*. London: John F. Shaw, n.d.

Horne, Thomas Hartwell. *A Protestant Memorial, for the Commemoration, on the Fourth Day of October, MDCCCXXXV, of the Third Centenary of the Reformation, and of the Publication of the First Entire Protestant English Version of the Bible, Oct. IV, MDXXXV*. 2nd ed. London: T. Cadell et al., 1835.

————. *Reminiscences, Personal and Bibliographical, of Thomas Hartwell Horne*. Edited by Sarah Anne Cheyne. London: Longman, Green, Longman, and Roberts, 1862.

Howitt, Mary, ed. *Biographical Sketches of the Queens of Great Britain. From the Norman Conquest to the Reign of Victoria. Or, Royal Book of Beauty*. London: Henry G. Bohn, 1851.

Hume, David. *The History of England from the Invasion of Julius Caesar to the Revolution of 1688*. 6 vols. 1778. Reprint, Indianapolis: Liberty Classics, 1983.

James, J[ohn] A[ngell]. "On Reading the Scriptures." *Tract Magazine and Christian Miscellany* (1869): 71–78.

"John Henry Cross." *The Child's Companion* 89 (May 1, 1876): 76.

Jones, Dora M. *At the Gates of the Morning: A Story of the Reformation in Kent*. London: Charles H. Kelly, 1898.

Kennedy, Grace. *Father Clement: A Roman Catholic Tale*. 1823. Reprint, Edinburgh: William Oliphant and Son, 1838.

Kenyon, Frederic G[eorge]. *Our Bible and the Ancient Manuscripts: Being a History of the Text and Its Translations*. 3rd ed. London: Eyre and Spottiswode, 1898. http://books.google.com.

Kingston, W. H. G. *The Last Look: A Tale of the Spanish Inquisition.* London: S. W. Partridge, 1869.

Lang, Alice. *The Adventures of Hans Müller.* London: Religious Tract Society, [1894?].

———. *From Prison to Paradise: A Story of English Peasant Life in 1557.* London: Religious Tract Society, n.d.

Le Bas, Charles Webb. *The Life of Wiclif.* London: J. G. and F. Rivington, 1832.

Lechler, [G. V.]. *John Wycliffe and His English Precursors.* Translated with additional notes by [Peter] Lorimer. New rev. ed. London: Religious Tract Society, n.d.

Lee, Sophia. *The Recess; Or, a Tale of Other Times.* Edited by April Alliston. Lexington: University Press of Kentucky, 2000.

Leslie, Emma. *At the Sign of the Golden Fleece: A Story of Reformation Days.* London: Gall and Inglis, 1900.

———. *Cecily: A Tale of the English Reformation.* London: Wesleyan Conference Office, 1881.

———. *The Chained Book.* London: George Cauldwell, [1878?].

———. *Conrad: A Tale of Wiclif and Bohemia.* 1880. Reprint, New York: Phillips and Hunt; Cincinnati, OH: Walden and Stowe, 1881.

———. *Daybreak in Italy.* London: Religious Tract Society, 1870.

———. *Peter the Apprentice: A Tale of the Reformation in England.* London: Religious Tract Society, n.d.

———. *Soldier Fritz and the Enemies He Fought: A Story of the Reformation.* London: Religious Tract Society, [1871?].

Lingard, John. *The History of England, from the First Invasion by the Romans to the Accession of William and Mary in 1688.* 6th ed., rev. 10 vols. London: Charles Dolman, 1855.

"Literary Notices." *Bradford Observer* 7, no. 1558 (December 17, 1863): 7. http://www.britishnewspaperarchive.co.uk.

Loserth, Johann. *Wiclif and Hus.* Translated by M. J. Evans. London: Hodder and Stoughton, 1884.

Madden, Richard Robert. *The Life and Martyrdom of Savonarola, Illustrative of the History of Church and State Connexion.* 2nd ed. 2 vols. London: Thomas Caviley Newby, 1854. http://books.google.com.

[Manning, Anne]. *The Cottage History of England.* London: Arthur Hall, 1861. http://books.google.com.

Marshall, Emma. *Dayspring: A Story of the Time of William Tyndale, Reformer, Scholar, and Martyr.* 2nd ed. London: "Home Words" Publishing Office, n.d.

The Martyr of Florence; Or, the Home of Fiesole. London: John F. Shaw, n.d.

M[ason], C. J. *Alice Sherwin: A Tale of the Days of Sir Thomas More.* New York: D. and J. Sadlier, n.d. http://books.google.com.

Massingberd, Francis Charles. *The English Reformation*. 3rd ed., rev. and enl. London: John W. Parker and Son, 1857.

Maurice, Charles Edmund. *Richard de Lacy. A Tale of the Later Lollards.* 1892. Reprint, London: British Library, n.d.

[Maurice, Mary Atkinson]. *Isabella Hamilton: A Tale of the Sixteenth Century*. London: John Farquar Shaw, 1852. http://books.google.com.

McAuley, Catherine. *The Correspondence of Catherine McAuley, 1818–1841.* Edited by Mary C. Sullivan. Dublin: Four Courts Press, 2004.

M'Crie, Thomas. *History of the Progress and Suppression of the Reformation in Italy during the Sixteenth Century; Including a Sketch of the History of the Reformation in the Grisons.* Edinburgh: William Blackwood, 1827. http://books.google.com.

Merryweather, Frederick Somner. *Gilbert Wright, the Gospeller.* London: S. W. Partridge, 1877. http://books.google.com.

Middleton, Erasmus. *Biographia Evangelica: Or An Historical Account of the Lives and Deaths of the Most Eminent and Evangelical Authors and Preachers . . .* 4 vols. London: J. W. Pasham, 1779. http://books.google.com.

Milman, Henry Hart. "Savonarola." In *Savonarola, Erasmus, and Other Essays*, 1–76. London: John Murray, 1870.

Milner, John [Francis William Blagdon]. *An Universal History of Christian Martyrdom, Being a Complete and Authentic Account of the Lives, Sufferings, and Triumphant Deaths of the Primitive as Well as Protestant Martyrs, in All Parts of the World, from the Birth of the Blessed Saviour to the Latest Periods of Pagan and Catholic Persecution.* London: J. G. Barnard, 1807. http://books.google.com.

M'Neile, Hugh. *The English Reformation, a Re–Assertion of Primitive Christianity. A Sermon, Preached in Christ Church, Newgate Street, on the 17th of November, 1858, the Tercentenary Commemoration of the Accession of Queen Elizabeth.* 2nd ed. Liverpool: Adam Holden; London: Longman, Green, Longman, and Roberts, 1858.

Murphy, John Nicholas. *Terra Incognita, Or the Convents of the United Kingdom.* London: Longmans, Green, 1873.

[Newman, John Henry]. Rev. of *Geraldine: A Tale of Conscience. The British Critic, and Quarterly Theological Review* 23 (1838): 61–82.

[Newman, John Henry, and James Mozley, eds.]. *Remains of the Late Reverend Richard Hurrell Froude.* 2 vols. London: J. G. and F. Rivington, 1838. http://books.google.com.

Newman, John Henry. *An Essay on the Development of Christian Doctrine.* Foreword by Ian Ker. Notre Dame, IN: University of Notre Dame Press, 1989.

———. *Loss and Gain: The Story of a Convert.* Edited by Alan G. Hill. Oxford: Oxford University Press, 1986.

O'Hanlon, Alice. *Erleston Glen: A Story of Lancashire in the Sixteenth Century*. London: Burns and Oates, 1878. http://books.google.com.

Oliver, Laetitia Selwyn. *Father Placid; Or, the Custodian of the Blessed Sacrament*. London: R. Washbourne, 1884. http://books.google.com.

"Our Library Table." *The Month: A Magazine and Review* 5 (1866): 535–50.

Page, James Augustus. *Protestant Ballads*. London: Whittaker and Company, 1852. http://books.google.com.

Peppergrass, Paul [Father John Boyce]. *The Spaewife; Or, the Queen's Secret. A Story of the Reign of Elizabeth*. New ed. Boston: Patrick Donahoe, [1876]. http://www.hathitrust.org.

Pepys, Charlotte Maria. *The Diary and Houres of the Ladye Adolie, A Faythfulle Childe, 1552*. London: Addey and Company, 1853.

Pike, G. Holden. "A Century of Bible Distribution." *Sunday Magazine* (1886): 736.

Pocklington, [Miss] L. *The Secret Room: A Story of Tudor Times*. 1884. Reprint, London: Religious Tract Society, n.d.

"Popish Tortures, Massacres, and Persecutions." *The Bulwark or Reformation Journal* 1 (1852): 295.

A Popular Manual of Church History. 1857. Reprint, Baltimore, MD: Kelly, Piet, and Company, 1876.

"The Present Crisis." *London-Scottish Reformed Presbyterian Magazine* 1 (January 1, 1869): 483–87. http://books.google.com.

Procter, J[ohn], O.P. "The Dominican Savonarola and the Reformation. A Reply to Dean Farrar." In *Publications of the Catholic Truth Society*. Vol. 28. 1895. Reprint, London: Catholic Truth Society, 1900. http://books.google.com.

"The Reign of Bloody Mary." *The Bulwark or Reformation Journal* 8 (January 1859): 182–83.

Rhind, W. Oak. *Hubert Ellerdale: A Tale of the Days of Wycliffe*. 1881. Reprint, London: S. W. Partridge, n.d.

R. J. M. "What Do We Read?" *American Catholic Quarterly Review* 22, no. 43 (October 1897): 673–93.

Robertson, Mrs. *Florence; Or, the Aspirant*. 3 vols. London: Whittaker Treacher, 1829.

Rule, William Harris. *Dawn of the Reformation. Savonarola. With Events of the Reign of Pope Alexander VI*. London: John Mason, 1855. http://books.google.com.

[Russell, C. W.] "Mary Tudor." *Dublin Review* 25, no. 50, n.s. (October 1875): 434–71.

Russell, Henry Patrick. *Cyril Westward: The Story of a Grave Decision*. London: Art and Book Company, 1899.

Russell, John. *Papal Aggression. Speech of the Right Honourable Lord John Russell, Delivered in the House of Commons, February 7, 1851*. London: Longman, Brown, Green, and Longman, 1851. http://books.google.com.

S., H. "Missionary Records. No. XXVII." *Church of England Magazine* 23 (October 1847): 234–36.

Sargeant, Anna Maria. *Tales of the Reformation*. London: Dean and Company, 1846.

[Sargent, George Eliel]. *Lilian: A Tale of Three Hundred Years Ago*. 1864. Reprint, New York: American Tract Society, [1865?].

Sayle, C. E. *Wiclif: An Historical Drama*. Oxford: James Thornton, 1887.

Scott, Walter. *The Abbot*. Edited by Christopher Johnson. 1820. Reprint, Edinburgh: Edinburgh University Press, 2000.

———. *The Heart of Midlothian*. Edited by Claire Lamont. 1818. Reprint, Oxford: Oxford University Press, 1982.

———. *The Journal of Sir Walter Scott*. Edited by W. E. K. Anderson. 1972. Reprint, Edinburgh: Canongate, 1998.

———. *The Monastery*. Edited by Penny Fielding. 1820. Reprint, Edinburgh: Edinburgh University Press, 2000.

Seymour, M. Hobart. "Danger to England from Treacherous Popery and Unwatchful Protestantism. Preached at St. Ann's Church, Blackfriars, on Sunday Afternoon, Nov. 3, 1839." *The Pulpit* 36, no. 909 (1839): 229–36.

"Signor Gavazzi." *Bulwark or Reformation Journal* 10 (February 1881): 51.

Southey, Robert. *The Book of the Church*. From the 5th London ed. Flemington, NJ: J. R. Dunham, 1844.

Stock, John. *A Sermon Preached in the Parish Churches of St. Mary Stratford Bow, and of All Saints, Poplar, Middlesex, on Sunday, October 4th, 1835, in Commemoration of the Third Centenary of the Reformation, and of the Publication of the First Entire Protestant English Version of the Bible, October 4th, 1835 [sic]*. London: A. and S. Alston, 1835.

[Stokes, George]. *The Lollards; Or, Some Account of the Witnesses for the Truth in Great Britain, from A.D. 1400 to A.D. 1546; With a Brief Notice of Events Connected with the History of the Early Reformation*. London: Religious Tract Society, 1838.

Stoughton, John. *Our English Bible: Its Translations and Translators*. [London]: Religious Tract Society, n.d.

Stowe, Harriet Beecher. *Agnes of Sorrento*. 1861. Reprint, Boston: Ticknor and Fields, 1865.

Straker, Fiorentina. *Immacolata, the Catholic Flower: A Convent Tale*. London: W. Knowles, 1860.

Strickland, Agnes [and Elizabeth Strickland]. *Lives of the Queens of England, from the Norman Conquest; With Anecdotes of their Courts, Now First*

Published from Official Records and Other Authentic Documents, Private as Well as Public. New ed., corr., 9 vols. London: Henry Colburn, 1844.

Stuart, Gilbert. *The History of the Establishment of the Reformation of Religion in Scotland.* London: J. Murray, 1780. http://books.google.com.

[Taylor, Frances]. *Tyborne: And "Who Went Thither in the Days of Queen Elizabeth." A Sketch.* London: Catholic Publishing and Bookselling Company, 1859.

Tennyson, Alfred. *Queen Mary: A Drama.* In *Tennyson: Poems and Plays,* 538–606. London: Oxford University Press, 1968.

"Tyborne." *Dublin Review* 48 (August 1860): 534–39.

Vaughan, Robert. *The Life and Opinions of John de Wycliffe: Illustrated Principally from His Unpublished Manuscripts; with a Preliminary View of the Papal System, and of the State of the Protestant Doctrine in Europe to the Commencement of the Fourteenth Century.* 1828. 2 vols. Reprint, New York: AMS Press, 1971.

———. "Wycliffe—His Biographers and Critics." *British Quarterly Review* 10 (1858): 360–422.

Villari, Pasquale. *The History of Girolamo Savonarola and His Times.* Translated by Leonard Horner. 2 vols. London: Longman, Green, Longman, Roberts, and Green, 1863. http://books.google.com.

Walpole, Horace. *The Castle of Otranto: A Gothic Story.* Edited by W. S. Lewis and E. J. Clery. Oxford: Oxford University Press, 2008.

Walshe, E[lizabeth] H[ely]. *From Dawn to Dark in Italy: A Tale of the Reformation in the Sixteenth Century.* 1864. Reprint, Boston: American Tract Society, [1865?].

Westcott, Brooke Foss. *A General View of the History of the English Bible.* London: Macmillan, 1868. http://books.google.com.

"Wycliffe and His Relation to the Reformation," *British Quarterly Review* 4 (1879): 334–68.

[Yonge, Charlotte Mary?]. "A Conversation on Books: Historical Tales." *The Monthly Packet* 31 (March 1881): 230.

Secondary Sources

Adams, James Eli. *Dandies and Desert Saints: Styles of Victorian Manhood.* Ithaca, NY: Cornell University Press, 1995.

Alexander, Michael. *Medievalism: The Middle Ages in Modern England.* New Haven, CT: Yale University Press, 2007.

Allibone, Samuel Austin. *A Critical Dictionary of English Literature and British and American Authors, Living and Deceased, from the Earliest Account to the Latter Half of the Nineteenth Century.* 3 vols. Philadelphia: J. B. Lippincott, 1891–1908.

Alliston, April. "The Value of a Literary Legacy: Retracing the Transmission of Value through Female Lines." *Yale Journal of Criticism* 4, no. 1 (1990): 109–27.

Anderson, Olive. "The Political Uses of History in Mid-Nineteenth-Century England." *Past and Present* 36 (April 1967): 87–105.

Ashworth, Suzanne M. "Susan Warner's *The Wide, Wide World*, Conduct Literature, and Protocols of Female Reading in Mid-Nineteenth-Century America." *Legacy* 17, no. 2 (2000): 141–64.

Aston, Margaret. "English Ruins and English History: The Dissolution and the Sense of the Past." *Journal of the Warburg and Courtauld Institutes* 36 (1973): 231–55.

———. *Lollards and Reformers: Imagery and Literacy in Late Medieval Religion.* London: Hambledon Press, 1984.

Atherstone, Andrew. "The Founding of Wycliffe Hall, Oxford." *Anglican and Episcopal History* 73, no. 1 (2004): 78–102.

———. *Oxford's Protestant Spy: The Controversial Career of Charles Golightly.* Bletchley: Paternoster Press, 2007.

Barnett, S. J. "Where Was Your Church Before Luther? Claims for the Antiquity of Protestantism Examined." *Church History* 68 (1999): 14–41.

Bassett, Troy J. "Living on the Margin: George Bentley and the Economics of the Three-Volume Novel, 1865–70." *Book History* 13, no. 1 (2010): 58–79. http://muse.jhu.edu.

Bebbington, David. *Evangelicalism in Modern Britain: A History from the 1730s to the Present.* 1989. Reprint, Grand Rapids, MI: Baker Book House, 1992.

Becker, Penny Edgell. "'Rational Amusement and Sound Instruction': Constructing the True Catholic Woman in the *Ave Maria*, 1865–1889." *Religion and American Culture* 8, no. 1 (1998): 55–90. http://www.jstor.org.

Bending, Lucy. *The Representation of Bodily Pain in Late Nineteenth-Century English Culture.* Oxford: Oxford University Press, 2000.

Bentley, James. *Ritualism and Politics in Victorian Britain: The Attempt to Legislate for Belief.* Oxford: Oxford University Press, 1978.

Betteridge, Thomas. *Tudor Histories of the English Reformations, 1530–1583.* Aldershot: Ashgate, 1999.

Bodenheimer, Rosemary. *Knowing Dickens.* Ithaca, NY: Cornell University Press, 2007.

Bonaparte, Felicia. *The Triptych and the Cross: The Central Myths of George Eliot's Poetic Imagination.* New York: New York University Press, 1979.

Booth, Alison. *How to Make It as a Woman: Collective Biographical History from Victoria to the Present.* Chicago: University of Chicago Press, 2004.

Bossy, John. *The English Catholic Community, 1570–1850*. New York: Oxford University Press, 1976.

Bostrom, Irene. "The Novel and Catholic Emancipation." *Studies in Romanticism* 2, no. 3 (1963): 155–76.

Bottigheimer, Ruth B. *The Bible for Children: From the Age of Gutenberg to the Present*. New Haven, CT: Yale University Press, 1996.

Bowen, John. *Other Dickens: Pickwick to Chuzzlewit*. 2000. Reprint, Oxford: Oxford University Press, 2003.

Brantlinger, Patrick. *The Reading Lesson: The Threat of Mass Literacy in Nineteenth-Century British Fiction*. Bloomington: Indiana University Press, 1998.

Bratton, J. S. *The Impact of Victorian Children's Fiction*. London: Croom Helm, 1981.

Brown, Callum G. *The Death of Christian Britain: Understanding Secularization, 1800–2000*. London: Routledge, 2001.

Brown, Candy Gunther. *The Word in the World: Evangelical Writing, Publishing, and Reading in America, 1789–1880*. Chapel Hill: University of North Carolina Press, 2004.

Bryan, Jennifer. *Looking Inward: Devotional Reading and the Private Self in Late Medieval England*. Philadelphia: University of Pennsylvania Press, 2008.

Burstein, Miriam Elizabeth. "Emily Sarah Holt and the Evangelical Historical Novel: Undoing Sir Walter Scott." In *Clio's Daughters: British Women Making History, 1790–1899*, edited by Lynette Felber, 153–78. Newark, NJ: University of Delaware Press, 2007.

———. "Protestants, Convents, and Seduction by Matthew 10:37." *Victorian Review* 37, no. 2 (Fall 2011): 16–20.

———. "Protestants Against the Jewish and Catholic Family, c. 1829 to c. 1860." *Victorian Literature and Culture* 31 (2003): 333–57.

———. "Reviving the Reformation: Victorian Women Writers and the Protestant Historical Novel." *Women's Writing* 12, no. 1 (2005): 73–84.

Cameron, Donald. "History, Religion, and the Supernatural: The Failure of *The Monastery*." *Studies in Scottish Literature* 6 (1969): 76–90.

Cameron, Euan. *Enchanted Europe: Superstition, Reason, and Religion, 1250–1750*. 2010. Reprint, Oxford: Oxford University Press, 2011.

Carpenter, Mary Wilson. *George Eliot and the Landscape of Time: Narrative Form and Protestant Apocalyptic History*. Chapel Hill: University of North Carolina Press, 1986.

———. *Imperial Bibles, Domestic Bodies: Women, Sexuality, and Religion in the Victorian Market*. Columbus: Ohio University Press, 2003.

Carroll, David. *George Eliot and the Conflict of Interpretations: A Reading of the Novels*. Cambridge: Cambridge University Press, 1992.

———. "George Eliot Martyrologist: The Case of Savonarola." In *From Author to Text: Re-reading George Eliot's* Romola, edited by Caroline Levine and Mark W. Turner, 105–21. Aldershot: Ashgate, 1998.

Carter, Grayson. *Anglican Evangelicals: Secessions from the* Via Media, *c. 1800–1850*. Oxford: Clarendon Press, 2001.

Case, Alison. "Against Scott: The Antihistory of Dickens' *Barnaby Rudge*." *Clio* 19, no. 2 (1990): 127–45.

Casteras, Susan P. "Virgin Vows: The Early Victorian Artists' Portrayal of Nuns and Novices." In *Religion in the Lives of English Women, 1760–1930*, edited by Gail Malmgreen, 129–60. London: Croom Helm, 1986.

Çelikkol, Ayşe. "Free Trade and Disloyal Smugglers in Scott's *Guy Mannering* and *Redgauntlet*." *English Literary History* 74, no. 4 (2007): 759–82.

Chadwick, Owen. *The Victorian Church*. Vol. 2. London: Adam and Charles Black, 1970.

Chancellor, Valerie. *History for Their Masters: Opinion in the English History Textbook, 1800–1914*. Bath: Adams and Dart, 1970.

Chapman, Alison. "Now and Then: Sequencing the Sacred in Two Protestant Calendars." *Journal of Medieval and Early Modern Studies* 33, no. 1 (Winter 2003): 91–123.

Chapman, Mark. "John Keble, National Apostasy, and the Myths of 14 July." In *John Keble in Context*, edited by Kirstie Blair, 47–58. London: Anthem Press, 2004.

Christian, George Scott. "'They lost the whole': Telling Historical (Un)truth in *Barnaby Rudge*." *Dickens Studies Annual* 32 (2002): 49–64.

Clery, E. J. *The Rise of Supernatural Fiction, 1762–1800*. 1995. Reprint, Cambridge: Cambridge University Press, 1999.

Colley, Linda. *Britons: Forging the Nation, 1707–1837*. New Haven, CT: Yale University Press, 1992.

Collinson, Patrick. "The Persecution in Kent." In *The Church of Mary Tudor: Catholic Christendom, 1300–1700*, edited by Eamon Duffy and David M. Loades, 309–33. Aldershot: Ashgate, 2006.

———. "Through Several Glasses Darkly: Historical and Sectarian Perceptions of the Tudor Church." In *Tudorism: Historical Imagination and the Appropriation of the Sixteenth Century*, edited by Tatiana C. String and Marcus Bull, 97–114. Oxford: Oxford University Press, 2011.

Conacher, J. B. "The Politics of the 'Papal Aggression' Crisis, 1850–51." *Canadian Catholic Historical Association* (1959): 13–27.

Cottom, Daniel. "The Waverley Novels: Superstition and the Enchanted Reader." *English Literary History* 47, no. 1 (1980): 80–102.

Craven, Mrs. Augustus. *The Life of Lady Georgiana Fullerton*. Translated by Henry James Coleridge. London: Richard Bentley and Son, 1888.

Crompton, James. "John Wyclif: A Study in Mythology." *Transactions of the Leicester Archaeological and Historical Society* 42 (1966–67): 6–34.

Culler, A. Dwight. *The Victorian Mirror of History*. New Haven, CT: Yale University Press, 1985.

Cummings, Brian. *The Literary Culture of the Reformation: Grammar and Grace*. Oxford: Oxford University Press, 2002.

Cutt, Margaret Nancy. *Ministering Angels: A Study of Nineteenth-Century Evangelical Writing for Children*. Wormley: Five Owls Press, 1979.

Dailey, Alice A. "Typology and History in Foxe's *Acts and Monuments*." *Prose Studies* 25, no. 3 (2002): 1–29.

Davidoff, Lenore, and Catherine Hall. *Family Fortunes: Men and Women of the English Middle Class, 1780–1850*. Chicago: University of Chicago Press, 1991.

Davies, Horton. *Worship and Theology in England: From Watts and Wesley to Martineau, 1690–1900*. 1961–62. Reprint, Grand Rapids, MI: William B. Eerdmans, 1996.

de Vere, Aubrey. *Recollections of Aubrey de Vere*. 3rd ed. London: Edward Arnold, 1897.

d'Haussy, Christine. "Les Récusants dans *Constance Sherwood*: Confesseurs et Martyrs in Ecrivains catholiques anglo-saxons." *Caliban* 24 (1987): 49–68.

Dickens, A. G., and John M. Tonkin with Kenneth Powell. *The Reformation in Historical Thought*. Cambridge, MA: Harvard University Press, 1985.

Dillon, Anne. *The Construction of Martyrdom in the English Catholic Community, 1535–1603*. Aldershot: Ashgate, 2002.

Dobson, Michael, and Nicola J. Watson. *England's Elizabeth: An Afterlife in Fame and Fantasy*. Oxford: Oxford University Press, 2002.

Dobson, R. B., ed. *The Peasants' Revolt of 1381*. London: Macmillan, 1970.

Dolan, Frances. *Whores of Babylon: Catholicism, Gender, and Seventeenth-Century Print Culture*. Ithaca, NY: Cornell University Press, 1999.

Dolnikowski, Edith. "Feminine Exemplars for Reform: Women's Voices in John Foxe's *Acts and Monuments*." In *Women Preachers and Prophets through Two Millennia of Christianity*, edited by Beverly Mayne Kienzle and Pamela J. Walker, 199–211. Berkeley: University of California Press, 1998.

Doran, Susan, and Thomas S. Freeman, eds. *Mary Tudor: Old and New Perspectives*. Houndmills: Palgrave Macmillan, 2011.

———. *The Myth of Elizabeth*. Houndmills: Palgrave Macmillan, 2002.

Dove, Mary. "Wyclif and the English Bible." In *A Companion to John Wyclif: Late Medieval Theologian*, edited by Ian Christopher Levy, 365–406. Leiden: Brill, 2006.

Drabble, John. "The Historians of the English Reformation: 1780–1850." PhD diss., New York University, 1975.

———. "Mary's Protestant Martyrs and Elizabeth's Catholic Traitors in the Age of Catholic Emancipation." *Church History* 51 (1982): 172–85.

Duffy, Eamon. Introduction to *J. A. Froude's The Reign of Mary Tudor*, 1–26. Edited by Eamon Duffy. London: Continuum, 2009.

Duffy, Eamon, and David M. Loades, eds. *The Church of Mary Tudor: Catholic Christendom, 1300–1700*. Aldershot: Ashgate, 2006.

Duncan, Ian. *Modern Romance and the Transformations of the Novel: The Gothic, Scott, Dickens*. Cambridge: Cambridge University Press, 1992.

———. *Scott's Shadow: The Novel in Romantic Edinburgh*. Princeton, NJ: Princeton University Press, 2007.

Edwards, John. *Mary I: England's Catholic Queen*. New Haven, CT: Yale University Press, 2011.

Ermarth, Elizabeth Deeds. *The English Novel in History, 1840–1895*. New York: Routledge, 1997.

Evans, G. R. *John Wyclif: Myth and Reality*. Downers Grove, IL: IVP Press, 2006.

Faught, C. Brad. *The Oxford Movement: A Thematic History of the Tractarians and Their Times*. University Park: Pennsylvania State University Press, 2003.

Felber, Lynette, ed. *Clio's Daughters: British Women Making History, 1790–1899*. Newark, NJ: University of Delaware Press, 2007.

Ferris, Ina. *The Achievement of Literary Authority: Gender, History, and the Waverley Novels*. Ithaca, NY: Cornell University Press, 1991.

Fisher, Devon. *Roman Catholic Saints and Early Victorian Literature: Conservatism, Liberalism, and the Emergence of Secular Culture*. Aldershot: Ashgate, 2012.

Fleishman, Avrom. *The English Historical Novel: Walter Scott to Virginia Woolf*. Baltimore, MD: Johns Hopkins University Press, 1971.

Flint, Kate. *The Woman Reader, 1837–1914*. Oxford: Clarendon Press, 1993.

Forbes, Duncan. *The Liberal Anglican Idea of History*. 1952. Reprint, Cambridge: Cambridge University Press, 2006.

Franchot, Jenny. *Roads to Rome: The Antebellum Protestant Encounter with Catholicism*. Berkeley: University of California Press, 1994.

Freedgood, Elaine. *The Ideas in Things: Fugitive Meaning in the Victorian Novel*. Chicago: University of Chicago Press, 2006.

Freeman, Thomas S. "Burning Zeal: Mary Tudor and the Marian Persecution." In *Mary Tudor: Old and New Perspectives*, edited by Susan Doran and Thomas S. Freeman, 171–205. Houndmills: Palgrave Macmillan, 2011.

———. "Inventing Bloody Mary: Perceptions of Mary Tudor from the Restoration to the Twentieth Century." In *Mary Tudor: Old and New Perspectives*, edited by Susan Doran and Thomas S. Freeman, 78–102. Houndmills: Palgrave Macmillan, 2011.

———. "Providence and Presecription: The Account of Elizabeth in Foxe's 'Book of Martyrs.'" In *The Myth of Elizabeth*, edited by Susan Doran and Thomas S. Freeman, 27–55. Houndmills: Palgrave Macmillan, 2002.

———. "Text, Lies, and Microfilm: Reading and Misreading Foxe's 'Book of Martyrs.'" *Sixteenth Century Journal* 30, no. 1 (Spring 1999): 23–46.

Fyfe, Aileen. *Science and Salvation: Evangelical Popular Science Publishing in Victorian Britain.* Chicago: University of Chicago Press, 2004.

———. "A Short History of the Religious Tract Society." In *From the Dairyman's Daughter to Worrals of the WAAF: The Religious Tract Society, Lutterworth Press, and Children's Literature*, edited by Dennis Butts and Pat Garrett, 13–35. Cambridge: Lutterworth Press, 2006.

Gamer, Michael. *Romanticism and the Gothic: Genre, Reception, and Canon Formation.* Cambridge: Cambridge University Press, 2009.

Garcia, Ramona. "'Most wicked superstition and idolatry': John Foxe, His Predecessors and the Development of an Anti–Catholic Polemic in the Sixteenth-Century Accounts of the Reign of Mary I." In *John Foxe at Home and Abroad*, edited by David Loades, 79–87. Aldershot: Ashgate, 2004.

Gaston, Patricia S. *Prefacing the Waverley Prefaces: A Reading of Sir Walter Scott's Prefaces to the Waverley Novels.* New York: Peter Lang, 1991.

Giebelhausen, Michaela. *Painting the Bible: Representation and Belief in Mid-Victorian Britain.* Aldershot: Ashgate, 2006.

Gordon, Bruce. "'This Worthy Witness of Christ': Protestant Uses of Savonarola in the Sixteenth Century." In *Protestant History and Identity in Sixteenth Century Europe: Volume 1, The Medieval Inheritance*, edited by Bruce Gordon, 93–107. Aldershot: Ashgate, 1996.

Gosse, Edmund. *The Life of Philip Henry Gosse, F.R.S.* London: Kegan Paul, Trench, Trübner, 1893.

Gray, Beryl. "Power and Persuasion: Voices of Influence in *Romola*." In *From Author to Text: Re-reading George Eliot's* Romola, edited by Caroline Levine and Mark W. Turner, 124–34. Aldershot: Ashgate, 1998.

Green, Ian. *Print and Protestantism in Early Modern England.* Oxford: Oxford University Press, 2000.

Greenberg, Devorah. "Eighteenth-Century 'Foxe': History, Historiography, and Historical Consciousness." In *John Foxe's The Acts and Monuments Online.* Sheffield: HRI Online Publications, 2011. http://www.johnfoxe.org.

———. "Reflexive Foxe: The *Book of Martyrs* Transformed, 'Foxe' Reinterpreted—Sixteenth through Twenty–First Centuries. " PhD diss., Simon Fraser University, 2002.

Gregory, Brad. *Salvation at Stake: Christian Martyrdom in Early Modern Europe.* Cambridge, MA: Harvard University Press, 1999.

Grenby, M. O. "Adults Only? Children and Children's Books in British Circulating Libraries, 1748–1948." *Book History* 5, no. 1 (2002): 19–38.

Gunn, Ann V. "Sir George Hayter, Victorian History Painting, and a Religious Controversy." *Record of the Art Museum, Princeton University* 53, no. 1 (1994): 2–32. http://www.jstor.org/stable/10.2307/3774681.

Haigh, Christopher. "The Recent Historiography of the English Reformation." In *The English Reformation Revised*, edited by Christopher Haigh, 19–33. Cambridge: Cambridge University Press, 1987.

Harkin, Patricia. "The Fop, the Fairy, and the Genres of Scott's *The Monastery*." *Studies in Scottish Literature* 19, no. 1 (1984): 177–93.

Hart, Francis. *Scott's Novels: The Plotting of Historic Survival*. Charlottesville: University of Virginia Press, 1966.

Heffernan, Thomas J. *Sacred Biography: Saints and Their Biographers in the Middle Ages*. Oxford: Oxford University Press, 1988.

Heimann, Mary. *Catholic Devotion in Victorian England*. Oxford: Clarendon Press, 1995.

Herringer, Carol Engelhardt. *Victorians and the Virgin Mary: Religion and Gender in England, 1830–85*. Manchester: Manchester University Press, 2008.

Hickerson, Megan L. *Making Women Martyrs in Tudor England*. Houndmills: Palgrave Macmillan, 2005.

Highley, Christopher. *Catholics Writing the Nation in Early Modern Britain and Ireland*. Oxford: Oxford University Press, 2008.

Hill, Rosemary. *God's Architect: Pugin and the Building of Romantic Britain*. London: Penguin, 2007.

Hinchliff, Peter. *God and History: Aspects of British Theology, 1875–1914*. Oxford: Clarendon Press, 1992.

Hobsbawm, Eric, and Terence Ranger, eds. *The Invention of Tradition*. Cambridge: Cambridge University Press, 1983.

Hoeveler, Diane Long. *Gothic Riffs: Secularizing the Uncanny in the European Imaginary, 1780–1820*. Columbus: Ohio State University Press, 2010.

Homans, Margaret. *Royal Representations: Queen Victoria and British Culture, 1837–1876*. Chicago: University of Chicago Press, 1998.

Homans, Margaret, and Adrienne Munich, eds. *Remaking Queen Victoria*. Cambridge: Cambridge University Press, 1997.

Horowitz, Evan. "George Eliot: The Conservative." *Victorian Studies* 49, no. 1 (2006): 7–32.

Howsam, Leslie. *Cheap Bibles: Nineteenth-Century Publishing and the British and Foreign Bible Society*. Cambridge: Cambridge University Press, 1991.

———. "The Nineteenth-Century Bible Society and 'The Evil of Gratuitous Distribution.'" In *Free Print and Non–Commercial Publishing since 1700*, edited by James Raven, 119–34. Aldershot: Ashgate, 2000.

Hubin, Allen J. *Crime Fiction IV: A Comprehensive Bibliography, 1749–2000, Addenda to the Revised Edition.* http://www.crimefictioniv.com/Part _32.html.

Hudson, Anne. *The Premature Reformation: Wycliffite Texts and Lollard History.* Oxford: Clarendon Press, 1988.

Hutcheon, Linda. *A Poetics of Postmodernism: History, Theory, Fiction.* London: Routledge, 1988.

Isabella, Maurizio. *Risorgimento in Exile: Italian Emigres and the Liberal International in the Post-Napoleonic Era.* Oxford: Oxford University Press, 2009.

Jaeger, Kathleen Grant. "Martyrs or Malignants? Some Nineteenth-Century Portrayals of Elizabethan Catholics." *Early Modern Literary Studies* Special Issue 7 (May 2001). http://extra.shu.ac.uk/emls/si-07/jaeger.htm.

———. "A Writer or a Religious? Lady Georgiana Fullerton's Dilemma." In *The Church and Literature,* edited by Peter Clarke and Charlotte Methuen, 271–82. Woodbridge, Suffolk, UK: Boydell Press, 2012.

Janes, Dominic. "The 'Modern Martyrdom' of Anglo–Catholics in Victorian England." *Journal of Religion and Society* 13 (2011). http://moses .creighton.edu/jrs/2011/2011-16.pdf.

———. *Victorian Reformation: The Fight over Idolatry in the Church of England, 1840–1860.* Oxford: Oxford University Press, 2009.

Jay, Elisabeth. *The Religion of the Heart: Anglican Evangelicalism and the Nineteenth-Century Novel.* Oxford: Clarendon Press, 1979.

Johnson, Christopher. "The Relationship between *The Monastery* and *The Abbot.*" *Scottish Literary Journal* 20, no. 2 (1993): 31–40.

Jones, Jason B. *Lost Causes: Historical Consciousness in Victorian Literature.* Columbus: Ohio State University Press, 2006.

Jones, Norman W. *Gay and Lesbian Historical Fiction: Sexual Mystery and Post-Secular Narrative.* Houndmills: Palgrave Macmillan, 2007.

Katz, David S. *God's Last Words: Reading the English Bible from the Reformation to Fundamentalism.* New Haven, CT: Yale University Press, 2004.

Kaufman, Heidi. *English Origins, Jewish Discourse, and the Nineteenth-Century British Novel: Reflections of a Nested Nation.* University Park: Pennsylvania State University Press, 2009.

Kearney, James. *The Incarnate Text: Imagining the Book in Reformation England.* Philadelphia: University of Pennsylvania Press, 2009.

Kenny, Anthony. "The Accursed Memory: The Counter-Reformation Reputation of John Wyclif." In *Wyclif and His Times,* edited by Anthony Kenny, 147–68. Oxford: Clarendon Press, 1986.

Ker, Ian. *John Henry Newman: A Biography.* Oxford: Oxford University Press, 1988.

Kerr, Donal A. *'A Nation of Beggars'? Priests, People, and Politics in Famine Ireland, 1846–1852.* Oxford: Clarendon Press, 1994.

Kerr, James. *Fiction against History: Scott as Storyteller.* Cambridge: Cambridge University Press, 1989.

King, John N. *English Reformation Literature: The Tudor Origins of the Protestant Tradition.* Princeton, NJ: Princeton University Press, 1982.

Knott, John R. *Discourses of Martyrdom in English Literature, 1563–1694.* Cambridge: Cambridge University Press, 1993.

Kort, Wesley A. *"Take, Read": Scripture, Textuality, and Cultural Practice.* University Park: Pennsylvania State University Press, 1996.

Krueger, Christine. *The Reader's Repentance: Women Preachers, Women Writers, and Nineteenth-Century Social Discourse.* Chicago: University of Chicago Press, 1992.

Kuchar, Gary. *Divine Subjection: The Rhetoric of Sacramental Devotion in Early Modern England.* Pittsburgh, PA: Duquesne University Press, 2005.

Lackey, Lionel. *"The Monastery* and *The Abbot*: Scott's Religious Dialectics." *Studies in the Novel* 19, no. 1 (1987): 46–65.

LaMonaca, Maria. *Masked Atheism: Catholicism and the Secular Victorian Home.* Columbus: Ohio State University Press, 2008.

Langland, Elizabeth. "Nation and Nationality: Queen Victoria in the Developing Narrative of Englishness." In *Remaking Queen Victoria*, edited by Margaret Homans and Adrienne Munich, 13–32. Cambridge: Cambridge University Press, 1997.

Larkin, Emmett. *The Making of the Roman Catholic Church in Ireland, 1850–1860.* Chapel Hill: University of North Carolina Press, 1980.

Ledger-Lomas, Michael. "Caroline and Paul: Biblical Commentaries as Evidence of Reading in Victorian Britain." In *The History of Reading, Volume 2: Evidence from the British Isles, c. 1750–1950*, edited by Katie Halsey and W. R. Owens, 32–47. Houndmills: Palgrave Macmillan, 2011.

———. "Mass Markets: Religion." In *The Cambridge History of the Book in Britain, Vol. 6: 1830–1914*, edited by David McKitterick, 324–58. Cambridge: Cambridge University Press, 2009.

Levine, Caroline, and Mark W. Turner, eds. *From Author to Text: Re-reading George Eliot's* Romola. Aldershot: Ashgate, 1998.

Levine, George. *Realism, Ethics, and Secularism: Essays on Victorian Literature and Science.* Cambridge: Cambridge University Press, 2009.

Lewis, Jayne. *Mary Queen of Scots: Romance and Nation.* London: Routledge, 1998.

Lincoln, Andrew. *Walter Scott and Modernity.* Edinburgh: Edinburgh University Press, 2007.

Littell, John Stockton. *The Historian and the Reformation*. New York: Young Churchman, 1910.

Loades, David. "Introduction: The Personal Religion of Mary I." In *The Church of Mary Tudor: Catholic Christendom, 1300–1700*, edited by Eamon Duffy and David M. Loades, 1–29. Aldershot: Ashgate, 2006.

———. *The Reign of Mary Tudor: Politics, Government, and Religion in England, 1553–1558*. New York: St. Martin's Press, 1979.

Loeber, Rolf and Magda Stouthamer-Loeber, eds., with Anne Mullin Burham. *A Guide to Irish Fiction, 1650–1900*. Dublin: Four Courts Press, 2006.

Lukács, Georg. *The Historical Novel*. Translated by Hannah and Stanley Mitchell. Lincoln: University of Nebraska Press, 1983.

Lynch, Jack. *The Age of Elizabeth in the Age of Johnson*. Cambridge: Cambridge University Press, 2003.

MacCulloch, Diarmaid. "The Myth of the English Reformation." *Journal of British Studies* 30, no. 1 (1991): 1–19. http://www.jstor.org/stable/175735.

———. "Putting the English Reformation on the Map: The Prothero Lecture." *Transactions of the Royal Historical Society*, 6th ser., 15 (2005): 75–95. http://www.jstor.org/stable/3679363.

Machin, G. I. T. *The Catholic Question in English Politics, 1820 to 1830*. Oxford: Clarendon Press, 1964.

Magnet, Myron. *Dickens and the Social Order*. Philadelphia: University of Pennsylvania Press, 1985.

Maison, Margaret. *The Victorian Vision: Studies in the Religious Novel*. New York: Sheed and Ward, 1961.

Maitzen, Rohan. "Plotting Women: Froude and Strickland on Elizabeth I and Mary Queen of Scots." In *Clio's Daughters: British Women Making History, 1790–1899*, edited by Lynette Felber, 123–50. Newark, NJ: University of Delaware Press, 2007.

Markovits, Stefanie. "George Eliot and Action." *Studies in English Literature 1500–1900* 41, no. 4 (Autumn 2001): 785–803.

Martin, Robert Bernard. *Tennyson: The Unquiet Heart*. London: Faber and Faber, 1980.

Mazzoni, Cristina. *Maternal Impressions: Pregnancy and Childbirth in Literature and Theory*. Ithaca, NY: Cornell University Press, 2002.

McArthur, Tonya Moutray. "Through the Grate; Or, English Convents and the Transmission and Preservation of Female Catholic Recusant History." In *The Catholic Church and Unruly Women Writers: Critical Essays*, edited by Jeana DelRosso, Leigh Eicke, and Ana Kothe, 105–22. Houndmills: Palgrave Macmillan, 2007.

McCracken-Flesher, Caroline. *Possible Scotlands: Walter Scott and the Story of Tomorrow*. Oxford: Oxford University Press, 2005.

McDannell, Colleen. *The Christian Home in Victorian America, 1840–1900.* 1986. Reprint, Bloomington: Indiana University Press, 1994.

McGann, Jerome. "Walter Scott's Romantic Postmodernity." In *Scotland and the Borders of Romanticism*, edited by Leith Davis, Ian Duncan, and Janet Sorensen, 113–29. Cambridge: Cambridge University Press, 2004.

McIntire, C. T. *England against the Papacy, 1858–1861.* 1983. Reprint, Cambridge: Cambridge University Press, 2008.

McKelvy, William. *The English Cult of Literature: Devoted Readers, 1774–1880.* Charlottesville: University Press of Virginia, 2007.

McNees, Eleanor. "The Resurgence of Savonarola in Victorian England." In *The Grand Tour Lives On*, edited by Alessandra di Luzio, 75–100. Bologna, Italy: CLUEB, 2006.

Melman, Billie. *The Culture of History: English Uses of the Past, 1800–1953.* Oxford: Oxford University Press, 2006.

———. "The Pleasures of Tudor Horror: Popular Histories, Modernity and Sensationalism in the Long Nineteenth Century." In *Tudorism: Historical Imagination and the Appropriation of the Sixteenth Century*, edited by Tatiana C. String and Marcus Bull, 37–56. Oxford: Oxford University Press, 2011.

Mighall, Robert. *A Geography of Victorian Gothic Fiction: Mapping History's Nightmares.* Oxford: Oxford University Press, 1999.

Milbank, Alison. *Dante and the Victorians.* Manchester: Manchester University Press, 1998.

Miller, John. *Popery and Politics in England, 1660–1688.* Cambridge: Cambridge University Press, 1973.

Milton, Anthony. *Catholic and Reformed: The Roman and Protestant Churches in English Protestant Thought, 1600–1640.* Cambridge: Cambridge University Press, 1995.

Mitchell, Rosemary. "Every Picture Tells a Catholic Story: Lingard's *History of England* Illustrated and the Transition in Catholic Historiography." In *Lingard Remembered: Essays to Mark the Sesquicentenary of John Lingard's Death*, edited by Peter Phillips, 125–42. London: Catholic Record Society, 2004.

———. *Picturing the Past: English History in Text and Image, 1830–1870.* Oxford: Clarendon Press, 2000.

Monta, Susannah Brietz. *Martyrdom and Literature in Early Modern England.* Cambridge: Cambridge University Press, 2005.

Moran, Maureen. "The Art of Looking Dangerously: Victorian Images of Martyrdom." *Victorian Literature and Culture*, vol. 32, no. 2 (2004): 475–93.

———. *Catholic Sensationalism and Victorian Literature.* Liverpool: Liverpool University Press, 2007.

———. "Pater's 'Great Change': *Marius the Epicurean* as Historical Conversion Romance." In *Walter Pater: Transparencies of Desire*, edited by Laurel Brake, Leslie Higgins, and Carolyn Williams, 170–88. Greensboro, NC: ELT Press, 2002.

Morris, Kevin L. "John Bull and the Scarlet Woman: Charles Kingsley and Anti-Catholicism in Victorian Literature." *Recusant History* 23, no. 2 (October 1996): 190–218.

———. "Rescuing the Scarlet Woman: The Promotion of Catholicism in English Literature, 1829–1850." *Recusant History* 22, no. 1 (May 1994): 75–87.

Morris, Pam. *Imagining Inclusive Society in 19th-Century Novels: The Code of Sincerity in the Public Sphere.* Baltimore, MD: Johns Hopkins University Press, 2004.

Mueller, Janel. "Pain, Persecution, and the Construction of Selfhood in Foxe's *Acts and Monuments.*" In *Religion and Culture in Renaissance England*, edited by Claire McEachern and Debra Shuger, 161–87. Cambridge: Cambridge University Press, 2006.

Müller, Sabine. "Romancing the (Unhappy) Queen: Emplotment Frühneuzeitlichen Weiblichen Königtums am Beispiel Mary Tudors (1553–1558)." *Zeitsprünge Forschungen zur Frühen Neuzeit* 10, nos. 3–4 (2006): 341–63.

Mumm, Susan. *Stolen Daughters, Virgin Mothers: Anglican Sisterhoods in Victorian Britain.* London: Leicester University Press, 1999.

Murphy, Andrew. *Conscience and Community: Revisiting Toleration and Religious Dissent in Early Modern England and America.* University Park: Pennsylvania State University Press, 2001.

Newman, Beth. "*The Heart of Midlothian* and the Masculinization of Fiction." *Criticism* 36, no. 4 (Fall 1994): 521–40.

Nockles, Peter. "A Disputed Legacy: Anglican Historiographies of the Reformation from the Era of the Caroline Divines to That of the Oxford Movement." *Bulletin of the John Rylands University Library of Manchester* 83, no. 1 (2001): 121–67.

———. "The Nineteenth-Century Reception." In *The Unabridged Acts and Monuments Online.* Sheffield: HRI Online Publications, 2011. http://www.johnfoxe.org.

Nolan, Emer. *Catholic Emancipations: Irish Fiction from Thomas Moore to James Joyce.* Syracuse, NY: Syracuse University Press, 2007.

Nolt, Steven M. *Foreigners in Their Own Land: Pennsylvania Germans in the Early Republic.* University Park: Pennsylvania State University Press, 2002.

Nord, David Paul. *Faith in Reading: Religious Publishing and the Birth of Mass Media in America.* New York: Oxford University Press, 2004.

Nordius, Janina. "A Tale of Other Places: Sophia Lee's *The Recess* and Colonial Gothic." *Studies in the Novel* 34, no. 2 (2002): 162–76.

Norman, Edward. *The English Catholic Church in the Nineteenth Century.* 1984. Reprint, Oxford: Clarendon Press, 1985.

O'Brien, Susan. "Making Catholic Spaces: Women, Décor, and Devotion in the English Catholic Church, 1840–1900." In *The Church and the Arts: Papers Read at the 1990 Summer Meeting and the 1991 Winter Meeting of the Ecclesiastical History Society*, edited by Diana Wood, 449–64. Oxford: Blackwell, 1992.

O'Day, Rosemary. *The Debate on the English Reformation.* London: Methuen, 1986.

———. "John Lingard, Historians, and Contemporary Politics, 1780–1850." In *Lingard Remembered: Essays to Mark the Sesquicentenary of John Lingard's Death*, edited by Peter Phillips, 82–104. London: Catholic Record Society, 2004.

Parish, Helen. *Monks, Miracles, and Magic: Reformation Representations of the Medieval Church.* New York: Routledge, 2005.

Parker, Daryl. "Histories of Violence and the Writer's Hand: Foxe's *Acts and Monuments* and *Titus Andronicus*." In *Reading and Writing in Shakespeare*, edited by David Moore Bergeron, 82–115. Newark, NJ: University of Delaware Press, 1996.

Patrick, James. "Newman, Pugin, and Gothic." *Victorian Studies* 24, no. 2 (1981): 185–207.

Paz, D. G. *Dickens and* Barnaby Rudge*: Anti-Catholicism and Chartism.* Monmouth: Merlin Press, 2006.

———. *Popular Anti-Catholicism in Mid-Victorian Britain.* Stanford, CA: Stanford University Press, 1992.

Pearson, Jacqueline. *Women's Reading in Britain, 1750–1835: A Dangerous Recreation.* Cambridge: Cambridge University Press, 1999.

Penny, D. Andrew. "John Foxe, Evangelicalism, and the Oxford Movement." In *John Foxe: An Historical Perspective*, edited by David Loades, 195–217. Aldershot: Ashgate, 1999.

———. "John Foxe's Historical Reception." *Historical Journal* 40, no. 1 (1997): 111–42.

Pereiro, James. *"Ethos" and the Oxford Movement: At the Heart of Tractarianism.* Oxford: Oxford University Press, 2008.

Perkin, J. Russell. *Theology and the Victorian Novel.* Montreal: McGill-Queen's University Press, 2009.

Phillips, Peter, ed. *Lingard Remembered: Essays to Mark the Sesquicentenary of John Lingard's Death.* London: Catholic Record Society, 2004.

Pickering, Samuel, Jr. "Evangelical Readers and the Phenomenal Success of Walter Scott's First Novels." *Christian Scholar's Review* 3 (1974): 345–59.

———. *The Moral Tradition in English Fiction, 1785–1850.* Hanover, NH: University Press of New England, 1976.

Price, Fiona. "Resisting 'The Spirit of Innovation': The Other Historical Novel and Jane Porter." *Modern Language Review* 101 (2006): 638–51.

Ragussis, Michael. *Figures of Conversion: "The Jewish Question" and English National Identity.* Durham, NC: Duke University Press, 1995.

Ralls, Walter. "The Papal Aggression of 1850: A Study in Victorian Anti-Catholicism." In *Religion in Victorian Britain: Interpretations*, edited by Gerald Parsons, 115–34. Manchester: Manchester University Press, 1988.

Raponi, Danilo. "An 'Anti-Catholicism of Free Trade'? Religion and the Anglo-Italian Negotiations of 1863." *European History Quarterly* 39, no. 4 (2009): 633–52.

Redworth, Glyn. "'Matters Impertinent to Women': Male and Female Monarchy under Philip and Mary." *English Historical Review* 112, no. 47 (June 1997): 597–631.

Reed, John Shelton. *Glorious Battle: The Cultural Politics of Victorian Anglo-Catholicism.* Nashville, TN: Vanderbilt University Press, 1996.

Reventlow, Henning Graf. *The Authority of the Bible and the Rise of the Modern World.* Translated by John Bowden. Philadelphia: Fortress Press, 1985.

Reynolds, Kimberley. "Rewarding Reads? Giving, Receiving, and Resisting Evangelical Reward and Prize Books." In *Popular Children's Literature in Britain*, edited by Julia Briggs, Dennis Butts, and M. O. Grenby, 189–208. Aldershot: Ashgate, 2008.

Rice, Thomas Jackson. "The End of Dickens' Apprenticeship: Variable Focus in *Barnaby Rudge*." *Nineteenth-Century Fiction* 30, no. 2 (1975): 172–84.

Richards, Judith M. "Reassessing Mary Tudor: Some Concluding Points." In *Mary Tudor: Old and New Perspectives*, edited by Susan Doran and Thomas S. Freeman, 206–24. Houndmills: Palgrave Macmillan, 2011.

Richmond, Velma Bourgeois. "Ford Madox Brown's Protestant Medievalism: Chaucer and Wycliffe." *Christianity and Literature* 54, no. 3 (Spring 2005): 363–92.

Robbins, Sarah. *Managing Literacy, Mothering America: Women's Narratives on Reading and Writing in the Nineteenth Century.* Pittsburgh: University of Pittsburgh Press, 2004.

Robertson, Fiona. *Legitimate Histories: Scott, Gothic, and the Authorities of Fiction.* Oxford: Clarendon Press, 1994.

Robson, Catherine. "Historicizing Dickens." In *Palgrave Advances in Charles Dickens Studies*, edited by John Bowen and Robert L. Patten, 234–54. Houndmills: Palgrave Macmillan, 2006.

Rose, Jonathan. *The Intellectual Life of the British Working Classes.* New Haven, CT: Yale University Press, 2001.

Rosen, David. "The Volcano and the Cathedral: Muscular Christianity and the Origins of Primal Manliness." In *Muscular Christianity: Embodying the Victorian Age*, edited by Donald E. Hall, 17–44. Cambridge: Cambridge University Press, 1994.

Rosman, Doreen. *Evangelicals and Culture*. 2nd ed. Eugene, OR: Pickwick Press, 2011.

Rupp, E. G. "The Influence of Victorian Nonconformity." *The Listener* 1359 (March 17, 1955): 468–70.

Sanok, Catherine. "*The Lives of Women Saints of Our Contrie of England*: Gender and Nationalism in Recusant Hagiography." In *Catholic Culture in Early Modern England*, edited by Ronald Corthell et al., 261–80. Notre Dame, IN: University of Notre Dame Press, 2007.

Santangelo, Gennaro Anthony. "Villari's *Life and Times of Savonarola*: A Source for George Eliot's *Romola*." *Anglia* 90 (1972): 118–31.

Sargent, Marion. "George Eliel Sargent and Emma Hewlett." In *Sargent Family History*, November 28, 1998. http://www.angelfire.com/ms/mysargent family/eliel.html.

Schiefelbein, Michael. *The Lure of Babylon: Seven Protestant Novelists and Britain's Roman Catholic Revival*. Macon, GA: Mercer University Press, 2001.

Schiefen, Richard J. *Nicholas Wiseman and the Transformation of English Catholicism*. Shepherdstown: Patmos Press, 1984.

Schofield, Scott. "Cain's Crime of Secrecy and the Unknowable Book of Life: The Complexities of Biblical Referencing in *Richard II*." In *Shakespeare, the Bible, and the Form of the Book: Contested Scriptures*, edited by Travis DeCook and Alan Galey, 40–56. London: Routledge, 2012.

Scott, Patrick. "The Business of Belief: The Emergence of Religious Publishing." In *Sanctity and Secularity: The Church and the World*, edited by Derek Baker, 213–24. Oxford: Basil Blackwell, 1973.

Scully, Robert E., S.J. "'In the Confident Hopes of a Miracle': The Spanish Armada and Religious Mentalities in the Late Sixteenth Century." *Catholic Historical Review* 89, no. 4 (2003): 643–70.

Seed, John. *Dissenting Histories: Religious Division and the Politics of Memory in Eighteenth-Century England*. Edinburgh: Edinburgh University Press, 2008.

Shaw, Harry. *The Forms of Historical Fiction: Sir Walter Scott and His Successors*. Ithaca, NY: Cornell University Press, 1983.

Shaw, Ian. "The Evangelical Revival through the Eyes of the 'Evangelical Century': Nineteenth-Century Perceptions of the Origins of Evangelicalism." In *The Advent of Evangelicalism: Exploring Historical Continuities*, edited by Michael A. G. Haykin and Kenneth J. Stewart, 302–23. Nashville, TN: B and H Academic, 2008.

Shaw, Jane. *Miracles in Enlightenment England*. New Haven, CT: Yale University Press, 2006.

Shea, Donald F. *The English Ranke: John Lingard.* New York: Humanities Press, 1969.

Sheets, Robin. "History and Romance: Harriet Beecher Stowe's *Agnes of Sorrento* and George Eliot's *Romola.*" *Clio* 26, no. 3 (1997): 323–46.

Shell, Alison. *Catholicism, Controversy, and the English Literary Imagination, 1558–1660.* Cambridge: Cambridge University Press, 1999.

———. *Oral Culture and Catholicism in Early Modern England.* Cambridge: Cambridge University Press, 2007.

———. *Shakespeare and Religion.* London: Methuen Drama, 2010.

Simpson, James. *Burning to Read: English Fundamentalism and Its Reformation Opponents.* Cambridge, MA: Belknap Press of Harvard University Press, 2007.

Simpson, Michael. "Telling Lives to Children: Young Versus New Historicism in *Little Arthur's History of England.*" In *Romanticism, History, Historicism: Essays on an Orthodoxy*, edited by Damian Walford Davies, 60–78. New York: Routledge, 2009.

Skinner, S. A. *Tractarians and the "Condition of England": The Social and Political Thought of the Oxford Movement.* Oxford: Clarendon Press, 2004.

Smith, Dennis Mack. *Victor Emanuel, Cavour, and the Risorgimento.* London: Oxford University Press, 1971.

Snook, Edith. *Women, Reading, and the Cultural Politics of Early Modern England.* Aldershot: Ashgate, 2005.

Spongberg, Mary. "*La Reine Malheureuse*: Stuart History, Sympathetic History, and the Stricklands' History of Henrietta Maria." *Women's History Review* 20, no. 5 (2011): 745–64.

Steinberg, Ronald M. *Fra Girolamo Savonarola, Florentine Art, and Renaissance Historiography.* Athens: Ohio University Press, 1977.

Stevens, Anne H. *British Historical Fiction before Scott.* Houndmills: Palgrave Macmillan, 2010.

Stewart, Kenneth J. *Restoring the Reformation: British Evangelicalism and the Francophone 'Réveil' 1816–1849.* Milton Keynes, UK: Paternoster, 2006.

Stott, Anne. *Hannah More.* Oxford: Oxford University Press, 2003.

String, Tatiana C., and Marcus Bull, eds. *Tudorism: Historical Imagination and the Appropriation of the Sixteenth Century.* Oxford: Oxford University Press, 2011.

Taylor, Charles. *A Secular Age.* Cambridge, MA: Belknap Press of Harvard University Press, 2007.

Taylor, Dennis. "Tennyson's Catholic Years: A Point of Contact." *Victorian Poetry* 47, no. 1 (2009): 285–312.

Taylor, Marion Ann. "Elizabeth Rundle Charles: Translating the Letter of Scripture into Life." In *Recovering Nineteenth-Century Women Inter-*

preters of the Bible, edited by Christiana de Groot and Marion Ann Taylor, 149–64. Atlanta, GA: Society of Biblical Literature, 2007.

Thompson, Andrew. *George Eliot and Italy: Literary, Cultural and Political Influences from Dante to the* Risorgimento. Houndmills: Macmillan, 1998.

Thuesen, Peter J. *In Discordance with the Scriptures: American Protestant Battles over Translating the Bible.* New York: Oxford University Press, 1999.

Tomko, Michael. *British Romanticism and the Catholic Question: Religion, History, and National Identity, 1778–1829.* Houndmills: Palgrave Macmillan, 2011.

Truman, James C. W. "John Foxe and the Desires of Reformation Martyrology." *English Literary History* 70, no. 1 (2003): 35–66.

Tumbleson, Raymond. *Catholicism in the English Protestant Imagination: Nationalism, Religion, and Literature 1660–1745.* 1998. Reprint, Cambridge: Cambridge University Press, 2008.

Tyacke, Nicholas. *Aspects of English Protestantism, c. 1530–1700.* Manchester: Manchester University Press, 2001.

Vallins, David. "The Feeling of Knowledge: Insight and Delusion in Coleridge." *English Literary History* 64, no. 7 (1997): 157–87.

Vaninskaya, Anna. "Dreams of John Ball: Reading the Peasants' Revolt in the Nineteenth Century." *Nineteenth-Century Contexts* 31, no. 1 (March 2009): 45–57.

Vargish, Thomas. *The Providential Aesthetic in Victorian Fiction.* Charlottesville: University Press of Virginia, 1985.

Vidmar, John. *English Catholic Historians and the English Reformation, 1585–1954.* Sussex: Sussex Academic Press, 2005.

Viswanathan, Gauri. *Outside the Fold: Conversion, Modernity, and Belief.* Princeton, NJ: Princeton University Press, 1998.

Von Nolcken, Christina. "Wyclif, the Wycliffites, and the *Oxford Dictionary of National Biography.*" *Medieval Prosopography* 25 (2004): 222–31.

Wacker, Grant A. *Augustus H. Strong and the Dilemma of Historical Consciousness.* Macon, GA: Mercer University Press, 1985.

Wagner, Corinna M. "'Standing Proof of the Degeneracy of Modern Times': Architecture, Society, and the Medievalism of A. W. N. Pugin." In *Beyond Arthurian Romances: The Reach of Victorian Medievalism*, edited by Jennifer A. Palmgren and Lorretta M. Holloway, 9–37. Houndmills: Palgrave Macmillan, 2005.

Walder, Dennis. *Dickens and Religion.* 1981. Reprint, London: Routledge, 2007.

Walker, Julia M. *The Elizabeth Icon, 1603–2003.* Houndmills: Palgrave Macmillan, 2004.

Walsham, Alexandra. *Charitable Hatred: Tolerance and Intolerance in England, 1500–1700.* Manchester: Manchester University Press, 2006.

———. "Inventing the Lollard Past: The Afterlife of a Medieval Sermon in Early Modern England." *Journal of Ecclesiastical History* 58, no. 4 (October 2007): 628–55.

———. *Providence in Early Modern England.* Oxford: Oxford University Press, 1999.

———. *The Reformation of the Landscape: Religion, Identity, and Memory in Early Modern Britain and Ireland.* Oxford: Oxford University Press, 2011.

———. " 'A Very Deborah?' The Myth of Elizabeth I as a Providential Monarch." In *The Myth of Elizabeth*, edited by Susan Doran and Thomas S. Freeman, 143–68. Houndmills: Palgrave Macmillan, 2002.

Watson, Nicola. "Gloriana Victoriana: Victoria and the Cultural Memory of Elizabeth I." In *Remaking Queen Victoria*, edited by Margaret Homans and Adrienne Munich, 79–104. Cambridge: Cambridge University Press, 1997.

Watt, James. *Contesting the Gothic: Fiction, Genre and Cultural Conflict, 1764–1832.* Cambridge: Cambridge University Press, 1999.

Weinstein, Donald. *Savonarola and Florence: Prophecy and Patriotism in the Renaissance.* Princeton, NJ: Princeton University Press, 1970.

Wells, Ruth Gilpin. *A Woman of Her Time and Ours: Mother Mary Magdalen Taylor, SMG.* Charlotte, NC: Laney-Smith, 1988.

Wheeler, Michael. *The Old Enemies: Catholic and Protestant in Nineteenth-Century England.* Cambridge: Cambridge University Press, 2006.

Whisenant, James. *A Fragile Unity: Anti–Ritualism and the Division of Anglican Evangelicalism in the Nineteenth Century.* Milton Keynes: Paternoster, 2003.

Wiblin, J. Gilbert. "A Quiet By–Lane of Huguenot Story (A Refugee Family of Roussel)." *Proceedings of the Hugenot Society of London* 14, no. 2 (1931): 191–210. http://archive.huguenotsociety.org.uk/34_Vol_XIV_Issue_2_1930-1.pdf.

Wihl, Gary. "Republican Liberty in George Eliot's *Romola.*" *Criticism* 51, no. 2 (Spring 2009): 247–62.

Williams, Sarah C. "Is There a Bible in the House? Gender, Religion, and Family Culture." In *Women, Gender, and Religious Cultures in Britain, 1800–1940*, edited by Sue Morgan and Jacqueline de Vries, 11–31. London: Routledge, 2010.

Wilson, Cheryl A. "Female Reading Communities in *Jane Eyre.*" *Brontë Studies* 30, no. 2 (July 2005): 131–39.

Wilt, Judith. *Secret Leaves: The Novels of Walter Scott.* Chicago: University of Chicago Press, 1985.

Wizeman, William, S.J. "The Religious Policy of Mary I." In *Mary Tudor: Old and New Perspectives*, edited by Susan Doran and Thomas S. Freeman, 153–70. Houndmills: Palgrave Macmillan, 2011.

Wolffe, John. *The Protestant Crusade in Great Britain, 1829–1860*. Oxford: Clarendon Press, 1991.

Woodhouse, Thomas. *Faithful Fictions: The Catholic Novel in British Literature*. Milton Keynes: Open University Press, 1991.

Wooding, Lucy. *Rethinking Catholicism in Reformation England*. Oxford: Oxford University Press, 2000.

Wright, T. R. *The Religion of Humanity: The Impact of Comtean Positivism on Victorian Britain*. 1986. Reprint, Cambridge: Cambridge University Press, 2008.

Yates, Nigel. *Anglican Ritualism in Victorian Britain, 1830–1910*. Oxford: Oxford University Press, 1999.

———. *Buildings, Faith and Worship: The Liturgical Arrangement of Anglican Churches, 1600–1900*. Rev. ed. Oxford: Oxford University Press, 2000.

Yeoh, Paul. "*Saints' Everlasting Rest*: The Martyrdom of Maggie Tulliver." *Studies in the Novel* 41, no. 1 (Spring 2009): 1–21.

Ziegler, Georgianna. "Reimagining a Renaissance Queen: Catherine of Aragon Among the Victorians." In *"High and Mighty Queens" of Early Modern England: Realities and Representations*, edited by Carole Levin, Jo Eldridge Carney, and Debra Barrett-Graves, 203–22. Houndmills: Palgrave Macmillan, 2003.

Zlatar, Antoinina Bevan. *Reformation Fictions: Protestant Polemical Dialogues in Elizabethan England*. Oxford: Oxford University Press, 2011.

Index

Miriam Elizabeth Burstein

is associate professor of English at the College at Brockport,
State University of New York. She is the author of
Narrating Women's History in Britain, 1770–1902.